Memory, Truth, and Justice in Contemporary Latin America

LATIN AMERICAN PERSPECTIVES IN THE CLASSROOM

Series Editor: Ronald H. Chilcote

Memory, Truth, and Justice in Contemporary Latin America

Edited by Roberta Villalón

ROWMAN & LITTLEFIELD
Lanham • Boulder • New York • London

Published by Rowman & Littlefield
A wholly owned subsidiary of The Rowman & Littlefield Publishing Group, Inc.
4501 Forbes Boulevard, Suite 200, Lanham, Maryland 20706
www.rowman.com

Unit A, Whitacre Mews, 26-34 Stannary Street, London SE11 4AB, United Kingdom

Copyright © 2017 by Rowman & Littlefield

British Library Cataloguing in Publication Information Available

Library of Congress Cataloging-in-Publication Data Available

ISBN: 978-1-4422-6724-4 (cloth)
ISBN: 978-1-4422-6725-1 (paper)
ISBN: 978-1-4422-6726-8 (electronic)

∞™ The paper used in this publication meets the minimum requirements of American National Standard for Information Sciences—Permanence of Paper for Printed Library Materials, ANSI/NISO Z39.48-1992.

Printed in the United States of America

Contents

Introduction

Memory, Truth, and Justice in Contemporary Latin America

Roberta Villalón

With the turn of the century, the process of dealing with the still unresolved human rights abuses under authoritarian regimes[1] and civil wars[2] in Latin America has been significantly reinvigorated. Truth, reconciliation, and justice efforts have been revisited, trials of people involved with violence, torture, abductions, murders, and disappearances have been (re)opened, and new interpretations and questions about what happened have been raised. The difficulties of coming to terms with not only the horror of extreme violence typical of (dirty and civil) wars but also the precariousness of justice processes postwar have permeated ebullient memory mobilizations and reconciliation efforts. Simple answers to the quintessential "Who is to be blamed?" and "How to move on?" have been put to rest, and a widespread recognition of the severe complexities of past, present, and future has taken hold. Did the violence actually begin before the establishment of military regimes or the eruption of civil wars because of indefensible structural inequalities? How can all the targets of violence be recognized with certainty without exacerbating latent conflicts? Are the limitations of democratization/pacification processes simply unavoidable, and, if so, will the struggles for memory, truth, and justice never end? Is current victimization a continuation of past oppression? How can the arbitrariness of abusive power relations be dealt with? Are justice, reconciliation, and social equality possible, or are they utopian ideals worth pursuing despite persistent dynamics of marginalization?

The emergence of what can be conceptualized as a second wave of memory, truth, and justice mobilizations—the first wave having occurred early on with transitions into democratic regimes and the signing of peace accords[3]—has not necessarily been a surprise. Scholars have theorized that the coming of age of a generation born and raised during times of widespread violence could awaken new interpretations and demands for addressing unsettled aspects of the past (Mannheim, 1952; Kaiser, 2005). Moreover, researchers have pointed out that the global upsurge of a culture of memory, given the acceleration and democratization of history in postmodern capitalism (Huyssen, 2000; Nora, 2002; Ricoeur, 2006) and the solidification of international human rights accountability (Hite and Ungar, 2013; Lessa and Payne, 2012; Roht-Arriaza and Mariezcurrena, 2006), would be fertile ground in which renewed efforts by previously marginalized groups to seek justice and rebuild memory could flourish.

At the same time, looking at the region as a whole and aware that each country experienced these processes in a different way, to a different degree, at a different time, and with unique contributing events,[4] three other factors have influenced the revival of memory, truth, and justice mobilizations. The first and arguably most relevant is what has been identified as "the impossibility of justice" (Arias and del Campo, 2009: 11; Rigney, 2012). Despite the expansion of democracy, the establishment of truth and reconciliation commissions, their reports documenting systemic human rights abuses, the trials and sentencing of the military in charge of designing, directing, and/or executing such violence, and the memorialization of the horror of the past conflict, justice has not been achieved. Among the main setbacks have been executive orders that ended the prosecution of the crimes committed during authoritarian regimes and civil wars and the use of amnesty laws, either to prevent prosecutions or to free those who had been convicted (Andreozzi, 2011; Centro de Estudios Legales y Sociales, 2011; Lessa and Payne, 2012; Santos, Teles, and de Almeida Teles, 2009).[5] These decisions generated a widespread sense of incompleteness and disenchantment with the promises made by the new regimes: political calculations and power imbalances seemed to have overtaken the rule of law once again. This public dissatisfaction (particularly among victims of violence and members of human rights organizations) was, however, not unexpected given that, in general, processes of transitional justice were bound to be tenuous at best. Besides the delicate balance that transitional governments had to maintain to appease the still volatile political environment with the threat of a resurgence of either military rule or polarized civil (armed) conflict (Lessa, 2013; Quinalha, 2013), the wide diversity of groups interested in seeking justice had different interpretations and expectations of what could actually constitute a "fair" solution—trials for all involved in violent activities, economic reparations to victims, memorialization of spaces where violence took place, funding for forensic investigations, or leaving the past in the past (Crenzel, 2008; Jelin, 1994; 2003; Loveman and Lira, 2002; Salvi, 2013; Stern, 2010).

The second factor was the remarkable persistence of processes of collective memory and justice against official accounts that remained partial with the ultimate goal of uncovering the facts and coming to terms with the various effects of such violent and traumatic events. This persistence rendered futile any effort to put a premature end to those processes. Indeed, neither the suspension of trials nor the declaration of amnesties that were intended to prevent the past from becoming "the gravedigger of the present" (Nietzsche, 2010 [1874]: 3) was able to repress collective memory and justice mobilizations. Memories were destined to resurface and groups to continue to dialogue with and dispute one another about the veracity and relevance of their truths and claims (Alexander, 2004; Eyerman, 2004; Freud, 1919; Schudson, 1989;

Sennet, 1998). The emergence of a second wave of memory, truth, and justice mobilizations in Latin America showed the perseverance of both dominant and marginalized groups in their efforts to legitimize and/or impose their versions of the past and support laws and policies that satisfied their interests (Burke, 1989; Foucault, 2011 [1975]; Jelin, 2003; Popular Memory Group, 2011 [1998]; Sarlo, 2005; Zerubavel, 1996). Their resilience was sustained by the commonality of injustice, amnesty, and impunity across borders: transnational awareness and collaboration contributed to the renewal of claims and the bracing of counter-hegemonic doxa and praxis (ideologies and practices) (Bourdieu, 1977; Marx, 1845). The continuous involvement of the Inter-American Court of Human Rights and the extraditions and trials of the military in the courts of other countries further reinforced mobilizations for memory and justice (Hite and Ungar, 2013; Lessa and Payne, 2012; Roht-Arriaza and Mariezcurrena, 2006).

Additionally, this perseverance was influenced by the centrality in the region of political mobilization and social movements on multiple issues (Eckstein and Garretón, 1989; Stahler-Sholk, Vanden, and Becker, 2014; Stahler-Sholk, Vanden, and Kuecker, 2008)—a rich culture of collective action and dissent that would persist and manifest itself with varying purposes and intensities in different times and places. Because of the inherent complexities and shortcomings of the processes of truth, reconciliation, and justice, human rights organizations increased their demands and new groups emerged to join them, introducing further issues (Hite and Ungar, 2013). Also, as time passed, political ideologies that had been repressed and/ or moderated began to gather old and new sympathizers (and in some cases achieved governmental power) while pushing for an expansion and reinterpretation of the human rights agenda set by the mobilizations of the first wave (Arnson et al., 2009; Ellner, 2014; Levitsky and Roberts, 2011). Thus neither the earlier armed conflict nor the deficiencies of justice in postauthoritarian or postwar times could curtail the long-standing culture of counter-hegemonic politics in Latin America or the ultimate motivation to pursue truth and justice.

A third factor that was influential in the second wave was a context of economic volatility and inequality (ECLAC, 2013) that, together with mounting violence, corruption, and impunity, stirred distrust of governmental and law enforcement institutions (Desmond Arias and Goldstein, 2010; Hite and Ungar, 2013; Medina and Galván, 2014; Morris and Blake, 2010; Wielandt and Artigas, 2007). Besides being disenchanted with the interrupted process of truth and justice, growing numbers of people became generally skeptical of "the political," conceptualized as everything related to government officials, traditional politicians, and formal institutions, particularly as the detrimental consequences of neoliberal schemes spread and deepened, and new administrations found insurmountable difficulties in bringing back growth and development.[6] The combination of institutional unreliability, low accountability, and social inequality fed criminal activities and violence (particularly with the spread of international trafficking of narcotic drugs, the rise of the related gangs, and the competition of nonstate armed groups for the control of resources), provok-

Different
Violance !

ing an environment of insecurity and fear.[7] This violence, now in a post–cold war context, was identified as different from the systematic terror of repressive regimes. However, it could not be thought of as completely divorced from either the recent past (with its polarized conflicts, abuses of power, and effects of neoliberal schemes) or the fragile state of justice. Efforts to show the continuities between the authoritarian past and the democratic present had been made by activists and scholars, but some political groups also capitalized on these links to (at least rhetorically) offer an alternative promise of a politics of justice, transparency, economic growth, stability, and redistribution (Davis, 2008; Desmond Arias and Goldstein, 2010; Faulk, 2013; Koonings and Kruijt, 1999; 2004; Sader, 2008; Silva, 2009).

Independently of what was expected by researchers of collective memory or the possible influence of the above factors, the reinvigoration of memory, truth, and justice mobilizations deserves attention in its own right because of its continental geographical spread, its conceptual depth, and, consequently, its political, social, and cultural relevance. It was with this second wave that the main strategists of systematic violence and its perpetrators from all military echelons were taken (back) to court, tried, found guilty, and incarcerated. It was also this time around that more disappeared people were found (deceased, as in the case of the discovery of mass graves, and alive, as in the case of the recovery of abducted grandchildren) despite official efforts to halt the search. And, last but not least, it was at this point that the collaboration of civil society with state/military powers was fully recognized, resulting in trials involving the participation of civilians in the repressive system and the revisiting of the way the actions of members of the paramilitary and other armed groups contributed to the normalization of the abuse of violence. All in all, the second wave displayed renewed vigor in dealing with the horror of bloodshed in all of its complexity—as it pertained to state, military and civilian groups; as it linked political ideologies with racial/ethnic, gender/sexual, and class regimes both domestically and internationally; and as it reflected embedded societal contradictions and ambivalence about the very meaning and possibility of justice and equality.

Memory, truth, and justice processes—here conceptualized as bottom-up collective efforts to counter the partial "official history" of what occurred during violent pasts with the aim of achieving a more complete understanding and a fair, legitimate resolution—involve the creation and application of various frames of doxa and praxis (Halbwachs, 2004; Goffman, 1974). These frames work as "principles of selection, emphasis, and presentation composed of little tacit theories about what exists, what happens, and what matters" (Gitlin, 1980: 6), prioritizing certain aspects while dismissing others that indeed might be important. These very frames influence memory, truth, and justice processes over time and space, resulting in the development of trajectories of thought and mobilization that start as counter-hegemonic but push to become hegemonic—that is, to become the one authentic version of the past. In turn, such progression generates the surfacing of new counter-hegemonic reframings that question the normalization of one particular reading of history with the hope of revealing aspects that might have been silenced or that might have not been visible before (Villalón, 2013). Divergent interpretations of "a past 'that does not pass'" emerge (Jelin, 2003: 101), since history, "a continuous recomposition of the past in the present," lives to be rewritten (Chizuko and Sand, 1999: 137). Through this contentious politics of representation in collective memory making and justice seeking, people and groups with various ideologies and capitals strive "to affirm the legitimacy of 'their truth'" (Jelin, 2003: 26), while hierarchies of knowledge and power are socially (re)organized (Bietti, 2009).

Thus, the politics of "framing public memories" (Philips, 2004: 1) can be thought of as a long-term dialogue between parties with diverse views and power, all struggling for legitimacy and recognition of their versions of the past and, thus, their expectations for the future (Cohen, 2001; Jelin, 2003; Weine, 2006). This kind of politics is a process of contestation that develops over time and space in which diverse and changing social actors become involved (Jelin, 2003; Roniger and Sznajder, 1999; Stern, 2010). The various (re)framings are necessarily multilayered and reflective of psychological, sociological, political, cultural, and ideological intersections that may allow for certain aspects to be brought forward or relegated to the background, to be connected in particular ways, and thus to yield new understandings. For example, these processes have altered the comprehension of how torture, killings, and disappearances were implemented: was political affiliation a determining factor or did other parameters, like gender, sexual orientation, racial/ethnic background, or social class, influence the systematic instrumentation of violence? Moreover, these reframing processes have led to new classifications of the historical periods that are identified as violent: did the violence begin with the military coup or the official declaration of war or did it precede these? These shifts have allowed for reevaluations of victimhood and justice, resulting in the emergence of adjusted demands over who is to be held responsible for human rights abuses and what reparations or reconciliation strategies need to be implemented.

Memory, truth, and justice processes not only implied the development of these various reframings, but also dealing with what can be conceptualized as a "wounded cultural background" plagued with the perversion, trauma, fear, and denial generated by the atrocious character of past matters (Alexander et al., 2004; Kaiser, 2005; Robben, 2007; Scarry, 1985; Fried Amilivia, 2009; Lira and Castillo, 1993; Hirsch, 2008; Koonings and Kruijt, 1999; Cohen, 2001; Sutton and Norgaard, 2013; Sutton, 2015). Within wounded cultures, one finds phases of widespread social retraction combined with moments of social mobilization that seemed to break through the paralyzing effects of trauma and fear and advance the long-term, transgenerational healing efforts against denial and injustice. Complementary to these coping processes, one finds artistic creations that furthered memorialization, justice seeking, and reconciliation processes. Capable of generating "meaning and intelligibility" (Vivanco and Fabry, 2013: 14), artistic responses to events that abruptly break the order of being have long been among the main means for making sense of and challenging the incomprehensibility and unspeakability of violent disruptions (Adorno, 1973 [1966]; 1978 [1951]; Agamben, 2009; Milton, 2014a; Scarry, 1985; Stern, 2014).

In the case of Latin America, artistic media have been produced to challenge atrocities and "restore the humanity" of citizens and communities (Milton, 2014b: 2; Stern, 2014), thus contributing with the broader memory, truth, and justice processes and the coping with wounded cultural backgrounds. Artistic creations and cultural spaces, like memory galleries and museums, have become means of bearing witness, humanizing horror and its victims, bringing understanding, encouraging reflection and discussion, promoting remembrance, expressing dissent, challenging misleading versions of events, and fostering the sensibilization and conscientization of violence, human rights abuses, and injustices during and after conflict (Bilbija and Payne, 2011; del Pino, 2014; Gómez-Barris, 2009; Milton, 2014a; Richard, 2007; Ritter, 2014; Vich, 2014). Artistic expressions and cultural arenas have been "indispensable to break the silence" (Stern, 2014: 260) and have played a decisive role in keeping memories and mobilization for justice thriving by showing that "something is still alive among the rubble" (Stern, 2014: 263). Moreover, they have served to destabilize the distinction between memory and forgetfulness (Sarlo, 2005) while highlighting the resilience and inevitability of memory. Through artistic representation and cultural productions and spaces, memory has defied efforts to "force closure over violence and its afterlife" (Gómez-Barris, 2009: 29).

While art and culture have played critical roles in collective memory and justice, their significance cannot be separated from that of other social mobilizations or legal and political efforts for truth and reconciliation. Far from establishing a hierarchy among "labors of memory" (Jelin, 2003: 5), artistic creations and cultural spaces are conceptualized as part and parcel of memory, truth, and justice processes, and as such cannot escape the context and history from which they emerged. Hence, they are not immune to past and current structures and practices of inequality (Milton, 2014a) that prioritize the versions of the past and claims for justice of certain groups. They reflect the conflictive nature of the past (Sarlo, 2005) and the present (Scarry, 1985) while embodying juxtapositions of hegemonic and counter-hegemonic forces (Gómez-Barris, 2009; Huyssen, 2000; Rojas, 2000; Stern, 2014; Sturken, 1997).

The complexity of memory, truth, and justice processes calls for studies to be developed from a relational perspective that avoids dichotomous or linear ways of reasoning. A positivist scientific dogma pushes scholars to form definitive, authoritative, "monolithic and essentialist" explanations that leave little room for doubt and fail to fully represent the intricacies and historic-political malleability of social processes like that of memory building (Hirsch and Smith, 2002: 6). Indeed, the changing, contradictory, and complicated nature of processes of reframing collective memory, particularly of violent traumatic pasts, calls for a Southern, postcolonial, feminist epistemology (Bortoluci and Jansen, 2013; Collins, 2000; Connell, 2007; Go, 2013; Harding, 1998; Mignolo, 2012). What can be labeled as a "critical epistemology from below" recognizes that knowledge about the past can be "used to rationalize, reinforce, normalize, and naturalize social inequalities" (Jaggar, 2008: xi). Research endeavors and methodologies are inseparable from emotions, politics, power, and "social and ethical values" (Jaggar, 2008: xi), all particularly critical to advance memory, truth, and justice movements.

Edited from this epistemological perspective, this volume is an example of activist scholarship — one convinced that ultimately the main purpose of academic research is contributing to community efforts to dismantle oppressive practices and structures and bring about social change and justice (Dubet, 2012; Hale, 2008; Mills, 1959; Naples, 2003; Shayne, 2014). This standpoint becomes particularly significant in memory and justice studies given that, as Foucault has argued,

> Memory is actually a very important factor in struggle (recall, in fact, struggles develop in a kind of conscious moving forward of history), if one controls people's memory, one controls their dynamism. And also one controls their experience, their knowledge of previous struggles. . . . Popular struggles have become for our society, not part of the actual, but of the possible. (Foucault, 2011 [1975]: 253)

Furthermore, an activist scholar approach is meant "to counter hegemonic practices in research and beyond" (Villalón, 2014: 269)—to study the "social production of memory" in an effort to debunk inequalities of knowledge and power (Popular Memory Group, 2011 [1998]: 254). This is an analysis that must be "relational," concerned with both "the relation between dominant memory and oppositional forms across the whole public (including the academic) field" and "the relation between these public discourses in their contemporary state of play and the more privatized sense of the past which is generated within a lived culture" (257). Because "political domination involves historical definition [and h]istory—in particular popular memory—is a stake in the constant struggle for hegemony" (258), the second wave of memory, truth, and justice mobilizations in Latin American could not go unnoticed.

The scholarship included in this volume reflects the importance of current mobilizations for memory, truth, and justice in the region. Studies about countries with a longer repertoire of policies and scholarship on memory and justice (such as Argentina and Chile), as well as research about countries that were newer to them (such as Guatemala, El Salvador, Brazil, Colombia, Peru, Bolivia, and Uruguay) make up this unique compilation. This volume exposes complexities and contradictions in the processes of collective memory and justice seeking by looking into the way they form over time, change in character and reach, create new meanings, raise new demands, and influence other policy, legal, and cultural spheres.

The compilation is organized in four parts. The first part looks into the processes of framing and reframing collective memory illustrating dynamics of power and the play of hegemonic and counter-hegemonic forces. The second part focuses on the significance of establishing parameters to define the beginning and ending of historical periods in identifying who is to be blamed and who deserves to receive reparations. The third part explores the formation and weight of wounded cultures and the difficulties beneath healing processes, as they both influence the possibility of achieving justice. The fourth part studies how artistic and cultural media creations emerge in contexts of struggles for memory and justice, and help in advancing claims of recognition and legitimacy. As a whole, the studies compiled in this volume allow for a more nuanced comprehension of past violence and collective memory, truth, and justice processes by breaking up dualistic interpretations that contrast victims and perpetrators, socialism and capitalism, pre- and postwar, fact and falsehood to explore the grey areas in between and reveal the misleading effects of dichotomous rationalizations.

This compilation highlights the value of critical examination of the processes of memory and justice as they continue to develop in the region. This standpoint informs the authors' focus on cases that are noteworthy both historically, because of their novel and influential character and quality, and culturally, because of their sociopolitical significance within and across geographical borders. Thus their analyses become relevant both academically and socially: their research is not only theoretically and empirically rich but also applicable to collective efforts for reconciliation and justice. These studies inform our understanding of the influence of preexisting processes on the emergence of a second wave of memory, truth, and justice mobilizations—for example, how the generation born and raised during dictatorial times in the region came of age in precarious contexts of impunity, corruption, social inequality, and violence and, inspired by a culture of collective action and political dissent, reconceptualized the past, questioned the present, and mobilized to raise new demands for justice. At the same time, they document and investigate novel developments and framings in the region: while convinced of the positive consequences of enduring mobilizations for memory and justice, the authors still point to their limitations and contradictions. Those problematic issues, however, are shared with the purpose of contributing to ongoing processes of memory, truth, and justice.

Readers of this compilation will find material empirically and theoretically relevant to the development of both scholarly and political knowledge about memory and justice. Because "the practice and analysis of cultural memory can in itself be a form of political activism" (Hirsch and Smith, 2002: 13), I end this introduction convinced of the value of engaging in these kinds of research projects from an activist, critical perspective. The daughter of parents who were classified as subversive and threatening to the nation and were persecuted because of their ideologies and occupations in Argentina's last military regime, I intend my editing of this volume to contribute to collective memory making and long-lasting struggles for justice and equality. I hope that the research presented here will add to ongoing processes of imagining alternative futures (Sjoberg, Gill, and Cain, 2003)—futures that are not trapped in an unresolved past, an unfair present, or a given order, but grow out of constructive contestation, reflection, communal understanding, and collaboration.

NOTES

This chapter, the introductions to parts 1, 2, 3, and 4, and the conclusion have reproduced sections of the introductions to each of the three-part special issue on The Resurgence of

Memory, Truth, and Justice Mobilizations in Latin America that I edited for *Latin American Perspectives* (Villalón, 2015; 2016a; 2016b). This volume includes a selection of articles from *Latin American Perspectives* 42 (3), 43 (5) and 43 (6).

1. By "authoritarian regimes" I mean repressive political settings including military governments and formal democracies in which the participation of political parties was regulated by the ruling forces, preventing competing parties from functioning within legitimate institutional channels, as in the cases of Mexico under the Partido Revolucionario Institucional or Argentina with the proscription of Peronism

2. By "civil wars" I mean cases in which it was openly acknowledged that two or more political groups were at war within their national territory and/or were disputing national sovereign power over a certain territory (as in El Salvador, Guatemala, or Colombia, for example) and cases in which armed conflict between groups took place even if officially it was not labeled a civil war (as in Argentina, Chile, Peru, or Uruguay, for example).

3. In keeping with the umbrella terms that I am using to refer to repressive regimes and armed conflict, by "transitions into democratic regimes" I mean transitions from military to democratic governments and transitions from formal democracies to "real" democracies. (The use of qualifiers for democracies reflects long-standing debates about the various types and degrees of freedom, representativeness, and legitimacy of this type of governance; on Latin America, see, for example, Gledhill [2000] and O'Donnell [2004].) "The signing of peace accords" includes cases in which civil wars were openly recognized and peace accords signed among parties and cases in which guerrilla, paramilitary, or civil/military armed conflict was present and there was a de facto cease-fire, whether reached by force or informally agreed upon (see Arnson, 1999, 2012; Leiner and Flämig, 2012).

4. For example, certain events helped to galvanize domestic and international efforts for accountability, such as the arrest of Pinochet in England in 1998, which restarted a chain of criminal prosecutions in Chile; the public search for Juan Gelman's disappeared granddaughter in Uruguay around 1996, which led to the creation of the Peace Commission; the sentencing of the Argentine naval officer Adolfo Scilingo to 640 years in prison in Spain for crimes against humanity in 2005; and the ratification of the conviction of Alberto Fujimori for human rights violations in 2009 by the Supreme Court, through which circumstantial evidence was established as legitimate and satisfactory given the destruction of material evidence or its immateriality (Burt, 2013; Roht-Arriaza and Mariezcurrena, 2006).

5. States have historically used amnesties "to promote political settlements, reconciliation, and stability" by extinguishing "liability for specific crimes committed by particular individuals and/or groups" (Lessa and Payne, 2012: 3, 4) in the past. Amnesties are usually extraordinary, ad hoc measures that work retroactively. In the post-authoritarian context of Latin America, different types of amnesties (self-amnesties, pseudo-amnesties, blanket amnesties, conditional amnesties, and de facto amnesties) were adopted by members of outgoing military regimes "to shield themselves from accountability" (4) or by agents of democratic governments who also sometimes made use of pardons that exempted "convicted individuals from serving their sentences without expunging the underlying convictions" (5). In all cases, the ultimate effect of these legal measures was to bar "criminal prosecution against certain individuals accused of committing human rights violations" (4).

6. Each country followed its own path, but in general structural adjustment policies and neoliberal reforms proved to be not only detrimental but also hard to let go of, given foreign debt obligations and the advance of global capitalism, which increased the vulnerability of

every economy to other countries' performances. The economic volatility of countries in postauthoritarian times included periods of decline as well as growth, rising as well as declining unemployment, increasing as well as decreasing income inequality. On the whole, the past few years have shown the most improvement compared with the 1980s, the 1990s, and the first decade of the 2000s (ECLAC, 2013). However, absolute, functional, and relational inequalities continue to represent and be perceived as a serious concern and a "pending debt" (ECLAC, 2014: 20).

7. The violence in certain countries, such as Colombia, Mexico, Bolivia, and El Salvador, has been openly linked to the rampant trafficking of drugs and the U.S. War on Drugs. These countries have shown weakness in controlling sectors of their territory where the actual ruling parties have become either drug traffickers, paramilitaries, or guerrillas that have driven populations away (both internally and transnationally). Gang violence and armed conflict with the tacit complicity of the state or an inability to reverse the situation have increased over the years. The controversial role of the state has been understood as a continuum from pre-democratic times (this popular interpretation may or may not be accurate, but it has added to the general distrust of formal institutions). In contrast, the violence in other countries, such as Argentina and Brazil, has not been directly associated with drug trafficking, but these countries have become more and more involved in transnational illicit trade networks and have a significant number of areas where gang violence rules. In these cases, there is also distrust of formal institutions of law enforcement such as the police, which have proven to be not only extremely corrupt but also inefficient, and an association between the increase in criminality, violence, and insecurity, and a lack of governmental power. Drug-related conflict has been concentrated in certain geographical sectors in each country, a spatial segregation that shows not only state weakness and/or complicity but also the ways in which systems of inequality drive some populations into marginal/ized areas (see, for example, Desmond Arias and Goldstein, 2010; Koonings and Kruijt, 2004; and ECLAC, 2014).

Part I

FRAMING COLLECTIVE MEMORY: COUNTER-HEGEMONIC AND MASTER NARRATIVES

Roberta Villalón

The chapters in this section of the volume focus on how collective memory is framed and reframed over time, illustrating dynamics of power and the play of hegemonic and counter-hegemonic forces. First, Crenzel's "Genesis, Uses, and Significations of the *Nunca Más* Report in Argentina" shows that this publication, originally the result of opposition to the veiled (and biased) nature of the military's official narrative of the so-called Dirty War, became a canonical text (that is, a new master narrative) from which to extract a unified understanding of human rights violations during the military regime in Argentina. Crenzel argues that the *Nunca Más* report portrayed victims as universal (depoliticized) subjects of law abused by the military regime and that it was used not only as evidence in the first round of trials against the military in Argentina but also as a model for other Latin American countries going through similar processes. By analyzing the politics underlying the creation and uses of the report, he ponders its value, complexity, and inconsistencies from a historical socio-logical perspective. His research demystifies the report and, while acknowledging its relevance as a master narrative, uncovers its biases—biases that should be thought through if there is interest in pursuing more in-depth understandings of an abusive past and a contradictory present.

Complementing Crenzel's provocative piece, Salvi's chapter analyzes how the mili-tary tried to take over the human rights perspective presented in the canonical *Nunca Más* report by claiming that those who were abducted, tortured, and/or murdered/disappeared were not the only victims of the regime and its system of repression but that everyone, including the military active at the time and their families, was a victim deserving recognition and justice. In "'We're All Victims': Changes in the Narrative of 'National Reconciliation' in Argentina," Salvi points to the way the rhetoric of national reconciliation has changed hands and meanings over time: used by the military to avoid trials of human rights violations, presented as the reason to forget about the scars of the "antisubversive war," and employed as a call for unity in the duty to remember the common pain that "all" Argentines have suffered. Salvi's analysis of the official human rights narrative as a double-edged sword whereby the victorious can become victims and the universal can be deconstructed as partial points to a controversial stage in the process of memory, truth, and justice: identifying a collective guilt in which no one is guilty because everyone is.

Hiner and Azócar's work "Irreconcilable Differences: Political Culture and Gender Violence during the Chilean Transition to Democracy" emphasizes the relevance of the contradictions and ironies of political processes of memory and justice. Focusing on the effects of the meta-rhetoric of national reconciliation in the sphere of gender violence policies, they show that this master framework was detrimental because it not only limited the process of truth and justice for victims of the military regime but also gave policy making an all-encompassing conservative tone. In the case of family violence, the imposition of a culture of reconciliation had notoriously negative consequences: it resulted in the prioritization of family unity over the well-being of victims of domestic violence. With their analysis, Hiner and Azócar uncover the controversial effects of applying a reconciliatory strategic framing beyond the human rights violations of the military regime: While the public/private, political/apolitical divides are in practice nonexistent, they continue to be dogmatically conceptualized as real. This fiction can only be detrimental, particularly to those in a vulnerable or marginalized position.

These three chapters challenge readers and scholars to develop more comprehensive research as their authors believe is the best means to tackle the complexities and the seemingly unavoidable paradoxes of processes of memory and justice as they develop over time and space.

Additional readings to complement this section can be found in *Latin American Perspectives* 42 (3) (see Sutton, 2015) and 43 (6) (see Mendoza, 2016; Fried Amilivia, 2016).

1

Genesis, Uses, and Significations of the *Nunca Más* Report in Argentina

Emilio Crenzel

The *Nunca Más* (Never Again) report was prepared by the Comisión Nacional sobre la Desaparición de Personas (National Commission on the Disappearance of Persons—CONADEP), created by constitutional president Raúl Alfonsín in December 1983, following Argentina's return to democracy, to investigate the fate of thousands of persons who were disappeared through the state's repressive actions.[1] *Nunca Más* exposed the characteristics and extent of the system of forced disappearances and established the responsibility of the state in its implementation. It became a bestseller, selling an unprecedented number of copies for a publication on the subject, was translated into English, German, Hebrew, Italian, and Portuguese, and was published abroad, with a total of 510,000 copies sold as of May 2009.[2]

Nunca Más gained greater public importance when the military juntas were brought to trial in 1985 and the investigation on which the report was based became the backbone of the strategy used by the prosecution, which also adopted its style of narrative and presentation of the facts. The court accepted the report as evidence, thus legitimizing its content as truth. The report's importance was further enhanced when the CONADEP was adopted as a model for various truth commissions formed throughout Latin America from 1985 to 2003 to expose the crimes committed under the various processes of state terrorism and civil wars that had afflicted the countries of the region from the 1970s to the 1990s (Acuña et al., 1995; Sikkink and Walling, 2006). In Argentina, starting in the mid-1990s, the *Nunca Más* report was postulated as a means for conveying an awareness of this past to the country's younger generations: it was incorporated into school curricula and disseminated through subsequent printings aimed at the general public. It acquired new meaning with the prologue added by the Néstor Kirchner administration in the 2006 edition, published for the thirtieth anniversary of the 1976 coup d'état. Through these processes, *Nunca Más* became Argentina's canonical account of the disappearances (Crenzel, 2008). It has been studied from different perspectives. A first group of works examined its impact on the field of transitional justice (Barahona de Brito, 2001; Funes, 2001; Grandin, 2005; Hayner, 1994; 2001; Marchesi, 2001), while a second group sought to understand the continuities and changes that it presented as a representation of human rights violations (Basile, 1989; González Bombal, 1995; Vezzetti, 2002). Until now, however, the history of the report has never been addressed as a specific object of study. Given the canonical nature of *Nunca Más* as an interpretation of the country's past of political violence, the history of the report will also serve to shed light on the politics of memory as applied to forced disappearances in Argentina.

CHANGES IN THE CULTURE OF DENUNCIATION: THE "DICTATORSHIP NEVER AGAIN" SLOGAN

The systematic practice of forced disappearances that began with the coup d'état of March 1976 presented two radical changes with respect to the degrees and forms of political violence experienced in Argentina throughout the twentieth century: a determination on the part of the state to exterminate its opponents and the perpetration of political killings as clandestine operations. These features set Argentina's dictatorship apart from the other regimes that spread through the Southern Cone of Latin America in the 1970s. In 1984 the CONADEP recorded 8,960 cases of forced disappearances of persons. Human rights organizations maintain that as many as 30,000 people were disappeared. In Uruguay, prolonged imprisonment was more commonplace, and most of the 100 cases of disappearances of Uruguayan nationals occurred on Argentine soil; in Chile, two-thirds of the mortal victims of the dictatorship were killed publicly (SERPAJ, 1989), with the disappeared representing 33 percent of all deaths (CNVD, 1991), and in Brazil some 100 people were disappeared (Arquidiócesis de São Paulo, 1985).

From 1973 to 1976, under the constitutional administrations of the Peronist party, political violence escalated on the side of both the guerrillas and paramilitary groups such as the Alianza Anticomunista Argentina (Argentine Anticommunist Alliance), which murdered hundreds of political opponents with official backing. While in the first half of the 1970s there were only isolated cases of disappearances, starting in 1975, under the presidency of María Estela Martínez de Perón and following two decrees issued by her authorizing the armed forces to wipe out all subversive elements, forced disappearances became increasingly common.[3] After the coup d'état of March 24, 1976, forced disappearances became a systematic practice. In fact, 90 percent of all disappearances occurred after the coup. Perpetrated by military or police forces, the disappearances combined generally public instances (kidnappings) with clandestine instances (imprisonment in clandestine detention centers, where victims were tortured and ultimately disappeared). In all cases, the military dictatorship denied any responsibility for them. It was only in December 1977 that, speaking to the foreign press, the dictator Jorge Videla mentioned the disappeared as an unintended by-product of the "antisubversive war." The disappeared, he said, were subversives who had gone underground, fled the country, or been killed in armed clashes that left their bodies beyond recognition. Thus he described the disappeared as guerrillas and attributed their disappearance to the state of war (Verbitsky, 1995: 78).

Months before, new human rights organizations such as the Madres de Plaza de Mayo (Mothers of Plaza de Mayo), the Abuelas de Plaza de Mayo (Grandmothers of Plaza de Mayo), and Familiares de Desaparecidos y Detenidos por Razones Políticas (Relatives of the Detained-Disappeared for Political Reasons) had been formed. They presented their demands not only to the military authorities but also to local human rights bodies such as the Asamblea Permanente por los Derechos Humanos (Permanent Assembly for Human Rights—APDH, which received 5,580 reports of disappearances), the United States Congress, several European parliaments, transnational human rights networks, and supranational bodies such as the Organization of American States.

During this process, a common style of denunciation emerged among the various individuals and organizations, both within Argentina and in exile, which reported the disappearances—a style that was shaped by the new relations forged with transnational human rights networks. Prior to the coup d'état, political repression was denounced from a revolutionary activist perspective that stressed the relationship between state violence and capitalist society, historically contextualized the violence, and exalted the political commitments of those who had suffered it (see Foro de Buenos Aires, 1973). After the coup, this discourse was displaced by a humanitarian narrative that, in terms of a moral imperative, called for empathy with the victims. Moreover, this type of account privileged a factual and detailed description of the violations committed, the persons responsible for such violations, and the victims, whose depiction focused on their moral qualities and basic identifying particulars such as age, sex, nationality, and occupation, thus positing their innocence and lack of involvement in "subversion." In this way, the individuals and organizations that reported the disappearances sought to challenge the stigmatizing discourse of the dictatorship that equated the disappeared with guerrillas, even if in highlighting the innocence and moral values of their disappeared relatives, they failed to question the premises and limits established by the dictatorship with respect to who merited the right to be considered a subject of law.[4] In this context of cultural and political change, the phrase "nunca más" (never again) began to be increasingly used by human rights organizations and groups of exiles in connection with the crimes perpetrated by the dictatorship and the historical cycle of military interventions inaugurated in 1930 (see Jensen, 2004: 645; Rojkind, 2004: 287).[5]

However, up until its military defeat in June 1982 in the war with Britain over the Malvinas/Falklands Islands, the dictatorship succeeded in neutralizing any reports of this crime. After the war, human rights organizations channeled the country's discontent with the regime and emerged as a difficult-to-ignore actor in the public sphere. With the aim of preventing a revision of the past, on April 28, 1983, the dictatorial government issued the "Final Document of the Military Junta on the War against Subversion and Terrorism," acknowledging its responsibility in the "antisubversive war" but leaving the examination of its actions to "divine judgment" and declaring that the armed forces had been called on to wipe out subversion by a "constitutional government," in reference to the decrees authorizing its involvement in the war issued in 1975 by Perón's widow in her capacity as president (*Convicción*, 1983). The legal counterpart to this message was the National Pacification Act (Law 22,924), passed on September 23, 1983, a month prior to the elections. This law, which came to be known as the "self-amnesty" law, extinguished all causes of action arising from crimes committed during the "antisubversive war," calling for the past of fighting, dead, and wounded "to never again be repeated" and for the country to "forgive mutual aggressions and engage in national peace-building efforts in a gesture of reconciliation."[6] Thus, the dictatorship proposed a "never again" that closed the book on the past and guaranteed impunity. The law was rejected by public opinion (see González Bombal and Landi, 1995: 158), and the human rights organizations then demanded that the future civilian government establish a bicameral commission to investigate state terrorism, which they claimed would guarantee the imperative of "never again." In this way, the phrase "never again" came to be associated for the first time with the demand for justice.

THE CONADEP INVESTIGATION AND THE *NUNCA MÁS* REPORT

After winning the presidential elections as the candidate of the Unión Cívica Radical, Raúl Alfonsín took office on December 10, 1983. Three days after his inauguration he ordered the prosecution of seven former guerrilla leaders and the members of the first three military juntas of the dictatorship. His decision was labeled "the theory of the two demons" because it limited accountability for political violence to the two sets of leaders and explained state violence as a response to guerrilla violence. Alfonsín also proposed that in the first instance the trials be heard by the supreme council of the armed forces and distinguished three groups of perpetrators: "those who planned the repression and issued the orders; those who acted beyond the orders, prompted by cruelty, perversion, or greed; and those who carried out the orders strictly to the letter." This allowed for the existence of "excesses" without specifying what such excesses were and therefore failing to define who had acted beyond orders.[7] Alfonsín's proposal fueled the demand of the human rights organizations for a bicameral commission, as these organizations believed that the military courts could not be trusted to hand down sentences. This initiative garnered increasing support from center-left parties, the Peronist party, and even some sectors of the government (Jelin, 1995: 128).

The president's advisers then suggested that he create a commission of "notables" modeled on the special commissions of prominent civil society personalities formed by the United States Congress to address specific issues. Alfonsín feared that establishing a bicameral commission would set legislators against each other as they vied to impose harsher sanctions on the armed forces, creating an extremely tense situation with the military (Nino, 1997: 112, 119).[8] He invited members of the human rights organizations calling for a bicameral commission to join the commission of notables in the hope of dissuading them from moving ahead with their proposal while at the same time legitimizing his own initiative. Nobel Peace Prize laureate Adolfo Pérez Esquivel declined the invitation, as did Augusto Conte and Emilio Mignone, both directors of the Centro de Estudios Legales y Sociales (Center for Legal and Social Studies— CELS). Alfonsín then invited Ernesto Sábato to join the commission instead (Adolfo Pérez Esquivel, interview, Buenos Aires, December 13, 2004).[9] Other personalities who were invited to form part of the commission included Eduardo Rabossi, lawyer and presidential adviser; Gregorio Klimovsky, epistemologist and APDH member; Hilario F. Long, former president of the Universidad de Buenos Aires; Marshall Meyer, rabbi and APDH member; Ricardo Colombres, former justice minister; Jaime de Nevares, bishop and APDH member; Magdalena Ruiz Guiñazú, journalist and human rights advocate; René Favaloro, heart surgeon; and Carlos Gattinoni, pastor and member of the APDH and the Movimiento Ecuménico por los Derechos Humanos (Ecumenical Movement for Human Rights—MEDH). All were prominent figures, and most had been human rights advocates or, as had Sábato, had changed their positive view of the dictatorship when it started evidencing signs of crisis.

The CONADEP was rejected by every human rights organization except the APDH and by the opposition, with only three Radical Civic Union representatives agreeing to join (*Clarín*, December 21, 1983).[10] Despite this, its direction reflected the power wielded by the country's human rights organizations. That influence was heightened when APDH members Graciela Fernández Meijide and Raúl Aragón agreed to act as the commission's secretaries for depositions and procedures, respectively, and when Fernández Meijide called on the organizations to volunteer activists to take depositions. Despite having opposed the establishment of the CONADEP, all of the human rights organizations, except the Madres de Plaza de Mayo, agreed to hand over all the testimonies they had gathered, in addition to giving statements before the commission and contributing personnel.[11]

The CONADEP soon exceeded the mandate set by the executive. With the help of the human rights organizations, it gathered thousands of new testimonies in areas surrounding large cities and in more remote locations around the country where the relatives of the disappeared had had nowhere to report the disappearances.[12] It also increased the number of statements from survivors, from whom there had been very few testimonies available. These statements led to the identification of previously unknown clandestine detention centers, provided additional information on other major centers, and revealed how prisoners were moved from one center to another, thus proving that the centers were part of a network. It also gathered testimonies from some perpetrators and from involuntary witnesses of these crimes who confirmed the reports (*Clarín*, March 14, 1984). The CONADEP organized this material according to clandestine detention center, understanding as such any place where a disappeared person had been held captive, even if only for a few hours. This led it to conclude that "any police or military unit could be turned into a secret detention facility at the discretion of the unit's chief, thus proving the systematic nature of state terrorism" (Alberto Mansur, CONADEP legal affairs secretary, interview, Buenos Aires, September 1, 2004).

The commission inspected close to 50 clandestine centers distributed throughout the country, coming up against military or police personnel whose reactions included attempting to prevent inspections, denying reports, and withholding information regarding the unit's physical infrastructure or personnel, as reported by witnesses (*Clarín*, March 1, 1984). In most cases the witnesses were able to identify general aspects of the places in which they were held captive, as well as details they would not have known if they had not been there before. The commission then held press conferences with the participation of these witnesses in which they offered a new public truth of what had happened, and it submitted the information gathered as evidence to the courts. These initiatives led to a shift in the way the CONADEP was perceived; its usefulness was no longer questioned, nor was it criticized for the ties some of its members had with the dictatorship. Instead, it now came to be associated with subversion (*La Voz*, May 29, 1984; *Clarín*, May 31, 1984, and June 14, 1984).

The convergence of the CONADEP and the survivors and relatives of the disappeared was also expressed through a television program, titled *Nunca Más*, in which the commission presented a preliminary report of its findings to the general public. This program was aired despite pressure from military circles to prevent this. In the introduction to the program, Interior Minister Antonio Tróccoli warned viewers that the violence suffered by the country had been sparked by "subversion and terrorism," equating these with state terrorism. Moreover, in line with Alfonsín's decrees, he stressed the need to bring to trial "the high commands of the groups responsible for unleashing the violence" and called for "never again." The rest of the program featured relatives of disappeared persons and disappearance survivors, as well as Estela Carloto and Isabel Mariani, vice president and president of the Abuelas de Plaza de Mayo, respectively, and members of the Madres de Plaza de Mayo, who described the abuses suffered and their struggle and demanded "trial and punishment for all perpetrators" to guarantee that the disappearances would "never again" be repeated. Their testimonies were backed by the CONADEP, represented by Sábato. The program was viewed by 1,600,000 people. Thus the voices of survivors and relatives of the disappeared reached a mass audience (*Somos*, 1984).

The *Nunca Más* program presented two different conceptions of "never again." While Alfonsín's minister associated the imperative with the need to bring the top military and guerrilla leaders to justice, the human rights organizations associated it with trial and punishment for all guilty parties. In spite of this difference between them, the human rights organizations and the CONADEP clearly agreed on where the legal proceedings should be conducted. Ignoring government pressures, the

CONADEP decided that it would submit all the testimonies and evidence it had gathered to civilian courts except when the reporting party expressly authorized submission to a military court, thus giving the relatives and survivors the power of deciding where the criminal actions brought by them would be prosecuted.[13] The two also worked together when it came time to write the report; the commission asked the human rights organizations to contribute any final input they might have and for the most part included that input in the report.[14] In addition, Sábato's decision to build the report around the testimonies gathered placed the voices of survivors and relatives of the disappeared in the center of the account. Along that same line, the CONADEP decided to present the disappeared exclusively through their basic identifying particulars, excluding their political commitments, thus resuming the humanitarian narrative that had prevailed in the denunciation of this crime during the dictatorship. It also chose to refrain from examining the responsibility of the Peronist party and political party leaders in general in the disappearances committed prior to the coup so as not to diminish the impact of its report, which in this way would have condemned only the dictatorship. The "Never Again" slogan, which according to the CONADEP members was accepted by all without discussion as the title for the report, translated this aim.[15]

THE *NUNCA MÁS* REPORT

As seen above, the CONADEP's investigation entailed the convergence of efforts by human rights organizations and the Alfonsín administration. The *Nunca Más* report expressed this convergence by combining the government's interpretation of the past of political violence with the humanitarian narrative forged by those who denounced the disappearances during the dictatorship. In line with the decrees ordering the trials of the guerrilla leaders and the military juntas, the prologue to the report presented the country's past political violence as a product of ideological extremes without putting it into historical context or explaining its causes. The report condemned the violence prior to the coup but focused on the "response" of the state as of 1976.[16]

By stressing the responsibility of the dictatorship in the disappearances, the report limited its object to the dictatorial period. Although the body of the report mentioned cases of disappearances that occurred in 1975, under the Martínez de Perón government, these facts were omitted from the prologue. Its periodization of violence according to the country's different institutional moments was complemented by its presentation of political democracy as a guarantee for preventing the horror from being repeated (CONADEP, 1984: 9, 15). This periodization was consistent with a policy of memory ignoring the political and moral responsibility that civil and political society may have had in the disappearances perpetrated prior to the coup. This policy was reproduced in the report's portrayal of society as a whole as taking one of two always innocent positions in the face of state terror: either its potential victim or an uninvolved observer that, if it justified the state's actions, did so only as a result of the widespread terror.[17] Despite these propositions, the body of the report evidenced the complicity of certain sectors of society—such as the educational authorities and the business establishment—in the disappearances, although it refers to them institutionally only in the case of the judicial system. This is particularly true with respect to the Catholic Church (CONADEP, 1984: 259, 379, 397).

The report presented the disappeared as opponents of the dictatorship, social and even revolutionary activists, and "friends of any of these people," thus constructing a universe of victims that excluded the guerrillas.[18] This delimitation was expanded in the body of the report to include political activists. The disappeared were almost exclusively identified by their names, presented as "individuals or human beings," "kidnapped, detained or disappeared individuals, or captives or prisoners," or classified according to their age and gender. This way of presenting the victims was complemented by the use of subsection headings such as "Children and Pregnant Women Who Disappeared," "Adolescents," "The Family as Victim," and "The Sick and Disabled," which highlighted the wide range of victims targeted for disappearance and the defenselessness and "innocence" of the disappeared. Thus, the report grounded its denunciation in the moral condition of the victims rather than in the universal character of their rights (CONADEP, 1984: 9, 10, 294, 345–346). Moreover, through the more than 400 names mentioned in the testimonies, it revealed the identity of the perpetrators. In six out of every ten cases they were explicitly identified as military or police officers. It also illustrated the repressive coordination of the dictatorships of the region and, near the end, briefly outlined their doctrine. This style of presenting the findings prioritized the description of the abuses over any mention of political considerations. Even so, it defined the abuses as violations of Western religious and political principles, refuting the discourse of the dictatorship that justified its actions in the name of "Western Christian" civilization (CONADEP, 1984: 8, 15, 265–276, 347–349).

The strategy employed in the *Nunca Más* report for presenting the facts was based on its exposure of the disappearances as a system. It charted the different stages of the crime: abduction, torture, clandestine captivity, and death of the disappeared. It put the number of disappearances at 8,960—although noting that this was not a definite figure—and the number of clandestine detention centers detected at 340. The number of clandestine centers and their distribution served to recreate the national dimension of the clandestine system. Moreover, by revealing that most centers were located in military or police facilities, the report refuted the military's denial of any responsibility in the disappearances.

The report's account drew primarily on the voices of survivors and relatives of disappeared persons, which represent 75 percent of the 379 testimonies included. The repeated reference to certain places, dates, and names in the testimonies restored the reality, spatiality, and temporality of the facts and the identity of the victims.[19] But the report also incorporated testimonies from perpetrators, which, while representing only 2 percent of the statements, together with statements from "involuntary witnesses" of disappearances served to confirm the voices of the relatives and survivors. This diversity of voices created a new result, a chorus of testimonies, that proposed a unified representation of the disappearances.

With respect to criminal responsibility, the report reflected the lack of consensus within the CONADEP on this issue and the differences between human rights organizations and the Alfonsín administration in terms of the scope of criminal justice. On the one hand, it established the responsibility of the military juntas in planning the crime. On the other hand, it presented clandestine centers according to the forces under their command, organized the disappeared according to the military units they were held in, suggesting the responsibility of the commanding officers of these units, and underlined that "any sign of disagreement within the armed and security forces over detention or elimination methods was brutally punished. . . . Any attempt to escape from the structure of repression, which members referred to as the 'pact,' could entail their persecution and even elimination" (CONADEP, 1984: 8, 253–259, 300). This suggests that the view taken in the report reproduced Alfonsín's distinction of degrees of responsibility. This position had been seriously undermined in February 1984 in a debate in the Senate, which concluded with the inclusion (on the initiative of Elias Sapag, a representative for the Neuquén People's Movement) of an amendment that denied the defense of due obedience to anyone who had committed "atrocious and abhorrent acts" (Nino, 1997: 119). However, *Nunca Más* challenged the official stance and came closer to the position held by humanitarian organizations when it warned that the "cases included in the report do not represent 'excesses,' as no such thing existed, if by 'excesses' we understand isolated and particularly abhorrent acts. . . . Abhorrent acts were not the exception but a common and widespread practice. The 'especially atrocious acts' numbered in the thousands. They were the 'norm.'" Thus, the report also rendered the Senate's amendment meaningless. It did so, moreover, by positing that it was "essential to conduct a judicial investigation to determine the makeup of the task forces that were part of the repressive structure," thus expanding legal inquiries to include middle- and lower-ranking officers, whom the government had intended to exclude (CONADEP, 1984: 15, 16, 223, 256, 481).

THE *NUNCA MÁS* REPORT AND THE PROSECUTION OF THE PAST

Released in November 1984, by March 1985 *Nunca Más* had sold 190,000 copies, including an edition in Braille and the first foreign edition, published by EUDEBA and the Spanish publishing house Seix Barral. This figure represents 42 percent of the 510,000 copies published as of May 2009 (Sandra Günther, interview, Buenos Aires, August 20, 2004).[20] This impact was linked to the credibility of the just-restored democracy, the prestige of the members of the CONADEP, and, in particular, public expectations surrounding the imminent trial of the military juntas. Domestically, the book was in great demand and drew a socially and ideologically

diverse readership. However, because of the harshness of its contents, it was emotion-
ally disturbing and difficult to understand, and readers often felt compelled to put
it down (Fontán, 1985: 38; Luis Gregorich, interview). In the public sphere, the report's assessment was conditioned by criminal prosecution objectives. This, however,
was not a cause for division between the human rights organizations and the military and its supporters. For Carlos Zamorano (1984) and Emilio Mignone (1984),
leaders of the LADH and the CELS, the *Nunca Más* report was a "strong piece of
evidence for the prosecution" that demolished the military thesis of "excesses" and
the official position of "degrees of responsibility." For the Madres de Plaza de Mayo,
in contrast, it did not present the truth and denied justice by suggesting that the repression was a response to the guerrillas when in fact the guerrillas had already been
decimated; it concealed the real objective behind the coup, which was to impose an
imperialist economic model, and it declared the death of the disappeared through
a "partial and deliberate selection" of testimonies "without any evidence to prove
them" (*Diario de las Madres de Plaza de Mayo*, 1984; 1985).

For their part, military supporters published their own book with the aim of
creating a debate. The book, *Definitivamente Nunca Más: La otra cara del informe
de la CONADEP* (Definitely Never Again: The Other Side of the CONADEP
Report), was written by lawyers of the Foro de Estudios sobre la Administración
de Justicia (Forum for Studies on the Administration of Justice—FORES), created
shortly after the coup, and it was released in May 1985 (Lynch and Del Carril,
1985: 100, 102). According to the FORES, the *Nunca Más* report omitted the fact
that the use of illegal methods began during the administration headed by Perón's
widow, María Isabel Martínez de Perón. The book further stated that the report
was based on testimonies of affected parties without "any attempt to verify if there
was any truth in them," with the aim of "passing judgment on the armed forces in
advance" and turning "guerrilla members into martyrs and those who combated
them into murderers and torturers." It also pointed out that the report failed to
prove that the illegal methods employed were a result of orders issued by superiors
as the prosecution argued in the military junta trials (Lynch and Del Carril, 1985:
19–20, 23–25, 71, 81–83, 95–99, 103–117).

In those trials the prosecutor, Strassera, grounded his strategy precisely in the
account given in the *Nunca Más* report, drawing on the evidence gathered by the
CONADEP. He presented the cases in which the victims were farthest from any
political commitment, highlighted the violation of the victims' rights and their
defenselessness, sought to condemn the dictatorship alone, and closed his allegations with the emblematic words "never again." The defense lawyers, for their part,
tried to expose the political activism of the disappeared and the witnesses with the
aim of denying their citizenship. Both strategies illustrate the limits of the concept
of citizenship in the newly restored democracy by failing to recognize the universal
nature of human rights.[21]

Nonetheless, the trials enhanced the legitimacy of the *Nunca Más* report. In Argentina there were several new printings of the book, and it was discussed in special

events organized by the state and by the human rights organizations (Alberto Mansur, interview, San Martín, September 1, 2004; Eduardo Rabossi, interview, Buenos Aires, August 19, 2004; Graciela Fernández Meijide, interview, Buenos Aires, October 20, 2004). It was through the efforts of these two actors that the report was translated abroad. In 1985 *Nunca Más* was published in Portuguese in Brazil, and in 1986 it was released in Italy through the initiative of relatives of the disappeared. It was published in English in London, by Faber and Faber, and in the United States, by Farrar Straus Giroux, with the support of Ronald Dworkin, a scholar who had advised Alfonsín on his human rights policy.[22] Also, at the regional level, in a context of democratization and debates over how to process the region's histories of political violence, *Nunca Más* was distributed through transnational human rights networks, and it was considered by governments as a model for building a new truth regarding their recent pasts (see CONADEP, 1984; Markarián, 2006: 176; Sikkink and Walling, 2006). Several truth commissions adopted *Nunca Más* as the title for their own reports (see Arquidiócesis de São Paulo, 1985; CIPAE, 1990; SERPAJ, 1989; Proyecto Interdiocesano de Recuperación de la Memoria Histórica, 1996).

The legitimization of *Nunca Más* can be said, then, to have resulted from a movement that emerged from the state and civil society and from both within and outside the country. Through these processes, the report established a new way of constructing a memory of the recent past, a concept that is proposed here to illustrate the structures of meaning that became dominant in the public sphere as various practices and discourses created frameworks for selecting what was memorable and introduced interpretative and narrative approaches for thinking about, evoking, and conveying the past.

However, divisions arose among *Nunca Más* supporters over their different expectations with respect to the criminal punishment that the perpetrators of the disappearances deserved. In December 1986 Alfonsín introduced a bill in the Congress for what would become the Full Stop Act, establishing a 60-day deadline for the filing of lawsuits, after which the cases would be extinguished. In May 1987 he introduced the Due Obedience bill, whereby all actions except those involving changes in identity, abduction of children, and misappropriation of property were deemed to have been committed under coercion and subordination to orders from superiors. The bill was accompanied by a message from the executive stating that the imperative of "never again" had been guaranteed by the trials and the end of indifference, in an allusion to the revealing nature of the report (*La Prensa*, May 14, 1987). For the human rights organizations, in contrast, "never again" was a goal that had not yet been fully attained and was threatened by pressures from the military but also by the official position that these laws represented (*Clarín*, April 30, 1987). These processes impacted the publishing history of *Nunca Más*. During the four years following the passage of the Due Obedience Act, the report was not published again in Argentina or abroad. The last printing from EUDEBA was published in July 1987, simultaneously with the German translation, which came out in 10,000 copies (Petra Dorn, electronic communication, July 16, 2004).

Upon taking office in 1989, the Peronist President Carlos Menem gave new meaning to the "never again" slogan, linking it to the policies of reconciliation and pacification of society that were summed up in the pardons he granted to members of the military juntas (*Clarín*, October 15, 1989; December 8, 1990). At that point, most humanitarian organizations saw the *Nunca Más* report as an instrument that could be used to challenge these policies, and they asked the authorities of the Universidad de Buenos Aires to publish it again.[23] This new printing came out in July 1991 and was presented by human rights organizations and the bishop Jaime de Nevares in his capacity as a former CONADEP member, without the participation of representatives from the state or political parties.[24] This absence was reflected in the document read by the human rights organizations at the launching ceremony, in which they declared that the report was the result of efforts of relatives of the disappeared, survivors, and the CONADEP, omitting all reference to the commission's governmental origins.[25] Despite this initiative, in a context marked by hyperinflation and the implementation of economic adjustment programs, the public's interest in the recent past waned, and this publication and those released by EUDEBA from 1992 to 1994 totaled 11,000 copies in all, only 2.5 percent of the copies published as of 2009.

NUNCA MÁS AS A VEHICLE OF MEMORY

However, the public debate on political violence was suddenly sparked again in February 1995, when the naval captain Adolfo Scilingo publicly confessed his participation in disappearance operations in which prisoners were dropped to their deaths from airplanes into the sea (*Página/12*, March 3, 1995). In this context, from March through August 1995, EUDEBA released 16,000 copies of *Nunca Más*, surpassing in only five months the number of copies issued in the 1991–1994 period. Simultaneously, various civil society groups called for new editions of the report. These initiatives had a number of peculiarities. On the one hand, they sought to employ *Nunca Más* as a vehicle for transmitting to younger generations the memory of the past violence. On the other, alongside a verbatim reproduction of the original text they featured other content and images through which the human rights organizations presented their own interpretations of the disappearances while at the same time denouncing current circumstances, thus making an exemplary use of *Nunca Más* (see Todorov, 2000).

The first of these new editions of *Nunca Más* was published by the daily newspaper *Página/12* in 30 installments that appeared from 1995 to 1996, with a circulation of 75,000 copies each. This serialized publication featured collages by the artist León Ferrari[26] in which the disappearances were represented as a product of "Western Christian" civilization. For Ferrari, massacres and genocides were explained by Christian morals, and therefore he saw the crimes committed in Argentina as another consequence of the Christian value system. His collages combined

Christian iconography with photographs of the perpetrators of the disappearances, pictures of high-ranking Nazi officers, and engravings of the Inquisition, witch hunts, and Spanish violence in the Americas. In this way, the same Western political and religious principles that the CONADEP considered had been violated by the dictatorship were now presented as causes of the horror, while democracy was no longer seen as posing a barrier to its repetition. Nonetheless, like the CONADEP report, the collages did not delve deeper into the country's history for explanations of the disappearances, and the disappeared were presented merely as human beings, omitting their political commitments.

The second edition of *Nunca Más* in this period was published for the twentieth anniversary of the coup d'état, just as the situation of social exclusion created by Menem's neoliberal policies had begun to be read as a result of the model established by the dictatorship. At the same time, a documentary by the journalist Eduardo Aliverti titled *Malajunta* was screened throughout the country (*Página/12*, September 21, 1996). The film set out to describe the cultural policy of the dictatorship, including testimonies of artists and intellectuals who were persecuted during that period.[27] The people interviewed in the documentary reproduced the narrative of the *Nunca Más* report by presenting themselves as innocent and bewildered victims of repression, and the disappeared were identified by their occupations, excluding the guerrillas from their universe. However, in contrast with *Nunca Más*, *Malajunta* established a link between the dictatorship's repressive actions and those of the Peronist government, thus highlighting a continuity in the repression, and the people interviewed considered society as complicit with the disappearances, which they associated with the regime's economic policies.

The third of these initiatives involved the incorporation of *Nunca Más* into the classroom as a means of conveying this past to the younger generations.[28] In February 1997 EUDEBA published 3,000 copies of a text titled *Haciendo memoria en el país de Nunca Más* (Remembering in the Land of Never Again), written by three education experts and distributed nationwide by the Ministry of Education. In contrast to *Nunca Más*, the text examined the political and ideological framework of the dictatorship, reviewed Argentina's history since the nineteenth century, established a connection between state terror and the economic programs of the regime, and portrayed the disappeared as activists and even as guerrillas. Moreover, by presenting the situation of increasing social inequality and police violence that prevailed in the country at the time of its publication, *Haciendo memoria* challenged the claim that democracy would guarantee the imperative of *Nunca Más* (Dussel, Finocchio, and Gojman, 1997: ix–x, 9–25, 33–34, 100–102).

Another edition appeared in March 2006, prepared by EUDEBA for the thirtieth anniversary of the coup. This time the report included a prologue penned by the National Human Rights Secretariat, formed by Eduardo Duhalde and Rodolfo Mattarollo, prominent defense lawyers of political prisoners and individuals who had denounced the dictatorship while in exile. This prologue did not establish a democracy-dictatorship dichotomy. Instead, it contrasted the Kirchner administration with the constitutional governments that came before it by criticizing the impunity laws passed in that period and the neoliberal policies implemented by the dictatorship and continued by the ensuing democratic governments and by describing the prologue of the original *Nunca Más* edition as a "symmetrical justification" of state violence in opposition to guerrilla violence.[29] It portrayed the present as a "historical" and "exceptional" moment, a product of the policies implemented by the government and its response to the "unwavering demands for truth, justice and memory that our people have been clamoring for throughout the last three decades" (CONADEP, 2006: 7). In this way, it presented a view of the relationship between Argentine society and the horror experienced by it that was the exact opposite of the one presented in the original prologue. But this new view was just as totalizing as the other in that it portrayed a society that stood undivided, as a monolithic whole, in the face of terror and impunity. It too failed to contextualize the country's political violence historically or to attribute responsibility for the disappearances perpetrated prior to the coup, and it reproduced the original CONADEP's sociodemographic portrayal of the disappeared, excluding the guerrillas, although it expanded this portrayal to include political activists (CONADEP, 2006: 8–9).

In sum, with the exception of the 2006 prologue, all the interventions implemented as of 1995 placed the disappearances within a time frame that transcended the dictatorship, either presenting them as part of a wider history of exterminations (Ferrari), highlighting the continuity of repression between the pre-coup government and the dictatorship *(Malajunta)*, or contextualizing it in terms of national history *(Haciendo memoria)*. Nonetheless, these efforts avoided a complex examination of this past. They also adopted interpretative approaches that contrasted with those contained in *Nunca Más* (Ferrari) or were absent from it by associating the horror with the economic model *(Malajunta, Haciendo memoria,* and the new prologue). But they failed to assign political and moral responsibility in this process, and from an opposite but equally totalizing view they presented society as a block, either justifying the horror (Ferrari, *Malajunta*) or denouncing it (the new prologue). This depoliticization of history was also reflected in the portrayal of the disappeared: *Malajunta* and the new prologue reproduced the description of the disappeared in terms of their sociodemographic characteristics, while Ferrari presented them as abstract human beings. All of these readings rejected the dictatorship-democracy dichotomy, positing instead the existence of economic and moral continuities between the two. And as a result, they all imbued *Nunca Más* with new meaning both as a text and as an imperative.

CONCLUSIONS

This article has examined the political and cultural processes involved in the preparation, uses, and resignifications of the *Nunca Más* report, a canonical text on the memory of Argentina's disappearances. It has shown that during the dictatorship the disappearances were denounced from a humanitarian stance that privileged the factual narration of the abuses and the presentation of the disappeared in terms of their basic identifying particulars, portraying them as innocent victims. The CONADEP engaged the representatives of this narrative in its work, appointing them to directive and technical positions within the commission, used the body of testimonies they gathered, legitimized their voices in the public sphere, allowed them to have an influence on the decisions made with respect to judicial proceedings, and involved them in the drafting of the report.

Nunca Más combined this humanitarian narrative with the premises established by the Alfonsín government for examining and judging the country's past political violence. It recognized the disappeared as subjects of law without revealing their political activism, posited the exclusive responsibility of the dictatorship in the disappearances, and upheld democracy as the guarantee for preventing the horror from ever happening again, thus obscuring the responsibility of political and civil society before and after the coup. By presenting a comprehensive account of the stages involved in the crime of forced disappearance and exposing its national scope and systematic nature, *Nunca Más* publicly challenged with unprecedented strength the dictatorship's denial of the crime. The official nature of the CONADEP and the prestige of its members rendered its account credible and secured it a massive readership.

The truth introduced by *Nunca Más* in its first major cycle of publication was shaped by its relationship with the process of justice and its use in and legitimization by the junta trials, which also enhanced the report's influence in the country and abroad. Thus, *Nunca Más* became the template for constructing a new memory of that past. It became the dominant way of thinking about, remembering, and representing the past. The coordination of *Nunca Más* with different judicial objectives set the human rights community against the government of Alfonsín in a dispute over who was the rightful interpreter of its contents, and this affected future publications of the report after the impunity laws were passed and the pardons were granted. In that period, the human rights organizations regarded the *Nunca Más* report as a means for denouncing the crime of forced disappearance and as a sign of the waning willingness of the state and political leaders to seek justice.

From 1995 on, *Nunca Más* entered a new cycle of mass dissemination as multiple actors sought ways of conveying the past to younger generations. In that context, it was no longer seen as a means for attaining punitive goals and became a vehicle of memory, opening the way for a debate over possible political and historical interpretations. In this process, it was reproduced literally while at the same time being resignified as exemplary memory on the basis of different readings of the violence perpetrated under the dictatorship. These accounts introduced new meanings, some even openly challenging the original report's view, by presenting state violence as existing prior to the coup, explaining the disappearances as a result of material goals or of political and religious values that the report posited as being violated by this crime, and abandoning the view of democracy as the political regime that guaranteed the "never again" imperative.

Nonetheless, these interventions reproduced some of the interpretative approaches of the report, eluded the historical examination of the past, overlooked any possible connections between political and civil society and the horrors perpetrated, and ignored the political activism of the disappeared. If the changes introduced by these interventions evidence the erosion of a system of memory established by the *Nunca Más* report, their continuations reveal the difficulties that Argentine society has had in recognizing the universal nature of human rights and in incorporating this past into a historical account that includes politics as a feature of its protagonists and a cause for ruptures. The uses of *Nunca Más* illustrate the public's acceptance of the report as a canonical text, while its resignifications evidence that it too was shaped by the political times of collective memory. These complex and contradictory processes explain why in today's Argentina "Nunca Más" is the only slogan that summarizes, in just two words, a sense of the country's past and future.

NOTES

The original version of this essay was published in *Latin American Perspectives* 42 (3): 20–38.

1. Created by the national executive's Decree 187, December 15, 1983, and published in the *Official Gazette* on December 19, 1983.

2. Calculated from data from Editorial Universitaria de Buenos Aires (EUDEBA), which released the report in book form.

3. See CONADEP database, National Human Rights Secretariat. In February 1975 President Martínez de Perón issued Degree 265 authorizing the armed forces to "carry out any military actions that may be necessary to neutralize and/or annihilate all subversive element activities" in the province of Tucumán. In October of that year, by Decree 2772, Provisional President Ítalo Luder extended those powers to the rest of the country.

4. Markarián (2006) has analyzed their makeup and prevalence among Uruguayan political exiles on the basis of contacts with transnational human rights networks.

5. Argentina's first military coup occurred in 1930, with the ousting of democratically elected president Hipólito Yrigoyen of the Unión Cívica Radical.

6. National Pacification Act, Law No. 22,924, *Official Gazette*, September 27, 1983.

7. See Nino (1997: 106–107) and presidential decrees 157 and 158 of December 13, 1983 (*Official Gazette*, December 15, 1983, 4–5).

8. The proposal did not take into account the failed experiences of commissions created in Uganda and Bolivia to investigate disappearances in those countries (see Hayner, 1994: 611–614).

9. On Alfonsín's invitation to Conte, see Unión Cívica Radical Representatives, Actas 5, December 21, 1983, 13. On the invitation to Mignone, see Mignone (1991: 160). Sábato is one of Argentina's most prestigious writers. During the dictatorship he had praised Videla after meeting with him (Duhalde, 1999: 113–114), but in 1981 he headed the Movimiento para la Recuperación de Niños Desaparecidos (Movement for the Recovery of Disappeared Children) jointly with Adolfo Pérez Esquivel.

10. The representatives were Santiago López, defense attorney for political prisoners and national representative for Chubut, Hugo Piucill, APDH member and national representative for Río Negro, and Horacio Huarte, lawyer and representative for the province of Buenos Aires.

11. On the support given by human rights organizations to the CONADEP, see CONADEP, 1983–1984: Actas 2 (December 27, 1983), 3–4; 4 (January 3, 1984), 8; 5 (January 5, 1984), 13; 6 (January 10, 1984), 16; 8 (January 24, 1984), 22; and 11 (February 10, 1984), 32. On the position of the Madres de Plaza de Mayo, see *Clarín*, December 29, 1983. However, according to the CONADEP (Actas 8 [January 24, 1984], 22, and 14 [March 6, 1984], 44), the Mothers of Disappeared Conscripts submitted 101 reports and the Mar del Plata chapter of the Madres de Plaza de Mayo contributed another 196.

12. Sixty-four percent of the reports received by the CONADEP came from small localities (Izaguirre, 1992: 41).

13. CONADEP (1983–1984): Actas 30 (June 26, 1984), 117; 4 (January 3, 1984), 8–9; 9 (January 31, 1984), 24; 14 (March 6, 1984), 47; 19 (April 10, 1984), 75; 32 (July 10, 1984), 124–127; and 33 (July 17, 1984), 128–132.

14. Relatives of the Detained-Disappeared for Political Reasons asked that the names of those responsible for the repression be included; the MEDH requested laws that would protect the families of the disappeared; and the Liga Argentina por los Derechos del Hombre (Argentine Human Rights League—LADH) called for education in human rights and the repeal of repressive laws (CONADEP, 1983–1984: Actas 24 [May 15, 1984], 100; 27 [June 5, 1984], 108; 30 [June 26, 1984], 115; 33 [July 17, 1984], 135, 35 [July 31, 1984], 144–145; and 40 [August 28, 1984], 162). The CONADEP also initially invited the human rights organizations to review the final version of the reports, but in the end this was not possible because of time constraints (Eduardo Rabossi, interview, Buenos Aires, May 11, 2005).

15. According to interviews with Raúl Aragón, Gregorio Klimovsky, Graciela Fernández Meijide, Alberto Mansur, Magdalena Ruiz Guiñazú, and Eduardo Rabossi. In 1955, the national inquiry commission created by the military government that ousted Juan Domingo Perón issued a report titled *El libro negro de la Segunda Tiranía* (The Black Book of the Second Tyranny).

16. "The armed forces responded to the crimes committed by terrorists with a terrorism far worse than that which they were combating, because as of March 24, 1976, they availed themselves of the power and impunity afforded by an absolute state, abducting, torturing, and killing thousands of human beings" (CONADEP, 1984: 7).

17. "A feeling of vulnerability gradually took hold of society, coupled with the dark fear that anyone, however innocent, might fall victim of the never-ending witch hunt. Some people reacted with overwhelming fear, while others tended, consciously or unconsciously, to justify the horror: 'They must have done something to deserve it,' they would whisper, as though trying to appease formidable and inscrutable gods, regarding the children or parents of the disappeared as plague-bearers" (CONADEP, 1984: 9).

18. "From people who wanted to change society through a revolution to socially aware adolescents who went out to shantytowns to help their residents. Anyone could become a victim: trade union leaders fighting for better wages; youngsters in student unions; journalists who did not enthusiastically support the regime; psychologists and sociologists simply because they belonged to suspicious professions; young pacifists; nuns and priests who had taken the teachings of Christ to underprivileged neighborhoods. And the friends of any of these people, and the friends of such friends, plus others whose names were given by someone out of vengeance or were obtained under torture from people in captivity. The majority of them were innocent. Not only had they not committed acts of terrorism, they did not even

belong to guerrilla combat units, as these preferred to fight back and either died in shootouts or committed suicide before they could be captured, with few of them still alive by the time they were in the hands of the repressive forces" (CONADEP, 1984: 9–10).

19. On the importance of these frameworks for remembrance, see Halbwachs (2004). On the rupture of such frameworks after the disappearances, see Da Silva Catela (2001: 116–119, 122–123).

20. The figure for the number of copies of the report published was provided by EUDEBA.

21. For example, Prats Cardona, defense attorney for Massera, asked the journalist Ruíz Guiñazú if she knew of anyone persecuted in the antisubversive war who had been innocent, and she replied that she did: the disappeared children (*El Diario del Juicio*, July 9, 1985).

22. Two editions of 3,000 copies each were published in Portuguese (Iván Gomes Pinheiro Machado, L&M editor, electronic communication, July 20, 2005), and as many copies were published in the Italian edition (Octavio Raimondo, Editrice Missionaria Italiana, electronic communication, October 5, 2006). Two editions were published in English, one with 1,500 copies and the other, an economical edition, with 10,000.

23. Memoria Abierta, Relatives, Document C.9.16. Memoria Abierta is a nongovernmental organization that assembles all the documentation collected by Argentina's human rights organizations in a single database. It has a large oral archive containing interviews with activists of the 1960s and 1970s.

24. "Guía para el acto," in Memoria Abierta, Relatives, Document C8.91.

25. Memoria Abierta, Relatives, Documents B8.95 and C9.62a.

26. Ferrari was part of an avant-garde artistic movement of the 1970s. During the dictatorship he was forced into exile and his son was disappeared. The newspaper *Página/12* first came out in May 1987 and has covered human rights abuses since its first number. The information regarding the print run of this edition was obtained through an electronic communication with Ricardo Badía, administrative manager of *Página/12*, December 1, 2003.

27. The documentary is narrated by the actor Alfredo Alcón Aliverti and features testimonies from David Viñas and Eduardo Galeano (writers), Miguel Angel Solá (actor), León Gieco (musician), Luis Puenzo (movie director), and Roberto Fontanarrosa (cartoonist). The only testimonies in the film that do not come from representatives of the cultural community are those of the prosecutor, Strassera, and several children of the disappeared.

28. This was implemented in the city of Buenos Aires by municipal order No. 49,192 of June 1, 1995 (*Municipal Gazette of the City of Buenos Aires*, No. 20,074, July 10, 1995, 102.604).

29. "If we are to lay down solid foundations on which to build our future, we need to be clear about something: we cannot accept any attempts to justify state terrorism as a form of counteraction to other forms of violence, as if it were possible to find a justifying symmetry in the actions of individuals, in the face of a deviation from the nation's and the state's inherent functions, which cannot be relinquished" (CONADEP, 2006: 8).

2

"We're All Victims"

Changes in the Narrative of "National Reconciliation" in Argentina

Valentina Salvi
Translated by Luis Alberto Hernández

On October 5, 2006, the first "act in tribute to the officers killed" in the Montoneros' attack on the Twenty-Ninth Mountain Infantry Regiment was held at the monument to General José de San Martín in the Buenos Aires plaza of the same name on a day designated as a "national day of the victims of terrorism." This event had a precedent in one celebrated on May 24 of that year at the monument to those fallen in the Malvinas and South Atlantic Islands War in the same plaza under the slogan "Soldier, do not ask for forgiveness for having defended your country." Both events were organized by the Comisión de Homenaje Permanente a los Muertos por la Subversión (Committee of Permanent Tribute to Those Killed by Subversion) and counted among their organizers relatives of the officers killed by the guerrillas during the 1970s, civilian groups gathered under the slogan *Memoria Completa* (Complete Memory), and retired officers who were members of the Unión de Promociones.[1]

Up until 2006, after the annulment of the Punto Final (Full Stop) and Obediencia Debida (Due Obedience) laws[2] and the reopening of the trials for crimes against humanity, the public space had not been the channel chosen by these groups to convey their demands and representations. Rather, for three decades their activities had been conducted behind closed doors, in military clubs and military churches, and they had applied political pressure on the state in a corporate manner, emerging into the public sphere when the pursuit of justice entailed a sense of direct and real threat (Brienza, 2009: 77). However, since 2006 some new factors have encouraged public demonstrations by this sector of Argentine society that has traditionally shown a distinct revulsion for them, among them the deinstitutionalization of the memory of the "struggle against subversion" in the armed forces, the reluctance of its authorities to award their stamp of approval to "acts of homage" to those "killed by subversion," and the silence or even passivity of active cadres regarding the fate of the officers prosecuted and convicted of human rights violations (Salvi, 2011b).

That October afternoon, Ana Lucioni[3] and José María Sacheri,[4] the only speakers at the event, ended their speeches by proclaiming that they spoke as "victims of a fratricidal war" and that they remembered the past and its dead with a "conciliatory message" in order to "save the future" for "the destiny of the fatherland" and for "the future of Argentina." In front of at least 1,000 attendees holding white banners on which, next to the names and photos of civilians and military killed by the guerrillas during the 1970s, was written "Víctima del Terrorismo—Nunca Recordado" (Victim of Terrorism—Never Remembered), Sacheri said,

> And we gather here today to pay tribute not just to our past but to our future, the future of our children and their descendants, the future of Argentina. We come here publicly to raise the flag of harmony, to definitely close Argentina's tragic past and lay the foundations of progress in peace, without discord, without violence, without resentment, hatred, or revenge.

The call for national reconciliation as a way of avoiding trials for human rights violations had been a constant in the discourse of the Argentine armed forces since the "Documento final de la Junta Militar sobre la guerra contra la subversión y el terrorismo" (Final Document of the Military Junta on the War against Subversion and Terrorism), broadcast April 28, 1983. However, that call had undergone resignification as a result of the turn at the end of the 1990s in the memory of the "struggle against subversion" from the figure of the "victors of the antisubversive campaign" to that of the "victims of terrorism."

This article seeks to explain the changes in the rhetoric of national reconciliation as a political strategy and a symbolic recourse promoted by civilians and retired military officers who remember and seek to justify the so-called struggle against subversion in order to deal not only with the representation of a violent past but also with the legal, political, and moral responsibility that derives from it (Jaspers, 1998). The goal, then, is to analyze how the figure of the "victims of terrorism" participates in the resignification of these memories.[5] Within this framework, my interest is to explain the way in which the rhetoric of national reconciliation helps to create a moral community capable of managing its own history while coping with the questions raised by society.[6]

FROM VICTORS TO VICTIMS

During the first democratic decade, the narrative of the struggle against subversion, shared by the officers who had participated in the Proceso de Reorganización Nacional (Process of National Reorganization) and the new military leadership and by the relatives of the officers killed by the guerrillas, assembled in Familiares y Amigos de Muertos por la Subversión (Relatives and Friends of Those Killed by Subversion—FAMUS), was characterized by a triumphalist and denialist tone. The military prosecuted for human rights violations, the officers on active duty, and the civilians close to them denied the clandestine and systemic character of the disappearances and the very existence of the disappeared. According to the "Documento final,"

> Many of the disappearances are the consequence of the manner in which terrorists operate. They change their real names and surnames and know each other by what they call "noms de guerre" and have plenty of forged personal documentation. This is all related to what is called "going underground"; those who decide to join terrorist organizations do so surreptitiously, abandoning their families and their social and working environments. It's the most typical case: the relatives denounce a disappearance whose cause they cannot explain or, knowing the cause, don't wish to explain. (*Convicción*. 1983)

From a perspective that prioritized the results obtained in the military field, the military felt like victors in the antisubversive war, and therefore the document demanded "recognition of the struggle for freedom, justice, and the right to life" for those who had "stoically endured the effects of an attack that they did not provoke or deserve." Moreover, the military also rejected the so-called theory of the two demons,[7] since they did not accept being equated with those against whom they had fought (the "subversive criminals") or the prosecution of their commanders alongside the guerrilla leaders (Altamirano, 2007: 20). General Mario Aguado Benítez, commander of the Fifth Corps, said in the first months of democracy, "Our enemies are never going to forgive us for defeating subversion" (*La Nación*, January 14, 1984). Similarly, after the publication of the report of the Comisión Nacional sobre la Desaparición de Personas (National Commission on the Disappearance of Persons—CONADEP), the retired first army chief of the democratic period, General Jorge Arguindegui, maintained that the trials of the military juntas that were about to start were a "Nuremberg trial but in reverse: there the ones judged were the defeated, not the victors" (*La Razón*, March 27, 1985).

At the same time, FAMUS[8] maintained that the members of the armed forces should be remembered for "their capacities and courage" and "their sacrifice," for "having given their best," putting "their families at high risk" in "absolute self-surrender" in order to "save the fatherland," and that having taken on the sacrifice of "fighting subversion" made them virtuous men worthy of recognition. For FAMUS, "the war had not ended" because the "murderers" had been transformed into "sacrificed victims" and the "heroes" into "prisoners of war." It denounced this situation in the second issue of its newsletter *Tributo* in 1982 and went on to say,

> It is now up to us, if we are well-born, to show gratitude to those who brought us PEACE and therefore we owe them our LIFE, our FREEDOM, and the possibility of living in a DEMOCRACY, but meanwhile the military chiefs are deprived of their liberty and the institution to which the Argentine people owe gratitude is being discredited. FAMUS invites all citizens to accompany our PRISONERS OF WAR, express well-deserved gratitude in the places where they are, and show them that, yes, IT IS AN HONOR HAVING FOUGHT AND HAVING WON.

These public statements were framed in the narrative of war and victory so dear to the armed forces and the commanders of the Proceso. They adopted the core of the representations that made possible the criminalization of the cadres, a war for the "survival of the nation," and, having "defeated the subversion militarily," constituted the basis for their demand for social and political recognition of the armed forces' role. They were convinced that having fought on behalf of the fatherland, peace, and democracy exempted them from having to offer any explanation to justice and society.

The same tone filled the pronouncements of the Carapintada rebellion of April 1987,[9] which received the name of "Operation Dignity" because it sought to give the army back its dignity at a moment when it was the target of "a campaign of public anger orchestrated by those who, when the opportunity arose, were defeated." Its main demand was to prevent the prosecution of "more comrades arrested and scorned merely for having fought and won a just and necessary war that made the current regime possible."[10] This triumphalist view of the past was grounded in the belief that the survival of democratic institutions was due to the military's having won a war against subversion. Besides halting the prosecution of the middle-ranking cadres of the army accused of human rights violations, the rebels sought to stop an alleged "smear campaign on the part of the mass media" and gain social recognition for the struggle against subversion.[11] This position with regard to the repressive past was not a banner raised exclusively by the rebels but also reflected the claims of broad sectors loyal to the army, including its high command. The "winners" could not accept, especially, that their commanders were being held in prison by a civilian court decision and considered amnesty imperative.[12] In a speech on May 29, 1987 (Army Day), the commander of the army, General José Caridi, said, "This victory has cost the army dearly: many years of struggle against an insidious, wily and cruel enemy, its merits and martyrs, the aggression and indifference of some citizens, the conviction of its commanders, and, finally, the committal for trial of numerous comrades" (Grecco and González, 1990: 51). Although this first decade under democracy ended with the pardons of the former commanders,[13] the armed forces were forced by civil society to answer for the forced disappearance of persons, and the war narrative was replaced by another that recognized the violence by the state. In the face of this reality, the military reaffirmed their role as the true defenders of the democratic institutions against the Marxist threat and continued to see themselves as saviors of the nation.

At the end of the 1990s, the memory of the struggle against subversion underwent a significant turn after the declarations by Captain Adolfo Scilingo and the former NCO Víctor Ibáñez, who recounted the details of the "death flights,"[14] and the announcement of General Martín Balza recognizing the torture and disappearances perpetrated by military officers.[15] These statements deprived the military of the ability to represent themselves as saviors of the fatherland against the Marxist threat or as victors in a just war against a subversive enemy (Badaró, 2009: 311). The former chief of the Second Army Corps and minister of planning under the military regime,

Major General Ramón Díaz Bessone, who was president of the Círculo Militar from 1994 to 2002, coordinated the three-volume collection *In memoriam* (1998), which established the bases for the turn of the military memory toward the figure of the military as victims. This "homage," considered by the military community as the counterpart of the CONADEP's *Nunca Más*, advocated for remembrance of the struggle against subversion as a just cause. Nevertheless, its claims of what was done by the army during the period of illegal repression are presented against a narrative of the recent past that begins with the suffering endured by the army officers and their relatives murdered by the guerrillas.

Díaz Bessone's book provided support for a new interpretative framework within which to evoke the recent past: Memoria Completa (Complete Memory). This happened at the same time as the progress made in the trials for crimes against humanity, starting in 2003 with the repeal of the Obediencia Debida and Punto Final laws, the scant space that the victims of the guerrillas had received in the memoirs of militants, the silence about the armed struggle in the memoirs produced by the human rights organizations, and the refusal of the state to recognize or accommodate any of these meanings of the recent past (da Silva Catela, 2010: 121). Since the mid-2000s, the associations of relatives, civilians, and retired military that rally behind the banner of Memoria Completa have emerged as a new actor in struggles over memory in Argentina. Aiming to popularize a narrative about the recent past that allows them to transcend the strong corporatist framework of the military circles, they seek to question the legitimacy of the human rights organizations and promote their demands with a discourse centered on "the victims of terrorism" aimed at a policy of national reconciliation.

From a binary perspective that replicates the rhetoric of confrontation among Argentines, Memoria Completa considers the social memory of the 1970s a "partial memory," an "unfair" one because it obscures the existence of a "revolutionary war" that produced "unrecognized victims." Memoria Completa has not only appropriated but also resignified two of the demands historically supported by the human rights organizations: memory and truth. It seeks to present a narrative about the recent past that is the more credible the more clearly it opposes the memory of the disappeared and the struggles of the human rights organizations (Salvi, 2011a).

With this purpose in mind, the figure of the "victims of terrorism" is emptied of political and moral ambiguities and purified in order to replace the immoral and antidemocratic generals of the Proceso with "innocent victims" in the pantheon of military heroes. In the list drawn up by Díaz Bessone in *In memoriam*, the murder in March 1960 of the four-year-old Guillermina Cabrera, the daughter of an army NCO, occupies the leading role in the military memory that has always been played by the kidnapping and murder of General Pedro Eugenio Aramburu by the Montoneros in 1970.[16] This reframing of the military memory around the figure of the victim, which seeks to take advantage of the socially accepted stereotype of the innocent victim by focusing on a child, whose innocence is beyond any doubt (Giesen, 2004: 47), denotes not only how morally reassuring this passivity is but also how socially obligatory is compassion for such a victim. Furthermore, the figure of Aramburu is too contradictory—strongly associated with the disputes between Peronists and anti-Peronists and with the putschist and antidemocratic image of the army—to continue to be the first and most prominent victim of the "revolutionary war."

Moreover, for these organizations of civilians and retired officers, the figure of the "victim of terrorism" tends to rival the figure of the detainee-disappeared. Colonel Julio Argentino del Valle Larrabure and Lieutenant Colonel Jorge Ibarzábal, who were kidnapped and murdered after the attacks on the military arms factory in Villa María and the Azul Regiment, have become martyrs of the struggle against subversion.[17] These officers, remembered as martyrs because they "fell defending the fatherland," have replaced generals of the Proceso such as Videla, Viola, Galtieri, and Menéndez, who represented a symbolic obstacle for the framing of the army as an innocent victim of terrorist and subversive violence.

Thus the military memory crystallized in the figure of the victim and ended up highlighting certain traits of the officers and silencing others in order to strengthen the idea that the military did not kill to save their country but died for it (Portelli, 2003a). In other words, it was no longer a matter of officers' fighting the enemies of the nation but one of officers' not giving up defending it. Furthermore, this turn toward the memory of the "victims of terrorism" was made possible by ignoring what the army did during the period of illegal repression—their responsibility for the systematic disappearance of people.

"WE'RE ALL VICTIMS"

With the turn toward the "victims of terrorism," Memoria Completa has anchored its discourse in traumatic events that serve as a basis for producing unity and adherence and for making demands and disputing meanings in public space. It seeks to receive recognition for the human losses not only from the state but also from civil society. To achieve this it uses the nationalization and equalization of the "dead of a fratricidal war." However, this requires that both the political violence and the illegal state repression be interpreted as a broad network of fraternal ties that incorporates the nation in its totality as a victim. As Ana Lucioni said in the Plaza San Martín, "We have all lost a loved one. We have all suffered the absence of a father, a son, a brother, a husband, or a friend."

As the human rights organizations have done with the disappeared, Memoria Completa seeks to project the "victims of terrorism" onto a common symbolic space in order to stimulate collective attachments. For this purpose, it appeals to the language of kinship and family ties to denote the ties that bind nationals to their country. Just like the primary image of the family, the fatherland represents the domain of love—the selfless emotional bonds that connect parents with their children, children with their parents, and siblings with each other. Sacheri's remarks in the Plaza San Martín are eloquent in this regard: "We the victims are not the only ones hurt in this war: the whole nation has been, but we can affirm that we the victims are the least culpable for these wars of terror and the ones who have been the hardest hit by these wars, to which we want to say, calmly but definitely, 'Enough!'" When Sacheri says that "the whole nation was lacerated" by "unwanted violence among Argentines," a memory that is called "complete" seeks to speak publicly on behalf of "all the dead." For this it is necessary to amalgamate and equate not only all the dead but also all the bereaved. The differences and hostilities of the past are abandoned and the current struggles and demands overcome in an all-inclusive "we" in which "all the dead are Argentines" (Márquez, 2004: 7):

> Twenty-five years after the end of the bloody and savage war of the 1970s we are left with a sad death toll of legal forces and terrorists, peaceful and violent people, men and women from the right and the left, innocent and guilty, good and bad, old and young, rich and poor. They all had a common denominator: they were all Argentines. They are the dead, our dead. (Márquez, 2004: 7)

The nationalization and equalization of the "victims" transform the memory of the "victims of terrorism" into a platform for the establishment of a public debt searching for acknowledgment. The particularity of this debt is that it introduces a dialectic through which the victim, having suffered harm, establishes the moral obligation of remuneration (Agamben, 1998a: 20). With the evocation of traumatic events, Memoria Completa seeks to strengthen the victims' public positioning: being presented socially as victims allows them to complain, protest, and present their demands in a framework of legitimacy and have their voices heard. This attitude, says Ricoeur (2003: 117), places the rest of society in their debt. The public debt not only helps to create a claim to which the rest of society is bound but also makes it possible to demand retribution. In summary, the turn toward the memory of the wounds allows the sectors that remember and claim the "struggle against subversion" to ask for recognition and political and symbolic reparations in the context of the silencing of social and state memories for the victims of the guerrilla war.

In addition, with the notions of "an internal war," "a fratricidal war," or "a fight among Argentines," Memoria Completa seeks to introduce into the scenario of struggles over memory a line of argument that equates all the victims and compensates for the suffering and violence. In contrast to the triumphalist discourse of the first years of democracy, which sought to differentiate between the victors of the antisubversive war and the subversives who had been turned into heroes and martyrs, Memoria Completa puts the emphasis on the human losses and brings together all the injured parties around its "common denominator."

What does the shift from the narrative of victors to one of victims do to the rhetoric of national reconciliation? At first, the idea of reconciliation was triggered by the need to forget the effects of an "antisubversive war," but here forgetting has a productive dimension: remembering past misfortunes has to be prohibited to make way for a national peace process. The idea of reconciliation as a national peace process was part of the justification for the amnesty law promulgated by the last military junta in

1983 and for the pardons of former commanders and generals granted by President Carlos Menem in 1990. At a second stage, after the annulment of the Punto Final and Obediencia Debida laws, the call for national reconciliation was reinforced not through forgetting but through a "duty of remembrance"[18] in which all Argentines were brothers and sisters in the evocation of shared suffering. In the face of the reopening of the trials, it was essential for the members of Memoria Completa to restore the discourse of national reconciliation to the public debate as a way of securing impunity in the negotiated and consensual form of a pardon. This was a political and extrajudicial strategy that sought to promote forgiveness and thus to close down the debate about the past and control its future manifestations (Ricoeur, 1999: 62).

The idea of national reconciliation rests on a set of ideological categories that are repeated in the slogan "Memoria Completa." These categories are derived from the rhetoric of war with the addition of those of debt and victimhood. When the narrative of war invades the entire discursive sphere, it not only approaches the past as a territory of conflict but also interprets the present that evokes it as its continuation. And since remembering means reopening old wounds, the national peace process can only emerge from healing the wounds of the past. This is exactly what Lucioni said:

> Today, after 31 years, we continue to feel the same pain for so much unnecessary bloodshed. . . . Consciously or unconsciously, they [all the combatants] were the bloody tools of particular interests that have nothing to do with the interests of the country. Therefore, today more than ever, we should pray for reconciliation, peace, and union among all Argentines.

But how does Memoria Completa intend to prevent the struggles and confrontations of the past from continuing in the present, with "the nation bleeding to death"? From this perspective, healing can only come from forgetting, from a mutual commitment not to remember the misfortunes of the past and to avoid the arm of justice, which represents a tool of revenge (Loraux, 1989). Future coexistence depends on the preventive erasure of the past—pretending that nothing happened and not asking questions about the causes of the conflicts that run through Argentina's political life. In other words, national reconciliation assumes the restoration of a conservative ideology according to which any form of disagreement or conflict—especially disagreement that derives from the need to assign blame and responsibility—is incompatible with social peace (Lira and Loveman, 1998).

Furthermore, the call for national reconciliation is put forward as a unitary and consensual discourse that invites all the parties to abandon their sectarian interests for the common good. This conciliatory and harmonious idea of reconciliation has as its starting point the assumption that violence is the result of a confrontation between two camps, the legal forces and the terrorists. This position, which was reproduced in the first years of democracy by the theory of two demons, maintains that there were two evils in Argentina and they were comparable. On the one hand, positing two equally perverse parties introduces an undifferentiated view of violence that obscures the specificity of state terrorism and political violence. On the other hand, it not only removes responsibility from the military involved in human rights violations but also proposes a sort of "double repentance" as necessary for reconciliation between two camps (Feld, 1998: 83). It is not so much that this double repentance is presented as the only way out of the conflict as that the equalization of blame denies, obscures, and conceals the conditions that made it possible to criminalize the armed forces.[19]

What new justifications emerge when the proposal for national reconciliation is based on the memory of the victims and the figure of the public debt? First of all, reconciliation is worded not as a "double repentance" but as a "mutual pardon." The demand for reparations and retribution that the figure of a debt establishes in the struggles for memory seeks to produce a reversal in the dialectics of forgiveness. As Ricoeur states (1999: 63), the person who caused harm can only ask for forgiveness, while only the victim has the power to grant it. With the memory of the "victims of terrorism," Memoria Completa seeks to appropriate forgiveness as a power deriving from the fact of presenting themselves publicly as injured parties and therefore as society's creditors. This is what the speakers said in the Plaza San Martín:

> All of us here are victims, those who participated in the wars of the 1970s and those who did not participate, because the whole of Argentine society was the victim of a past of violence that affected it in its entirety, without exclusions. . . . But we the victims are innocent of any mistake or horror committed, de jure or de facto, by the various national administrations since the second half of the twentieth century, We the victims, who have been bathed in the warm blood of our parents and have cried in silence each drop of water in the tears of blood, take the first step. I repeat, we offer our open hand even to those who killed and murdered our parents.

Memoria Completa presents itself as offering an "open hand" to its "attackers" and renouncing vengeance for the indignities and humiliations suffered by the "victims of terrorism." Therefore it considers it just for the terrorists of yesterday and the adversaries of today to put aside their desire for revenge or retaliation and grant amnesty to those who forgive them. This self-exculpating argument rests on an equation of the suffering of the "victims of terrorism" with the situation of the officers sent to jail for human rights violations. Thus the victim-victimizer relationship is reversed and the groups associated with Memoria Completa, spokespersons for the officers who have been indicted, appear in public forgiving their "attackers" even though no one has asked them to. As Ricoeur puts it (1999: 65), forgiveness is first and foremost a gift. While "giving" means handing over something that we possess without asking for anything in return, this relationship has its dangers. Forgiving when no one has asked one to means not only overlooking the possibility of a refusal or rejection—the drama of encountering the unpardonable—but also reintroducing the logic of debt. It establishes an unequal link in that the one receiving it is bound to reciprocate. Of course, being treated as victims publicly reinforces the claim for retribution and the obligation of recognition by turning Argentine society into the beneficiary of the reconciliation. Therefore, in a turn in the discourse, national reconciliation is formulated as a pardon that erases the acts committed, and the officers charged with and prosecuted for human rights violations are presented, through their spokespersons in the struggles for memory, as forgiving the victims of repression. This act of renunciation makes them titled to forgiveness for the crimes they committed during the period of state terrorism.

CONCLUSIONS

In this article I have discussed the turn taken around 2000 in the memory of the so-called struggle against subversion from the figure of the "victors of the antisubversive war" or "saviors of the fatherland" to that of the "victims of terrorism." From that moment on, the emphasis was placed especially on the associated changes in the rhetoric of national reconciliation, from the idea of double repentance involving two equally perverse parties to one of mutual forgiveness among the victims of a fratricidal war. My analysis of the two narratives has examined the way in which the rhetoric of national reconciliation deals with the legal, political, and moral responsibility of military officers and the armed forces for the illegal repression.

Hannah Arendt (1994; 2007) argues that collective blame conceals the criminal responsibilities of the perpetrators of massive crimes because it builds a kind of universal complicity among the members of a community or nation. At the same time, collective victimhood disguises the responsibility not by equalizing blame but by establishing feelings of solidarity and compassion in order to equalize the sufferings and, consequently, the behaviors. Both help to exonerate the perpetrators morally and legally, but while the first calls for developing a kind of collective remorse, since society as a whole appears to be guilty of the violence of the past, the second invokes feelings of compassion. Paraphrasing Arendt (2007), we might say that one encourages vicarious blame while the other fosters vicarious compassion. Vicarious blame assumes that no criminal blame is associated with the acts of the past, while vicarious compassion involves sympathizing with the victim even though that person was a repressor. Thus, collective victimhood reaffirms the solidarity with the victimizer in that it extends compassion for the damage and suffering endured by a group to the whole of society. Undifferentiated victimhood functions as an instrument of apology and massive exculpation. It is not a question of indicting and punishing everyone equally but one of forgiving and making full reparations so that no individual or institution can be regarded as responsible for the crimes committed. In short, with the turn toward the figure of "victims of terrorism" and the equalization of "all the victims," Memoria Completa creates a way of replacing the rule of "everyone" with the rule of "no one." In other words, the maxim of collective guilt, that "where everyone is guilty no one is" (Arendt, 2007: 151), is supplanted by another equally exculpatory one, that "where everyone is a victim no one is guilty."

NOTES

The original version of this essay was published in *Latin American Perspectives* 42 (3): 39–51.

1. The relatives and friends of the dead officers are assembled as the Asociación de las Víctimas del Terrorismo en Argentina and Familiares y Amigos de Víctimas del Terrorismo and present themselves as unrecognized direct victims of "subversive terrorism" as wives, children, nephews, fathers, and mothers of officers "killed by the subversion." Among the civilian organizations are the Argentinos por la Memoria Completa, Grupos de Amigos por la Verdad Histórica, Foro por la Verdad Histórica, Jóvenes por la Verdad, Verdad sin Rencor, Argentinos por la Pacificación Nacional, and the Asociación Unidad Argentina, which embody a "struggle for memory, truth, and the reconciliation of all Argentines" and against "the humiliation, harassment, and persecution of the fundamental institutions of the nation." Another organization that is concerned with the defense of the officers in prison for human rights violations is the Asociación de Familiares y Amigos de los Presos Políticos Argentinos. The Unión de Promociones is made up of retired officers whose objective is to defend and support their "detained comrades and their families."

2. In June 2005 the Supreme Court declared the Punto Final and Obediencia Debida laws unconstitutional, thus endorsing Law 25.779, by which Congress had overturned them in 2003.

3. President of the Comisión de Homenaje Permanente and the daughter of First Lieutenant Oscar Lucioni, who died on October 10, 1976, in an attack by the Montoneros.

4. A member of the Asociación de las Víctimas del Terrorismo en Argentina and the son of Carlos Alberto Sacheri, a nationalist philosopher killed by the Ejército Revolucionario del Pueblo (People's Revolutionary Army—ERP) on December 22, 1974.

5. The analysis starts from a theoretical and methodological perspective that, instead of focusing on what the social actors are capable of saying or thinking about certain symbols or meanings from the past, stresses the symbols and meanings that are available in their cultural frameworks and, in a given time-space juncture, are shaped by social actors to allow one or another interpretation of the past (Olick, 2007).

6. This work is based on observations of public events convened by the groups of Memoria Completa between 2006 and 2009 and a survey of secondary sources such as magazines, books, web pages, speeches, pamphlets, and communication materials produced by these organizations.

7. This interpretation materialized with the initiative of President Raúl Alfonsín of simultaneously prosecuting both the military high command and the leaders of the Montoneros and the ERP. Later, it became widespread with the preface to the report *Nunca Más*, written by Ernesto Sábato (Crenzel, 2008: 82).

8. The public activities of FAMUS showed a time line closely linked to the political-military agenda of the first decade under democracy, especially as a response to the research done by the Comisión Nacional sobre la Desaparición de Personas and the trial of the military juntas. During those years, it dealt with the allegations of human rights violations by proposing to improve the public image of the armed forces and damage the prestige of the Madres de Plaza de Mayo by exposing the drama of the military and police attacked by the guerrillas. This discourse was complemented not only by a bellicose stance toward the human rights organizations but also by an effort to justify the actions of the generals of the dictatorship

(Marchesi, 2005: 179). FAMUS became inactive in 1991 after the pardons of the former commanders and generals.

9. Also known as the Semana Santa (Holy Week) Uprising, led by Lieutenant Colonel Aldo Rico. The *carapintadas*, who painted their faces with shoe polish to distinguish themselves from the *generales carablancas* or armchair generals, were mostly officers indicted for human rights violations.

10. Letter dated February 18, 1987, months before the uprising, from Lieutenant Colonel Aldo Rico to his brigade commander (Verbitsky, 1987: 164).

11. After the conflict, the government fulfilled the principal demand of the rebels: stopping the trials. On June 4, 1987, the Law of Due Obedience established that the officers could not be accused of punishable crimes because they were following orders.

12. In the trial of the military juntas, Jorge Rafael Videla and Emilio Eduardo Massera were sentenced to life imprisonment, Roberto Eduardo Viola to 17 years in prison, Armando Lambruschini to 8 years in prison, and Orlando Ramón Agosti to 4 years in prison.

13. On December 23, 1990, President Carlos Menem fulfilled his announced wish to pardon the former commanders and generals Camps, Suárez Mason, and Richieri, among others.

14. Scilingo made his comments on the television program *Hora Clave* on March 12, 1995, and in an interview with the journalist Horacio Verbitsky that resulted in the book *El vuelo* (1995). Ibáñez's declarations on the Hadad and Longobardi program on April 24, 1995, confirmed those made by Scilingo.

15. Balza's message was delivered on April 25, 1995, in front of a television audience. Besides acknowledging the torture and disappearance of people, he admitted the illegitimacy of the acts committed by officers under his command during the period of unlawful repression and moved away from the idea of human rights as a campaign implemented to discredit the institution.

16. The daughter of Mayor David René Cabrera, Guillermina Cabrera died as a result of the explosion of a bomb planted in the family house by the Ejército de Liberación Nacional / Movimiento Peronista de Liberación Uturuncos, one of the first Peronist youth organizations radicalized in the 1960s. Aramburu was the leader of the dictatorship called Revolución Libertadora (Liberating Revolution), which overthrew the government of Perón in 1955, and was responsible for the execution of civilians and military loyal to Perón in June 1956.

17. On January 19, 1974, when the ERP attacked the Tenth Regiment of the First Armored Cavalry in the city of Azul in Buenos Aires Province, Ibarzábal was taken hostage, and after nine months in captivity he was killed. On August 10 of that year, the ERP attacked the Fábrica Militar de Pólvoras y Explosivos of Villa María, in Córdoba, and took Larrabure hostage. His body was found on the outskirts of the city of Rosario in August 1975.

18. Nora (2008) maintains that we live in a time that creates in each of us the obligation to remember and turns the recovery of belonging into the principle and the secret of identity.

19. Feld (1998; 2001) shows that the idea that there were "repentant officers" is part of a grand narrative created by the mass media in 1995 and that when these repentances were offered they were showcased on television, demanding a sort of counterpart to the "other part" as a way of moving toward "national reconciliation."

3

Irreconcilable Differences

Political Culture and Gender Violence during the Chilean Transition to Democracy

Hillary Hiner and María José Azócar

This article explores the way in which violence against women became a matter of public policy during the 1990s in Chile. Discourses associated with the transition to democracy and collective memory battles related to human rights, truth, and reconciliation contributed to the way in which violence against women was addressed. A hegemonic discourse of "reconciliation" and its association with Christian forgiveness served as an emblematic framework promoted by a political class that understood itself as a community of "gentlemen" and "brothers." This "gentlemen's agreement" affected not only human rights discourse (by excluding crimes such as rape and sexualized torture from the 1990–1991 Truth Commission's mandate), but also state discourse on violence against women, identifying conciliation as the preferred outcome of family violence sentencing in the 1994 family violence law.

This case explores the way in which hegemonic frameworks shape forms of violence in the interplay between law and human rights discourse, gender values, and state models. The political culture of reconciliation and consensus in Chile during the 1990s is generally regarded in a positive light and as conducive to political change, but the Chilean experience also demonstrates how dynamic the cultural battle over collective memory and the meaning of human rights can be. Indeed, it was precisely the limited contours of the reconciliatory framework that ultimately established the conditions for its own contestation, seen in the 2003–2004 Truth Commission report and the revised family violence law of 2005. These later expressions of state discourse on gender violence and human rights largely broke with the reconciliatory discourse of earlier times.

COLLECTIVE MEMORY AND GENDER VIOLENCE:
THEORY AND PRACTICE

Since the late 1990s a great number of texts have emerged that analyze collective memory in the wake of the Latin American dictatorships of the 1970s and 1980s, particularly with regard to political violence such as torture, forced disappearance, and exile. Scholars such as Elizabeth Jelin (2001), Steve Stern (2004; 2006a; 2010), Hugo Vezzetti (2002), and Beatriz Sarlo (2005) have published important works on collective memory and memory battles in the Southern Cone. There is scholarly consensus that both history and memory are constructed and that they interact in a complicated and sometimes contentious way. Considering the way in which certain collective memories are made hegemonic and therefore become incorporated into national and transnational histories, Jelin (2001: 48–50) speaks of "memory entrepreneurs," such as the leaders of human rights nongovernmental organizations (NGOs), politicians, and other elites who take the lead on collective memory issues in Argentina, while Stern (2004: 120–124) considers these actors along with ordinary Chileans. For Stern it is the "emblematic" nature of shared memories—constructed in relation to times and places that he terms "memory knots"—that allows him to conceptualize the formation of different and opposing memory camps in Chile: "Emblematic memory refers not to a single remembrance of a specific content, not to a concrete or substantive 'thing,' but to a framework that organizes meaning, selectivity, and countermemory" (2004: 105). In the same vein, Roberta Villalón (2013: 300) argues that the politics of framing public memory includes the reconstruction of individual and collective memories in intersection with gender, sexual, racial/ethnic, religious, and class lines that "may allow for certain aspects to be brought forth or put back, to be connected in particular ways, and hence, to yield new understandings." In this paper, we will use the notion of frameworks that organize memory meaning in considering the emergence of discourses concerning gender violence.[1]

Explicit links between the collective memory of the dictatorships and feminist analysis of gender or gender violence are fairly uncommon (Hirsch and Smith, 2002: 3), although women are often mentioned, particularly as relatives of the disappeared. Analyzing women's testimonies on political violence in Argentina and speaking in relation to the Madres de Plaza de Mayo, Elizabeth Jelin (2001: 108) states:

> Many women narrate their memories from the standpoint of the traditional role of women, living, as it were "for others." This is linked to identity making that is centered on serving and looking after loved ones, usually within family relations. The ambiguity of the active subject/passive caretaker position can manifest itself through a shifting of her identity, wherein she "narrates the other." . . . This implies choosing to be a witness-observer for the "other" (a detained and disappeared son, for example), while denying or silencing testimonies about her own experiences.

In contrast to these testimonies, from the early 1980s on, a series of testimonial accounts of state violence affecting women has emerged, most famously that of Rigoberta Menchú in Guatemala (Burgos, 1998 [1983]) but also those of other women in Central and South America who experienced political violence firsthand (Arce, 2004; Calveiro, 1998; Herzog, 1993; Partnoy, 1998; Stephen, 1994; Vidaurrázaga, 2007). However, because of the constraints of the *testimonio* genre, the majority of these texts are not explorations of links between political violence and gender, although both Calveiro and Vidaurrázaga do conceptualize female incarceration and sexual torture from an experiential point of view.

These testimonies and others were used by some pioneering women scholars in the 1980s and 1990s to theorize the relation between authoritarianism, political violence, and violence against women, among them Ximena Bunster (1985), Jean Franco (1992), Julieta Kirkwood (1990 [1986]), and Teresa Valdés (1988; Valdés and Weinstein, 1993) and women associated with Latin American Institute of Mental Health and Human Rights (Agger and Jensen, 1997; Lira, 1994; Lira and Piper, 1996; among others). Bunster (1985: 297) reports that torture was brutally "feminized" in Chile—that women were tortured both because of their own political beliefs and to extract information about the whereabouts of those close to them—and argues that "the more generalized and diffused female sexual enslavement through the patriarchal state has been crystallized and physically literalized through the military state as torturer." As scholarship on gender and political violence has moved into the twenty-first century there has been a steady stream of social science texts on areas affected by state violence and civil war, such as South Africa, Northern Ireland, Yugoslavia, Peru, and Central America, and on the relation between gender/sexual violence and transitional justice at both the local and the international levels (Boesten, 2012; Edwards, 2011; Mantilla, 2007; Ni Aoláin, 2009; Ni Aoláin, Haynes, and Cahn, 2011; Ross, 2003; Sharrat, 2011).

While it may appear from this review that gender violence has been consistently and specifically studied for more than 20 years, the fact remains that these studies are usually concerned only with political violence during the dictatorships, with intimate partner or domestic violence (Johnson, 2007) receiving considerably less attention and generally absent from collective memory and history studies. For example, there have been theoretical texts produced by lawyers and academics specialized in international law that conceptualize intimate partner violence as a grave human rights violation in Latin America (Cook, 1997), and there have been innovative studies by anthropologists relating domestic violence to other types of violence and unrest in Central America and Colombia (McIlwaine and Moser, 2001; Menjívar, 2011, Silber, 2011). There have also been studies on the development of domestic violence policy in Brazil (Santos, 2005), Costa Rica (Sagot, 2010), and Uruguay (Clavero, 2009). However, these studies, while valuable, do not dialogue with investigations of gender violence and collective memory. Texts that deal with collective memory, gender violence, and the transition to democracy in Chile, such as those of Nelly Richard (1993; 1998; 2008) and Lessie Jo Frazier (2007), do not deal with intimate-partner violence, while the work of the historian Heidi Tinsman (1995; 2002) on domestic violence has generally not included the transitional period since the 1990s (for exceptions see Hiner, 2012; 2013).

In this limited sense, then, this article is innovative in exploring the links be-tween domestic violence policy and the transition to democracy. The majority of texts on the transition in Chile tend to be either comparative political science and law-oriented texts on transitional justice (Arthur, 2009; Barahona de Brito, 1997; 2001; Collins, 2010; Ensalaco, 1994; Evans, 2007; Grandin, 2005; Hayner, 2001; Olsen, Payne, and Reiter, 2010; Pion-Berlin and Arceneaux, 1998; Sikkink and Walling, 2007) or social science and historical texts (generally produced by Chilean academics) that deal more generally with the political history of the Chilean tran-sition (including past human rights abuses) and its relationship to neoliberalism (Dooner, 1989; Fuentes, 1999; Lechner and Güell, 2006; Loveman and Lira, 2000; 2002; 2005; Moulian, 1998; Ruiz, 2000; Silva, 2002). From this diverse body of work we have borrowed several key ideas. One is that the transition to democracy was essentially a compromise. There continued to be a strong military presence and authoritarian enclaves in Chile, and therefore transitional justice[2] would be pursued only "as far as possible," favoring truth commissions over trials and the adoption of "reconciliation" discourse. Another is that legacies of the dictatorship such as reliance upon the free market to guide neoliberal economic policy and the reification of the Catholic "traditional" family as the bedrock of the nation would continue unabated. During the 1990s the Catholic Church consistently battled initiatives that it consid-ered to put the traditional family in jeopardy, including the legitimization of divorce, homosexuality, abortion, and use of the concept of gender itself.

What we remember and how and why we remember are key components of our ability to understand the present. The language that we have available to put our ex-periences into words is a factor in this; the ability to articulate aspects of the past such as authoritarianism, human rights abuses, and gender violence depends upon our knowledge of these discourses. Echoing Joan Scott's (1992) work on language and experience, Jelin (2001: 36) states, "It matters if we have, or don't have, the words to express what we have lived." Memory discourse and emblematic memory framings—a tentative "memory language," as it were—are constructed collectively over time in a way that is both contentious and temporally and spatially heterogeneous. In the case of Chile, memory language on gender violence has been primarily determined by the law—the courts, truth commissions, and legislative initiatives. The Argentine schol-ars Hugo Vezzetti (2002) and Emilio Crenzel (2008) have made a similar point for Argentina, with Vezzetti (2002: 28) seeing the truth commission there as producing "a truly re-organizational moment of meaning for the past [which] . . . has become a reference point for memory studies." Following this argument on "re-organizational moments," we argue that it was during the transitional period of the 1990s, in the events surrounding the National Truth and Reconciliation Commission and the pas-sage of the family violence law, that much of the "foundational" discourse on gender and violence in Chile was established.

Our research incorporates the perspectives on gender violence, law, and memory of our doctoral research and draws upon two sources: congressional reports, political speeches, and media reports (archival, published, and electronic) covering a period between 1990 and 2010 and semistructured interviews of 38 people, including people who were involved in key congressional discussions of family law, state officials, activists from grassroots organizations, and academics who participated in the design and implementation of family and criminal law reforms in Chile.

A CONTEXT OF CONSENSUS: RECONCILIATION AND RIGHTS DURING THE 1990s

During the 1990s Chile had two Christian Democratic presidents, both of whom governed through a coalition of center-left political parties called the Concertación de Partidos por la Democracia (Coalition of Parties for Democracy, from here on "Concertación"). The first of these presidents, Patricio Aylwin, was responsible for the transition to democracy after the 1988 plebiscite that ended 17 years of a military dictatorship led by Augusto Pinochet. Following Aylwin, Eduardo Frei, the son of a former president of the same name, took the helm in 1994, vowing to lead Chile into the next century as a modern, developed country. In both of these periods Pinochet exercised substantial autonomy as commander in chief of the armed forces and wielded considerable power over the political process of transition. Through his leadership of the armed forces and his connections with right-wing parties, he actively obstructed investigations into the dictatorial past.[3] In addition, he established the limits of the transition through the 1978 amnesty law and the 1980 constitution, which heavily favored the executive branch and gave conservatives the upper hand in Congress through a system of designated senators and a binomial electoral process that virtually guaranteed the maintenance of the status quo (Drake and Jaksic, 1999; Garretón, 1988; Moulian, 1998). This set of circumstances forced the Concertación to look for consensus within its ranks in order to effect change. The discourse of "reconciliation" was a key element of the cohesion of the coalition.

On the one hand, "reconciliation" was a strategic discourse designed by the Concertación—shrewdly or cynically—to achieve consensus.[4] On the other hand, it had its roots in Judeo-Christian theology, embracing the need to "refound" the spiritual *patria* or the link among all Chileans. The Christian overtones of this discourse should not surprise us, given the proximity of the Catholic Church to the Christian Democratic Party and the fact that its more progressive elements were staunch supporters of human rights and redemocratization (M. A. Cruz, 2004). In a context of economic turmoil and renewed social protest, on December 17, 1982, the Chilean Catholic bishops issued a statement titled "The Rebirth of Chile" in which they advocated a democratic transition based on Christian values (Conferencia Episcopal de Chile, 1984: 37):

> Hope is an essentially Christian virtue. It is based on our certainty that God assumed, upon the death of Jesus Christ, all of our pains and failures and, in his resurrection, has overcome all evil. His life is more powerful than death. We Chileans have suffered

plenty and we will not forget this lesson. We are capable of forgiving ourselves and of constructing, on Christian principles, a nation of brothers.

Likewise, during his 1987 visit to Chile, Pope John Paul II stated, "Chile is a country of understanding, not confrontation. We cannot make progress while deepening our divisions. It is time for forgiveness and reconciliation" (quoted in Aylwin, 1992: 132).

Thus it was clear from the very beginning of the Aylwin presidency that the issue of human rights was going to be dealt with "as far as possible."[5] As a consequence, when in 1990 Aylwin created the Comisión Nacional de Verdad y Reconciliación (National Truth and Reconciliation Commission, also known as the Rettig Commission), it was with the express purpose of reconciling all Chileans, even though it had the divisive mandate of clarifying disappearances and other violations of human rights.[6] The Rettig Commission was clearly an attempt at refounding the nation. As the historians Greg Grandin and Thomas Klubock (2007: 3; see also Grandin, 2005) have put it, "Truth commissions worked, at least in theory, similar to other myths and rituals of nationalism, to sacramentalize violence into a useful creation myth." At the same time, this mandate was made more politically palatable through the exclusion of torture and other criminal acts that did not result in death. Thus many victims of political violence were excluded from the proceedings, and sexual violence was not part of the conceptual framework of the commission's report. The Rettig Commission created a version of the past in which the majority of the most serious victims of the dictatorship's abuses were men (Hiner, 2009: 62).

On March 4, 1991, Aylwin (1992: 132) read the Rettig Commission's results and declared:

> For the good of Chile we must look to the future that unites us more than the past that separates us. . . . We must know who the offended that are called upon to forgive are and who the offenders that must be forgiven. I cannot forgive for another. Forgiveness is not imposed by decree. Forgiveness requires regret by one party and generosity by the other.

However, as many in the human rights groups made very clear, the problem with this formulation was that there could be no forgiveness without justice and justice was in short supply. The Rettig Commission's recommendations were not legally binding and did not identify offenders by name. Although its findings were transmitted to the judiciary, judicial prosecution was understood by the Concertación as a high-risk alternative.[7] Additionally, less than a month after Aylwin presented the truth commission results on television, the right-wing ideologue Jaime Guzmán was assassinated by the Frente Patriótico Manuel Rodríguez (Manuel Rodríguez Patriotic Front—FPMR), a far-left armed group. The assassination was manipulated by right-wing parties and the conservative mass media to serve as evidence that the Marxist "threat" was still alive and well and, therefore, that the two-demons theory was the correct way of analyzing the past (Hiner, 2009). Two years later, the trope of "reconciliation" was called upon once again to justify a law that would have severely limited human rights prosecutions. Although in the end it did not pass, it was seen as an indication that the president and the Concertación were willing to back away from human rights issues.

Aylwin's pragmatism, then, established the discourse of reconciliation as a discourse of the status quo with respect to judicial prosecutions and human rights abuses. This was reinforced by his personal conflicts with the courts, which seemed to indicate the danger of a breakdown in consensus. In the words of one of his former ministers, "He accused judges of lacking moral courage during the dictatorship, so he confronted them. In the end he did not obtain much because he was too conflictive, but because he could not touch the military he confronted judges, and in that moment he really made a mess of things. It was the antigovernment of Aylwin" (Interview #8, October 27, 2010). The Supreme Court and judges in general consistently remained silent on human rights abuses during the dictatorship, rejecting almost all of the human rights cases that were brought before them. Thus Aylwin, a lawyer himself, the son of a judge, and the brother of a well-known human rights lawyer, took very personally the task of introducing changes in the judiciary, proposing an ambitious agenda of judicial reform. In fact, shortly after his election he convened a commission of "distinguished jurists" to explore a proposal on constitutional and organizational changes to the judiciary. This commission concluded that the courts were in crisis and urgently needed reform. Aylwin looked to his justice minister, Francisco Cumplido, to prepare an ambitious proposal. The Cumplido laws were introduced on April 25, 1990, the same day that the Rettig Commission was announced.

As could be expected, the judiciary and right-wing parties accused Aylwin's government of overstepping its executive bounds, forcing Cumplido to abandon his proposals. However, the topic of judicial reform continued to enjoy a great deal of political support across the aisle.[8] Lawyers working in academia and left- and right-wing NGOs pressured Aylwin's successor, Eduardo Frei, to undertake an important reform of the penal code and the judiciary.[9] It was a reform that received a remarkable degree of support, even among some of Pinochet's former ministers. In the words of one of the promoters of this reform, "They [the right-wing politicians] were very uncomfortable with their image as human rights abusers, but they got an opportunity with this reform to defend a discourse on individual guarantees without criticizing the dictatorship" (Interview #33, August 28, 2010). The reform was implemented in 2000, and it created a new criminal justice system, similar to the U.S. model, with an attorney general and a public defender's office.

The political implications of this judicial reform were crucial for the transition. First, it reframed the debate on human rights, choosing to deal with the present and the rule of law during democracy instead of confronting the state's past human rights abuses. Second, because of the exclusion of human rights cases from the jurisdiction of new tribunals—a bargaining chip that was included in the new penal code reforms in order to guarantee their passage during Frei's presidency—the reform was framed as "less politicized" and more "technical" (therefore more "politically neutral") than

Cumplido's proposals. Finally, it presented an "apolitical" discourse in relation to the punitive power of the state, now exclusively concerned with the protection of individual rights and fair procedures. The conflictive topic of human rights abuses was to be resolved by the judicial system, which also discursively placed these abuses firmly in the past. The discourse of human rights would often come into direct conflict with the views of the military and the right-wing political parties, and therefore its applicability had to be analyzed on a case-by-case basis when framing issues of social justice. However, discourses such as those related to reconciliation and individual guarantees under the law enjoyed considerable support on both the left and the right. As a result, political elites learned to frame social reforms as "apolitical," "reconciliatory" in nature, and concerned with the "present" because this gave them a greater chance of being adopted. This is the basis of what we are calling the political culture of reconciliation that permeated Chile during the 1990s.

TRYING TO RECONCILE THE IRRECONCILABLE? FAMILY DISCOURSE AND VIOLENCE AGAINST WOMEN IN THE 1990s

On January 3, 1991, Soledad Alvear became the first director of the newly created Servicio Nacional de la Mujer (National Women's Service—SERNAM). From its inception SERNAM was designed to be a political "lightweight": its budget represented less than 0.1 percent of the total fiscal budget, it was not a cabinet ministry (although its director had ministerial standing), and it played a subsidiary role in the planning of public policy. As Susan Franceschet (2003: 22) has pointed out, this created a number of challenges:

> One of the consequences of SERNAM not being its own ministry is that it is prohibited by law from implementing its own programs. Instead, SERNAM is charged with proposing and creating public policies for other ministries or agencies to implement. The only projects SERNAM can directly carry out are pilot projects, which, once proven effective, are turned over to the relevant ministry or agency for future implementation.

In addition, because the directors of SERNAM were appointed by the president, both Alvear and her successor, Josefina Bilbao, were members of the Partido Demócrata Cristiano (Christian Democratic Party—PDC), and PDC women were more likely to espouse the party line of the need for national "reconciliation" and to have a conservative view of women and the family (Baldez, 2002; Blofield and Haas, 2005; Haas, 2010; Htun, 2003; Ríos, Godoy, and Guerrero, 2003). According to the agency's Ximena Ahumada, "From the moment SERNAM was created, it immediately began to work on family violence. This issue was defined as a ministerial priority, as it was considered a grave social ill suffered not only by those directly affected but also by their loved ones and whose consequences extended to all of society" (quoted in SERNAM, 1995: 60). The high profile that this program assumed was largely due to the fact that—at least in principle—it did not constitute a threat to any political party. Instead, it allowed for a high degree of political goodwill on both the right and the left. As a consequence, SERNAM had the political support to launch a number of initiatives, including gathering the first domestic violence statistics, carrying out national media campaigns, providing information on women's rights to the public, and supporting Chile's first family violence law. The idea of violence against women was challenged by the Catholic Church, the right, and some sectors of the Concertación (Blofield and Haas, 2005; Haas, 2010; Htun, 2003). After all, it could lead to divisive discussions of the structure of the Chilean family, reproductive rights for women, and the legalization of divorce. The discussion of violence against women had to be framed very carefully to promote consensus. This is when the hegemonic politics of national reconciliation offered an opportunity: instead of treating women as victims in their own right, some sectors—primarily the PDC, backed by SERNAM—treated domestic violence as an issue of the "family" and its solution as a matter of personal rehabilitation rather than as a matter of reframing the hegemonic understanding of the past.

It is important to recall that in the early 1990s violence against women was front and center on the world stage. The United Nations' World Conference on Human Rights, held in Vienna in 1993, explicitly condemned all forms of violence against women, and the Inter-American Convention on the Prevention, Punishment, and Eradication of Violence against Women was approved by the Organization of American States in 1994. As Margaret Keck and Kathryn Sikkink (1998: 171–172) point out,

> What existed first was not the general category "violence against women" but separate activist campaigns on specific practices—against rape and domestic battery in the United States and Europe, female genital mutilation in Africa, female sexual slavery in Europe and Asia, dowry death in India, and torture and rape of political prisoners in Latin America. It was neither obvious nor natural that one should think of female genital mutilation and domestic abuse as part of the same category. The category "violence against women" had to be constructed and popularized before people could think of these practices as the "same" in some basic way. Yet activists cannot make just any category stick.

Thus, when Aylwin assumed office in 1990, the common terms utilized by feminist activists were, accordingly, "violence against women" and "domestic violence." When a law regarding this matter was presented in September 1990 by the left-leaning representatives Sergio Aguiló and Adriana Muñoz, it was called a law on "domestic violence" (see Guzmán, Mauro, and Araujo, 2000; Haas, 2010: esp. Chap. 3). However, its name was changed to "family violence" at SERNAM's request (Senado, 1993):

> SERNAM brought to this commission a folder with different pieces of information, and one of the most important was that related to the prevention of family violence. . . . In

the information studied it was established that "family violence" and "domestic violence" allude to all forms of abuse that take place within the confines of familiar relationships and that this abuse affects all of the family's members. . . . The commission highlights the educational nature of the law, which values, above all, reconciliation, in order to "safeguard the family." . . . The commission has changed the name of the law to "family violence," and by "family violence" we mean all abuse—both physical and verbal—that prejudices the physical or mental health of the spouse or cohabitating partner and that of family members, older and younger, related by blood to said spouse or partner.

In spite of the best efforts of some sectors of the Concertación to recast violence against women as a "societal ill" related to the Chilean family, there remained considerable resistance on the part of the right-wing parties and some conservative sectors of the ruling coalition to the idea of legislation on this matter. On the one hand, the Concertación itself exhibited a variety of positions. The PDC, for example, tended to encapsulate the issue in the discourse of reconciliation and the family; Representative Sergio Ojeda stated that "family violence breaks with the basic societal nucleus, which is the family" (Cámara de Diputados, 1993). Other sectors within the Concertación were considerably more closely aligned with discourses that strengthened the rights of women and democratic values, and the original sponsor of the bill, Representative Adriana Muñoz, made this clear: "Family violence is a daily and intimate expression of a social order based on discrimination, violence, and authoritarianism of the powerful over the weak, and the woman is a clear example of that. And, although making violence visible within the family means entering into the privacy of the home, it is totally necessary" (Cámara de Diputados, 1993). However, discourses on the family could also be used by the right to reject the law: the center-right Renovación Nacional (National Renovation Party—RN) and the far-right Unión Demócrata Independiente (Democratic Independent Union—UDI) both criticized the law as opening the door to a questioning of the institution of marriage and the "natural" gendered order.

In the midst of the discussion of family violence in Congress, on July 9, 1992, Aylwin created the National Family Commission, which sought to establish a public policy agenda based on the family. Like the Rettig Commission, it was used as an instrument for confronting the obstinate past but at the same time for legitimizing state decisions as a new myth based on the supposed neutrality, diversity, and expertise of the commissioners. In the words of Aylwin (1992: 18), it was not the commission's goal "to go to the press, get involved in controversies or produce spectacular effects. Rather, it is a commission like the Rettig Commission, which accomplished its mission well, that aims to work in silence and with due gravitas." Nevertheless, as could be expected, what occurred with this commission was precisely the opposite. The flexible definition of family that it offered (not related solely to matrimony) was contested by politicians from the whole political spectrum but especially by the right and by the Catholic Church. As a person who participated in the commission (Interview #21, November 23, 2010) told us,

The only valid definition of family, in those days, was that of a family in matrimony. If the law of violence against women was approved, or if children born outside matrimony were considered as having the same rights as children born inside matrimony, it meant that the state was recognizing different types of families in Chile. And the right wing was not willing to accept that. In addition, the influence of the Catholic Church was crucial: the cardinal telephoned Patricio Aylwin and Josefina Bilbao, trying to stop our work.

Thus, the family violence law was paralyzed in Congress during the Aylwin presidency, and his National Family Commission was unable to reach any viable consensus.

As a consequence, Soledad Alvear turned to the law as a mechanism for negotiation. In 1993 she timidly started a discussion on the creation of family courts in an effort to translate the problem of family violence into a matter of judges and conciliatory procedures. It was expected that these new courts would attend to all the problems related to the family (including family violence) at once and that therapists would have a critical role in counseling judges to obtain conciliation of conflicts (Interview #38, July 26, 2010). This was a strategy that immediately gained political traction. As many interviewees told us, family law never captured the interest of the legal profession's "notables" (who were mostly men), and therefore the family courts reform did not offer an appealing "technicism" for translating the discussion on family violence into "proper" jurisprudential terms. As an expert in charge of the parliamentary negotiation of this reform told us, "This reform was far more difficult to translate, because parliamentarians gave more personal opinions than technical opinions. Everything related to family issues was about their own experience" (Interview #9, August 13, 2010). Thus, when the framework of reconciliation was used by the state in the negotiation of the family courts reform, the discussion was conducted mainly in therapeutic terms, depoliticizing gender violence as a matter of personal failure or lack of will to heal the past. In other words, the same hegemonic framework of reconciliation was used in discussion of the Rettig Commission and the family violence law. In both instances women were elided as subjects in their own right, and in the latter the judge was made secondary to the psychologist and the social worker, highlighting the "therapeutic" aspect of family violence outcomes.

In November 1993, the family violence law went to the Senate, which was considered much more politically conservative than the House and at the time was made up of designated senators, who were more favorable to the right. At this point the tone of the family violence debate became definitively favorable to the "family." Senator Eugenio Cantuarias (UDI) alleged that "there is no worse family violence than abortion and divorce. . . . A well-constituted family represents a solid and stable base for society, a badly conformed family is a risk for the entire community" (Senado, 1993 [Senate, Session 14, November 16th]). The PDC weighed in through Senator Nicolás Díaz, agreeing with Cantuarias that "the most brutal violence is that used to assassinate a child in the uterus" (Senado, 1993 [Senate, Session 14, November 16th]). Conservative, pro-family arguments such as these resulted in proposals that sought to limit the scope of the law and resulted in the highly controversial addition that women had to be "significantly affected by the violence" in order for it to be termed "family violence." This addition was duly rejected by the House and led to a House-Senate conference in January 1994.

Finally, a month after the election of Eduardo Frei and through negotiations by the current and former directors of SERNAM with the executive branch, Law 19.325 was passed in April 1994 and entered into the Official Gazette on August 27, 1994. Speaking at the ceremony marking the passage of the law, Frei described it as follows (*El Centro*, August 20, 1994):

> This law is passed in the spirit of rehabilitation. The victims look more toward recuperation than penalizing the aggressor, with the hope of reestablishing family relations on the terrain of a healthy relationship, free of trauma. Certainly, it would be better not to have to legislate about these topics. But, unfortunately, this reality exists and we can't ignore it. I want to insist that the law, even a complete and just law, is not enough. Our change of heart will be much more profound if it is based on conviction rather than on punishment.

In the end, as the president recognized, it was the spirit of reconciliation—the language of rehabilitation and recuperation that also typified discussions of human rights—that turned the tide and allowed for a consensus to form around the idea of protecting the "family." But this came at a high cost: survivors of domestic violence would soon find that reconciliation did not always lead to the effective judicialization of domestic violence. Thus, the rhetoric of conciliation in the process of memory making during the transition in Chile had different consequences depending on who the "moral entrepreneurs" using it were; lawyers involved in the discussion of human rights violations linked reconciliation with jurisprudential debates around the punitive role of the state, whereas in the realm of domestic violence, lawyers and judges were seen as secondary to therapeutic rehabilitation programs.

The discursive conflicts that emerged in connection with the first family violence law in Chile were studied by Virginia Guzmán, Amalia Mauro, and Kathya Araujo of the Santiago-based Centro de Estudios de la Mujer (Women's Studies Center—CEM) in 2000. In their report they conclude (2000: 87–88):

> Seen from the perspective of a process, discursive confrontation was initiated with a bill that was constructed around the interpretive frame of gender discrimination. With the arrival of the bill in the committees of the House of Representatives a new interpretive frame was added, that of human rights, and there was a shift from "woman" to "family" in the discussion and argumentation of legal protection. With the receipt of the project by the Senate committee the third interpretive frame emerged: that which posited the "family" as the object of legal protection. Along the way, the name of the law was changed from "domestic violence" to "family violence." The final approval of the law was the result of a political solution that was supported by the mindful intervention of the executive, which resulted in a compromise in which the different factions were allowed to incorporate some of their proposals.

As these researchers note, this was the first law passed in Chile that sought to regulate what had previously been considered a private matter, and it filled a legal void. However, from the moment of its passage it was clear that various points of the new law were going to impede the state's ability to prosecute violent offenders and protect survivors of domestic violence.

First, the law recognized domestic violence not as a crime but as a misdemeanor, which meant that the possible penalties for domestic violence were light: usually only fines, community service, or temporary restraining orders that removed the abuser from the home. Prison time was exceedingly rare and usually only applied when the case went to the criminal court because of severe bodily harm, rape, or murder. This was not "restorative justice," since there were no attempts at conferencing or other "alternative" court options in which victims were allowed to tell their stories (Curtis-Fawley and Daly, 2005; Daly and Stubbs, 2006; Hudson, 2002; Sokoloff and Dupont, 2005; Stubbs, 2007). Rather, it was the product of a law that did not identify domestic violence as a serious crime. Second, the route taken within the courts was not sufficiently expeditious or beneficial for domestic violence victims because what was considered the proper realm for these cases—family court—had not yet been created. It was primarily the civil courts that were responsible for family violence cases, but these courts commonly granted restraining orders only upon meeting both parties. Additionally, since the resources allotted to the courts and the police for enforcing the law were insufficient, it was easy to beat the system either by being "let off the hook" by judges and police who had not been properly trained in dealing with family violence or by escaping capture. Luz Rioseco, a lawyer who worked for an antiviolence women's NGO, described the situation as follows: "The law is not solving the problem because too much depends on the court in which the proceedings are initiated and on the sensitivity that particular judges may have concerning this topic" (*La Nación*, November 25, 1996).

Finally, the main goal of the law was to maintain the family united through reconciliation. In practice, even though the sentiment of reconciliation between the parties might be lacking, conciliation was the obligatory first stage according to the law. To make matters worse, the waiting period between the first call to the police and the court appearance could be so long that it promoted the abandonment of the case by survivors. Faced with few economic options and a lack of alternative living arrangements, many women would simply give up and resume their previous relationships. By 2003 it was estimated that 92 percent of family violence court cases ended in conciliation (*La Nación*, June 30, 2003), even though a 2001 survey done by SERNAM and the University of Chile pointed to an alarming rate of sexual, physical, and psychological violence committed against women in the Santiago area: 50.3 percent (SERNAM, 2009). As Fiona Macauley (2006: 111) has argued, "Although the conciliation process is generally much faster and more accessible, it has decriminalized the bulk of domestic violence, reserving the mainstream criminal courts for a small number of the most egregious cases. . . . Women [are] stranded between pressure to conciliate, on the one hand, and the unresponsiveness of the criminal courts, on the other."

CONCLUSIONS: THE PROBLEM AND THE POTENTIAL OF RECONCILIATORY FRAMING

The 1990s in Chile were a time of deep memory cleavages and political divisions that were dealt with by the ruling political elite with a mixture of realpolitik and consensus. In order to achieve consensus among its different political factions, the Concertación often used "reconciliation" to portray the nation as a family led by the symbolic father figure of the president who tried to reconcile his squabbling children through Christian example. Political learning on the part of Concertación elites caused them to frame potentially divisive political issues in the most "apolitical," ahistorical, and technical way. In the case of penal reform, they were able to reach consensus in this way, but the problem of social justice was more complex. Human rights, for example, could not be politically whitewashed and continued to be a political wedge issue into the twenty-first century, even though it had been cast as "gender-neutral" and beneficial to the national "family."

In this context, violence against women was construed as an issue of the family and individual liberties in an effort to achieve consensus and approve the first family violence law. However, the family could never be truly apolitical, and in the end the negotiations over the law resulted in an effort to maintain the family intact. This was achieved formally through conciliatory measures in the courts and informally through perhaps unintentional byproducts that frustrated women victims' possibilities for obtaining justice. From the point of view of victims of domestic violence, "reconciliation" was not enough.[10] Moreover, its association with the Christian concepts of "turning the other cheek" and forgiveness made it difficult for those affected by gender violence to achieve justice.[11]

"Family" and "reconciliation" framings gradually came into question as Chile moved into the twenty-first century. The Lagos and Bachelet presidencies incorporated more social justice and gender narratives into their framings of violence against women. Chile's participation in the 1995 United Nations Women's Conference in Beijing and the arrest of Pinochet in London in 1998 dealt serious blows to the Concertación's framings of violence and gender and led to a partial breakdown of "reconciliation" discourse. Recognizing the limitations of the Rettig Commission's report, Ricardo Lagos convened the Valech Commission, which dealt with political violence and torture and included a section on sexual violence and women's experiences of torture (Hiner, 2009). At the same time, in 2004 a divorce law was finally approved and a family court system established. In 2005 a new family violence law was passed that sought to correct many of the main problems with the previous one—identifying family violence as a crime, calling attention to "habitual abuse," tightening precautionary measures, and allotting more serious victim protection through the newly created attorney general's office and a state-run system of battered women's shelters. Thus, although the memory languages of the 1990s in Chile put a premium on the relatively conservative framings of family and national reconciliation, they served an important purpose in opening up discursive spaces on gender violence issues that were legitimized by the state and that could be further refined.

NOTES

The original version of this essay was published in *Latin American Perspectives* 42 (3): 52–72.

1. We regard gender violence as what Kimberle Crenshaw (1991) has called "intersectional" in that it involves not only gender but also race, class, ethnicity, age, and sexual orientation. We follow Sally Engle Merry (2008: 3) in defining it as "violence whose meaning depends on the gendered identities of the parties. It is an interpretation of violence through gender. . . . The meaning of the violence depends on the gendered relationship in which it is embedded. These relationships are used to explain and even justify the violence. . . . Understanding gender violence requires a situated analysis that recognizes the effects of the larger social context on gender performances. When men abuse women in intimate relationships, they use the violence to define their own gendered identities. . . . Gender violence is now an umbrella term for a wide range of violations from rape during wartime to sexual abuse in prisons to insults and name-calling within marriages."

2. Adopting the terminology of Christine Bell and Catherine O'Rourke (2007), we propose that in Chile the main thrust of transitional justice was liberalizing rather than restorative. Its use of truth commissions could be viewed as restorative, but it was liberalizing in its conceptualization of a moving horizon of aspiration and its focus on "nation building" through reconciliation.

3. There are many examples of Pinochet's insubordination and frank disregard for the new democratic government in the 1990s, including continuous efforts to discourage human rights initiatives and legal actions.

4. As Paul Drake and Ivan Jaksic (1999: 23) have pointed out, the "excuse" of a legacy of authoritarianism has been criticized as merely "the Concertación's way of avoiding conflict and change," especially since the neoliberal economic model of the dictatorship remained in place and there was little institutional challenge to either the 1980 Constitution or the 1978 Amnesty Law.

5. Even prior to the election of Aylwin, a number of "reconciliation" discourses were already circulating among human rights groups and legal scholars. The position that came to dominate was that of José Zalaquett (1988; 1992), a renowned legal scholar, member of Comité Pro-Paz Chile (COPACHI), and head of Amnesty International from 1979 to 1982, that truth was an intrinsic value of the democratic transition and that, because of the constraints of the Chilean democratic transition, in which where trials would not easily be undertaken, it was imperative to discover as much truth as possible through the creation of a truth commission like Argentina's Comisión Nacional sobre la Desaparición de Personas.

6. The truth commission's objectives were to "(1) establish to the most complete degree what happened regarding the grave stated occurrences [grave human rights abuses], including background information and circumstances; (2) investigate individual victim cases, establishing what happened to each one or establishing their whereabouts; (3) recommend reparative and restorative measures to be carried out by the judiciary; and (4) recommend legal and administrative measures that should be adopted in order to impede or prevent similar events in the future" (Secretaría General de Gobierno, 1996: 1307).

7. Chile's first high-profile human rights trial, in November 1993, ended in the imprisonment of General Manuel Contreras and Brigadier General Pedro Espinoza. The contentious nature of this trial and Contreras's open contempt for the justice system restrained the Concertación from sending more cases to the courts.

8. In fact, Jaime Guzmán declared in 1991 that judicial reform was the only unresolved task of Pinochet's regime (Correa, 1999: 283). Moreover, in 1992 a prominent right-wing businessman, Agustín Edwards, founded the NGO Fundación Paz Ciudadana in direct response to the judicial problems that he encountered when his son was kidnapped by the FPMR (Palacios, 2011: 54).

9. These proposals were justified from the perspective of human rights and good governance but also from a neoliberal perspective, in terms of the need to secure economic predictability of market transactions (see, for example, Dezalay and Garth, 2002; Trubek and Santos, 2006).

10. Indeed, the appropriateness of concepts such as "reconciliation" in domestic violence in transitional contexts has increasingly been questioned (Bell and O'Rourke, 2007). It is important to stress that we are not taking the institution of families as *the* natural location for gender oppression. Families can also be institutions of support and resistance to other forms of social oppression (Ferree, 1990: 868). Thus it is more useful to take families as a multilayered field in which various struggles take place at an individual and collective level. According to Ferree (2010: 421), "lacking such an analysis, family change has continued to be seen more as a crisis than an opportunity for challenging pervasive structures of societal inequalities."

11. This article should not be read as opposing reconciliatory measures such as the culturally competent restorative-justice approaches currently used for domestic violence cases in other contexts. As Judith Herman (2005: 576) has pointed out, "Religious teachings traditionally exhort victims to transcend their anger through forgiveness, rather than taking action against those who have offended them, and the virtues of forgiveness have always been especially recommended to women and to members of other subordinate groups, whose justified resentment might make those in power uncomfortable."

Part II

DEFINING HISTORICAL PERIODS, BLAME, AND REPARATION

Roberta Villalón

The chapters included in this section of the volume exemplify how framing the past brings up critical issues of defining the beginning and end of historical periods, which shapes questions of responsibility, victimhood, reconciliation, and reparation, as well as informs political alignments and alliances. First, in "The Memory of the National and the National as Memory," Poblete looks to the cultural and ideological realms to understand the transition from a world that treasured the social, the public, and the collective to a world ruled by a neoliberal political economy of consumerism and individualism. This transition was not simultaneous with the shift from military to democratic regimes, but began during military times and continued under democracy in Chile. The neoliberalization of culture shaped processes of collective memory in three ways: first, it concealed the virulent socioeconomic violence of global capitalism, focusing instead on the violence of the military with regard to human rights abuses; second, it constrained the expansion and uniqueness of the national and thus the possibility of the emergence of a national memory; and, third, it reified the social (public/collective/socialist) as part and parcel of the past. Conceptualized in such a manner, "the political present is thus defined as a perverse mix of continuity and rupture" (Poblete, chapter 4 of this volume).

The contentious process of defining historical periods is also addressed in García Jerez and Müller's piece, "Between Two Pasts: Dictatorships and the Politics of Memory in Bolivia." In a context that had seemingly defeated the global imperatives of neoliberal capitalism, a redefinition of the past and inequality transformed the focus of memory and justice. This transformation did not follow the expected path based on Morales's promises to bring social and economic recognition to victims of the dictatorship. Instead, it consisted in prioritizing the long-term memory of colonial oppression over the short-term memory of military dictatorship. García Jerez and Müller show that the MAS government's efforts to revisit victimhood were influenced by military issues, the dismantling of leftist traditional parties and organizations, and the *indigenista* paradigm shift. While acknowledging the relevance, the legitimacy, and the political logic of centering attention on the prolonged marginalization of indigenous populations, they question the divisive effects of building a long-term memory exclusive of more recent struggles in which a demographically diverse mass of Bolivians risked their lives for inclusivity and fairness.

The questioning of when conflict begins and ends, and therefore who is to be blamed for it and who is to be offered reparations, is also addressed by Márquez in "Colombia's Gallery of Memory: Reexamining Democracy through Human Rights Lenses." The Gallery, an itinerant space for memory building set up in public spaces where documentation and photographs of a diverse array of victims of Colombia's still ongoing conflict are displayed, points to the arbitrariness of the official determination of post-conflict violence. She explains how the Gallery has served, on the one hand, as a means of breaking the silence about past and present state violence and its still unrecognized victims and, on the other hand, as a cultural gathering space for collectives to mobilize to guarantee the human rights of victims regardless of their political orientation or demographic background. Márquez explains that the Gallery and the movements attached to it intervene in top-down narratives of pacification and reconciliation by marking the problematic securitization of democracy as a cover for state-sponsored abuses of power. This study underscores the power of counter-hegemonic strategies as critical to halt processes that intend to move forward and leave conflict behind through selective memory, truth, and justice politics.

These three chapters call readers to look into normalized historical phases: military regimes, democratic times, pre- and post-conflict eras are nothing else but sociopolitical constructions of the past. To think about their sense of being, logic, accuracy, purpose, and implications can help advance memory, truth, and justice processes.

Additional readings to complement this section can be found in *Latin American Perspectives* 42 (3) (see Straubhaar, 2015; Leal-Guerrero 2015) and 43 (5) (see Phillips-Amos, 2016).

4

The Memory of the National and the National as Memory

Juan Poblete

If it is true that every national culture is by definition a form of mediation between the specific and the universal, a framework for understanding the connections between the local and the global, then Chilean culture has been working double shifts for a long time. For the past 45 years it has been defined by a series of international and global narratives derived first from the cold war struggle and then from its post-1989 global neoliberal aftermath. Those narratives understood the history of Chilean social, political, and cultural processes as an important performative space. This space showed, first in a rather confusing but then in a quite vivid fashion, a transition only now fully evident from the world of the social to that of the postsocial—a transition from a welfare state–centered form of the nation to its neoliberal competitive state counterpart. To a significant degree, the cultural history of Chile in this half century has been an extended meditation on the status of the national as memory—on the forms and uses of a national collective memory of the social in a postsocial global context. Any transformative democratization in Latin America depends on our capacity to understand the interplay between the memory of the social past and the reality of the new and increasingly hegemonic normal present of the postsocial. In Lechner and Güell's (1999: 187) terms, "The social construction of memory is part of a broader process: the construction of social time." The latter depends on the way we experience our present in tension with a past and a future. My contention on the memory of the national (the history of the properly national moment for a given national society) and the national as memory (the extent to which the national itself is a link and an experience formed in and through memory) is precisely an attempt at providing a broader memory framework (perhaps an example of what Halbwachs called *cadre sociaux de mémoire*) for an understanding of those relationships and the social and political possibilities they determine.

This essay is conceived as an intervention in the field of studies of collective memory after political violence. However, it is not the "after" of violence but its ever-presentness that interests me here. I am concerned with the double articulation of collective memory under neoliberalism, the deep and recurring violence it has involved (beyond military force or human rights violations, which are crucial but relatively well-studied issues), and its self-articulation as a social memory apparatus. Neoliberal violence and the administration and rearticulation of social memory are two sides of the same coin. I posit both the political potential of the living memory of the social within the postsocial (as recently shown by the Chilean student movement) and the difficulty of national collective memory under current global conditions. I develop two central ideas: the concept of the postsocial and the neoliberal alienation of human memory and the memory of the human (both knowledges and affects) in a system that coordinates political and libidinal economies (i.e., ways of re/producing and administering social and individual life and wealth) within a social horizon characterized by "short-termism" and thus incapable of thinking intergenerationally. In the last section I analyze two films that deconstruct through careful metalinguistic procedures (insisting on the processes of symbolic violence that promote presentism and forgetfulness) the logic and history of such a transformation.

The Chilean case, it is now clear, made fully visible a form of neoliberal violence and memory processes that have come to define what we understand as the contemporary political and social predicament. What initially was seen as the relatively unsurprising violent imposition of a new political regime in a Latin American country, albeit one that claimed to be exceptional in this regard in the regional context, has turned out to be an exceptionally vivid but otherwise accurate incarnation of the global effectiveness and the revolutionary capacity of neoliberalism and its attendant forms of violence: a restructuring of the social that reaches well beyond Chile. The neoconservative Chilean revolution ended up being less another coup d'état in a small Latin American country than a sign of what was to come globally in the form of Reaganism and Thatcherism. It entailed a form of radical change in our understanding of the social and its defining processes, actors, and goals—a transformation whose forms of violence turned out to be manifold and by no means dependent on the imposition of a military dictatorship.

This neoliberal globalization as epochal change has involved both the imposition of new forms of subjectification and postsocial culture and the nostalgic remembrance of a previous historical moment. Four movements are combined in this process and in the cultural experience of the new neoliberal epoch: they look into the present of the nation and out to the world; backward to the past, and forward to the uncertain future. I propose that, despite its rather insignificant size in the international context, Chile has performed an outsized historic and cultural role in the international comprehension of the duality of neoliberal globalization. This duality refers to the imposition of both a new political economy (often referred to as "neoliberal trickle-down economics") and a new libidinal economy based on the stimulation of individual consumption and debt and, above all, to their degree of imbrication and their contrast with previous ways of structuring the social and individual experience. Moreover, I claim that such a configuration has been crucial at the level of the constitution of national memory—in other words, that in remembering the forms of the social past or the past forms of the social we also confirm that, under neoliberal globalization, the national becomes, to a significant degree, such a memory counterpoint. The national in its new openness and disaggregation is now always lived as a permanent contrast between the national social in different stages of dissolution or radical transformation and the national globalized or postnational and its different forms of organization, socialization, subjectification, and memory.

THE MEMORY OF THE SOCIAL AND THE CHILEAN COUP

My hypothesis implies a relative and perhaps paradoxical displacement of two of the main objects of what could be considered the intersecting fields of political research and memory studies on the Chilean process of the past 40 years. In this view, Chilean culture was seen as insistently remembering the 1973 Pinochet coup and the dictatorial violence that followed it, on the one hand, and then living and analyzing a long transition toward democracy. If my hypothesis is correct, however, what was being remembered or memorialized was, at least from a global perspective, less that of political trauma and transition (now turned into symptoms of a broader configuration) than a violent, global, and no less decisive transformation. Before I go on to develop this idea, and in order to understand how it differs from and is linked to memory studies, I will use the work of Elizabeth Jelin, Steve Stern, and Nelly Richard as points of reference.

Steve Stern's trilogy *The Memory Box of Pinochet's Chile* (2004; 2006b; 2010) uses the idea of a memory box—both the holder of multiple, often contradictory, and partial accounts of the past and the object of struggles aiming at closing or opening such consideration of the past—to explain the emergence of a memory impasse in Chile. Such an impasse was beyond the simple binary of memory/forgetting and included active efforts to forget as well as the obstinate presence of the memory of horror and rupture on both the political left and the right. In addition to Stern's useful postulation of a link between individual and social memories through the positing of "emblematic memories," memories capable of shaping the meaning and value of other narratives, and beyond his insightful description of four memory frameworks in Chile ("salvation, rupture, persecution, and awakening" [2006b: 145]), what I would like to rescue from his work here is his highlighting of one of the results of the Chilean memory impasse: "not so much a culture of forgetting as a culture that oscillated—as if caught in moral schizophrenia—between prudence and convulsion" in its efforts to overcome and deal with the legacy of the Pinochet years (xxix).

Elizabeth Jelin's (2002) *Los trabajos de la memoria*, the first volume of a series of edited books titled *Las memorias de la represión*, provides an excellent panoramic view of memory studies in connection with political violence. In addition to an emphasis on the active nature of the memory processes associated with political violence—through concepts such as the work of memory, the need to learn to remember, and the struggles between dominant, official, and suppressed or unofficial memories—and the multiplicity of agents, critical points in time (commemorations), and loci of memory, Jelin distinguishes between operative narrative memories, capable of endowing the past with a functional meaning, and traumatic or wounded memories, which cannot find a narrative meaning and manifest themselves as symptoms in a never-ending process of mourning. In a similar vein, Patricio Marchant has referred to the 1973 military coup that frames the periodization of contemporary Chile (before, during, and after) as a "coup against representation," a radical perturbation of ways of thinking and speaking about the social. This break in signification, Idelber Avelar (1999), Alberto Moreiras (1993), and Nelly Richard (2006) have insisted, defines the space of the postdictatorship and poses the challenge of finding an alternative to the responses already offered: the expert and accommodating answers of the social sciences, the communist efforts to refurbish epic past languages, and the indifference of consumers in the market.

For Richard that language is provided by the artistic and literary Chilean avant-gardes who respond to the categorical disaster of the coup and the loss of meaning of the social with an insistence on not losing sight of the meaning of the loss itself. Following the work of Moreiras on postdictatorial thought, Richard (2004 [1998]: 22) characterizes the cultural horizon of the Chilean post-dictatorship thus:

> The postdictatorial condition is expressed as a "loss of object" in a definite situation of "mourning." . . . The melancholic dilemma between "assimilating" (remembering) and "expelling" (forgetting) traverses the postdictatorial horizon, producing narratives divided between a muteness—the lack of speech linked to the stupor of a series of changes that, given their velocity and magnitude, cannot be assimilated to the continuity of a subject's experience—and overstimulation: compulsive gestures that artificially exaggerate the rhythm and signs to combat depressive tendencies with their artificial mobility.

Faced with this situation, the hegemonic Chilean culture of the postdictatorship has, in its effort to push for consensus, simultaneously exaggerated its novelty and its degree of rupture with the authoritarian past and hidden the non-new—the significant degrees of continuity of the legal structures created by the dictatorship and the postdictatorial governments' policies. The political present is thus defined as a perverse mix of continuity and rupture.

In this quick review of a few important writers working on memory studies and political violence, there are a few crucial points that will interest me here: first, the oscillation between past and present in the definition of political life and its capacity to limit the imagination of the political horizon of the possible; secondly, the emphasis on narrative and social frameworks as determining the nature of memory; and, finally, the coexistence in the historical present of operative and traumatic narratives, sense making, and interruption.

More generally, however, within memory studies the Chilean coup and its aftermath have traditionally been thought of as both exceptions to the rules and predictable, brutal, Southern Cone processes exclusively associated with right-wing military dictatorships and their human rights violations and excesses. This has generated very productive concepts and dynamics—such as the emergence of human rights as a global and national political issue, the cultures of transition to democracy and their manifold searches for the right combination of truth determination and political feasibility, and an acknowledgment of new political and social actors such as social movements, nongovernmental organizations, and women. Those memory studies, however, may have ended up obscuring another potential framework for an understanding of such political developments and human rights violations. I am proposing that the latter were only the most visible part of a much wider and all-encompassing global process. Naomi Klein (2007: 7) has referred to the Chilean coup as "the first test" or the "birth pangs" of what she deems the shock doctrine of disaster capitalism, whereby in the guise of a crisis that requires extraordinary measures and taking advantage of the public's disorientation and shock (in this case from violence and hyperinflation) a "rapid-fire transformation of the economy—tax cuts, free trade, privatized services, cuts to social spending and deregulation"—is imposed. Reading the history of global neoliberalism and referring to the paradigmatic influence of the Chilean case, David Harvey (2005: 9) concludes that it "provided helpful evidence to support the subsequent turn to neoliberalism in both Britain (under Thatcher) and the United States (under Reagan) in the 1980s. Not for the first time a brutal experiment carried out in the periphery became a model for the formulation of policies in the centre."

My hypothesis on the memory of the national and the national as memory adds a temporal dimension to such a consideration of the exemplarity of the Chilean case. This temporal dimension explains the tension between the present, the past, and the future and the cultural and political productivity of that tension.

If states, including the Chilean military dictatorship, use the "breakdown" of the political system and the figure of the "clean slate" as a founding narrative for a national memory capable of creating the foundational basis of their often authoritarian projects, then the postsocial is less a degree of rupture or a break than a form of permanent dialectic between the social past and the postsocial present. This in turn defines the future as an uncertain mix of loss, inevitability, and potential.

THE ARGUMENT

At this point a restatement of my hypothesis may be in order. By "the social," following Jacques Donzelot (1991), I understand simply the sphere of governmental intervention in society that emerged in the second half of the nineteenth century—first in France and later more broadly—as a way of dealing with the tensions between right-

and left-wing understandings of republicanism, stressing individual and collective rights, respectively. The social is a specific sphere of state intervention in the creation of solidarities that do not threaten the ultimate sovereignty of the voting people. Through the carving out of social solidarities as a specific sphere of governmental intervention, the state becomes an actor relatively separate from social relations and more of an arbiter or a "guarantor of social progress" (Donzelot, 1991: 173). By increasingly extending the realms of the social, the state became the welfare state, a social democratic compromise between liberal democracy and socialism, both a way of increasing opportunity for the actual exercise of individual freedoms and a way of reducing social risk and market irrationality by promoting social security. The welfare state administered the social for close to a century, but it is now clearly under attack. The steady neoliberal creation of a new political and social "common sense" has taken full advantage of the tensions between the claims of the welfare state and its impacted capacity to continue delivering the social goods it promised to all its citizens. Instead, the neoliberal new normal has imposed what, from a critical viewpoint, I am calling "the postsocial." Thus by "postsocial," I understand a social configuration that results from the transformation of the welfare state, with the end of its ethos of the social as a solidarity-based commitment administered by the state and its replacement by a competitive state whose rationality derives from the neoliberal version of the economy and whose ethos, instead of socializing and distributing risk in solidarity, individual-izes and privatizes it. Obviously, the postsocial does not imply the disappearance of society, but it does involve its radical restructuring.

In the vast field of relations between the economy and culture, we have moved historically from a situation in which the economy was at the service of a certain social transformation defined by noneconomic (political, social, and cultural) values to a new scenario in which society is transformed at the pace signaled by economic values. From societies endowed with certain economies and markets we have transitioned to market societies. This transition and transformation have involved a form of memory practice present in both larger political and everyday life. A certain form of organizing society that we called the "social" becomes, in the postsocial, the object of national memory. The social is nostalgically or achingly remembered in an insistent counterpoint with a new postsocial way of structuring experience, political horizons, and memory.

My hypothesis, then, is that if under conditions of neoliberal globalization the economy has seemingly phagocytized society—if it has transformed its values in the fusion of society and economy in so-called market societies—this process can and perhaps must be described as the shift from the social to the postsocial. This transition, the deeper and global transition of which the Chilean one was only one example, is defined by two complementary transformations: first, the new legitimation of zones of inequality, with their attendant internalized border zones, and the stabilization of zones of exception, and, secondly, the privatization of the memory of the social and its replacement by the form of forgetfulness and presentism produced by consumption. The first transformation refers to the organization and ends of the social, while the second is connected to the forms of organization of memory in postindustrial societies.

My thesis on the memory of the national (the history of the properly national moment for a given national society) and the national as memory (the extent to which the national itself is a link and an experience formed in and through memory) is therefore an attempt at seeing memory dynamics in the context of the permanent haunting of the postsocial (national as memory now) by the half-gone, half-present evocation of the social (memory of the national in the past). It is also an effort to insist that the postsocial is not an irreversible state but instead a condition open to powerful challenges by the reemergence of forms of social protest and organization of which the Chilean student movement of the past couple of years has been an inspiring example—an eruption and disruption stemming from a past capable of interrupting the totalizing nature of the present.

THE WORKING OF MEMORY IN THE TRANSITION FROM THE SOCIAL TO THE POSTSOCIAL

During the first 70 years of the twentieth century, the state found in the conjunction of industrial capitalism and the welfare state its main form of legitimation. It was the Keynesian compromise that gave workers salaries that allowed their consumption of goods in the economy, because it understood production and consumption as processes integrated within a spatial dynamics of coexistence in a particular national market and society. While the state at the time tended toward the universalizing expansion of social rights and social welfare, the same state searches now—in the context of a relative separation between power and politics—for a different form of legitimation. It finds it not in the provision of a modicum of security in the form of welfare for all its citizens but in the need to cut, for budgetary reasons, those services and often in the provision of police security and the exploitation of the fear of some citizens (the so-called taxpaying ones) of others, excluded or semiexcluded (the tax-eating ones).

This reterritorialization of the social, the political, and the cultural defines globally the social geography of the postsocial. Among its constitutive factors one could mention a privatization of social risk and its administration (in which pensions, social security, education, and many other social services once solidly established depend on each individual's contributions and the vagaries of the financial market, with the ensuing increase in instability and anxiety); a change from an economy in which many of the good jobs were in manufacturing with high labor intensity to a postindustrial economy of services of less labor intensity; and thus a radical flexibilization of the labor force and with it a much higher tolerance for or even legitimation of inequality in the distribution and concentration of wealth.[1]

Instead of socializing and distributing risk in solidarity, the new dominant ethos individualizes and privatizes it, resulting in dynamics of both relative inclusion and exclusion affecting sizable sectors of the population and the stabilization of zones of exception concerning, most crucially, the young and poor. These zones of exception can be used to mobilize fear and distrust among the citizenry and confirm its spatial stratification in a territory crisscrossed by internal borders, dividing the social into subterritories in need of high surveillance (Poblete, 2012; Sánchez, 2006).

In this new postsocial condition, everyday life and its experience are constituted to a significant degree by the memory of a different form of the national and the social and by their constant contrast with their occlusion in the present. In the post-social, the sites of memory and the dynamics of evocation and loss are multiplied in such everyday occurrences as the visit to the doctor or the configuration of the workplace, the call to a customer service hotline or a stop at a government office. What we experience in each case is not a clear form of political violence or a blatant violation of our human rights but a diffuse discomfort that has slowly become more distinct. We collectively live—although this is surely different for those under and over 40—within the constant contrast between a sense of the way things used to be (and its memory) and the way things are now.

The second process that the transition from the social to the postsocial presupposes is the privatization of the memory of the social and its unsatisfactory replacement by forgetfulness in consumption. According to Bernard Stiegler (2010), to the extent that the industrial capitalism of production became the postindustrial capitalism of consumption that has now entered into the crisis of financial capitalism, that capitalism ended up phagocytizing the state and the economy itself. Whereas the state had been throughout the first two-thirds of the twentieth century the single agent in charge of adjusting the fit between the apparatus of economic production and the social system, toward the end of the century that state was sidelined by transnational and speculative capitalism bent on blaming the state for limiting its creative capacities—a predatory capitalism whose only horizon is the short-term and whose results are the proliferation of so-called externalities (from human to ecological consequences) and the incapacity to think an intergenerational horizon, with the attendant reduction of the economic to immediate speculation and the destruction of credit—of faith and trust in social investment in the social.

Whereas every true economy presupposes among the participants a commerce of savoir faire (knowledge of how to do) and savoir vivre (knowledge of how to live)—an exchange of life and creative materialized ideas—Stiegler sees contemporary capitalism as not properly an economy but an antieconomy, reduced as it is to monetary exchanges. This antieconomy leads to the destruction of savoir faire and savoir vivre, a mutation of the nature of work, and a functionalization of production, consumption, and social relations, now inseparable from the technological apparatus. For Stiegler, Plato was the first critic of proletarianization to the extent that he opposed the transfer of live forms of memory and experience to written discourse, a technology that, for him, alienated such memory. The process that leads us to transfer more and more of our human memory to machines (as manifested in everyday situations such as the autocorrection of spelling in the machine on which I am writing) is the last result of a broader process of proletarianization (a term that for Stiegler is not synonymous with economic impoverishment) that has at least three modern moments.

It began in the nineteenth century with the destruction of the savoir faire of workers (of their physical working gestures) by its transfer to machines, which made possible the creation of a proletarian labor force. It continued in the twentieth century with the destruction of the savoir vivre of workers qua consumers and has gone on now with the crisis of such forms of production and consumption in a generalized process of cognitive and affective proletarianization. In this process what is alienated to machines—what is externalized—is, in addition to savoir faire and savoir vivre, savoir theorizer, the capacity to think about our experiences and produce knowledge (Stiegler, 2010: 30). The proletarians of the muscular system, produced by the machine appropriation of their savoir faire, are now joined by the proletarians of the nervous system, who produce cognitive labor without controlling the knowledge thus produced. "Grammaticalization" is the name Stiegler gives to this externalization of memory in its various forms: bodily and muscular, nervous, cerebral, and biogenetic. Once grammaticalized, these different forms of memory can be manipulated by systems of biopolitical and sociopolitical control that regulate, in a "general organology," the articulation of bodily organs (muscles, brain, eyes, genitals), artificial organs (tools and machines), and social organs (from the family to the nation as forms of organization of the social and its reproduction). From this viewpoint, proletarianization is, literally, a short circuit, an interruption and short-termism, a separation of the worker as producer (but also of the consumer as producer) from the control of the conditions of production and the products thus generated, and an interruption of what Stiegler calls "transsubjective individuation," which is the goal of all real knowledge and experience.

I have thus identified a second distinctive dynamic of the experience of the postsocial national within my framework for an understanding of the national as memory today and the memory of the national in the past. While the first dynamic is the constant counterpoint between the postsocial present and the memory of a previous configuration of the social, the second is the articulation of a political economy with a libidinal economy that regulates both production and consumption, generating a series of negative externalities (from the destruction of nature to the disarticulation of the social environment, both the basic conditions of forms of individuation and sociality that are truly productive and sustainable) and what Nelly Richard (2006: 10) calls "technologies of dismemory." At the national level the result of this double process—of rearticulation of the social and alienation of memory, dominated by the short circuit and short-termism—is an incapacity for projecting the national (the memory of its savoir faire, vivre, and theorizer) as a long-term collective future. This, I think, is how the memory of the social national is activated and how the postsocial national is lived as counterpunctual memory.

ARTICULATING POLITICAL AND LIBIDINAL ECONOMIES

Like the social—described by what Bruce Curtis (2002: 85) calls its "artefactual" character, "that it is a product of projects, practices, and techniques which equate and unify empirically disparate objects and relations"—the neoliberal postsocial is the result of active efforts at shaping the lives and souls of its citizens, multiple techniques and practices that help produce it and objectify it. Maurizio Lazzarato (2009: 109), analyzing what he calls "neoliberalism in action," refers to some of the techniques that have helped transform society into "an 'enterprise-society,' based on the market, competition, inequality, and the privileging of the individual." They include the apparatus of financialization of the economy and society and strategies such as "individualization, insecuritization, and depoliticization used as part of neoliberal social policy to undermine the principles of mutualization and redistribution that the Welfare State and Fordism had promoted."

I have elsewhere (Poblete, 2015a) analyzed two Chilean films of the past decade—*Taxi para tres* (2001) by Orlando Lübbert and *Super: Todo Chile adentro* (2009) by Fernanda Aljaro and Felipe del Rio—in order to highlight, first, that the invitation to consume and buy on credit in a context of significant social inequality produces subjects in debt, individuals whose "conduct, capacities, needs, aspirations and desires" (Schild, 2007: 179) are thus normalized; and, secondly, that the humanist critique of such a social configuration becomes internalized by that system's ability to commodify everything, including dissent. I would like to conclude by analyzing two additional recent Chilean films that help explain the consequences and costs of such neoliberal techniques for the restructuring of the social and the production of the postsocial and its memory dynamics: *Tony Manero* by Pablo Larraín (2008) and *Nostalgia de la luz* by Patricio Guzmán (2010). The first will help us understand the psychic mechanisms behind the original neoliberal violence and its present aftereffects, while the second will be read as a reflection on the artifactualness of the production of memory in the contrasting contexts of the social and the postsocial in Chile. Both films vividly index the double process of rearticulation of the social and the attendant memory (and erasure of memory) dynamics implied by the neoliberal regime.

Tony Manero is one of the most radical Latin American film explorations of the deep social violence involved in the continental implantation of neoliberalism. While seemingly inscribed as yet another Third World reflection on the world of fandom, media consumption, and creative spectatorship in the midst of mass-mediated communication and social relations along the lines of *Strictly Ballroom* or *Slumdog Millionaire*, *Tony Manero* ends up offering a trenchant critique of neoliberalism as represented by the arrival in Chile of both a new model of society and a form of mass-mediated modernity that found in global Hollywood one of its main vehicles of reproduction.

Set in 1979, at the end of one of the most violent periods of repression of the Pinochet dictatorship and at the beginning of its institutionalization and attempted legitimization through both the drafting of a new constitution and the imposition of a new model of (market) society, a society for which competition and consumption will become the fundamental pillars and paradigms of all social relationships, *Tony Manero* is an extraordinary and disconcerting film experience. On the one hand, we as spectators cannot but identify, at least partially, with the main character and his underdog effort to perform as well as Tony Manero in *Saturday Night Fever* and win a TV contest of John Travolta look-and-dance-alikes. On the other, our repulsion over the multiple murders and crimes that this Chilean Manero feels obliged to commit in order to bankroll his artistic and creative endeavors forces us to see the much less glittering underside of the spectacle, its political and psychic unconscious. This is accomplished through an uncomfortable and disconcerting juxtaposition of the shiny world of fandom and creative emulation with the much grimmer, darker, and grainier world of poverty and brutal physical and social violence. The film, however, ends up not simply representing an external, violent social and political reality but also redefining its mode of filmic incorporation. Eventually, the violence for the spectator resides less in the crimes coldly perpetrated by this sociopath than in the psychic contrast or alternation between radically different genres that the film viewer is forced to activate and experience simultaneously. The result of this enactment of symbolic struggle and violence in the mind of the spectator is as close to an effective representation of the long-term and long-lasting historical violence inflicted by the dictatorship on Chilean society as any of the many films that have more realistically attempted to depict it. The reason is simple: rather than exploring a world out there, a historical experience preexisting its film representation, *Tony Manero* seeks to represent it through one of the psychic mechanisms that allowed for the simultaneous imposition of a market society predicated on the radical freedom of the uncoerced consuming individual and a brutal form of collective outward and inward violence, a reproduction of a call to live in the permanently glittering world of consumption in the here and now at the expense of any sense of historical memory or justice. Moreover, the film seeks to do so using a form of filmic cognitive dissonance that reinscribes the Hollywood encyclopedia of topics, genres, and styles into its real political economy in an attempt to represent in film the subordinated memories of Latin American experiences (Poblete, 2015b).

Nostalgia de la luz is the latest of a long and illustrious series of documentaries by Patricio Guzmán that explore the national memory process around the Chilean road to democratic socialism, its tragic end in September of 1973, the violent dictatorial aftermath, and the protracted postdictatorship period. This series has included *La batalla de Chile, Salvador Allende, Chile la memoria obstinada*, and *El caso Pinochet*. Guzmán's latest film is a particularly honest and beautiful reflection on both documentary film as a practice, capable of rendering historical experience visible, and the technologies of memory and forgetting under neoliberal conditions that tend to obscure such experience or render it partial and inoperative.

The film is structured around the contrast between three forms of the here (spaces) and now (times) of the nation. There is, first, an almost mythical present in the past, when Guzmán was young and in Chile: "Life was provincial. Nothing ever happened and the presidents of the Republic walked the streets without bodyguards. The present time was the only one that existed." Then there is, by contrast, the almost unbearable present of the current neoliberal moment, a present defined by its incapacity to produce a coherent narrative of the historical memory of the nation and haunted by the never-ending search of those who seek to recover the bones of their disappeared relatives. As the documentary comes to a close, Guzmán concludes with a third form of the present: "I believe that memory has a force of gravity. It always attracts us. Those who have a memory are capable of living in the fragile present time. Those who don't have one cannot live anywhere." This third, fragile form of the present is paradoxically defined by its unique capacity to enable social action by effectively remembering the history of the nation, thus providing its subjects with a solid grounding for future action. Time as memory becomes the condition of any acceptable location or national spatiality.

The two dimensions, temporal and spatial, historical and geopolitical, are fully intertwined. Whereas Chile was once "an oasis of peace, insulated from the world," history happened twice, via a revolutionary and a counterrevolutionary process. Both meant a displacement of the relevant spatialities and temporalities of the nation: "This quiet life came to an end one day. A revolutionary wind threw us in the middle of the world. . . . Later, a coup d'état swept democracy, dreams, and science away." While, as Guzmán says right before the closing credits, "Every night, slowly, impassively, the center of the galaxy flies over Santiago," the challenge of *Nostalgia de la luz* is how to comprehend the scales and coordinates of the nation, the scales of the times and places that allow a proper understanding of its global and cosmic history and location.

In order to do that, Guzmán turns his attention inward and outward: inward, on his own past and his desire to reconstruct the memory of the nation and on the affective life of those who search in the desert for their disappeared relatives or live with the legacy of those disappearances; outward, on the documentary genre itself and the many artifacts, instruments, knowledges, and strategies that allow human beings to both apprehend the connections between the past, the present, and the future and find their place in the world. In this exploration of both the documentary technologies for rendering the social visible and the transcendental categories of time and space that make possible the conceptualization of the experience of the nation, the Atacama Desert becomes a cypher figure of that nation. The desert is the location of multiple forms of life and their traces, from prehistoric times to contemporary human rights violations and scientific archaeological and astronomical explorations, including nineteenth- and early twentieth-century commercial exploitation of saltpeter. It is also the scene of affective and political searches into and for the memory of the nation.

Turned into a text and a scene ("The transparent and thin air allows us to read this great open book of memory, page by page"), the desert functions as a memory box, holding both the record of the distant, mid-range, and recent past and the possibility and grounding of a future for the nation. The key connector is the fragile present, revealed now as always already penetrated by the past, a time/space construct produced as much by the instruments and knowledges that let us apprehend it as by the structure of our perceptual apparatus. In both cases, light mediates and allows the perception and understanding of the present time/space of Chile as always already a reflection and manifestation of the past, a present that exists only as memory.

The documentarist's work—itself one more in a long line of knowledges and practices that produce the social national, including archaeology (the distant prenational past), history (the republican and postsocial past), and astronomy (the cosmic and global location of the nation)—must reveal the natural and social constructedness of all national times (past, present, and future) and their reliance on a "manipulation" of the data that always come from the past. From this viewpoint, all knowledges of the nation are memory practices. Like astronomers—who know that for their current perception of the universe through telescopes "the past is the great tool," as the film states (to the extent that they analyze light that has taken a long time to reach us)—the documentary filmmaker must be able to learn from the professional knowledges of the archaeologist, the historian, and the astronomer on and for the manipulation and interpretation of the past. He must also combine the affective knowledges of those who suffered imprisonment in the desert but learned to survive by looking up at the sky or by preserving in memory the spatial dimensions of their concentration camp with the affective and memory practices of the relatives who search for their lost ones like astronomers of the land or archaeologists of the present and the future. Connecting these processes of memory and interpretation is necessary if the documentary filmmaker is to reveal the secret of the nation: that the present and thus the future are always already haunted and constituted by the past, always already memory processes.

Those instruments and knowledges reveal that, as much as the desert, the nation is a layered time/space for which memory processes are fundamental and constitutive, even in the midst of the neoliberal postsocial tabula rasa.

CONCLUSION

In a well-known essay on what he calls "irruptions of memory" and "expressive politics" in the Chilean transition to democracy, Alexander Wilde (1999: 475) defines the former as "public events that break in upon Chile's national consciousness, unbidden and often suddenly, to evoke associations with symbols, figures, causes, ways of life, . . . associated with a political past that is still present in the lived experience of a major part of the population." These irruptions, including political violence and the discovery of mass graves, but also shows of force by the military and the Pinochet trial in London, were part of and challenges to the expressive politics of postdictatorship democratic governments. In rekindling the political struggles and forms of violence of the past and their memories, they reminded people of the limitations of actually existing democracy in Chile. They extended the duration of the transition by questioning the depth of the democratic regime and its moral authority, given the existence of "unreconciled memories of a divided past" (Wilde, 1999: 496). The student movements I mentioned before are another form of irruption of the past in the present, this time not of the dictatorial past but of the predictatorial epoch of the social, a time when accessible public education, proper political representation, and equality for all were seen not only as worth fighting for but also as feasible political goals. Disrupting the hegemony of the possible under the postdictatorial transition, all three goals have now been centrally embraced by the current and significantly more radical second Michelle Bachelet presidential administration.

What my hypothesis about the postsocial has attempted to explain is another long-term transition of which the Chilean transition has turned out to be only a part, a form of "lived experience" based both on memories of the national qua social and on their contrast with the national as impacted memory under neoliberal postsocial regimes with their attending memory-administration machines. Consequently, I have attempted to highlight not the forms of past violence (military force and human rights violations) that we have come to identify with memory and political violence studies but the ever-present neoliberal violence and its self-articulation as an apparatus for the production and administration of social and individual memory. As a memory apparatus, neoliberalism depended on a dual evacuation of historical time. Individuals in constant pursuit of personal satisfaction in a market society were pushed to shed the past so that the present could persist unchanged (the developed future being just a radical and massive extension through consumption of the trickling-down successes of the present as currently enjoyed by a few). But the historical social past was also recreated as simultaneously irrelevant and dangerous for such an extension. By definition any idea stemming from the social past (especially the socialist past) was deemed irrelevant for the present and future at the same time that it was conceived as threatening them (at best as a negative counterexample). A future-as-extended-present that could so decisively dispose of the past was then affirmed precisely on such radical erasure, always dependent on its radical newness.

What *Tony Manero* and *Nostalgia de la luz* allow us to see and experience anew is first the symbolic violence involved in the implantation of a present-oriented society of profit-maximizing individuals (what I have called here the "postsocial") and then that if this totalizing and dehistoricizing "now" has involved significant political, social, and cultural work invested in forgetting, its overcoming will require substantial countermemory work recalling the languages, practices, and cultural meanings of the social past. Those memories of multiple pasts and their daily counterpoint with the fabric of the present are both the source of Chile's comfort and discomfort with its own form of modernity and the spring from which true challenges to the status quo may emerge.

NOTES

The original version of this essay was published in *Latin American Perspectives* 42 (3): 92-106.

1. Juan Carlos Castillo (2012) points out that, contrary to a normative perspective that would presuppose that higher degrees of inequality would generate a stronger social demand for equality, the data from public opinion surveys indicate that in Chile they have produced more legitimation of inequality. Chilean society as a whole now accepts and justifies greater inequality than it did in the past.

5

Between Two Pasts

Dictatorships and the Politics of Memory in Bolivia

Francisco Adolfo García Jerez and Juliane Müller
Translated by Margot Olavarria

During the second half of the twentieth century in Bolivia, state repression, massacres, and arrests by the military accounted for more than 650 assassinations and left tens of thousands wounded, imprisoned, or exiled. In fact, about 150 disappeared continue to be recorded (ASOFAMD, 2008: 17; Guzmán, 2012: 95). In response to these crimes, Bolivia was one of the first countries in Latin America to establish a truth commission. Set up at the beginning of the 1980s, by the 1990s it had approved a series of initiatives for the compensation of the victims, and these were complemented by those of the governments of Evo Morales. However, despite these efforts and as a consequence of their limited success, organizations that could be described as authentic "entrepreneurs of memory" (Jelin, 2002) have expressed dissatisfaction, and this has resulted in public condemnation by Amnesty International, the Asociación de Derechos Humanos de Bolivia (Human Rights Association of Bolivia), and Human Rights Watch with regard to, among other issues, the impossibility of gaining access to military archives alluding to the dictatorships (Amnesty International, 2012; Human Rights Watch, 2014) and in the organization by the Plataforma de Luchadores Sociales (Social Fighters' Platform–PLS) of a vigil in front of the Ministry of Justice since March 2012. The action demands a change in Morales's policies concerning memories of the dictatorships. "No Forgetting, No Forgiving," "Truth, Justice, Reparation, No More Impunity," and "For a Conscious People of Historical Memory" are some of the slogans that can be seen at that vigil (see figures 5.1 and 5.2).

These protests on the part of the victims' and human rights organizations led us to ask why governments that identify themselves as socialist, sensitive to historical discrimination, and populist are not working to resolve definitively the demands of the dictatorships' victims. Therefore, the objective of this article is to analyze the influence of the Morales governments on the politics of memory (García Álvarez, 2009), especially in connection with the dictatorships between 1964 and 1982 (Dunkerley,

Figure 5.1. Vigil of the Plataforma de Luchadores Sociales in front of the Ministry of Justice.
Source: Francisco Adolfo García Jerez

Figure 5.2. Mural with portrait of Marcelo Quiroga Santa Cruz.
Source: Juliane Müller

1984; Malloy and Gamarra, 1988; Mayorga, 1978).[1] Far from intending to minimize the complex governmental task that the MAS government has had to face, we want to distinguish the contradictions of political practice from the contradictions that emerge from the structural framework (Kohl, 2010). With regard to the first, apart from those stemming from the proposal to construct a new highway across part of the Territorio Indígena y Parque Nacional Isidoro Sécure (Isidoro Sécure Indigenous Territory and National Park) without the permission of the indigenous communities, in violation of the new constitution (Almarez et al., 2012; Lorenzo, 2011), another contradiction of political practice is directly linked to the apparent disinclination of the MAS government to develop an effective policy for the restoration of memory, justice, and reparations for the victims of the dictatorships.

Analyzing the politics of historical memory in the Bolivian case and the factors that influence it allows us to understand that it is part of an area of struggle in which global trends involving international agendas and transitional jurisprudence converge with particular historical factors and conjunctures. While the Bolivian case underlines a key factor shared with other South American countries with regard to truth and justice, the role of the military, the reconfiguration of the Bolivian left and the indigenous and anti-neoliberal nationalist discourse are the consequence of historical variables and particular sociopolitical conjunctures that are significant for understanding the reframing of categories of international rights at the national level and their articulation with specific policies about memory.

TRANSITIONAL JUSTICE AND THE POLITICS OF MEMORY

The society's interest in recovering memory has to be framed in terms of a global trend toward memorializing traumatic events and granting prominence to victims of state terror and genocide.[2] The world wars of the twentieth century and the Nazi Holocaust promoted a transnational movement for the symbolic and material recovery of its victims (Bloxham, 2001). Studies of memory, on the one hand, and of transitional justice, on the other, emerged from the political and social consciousness of the importance of the compensation of victims and the condemnation of those responsible (Olick and Robbins, 1998). While the first have focused on memory in a broad sense, the latter have focused on democracy and stability in postdictatorship contexts, the political transformation of socialist countries, and the "post-conflict security framework" (Teitel, 2008: 3) of the countries of Central America, Eastern Europe, the Middle East, and Africa. The focus has been on truth and justice—research on the events, for example, by ad hoc commissions and the judicial prosecution of those responsible, the economic compensation of victims, and their symbolic repatriation (Lessa, 2013; Van Drunen, 2010).

In the Latin American context, studies of Guatemalan and Salvadoran reality after these countries began their democratization processes in the 1990s have called attention to the role of transitional justice in the pacification and democratization of societies divided by intense violence by the state and armed groups (Dosh, 2002). Parallel to these studies, research groups have emerged around the dictatorships of the Southern Cone, responding to the agenda of social organizations that had conducted the first studies and reports, especially in Argentina and Chile. One of these was the research and training program financed by New York's Social Science Research Council in 1999, whose objective was to coordinate research by 60 young scholars on political repression in Southern Cone countries (Lida, Gutiérrez Crespo, and Yankelevich, 2007). In 2001 the Núcleo de Estudios sobre Memoria was formed, made up of experts and academics interested in the study of historical memory, mainly in Argentina, Chile, Brazil, Paraguay, and Uruguay (http://memoria.ides.org.ar/). Its principal themes were the use and custody of military archives, the emergence of social movements, and the analysis of commemorative rituals and places of special interest for those mnemonic processes.

In this article we aim to continue the studies of South American dictatorships that link memory with justice and truth (Bickford, 2000; Jelin, 1994; 2002; 2007; Stern, 2006a; Van Drunen, 2010). Given the scarcity of research on the topic for Bolivia,[3] we will not examine the nature of memory or its processes of construction or the construction of historical memory by social organizations. Instead, we are interested in the politics and narratives of memory—not just those related to the dictatorships of the twentieth century but also those associated with other periods of injustice and systemic violence. In this way, the politics of memory and its management must be considered, following Pierre Bourdieu (1984), as symbolic capital that is put into play in the political sphere. Moreover, as the work of Graham, Ashworth, and Tumbridge (2000) urges us to understand, the past is a social field subject to conflicts and tensions and subject to differing interpretations that may even be contradictory or incompatible. It not only sanctions past narratives but also legitimates current social relations and structures and future narratives (Albro, 2006).

An indispensable context for understanding the field of memory in Bolivia is structural inequality and the counterposition of an official mestizo-creole historiography with one that is indigenous and has been subaltern. Whereas the former is based on the 1825 Independence and the National Revolution of 1952, the memory of the Aymara-Quechua insurgencies of 1781 disrupts this genealogy by challenging the idea of an integrated nation and recovering the memory of indigenous resistance and insurrection (Rivera Cusicanqui, 2003 [1984]; Stephenson, 2002; Thomson, 2003; Ticona Alejo, Albó, and Choque Canqui, 1996). These memory and subaltern studies, following Rivera Cusicanqui (2003 [1984]), have given us the terms "long memory" and "short memory," the first referring to indigenous resistance to the Spanish presence, internal colonialism, and the subsequent creole hegemonies and the latter to the revolutionary power of unions and peasant militias of the 1952 Revolution. Apart from Rivera Cusicanqui, Javier Hurtado (1986) uses "long history" and "short history" to describe these two periods of oppression and resistance. More recently, Xavier Albó (2009) has referred to the "long ethnic memory" of indigenous political subjects.

In Rivera Cusicanqui's work, the different insurrectional horizons are articulated. She attributes to these categories an epistemological dimension that reflects a particular conceptualization of time-space of Andean cultures and a special dialectical process in Bolivian history. That long memory is present in twentieth-century uprisings gives rise to cycles of popular and civilian protests grounded in a historical consciousness that predates industrialization and working-class formation (Murillo, 2012). Empirically grounded in oral history analysis, this approach conceptualizes different moments in time as intertwined in the process of building "communicative" and "cultural memory" (Assmann, 2008).

These works are indispensable for understanding the cultural processes of memorialization that have been deployed in Bolivia. In our article, however, rather than the nature of memory on a theoretical-epistemological level or as a social phenomenon, we examine its use in the political sphere. We start from the premise that the articulation of different horizons tends to be omitted when they enter the political sphere and official discourse. We are especially interested in how allusions to different memories and insurrectional moments have been used to serve the political interests of the moment, accommodating themselves to and partially displacing each other according to the requirements of the intended societal project. Moreover, as the lineal time of the nation-state advances into the future (Alonso, 1994), new time layers of events are added that form an ever more recent short memory. As we will show, the politics of memory under the MAS oscillates between long memory and a new short memory of anti-neoliberal peasant and urban protests against U.S. and European political and corporate interests that has partially displaced not only the memory of the 1952 Revolution but also the historical memory of the dictatorships.

TRUTH AND JUSTICE INITIATIVES

According to a report released by Asociación de Familiares de Detenidos, Desaparecidos y Mártires por la Liberación Nacional (ASOFAMD, 2007), five different repressive contexts shook Bolivia during the twentieth century. The first, from 1964 to 1968, was headed by René Barrientos, under whose government the military assassinated dozens of miners who had supposedly supported Che Guevara's guerrillas (Puente, 2011). In 1970, under the government of General Alfredo Ovando, the army defeated the Teoponte guerrillas, who were mostly students, killing 65 of them at the president's order ("I only want dead bodies, not prisoners") (Puente, 2011: 110). During the government of General Juan José Torres, Hugo Banzer organized a coup d'état that led to 14,750 arrests, 19,140 exiles, and 77 disappearances of Bolivians in Bolivia, Argentina, and Chile (Alanes, 2012: 66; Sivak, 2001); in the Valley massacres in Tolata, Epinaza, and Melga, some 200 peasants were killed protesting against some of that government's decisions (Dunkerley, 1984). On November 1, 1979, just three months after the general elections, a coup d'état perpetrated by

General Alberto Natusch provoked a popular uprising that was violently suppressed and caused, according to ASOFAMD (Alanes, 2012: 68), the deaths of more than 100 persons, another 200 wounded, and 20 missing people (known as the Todos Santos massacre). Finally, on July 17, 1980, a military group under Luis García Meza and Colonel Luis Arce Gómez, linked to drug trafficking, and advised by the German Nazi Klaus Barbie, overthrew the interim government of Lidia Gueiler, killing the socialist leader and congressman Marcelo Quiroga Santa Cruz and congressman Carlos Flores Pedregal. Another 26 persons disappeared during García Meza's regime (Alanes, 2012: 70; ASOFAMD, 2008: 24).

Because of the state violence and human loss suffered under the dictatorships and their similarities with other Latin American dictatorships (Bickford, 2000; Jelin, 1994; Zalaquett, 1999), we believe that there should be a deeper analysis of them than they have so far received. According to Garretón, González Le Saux, and Lauzán (2011), Bolivia's Comisión Nacional de Investigaciones de Desaparecidos Forzados (National Commission of Investigations of Forced Disappearances), established in 1982, was one of the first in Latin America, although it was paralyzed by the weakness of its mandate. Other important national initiatives were a law establishing compensation for victims of political violence and the creation of two commissions—in 1995 and 1997—with the aim of searching for the bodies of Ernesto Che Guevara and Marcelo Quiroga Santa Cruz. The Consejo Interinstitucional para el Esclarecimiento de Desapariciones Forzadas (Interinstitutional Council for the Clarification of Forced Disappearences—CIEDEF) was created in 2003 with the objective of integrating all the policies covering this field. In 2004 the government of Carlos Mesa approved Law 2640, whose principal objective was to establish procedures for compensation of the political victims of unconstitutional governments. Among the measures contemplated were awards of honors by the government, special social benefits, and economic compensation of the victims of such abuses. In tribute to the Jesuit, journalist, and filmmaker Luis Espinal, kidnapped and killed on March 21 and 22, 1980, March 21 was declared the Day of the Bolivian Cinema. In 2008 a national plan of action on human rights was approved, and the creation of a new truth commission was one of its main components. A biography of the murdered student Renato Ticona Estrada was published in that year, and in 2009, through a ministerial resolution, the Supreme Court authorized the declassification of part of its military archives.

Many of the local and national initiatives related to the public acknowledgment of victims took shape in public spaces, through the naming of streets and avenues and the building of memorials to honor primarily the distinguished victims of the dictatorships: between 1983 and 2005, the Heroes of January 15 memorial walk and Martyrs of Democracy Street (both named for the eight leaders of the Movimiento de la Izquierda Revolucionaria (Movement of the Revolutionary Left—MIR) executed on Harrington Street on January 15, 1981); the plaza and memorial way dedicated to Marcelo Quiroga Santa Cruz, who was murdered at the entrance of the Central Obrera Boliviana (Bolivian Workers' Central—COB) headquarters in La Paz in 1980; and a plaza and school named for the student and leftist activist José

Carlos Trujillo Oroza, who was detained and disappeared. Under the MAS governments we should highlight, among others, the plaza named after Renato Ticona Estrada, the authorization by the La Paz municipality of the placing of a plaque in honor of the murdered Jesuit Mauricio Lefebvre, the brief opening of the Museum of Memory in 2011 in the basement of the Ministry of Government, and the 2012 inauguration of the temporary exhibition titled The Light of Memory.

As we have said, despite these efforts by Evo Morales's governments at acknowledgment of the dictatorships' victims, victims' associations and human rights organizations have remained dissatisfied. Besides the already-mentioned vigil of the PLS in front of the Ministry of Justice, criticism has been directed at the CIEDEF and the human rights plan for their limited resources and interinstitutional coordination. Many of these organizations have pointed out that only 1,800 of the 6,200 dossiers presented for consideration under Law 2640 have been accepted (Amnesty International, 2012). This law was modified on April 30, 2012, to streamline the economic compensation, but in the opinion of the PLS (García Jerez, 2012) and Amnesty International (2012) its application is insufficient in that only 20 percent of the total compensation sought by each recognized victim has been granted. These organizations also denounce the extreme bureaucracy involved in acquiring victim status, which requires demonstrating that status, paradoxically, with an official document to which, even if one exists, full access is denied.

One of the main criticisms of these initiatives for social recognition voiced in our recent study was the focus on particular individuals to the detriment of others despite the fact that the law contemplated the granting of public honors to all proven victims (García Jerez, 2012; Garretón, González Le Saux, and Lauzán, 2011). Social recognition has focused on political figures such as Quiroga, Trujillo, and the MIR members assassinated in 1981. There have been few devices for triggering public remembrance of a collective character—for example, calling attention to the so-called security houses, apartments in which politicians who sympathized with the opposition were tortured with impunity—and the only attempt to establish a memory museum barely outlasted its inauguration.

THE POLITICS OF MEMORY OF THE DICTATORSHIPS UNDER THE MAS

Given the political dimension of memory and its management, we think it is appropriate to ask why the MAS governments have not responded to the demands of the social organizations in a definitive way. The question is especially timely in that evocations of the past have become the focus of constant attention in Bolivian public life. In response to this question, we highlight three explanatory factors: the military issue, the collapse of parties and traditional organizations of the left, and the articulation of a new narrative based on indigenous and anti-neoliberal nationalism whose objective is the consolidation of the MAS's government project.

The Military Issue

The military issue (Acuña and Smulovitz, 1995) is the impossibility of carrying out one of the principal demands of the human rights and historical memory organizations: justice (Jelin, 2007). Faced with the possibility that high-ranking military officials, sometimes still on active duty, could be found responsible for violations and that this would trigger a crisis of the state, governments such as that of Argentina have opted to avoid this situation in their first years (Jelin, 1994). In Bolivia, despite the fact that 30 years have passed since the last dictatorship, this factor is still present—a circumstance that derives from the process of transition to democracy, initiated in 1982, itself. The precariousness of the Unión Democrática Popular (Democratic People's Union—UDP) government in the context of the fragmentation of the political left and an opposition that vetoed any decision led to the military's becoming one of the main agents of internal security, charged with avoiding possible armed insurrection. This, as Quintana (1998: 24) has put it, "impeded the immediate prosecution of those responsible for the dictatorship." In fact, as Barrios (1992) asserts, from the beginning of democracy, the functioning of the national defense committees established to reformulate civilian-military relations was not entirely satisfactory. These committees were unable to obtain access to information about the armed forces, and their supervisory role was understood as "meddling in the affairs of the military institution, which had a certain 'historical immunity'" (Barrios, 1992: 3).

This was one of the explanations that members of victims' associations gave us for the ineffectiveness of the current MAS government with regard to the demand for justice. This demand was manifested in 2012 in a declaration titled "Bolivia: Thirty-Three Years since the Todos Santos Massacre." It called for the recovery of historical memory, "punishment for material and intellectual perpetrators," and "integral reparations for victims." According to the signatories of this declaration,[4] "victimization and impunity are still present today, when there are more than 100 victims who remain unqualified by the government through the Ministry of Justice's qualification committee" (PLS, 2012). On one of our visits to the vigil organized by the PLS, some of its members, after hearing the news on the radio of Argentina's judicial system's decision to sentence General Jorge Rafael Videla in the summer of 2012, lamented the ineffectiveness of Bolivia's judicial system in such matters (García Jerez, 2012). This was not the first time such a concern had been raised; in 2010 family members of human rights victims had demanded that the attorney general "investigate and prosecute 109 persons linked to the 1980 dictatorship, ex-military officers and 12 foreign mercenaries among them" (*La Razón*, July 24, 2010).[5] The president of the Fundación contra la Impunidad (Foundation against Impunity) stated in the same report that "the majority of the military members identified are in the country, enjoying their retirement, while two mercenaries are living in Santa Cruz" (*La Razón*, July 24, 2010).[6] Meanwhile in November of the same year the army was awarded the Orden Parlamentaria al Mérito Democrático Marcelo Quiroga Santa Cruz, an action that provoked indignation among victims and human rights organizations because the award was given to the same institution that had been responsible for Quiroga's death. ASOFAMD claimed that in order to receive this decoration, the army should at least have had to declassify its archives (*La Razón*, November 19, 2010). The military's impunity not only affected trials but also led to the impossibility of gaining access to a significant part of those archives (Amnesty International, 2010; 2012; ASOFAMD, 2007; Garretón, González Le Saux, and Lauzán, 2011), one of the most important sources of documentation about what happened during the dictatorships and one of the most effective instruments for charging those possibly responsible (figure 5.3).

Figure 5.3. Poster denouncing the policy of declassifying the military archives.
Source: Juliane Müller

The passivity of the MAS governments in dealing with victims' claims for justice may be reflected in what Stefanoni (2006: 43) calls an attempt to reinstate the 1964 Pacto Militar Campesino (Military-Peasant Pact). This time it was not a matter of the co-optation of the peasantry by the armed forces but the reverse: a pact "articulated from an indigenous-grassroots government that incorporated the armed forces into the current nationalist process." Morales's ordering the military to occupy some oil wells in the nationalization process was evidence of this, as was his sending 28 generals of three different promotions to the reserve once he came to the presidency. In a more symbolic way, the Flag Day parade in 2006 included both the military and indigenous groups with the objective of displaying their desired unity (Mejías, 2007).

These initiatives, according to Morales, were intended to end the "times of dictatorship and conflict between the armed forces and the people" (Mejías, 2007: 449). It could be argued, following Stefanoni and Mejías, that the MAS governments were seeking to co-opt various state institutions for their political project. From this perspective, the possibility of sentences for those responsible for crimes and violations committed during the dictatorships could be interpreted as a serious obstacle to this co-optation. Not in vain, as Orellana (2006: 104) points out, has the "democratic revolution" of Morales's government tended toward the pursuit of "peaceful coexistence with the old power" rather than "a radical transformation of the state structure."

From the Decline of Marxism to a "New Multitude"

The decline of the traditional organizations of the Bolivian left is a consequence of internal and external historical factors. Many of these organizations date from the incorporation of a significant number of indigenous people, miners, and peasants after the Chaco War of 1932–1935, when the liberal model ultimately failed (Klein, 2011). Among the political parties whose ideological substratum was Marxist were the Partido Obrero Revolucionario (Revolutionary Workers' Party—POR), the Partido de Izquierda Revolucionaria (Revolutionary Left Party—PIR), and the Partido Comunista de Bolivia (Communist Party of Bolivia—PCB) (Dunkerley, 1984; Puente, 2011). It was with the rise to power of the Movimiento Nacionalista Revolucionario (Nationalist Revolutionary Movement—MNR) that one of these organizations, the Federación Sindical de Trabajadores Mineros de Bolivia (Mine Workers' Labor Federation—FSTMB), founded in 1944, achieved powerful mobilizing capacity. The FSTMB became part of the original platform of the proletarian masses and, once integrated into the COB, of the organizational framework of the 1952 Revolution (Degregori, 1999; Klein, 2011).

With the gradual shift to the right of the MNR, the organizations of the left lost influence. It is only under the dictatorships that they reemerged, this time under the leadership of the Federación de Mineros, the Bloque Independiente, and Jenaro Flores's Movimiento Revolucionario Tupak Katari and more traditional organizations such as the COB and the PCB. The establishment of the Asamblea Popular in May 1971 was significant in that, as a representation of the Bolivian left, it brought together many union delegations and leftist parties (Klein, 2011; Puente, 2011). It was the "national-popular alliance" (Hylton and Thomson, 2007) of the COB, the recently founded Confederación Sindical Única de Trabajadores de Bolivia (Single Labor Confederation of Peasant Workers of Bolivia—CSUTCB), and the leftist parties and progressive sectors of the middle class that capitalized on the opposition to the various dictatorial regimes between 1977 and 1982 and acquired prominence in public life once democracy was restored. The establishment of the UDP and its electoral success in 1980 positioned these organizations at the head of government in 1982, once the last military rulers had been defeated. However, their inability to manage the economic crisis (Klein, 2011), the persistence of old structures of the 1952 state, and the discrediting of the COB with the peasant and indigenous organizations frustrated the expectations that had been placed in them (Puente, 2011). More specifically, the miners' movement collapsed under the political repression and privatization of the mines undertaken by the government of Víctor Paz Estenssoro, which resulted in the elimination of more than 20,000 jobs and the migration of many families of miners to the cities and the coca cultivation areas. This, together with other neoliberal policies, contributed to the dispersion and depoliticization of the labor movement and, in general, of middle-class leftist sympathizers (Hylton and Thomson, 2007).

It was in this context that the objective conditions were created for the articulation of a new movement in the 1990s capable of bringing together the social sectors that lacked leftist organizational moorings. This new social-political force was made up primarily of the coca growers' movement of the Chapare, which toward the end of the 1980s took control of the CSUTCB from the Kataristas, and later the MAS, with an increasingly broad social base. In contrast to that of the Kataristas, which fragmented into multiple subgroups and parties and lost its political influence, the coca growers' movement and the MAS managed to bring together different social and indigenous sectors and rise via the political system (Van Cott, 2005). Moreover, the struggle between the indigenous-peasant unions and the proletariat for the leadership of the COB and the latter's resistance to changing its orthodox notion of the industrial proletariat's vanguard role led the peasants, and especially the coca growers, to focus on other organizations, such as the Federaciones del Trópico, the CSUTCB, and a coalition including neighborhood and other urban and peri-urban associations, marginalizing the COB from future mobilizations and actions (Hylton and Thomson, 2007).[7]

The social movements of the 1990s and the beginning of the twenty-first century focused their protests against the U.S. Drug Enforcement Agency (DEA) and the large multinational corporations in the energy and basic services sector. The "water war" in Cochabamba in 2000 and the "gas war" in El Alto and La Paz in 2003, protests against privatization and external sale of natural resources that caused the departure of President Gonzalo Sánchez de Lozada, and the victory of the MAS in the 2005 elections can be understood as the result of the convergence of different subjects into a "new multitude" (Postero, 2010; also see Albro, 2005). In contrast to the classic labor organizations, this new political subject was able to capture the demands of the current Bolivian working class with more flexible and horizontal organization and indigenous forms of moral authority (Postero, 2010). As Ellner (2012) points out, the MAS itself rejected the old idea of the vanguard role of the traditional Marxist organizations in favor of a hybrid system that combined elements of both radical and representative democracy.

It may be this trajectory that explains why the MAS did not feel entirely indebted to either the parties or the traditional forces of the left. Moreover, ideologically, in the words of vice-president Álvaro García Linera (2006), the MAS governments were committed more to the development of an Andean-Amazon capitalism than to an intrinsically anticapitalist mode of production (also see Orellana, 2006; Webber, 2011: 189–190). Thus it did not fully reflect the ideology of those parties and their memories of the dictatorships, and this view led to the predominance of the indigenous element and a rejection of the neoliberal variant of capitalism to the detriment of the victims' associations and former leftist militants.

A New Narrative: The Indigenous and Anti-Neoliberal Nationalist

The emergence and consolidation of an indigenous national discourse[8] was apparent in the unofficial inauguration of Evo Morales as president of Bolivia. At the ruins of Tiwanaku, Morales, being recognized as the greatest indigenous authority by Andean religious specialists, called on the ancestors and Pachamama for their blessing. The next day, in another ceremony, this time in the Plaza Murillo in La Paz, Morales spoke of his societal project: a "cultural democratic revolution" as a legacy of the idea of a new Inca Empire of Tupak Katari, the "great homeland" of Simón Bolívar, and the "new egalitarian world" of Che Guevara. At the same time, he called for a moment of silence in memory of the "martyrs of liberation," among whom he included the indigenous insurgents of the colonial period, the intellectuals and priests disappeared by the military dictatorships, the coca growers murdered while opposing the policies of the DEA, and the urban activists of the neoliberal period (Postero, 2010). In these two speeches, one alluding more to the colonial period and the other more to contemporary Bolivian history, Morales, as Howard (2010) and Canessa (2006) point out, avoided presenting himself as exclusively indigenous in order not to endanger the plurality of the MAS project. It was crucial to bring together a significant number of social sectors on the basis of what Do Alto (2005) has called "a reciprocal exchange of legitimations." However, the consolidation of the government project required a more solid narrative that has rested on tropes of indigenous and anti-neoliberal struggles that would be supported in a multiplicity of semiotic channels (Howard, 2010). This narrative has become especially salient since the already mentioned case of the Isiboro Sécure Indigenous Territory and National Park and the case of Mosetén, where the MAS government has attempted to extract petroleum against the will of the indigenous communities (Canessa, 2012). As the eco-indigenous discourse, very much present during the first MAS legislative period, entered into contradiction with the economic interests of the state, the government has attempted to recover its moral authority by guaranteeing the commitment of the new multitude through narratives and semiotic channels based on elements of long and short memory. As Fontana (2013: 35) argues, one of its rhetorical strategies has been the use of "merging categories," narratives that combine new collectives and very recent protests such as those of the 1990s and 2000s with mythological notions.

Hence, along with the recurrent use of cosmological terms from the Aymara culture such as Pachamama and *pachakuti* (the future in the past),[9] the government began to recover and recall events and figures from the Republican period, such as the Zárate Willka insurrection in reaction to the Federal War of 1898–1901 (Webber, 2010). The most noted example of this rhetoric is the association of Tupak Katari with Evo Morales. For the MAS, both Tupak Katari and Evo Morales symbolize the grassroots and indigenous masses against colonizing and imperialist forces (Hylton and Thomson, 2007).[10] Therefore, for the MAS, Morales's electoral victories represent one more milestone in the 500-year-long resistance to the nonindigenous conqueror, while the struggle against neoliberal policies and the DEA and their dead are one more part of the memory of indigenous liberation and its martyrs. The claim that the natural resources belong to the Bolivian—in the end, native Bolivian—population is a statement that perfectly connects long indigenous with recent anti-neoliberal protests. Moreover, the coca leaf is a strong "merging" concept that relates indigenous cultural history with anti-imperialist policies.

The recovery of long memory and a certain displacement of the memory of 1952, did not, however, originate with Evo Morales's coming to power but began in the 1960s with the emergence of a new indigenous consciousness. The nationalist revolution of 1952 had institutionalized the dispossessing of indigenous people of their languages, practices, and beliefs and converted them into peasants, with the intention of materializing a new mestizo national identity (Degregori, 1999). This failed attempt of the new regime, however, became in the 1960s an anticolonial reading of the Bolivian reality and indigenous confirmation by a group of Aymara university students, the Kataristas (Hurtado, 1986; Ticona Alejo, 1996). It was they who tried to break the Military-Peasant Pact after indigenous liberation and the recovery of their ethnic identity. Although Sinclair Thomson points to the existence, already in the 1940s, of thinkers and novelists who recovered the memory of Tupak Katari in their texts, it was in the 1960s and 1970s that the Partido Indio (Indian Party) of Fausto Reinaga and most of all the Kataristas, both under Flores and later under Felipe Quispe, who repositioned and situated Tupak Katari and other figures of the indigenous rebellions against the Spanish colonial authorities in the public sphere, aiming to make them part of their political discourse (Dunkerley, 1984: 213–214; Thomson, 2003). This rereading of the past would be used by the MAS for its refoundational project.

While this heritage adopted by the Morales governments explains the interest in long memory at the expense of other layers of cultural memory, it does not explain why they did not conceive the possibility of reusing memories of the dictatorships' victims (those whom Morales had recognized as "martyrs of liberation") for their cultural democratic revolution. Beyond the decline of the traditional organizations of the left at the beginning of the 1990s, in our opinion the MAS did not find many elements for a possible indigenous reinterpretation in the memory of the dictatorships or even in the ascent and repression of the first Kataristas (Dunkerley, 1984; Hurtado, 1986), although many of the victims of the bloodiest massacres in fact were indigenous, as were the Siglo XX and Catavi miners killed on June 24, 1967, and the Quechua peasants of the Valle del Alto in Cochabamba murdered in January 1974. It seems that the mnemonic material from the dictatorships—closely linked to Marxist organizations and relatively remote from the ethnic—did not quite fit its narrative of clearly indigenous and anti-neoliberal inspiration, in which an oscillation between long memory and the very short one offered Morales and the MAS notable symbolic resources for the building of a narrative future (Albro, 2006) based on "utopian visions of Andean culture" (Postero, 2007: 1) and state-centered industrial development.[11]

CONCLUSIONS

It seemed that the scenario in MAS Bolivia would be highly suitable for the development of a politics of memory of the dictatorships based on social and economic compensation and justice. However, this expectation has not been totally met, and in our opinion this is the case because of the military issue, the decline of the traditional leftist organizations, and the necessity of constructing a new narrative for the consolidation of the MAS project. The MAS's ascent to government marked a turn in the field of the politics of memory. This has meant that evocations of long and very short memory have become its hegemonic axis, partially displacing the memory of the 1952 Revolution and the historical memory of the dictatorships, neither of which seems to provide sufficient symbolic material in the way of prominent figures or cosmological and ethical concepts to sanction its project for change. Public recognition of victims has concentrated on certain heroes of the resistance to repressive regimes, and while Morales mentioned them in his inauguration speech, they have not been fully reworked as mnemonic material for constructing a new narrative capable of legitimizing his policies among the social bases.

Despite some institutional initiatives in favor of compensation for the dictatorships' victims, we think that the displacement of memories of the dictatorships has had some ill effects. One of them has to do with the lack of economic and social recognition of the victims, which is generating a feeling of discouragement and distrust on the part of the human rights organizations that are working to recover historical memory under the MAS governments. At the same time, the MAS governments are losing the opportunity to articulate the memories of various phases or horizons of Bolivian history. After all, as Rivera Cusicanqui (2003 [1984]) and others have shown, different horizons and memories are juxtaposed into complex forms of collective and individual identity. Moreover, Nash (1993) (see also Albro, 2009) has described the way the collective action of socialist miners and workers combines class solidarity based on memories of past events such as the massacres of the dictatorships with Andean ritualized practices of resistance. To respect and reproduce this kind of juxtaposed memory in political discourse and practice would be a way of avoiding the risks inherent in the current strategy of MAS, among them Andes-centrism (Postero, 2007), the tendency to play certain social groups off against others, and the neglect of anonymous victims who have struggled for a more just Bolivia. It would mean taking on the totality of memories of the dictatorships—of their victims and of the political forces in which many of them worked toward a different, classless and more democratic Bolivia. All of this would make the new nationalist narrative more holistic and inclusive.

Thus our analysis of this case shows that, beyond global trends, international associative networks, and transitional justice in favor of historical memory, each national context generates a frame to deploy for resolving the issue. In these strategies, far-reaching political objectives (such as the consolidation of a national project) and immediate political interests (such as the pursuit of internal social equilibrium) converge. But they also embody historical factors that partially displace groups and their claims, such as the emergence of contradictions that, inherent in the complex task of governance, determine the magnitude and direction of these policies of redress.

NOTES

The original version of this essay was published in *Latin American Perspectives* 42 (3): 120–139.

1. We used mainly secondary sources but also reformulated some of the data gathered during ethnographic work conducted in June and July 2012 on the role of urban space in La Paz in the projection of memories of the dictatorships. This fieldwork involved semistructured interviews with the leaders of victims' organizations (the Asociación de Familiares de Detenidos, Desaparecidos y Mártires por la Liberación Nacional, the Instituto de Terapia e Investigación sobre las Secuelas y la Violencia Estatal, the Plataforma de Luchadores Sociales contra la Impunidad, por la Justicia y la Memoria Histórica del Pueblo Boliviano, Víctimas de Violencia Política, la Asociación de Derechos Humanos de Bolivia and the Movimiento de Mujeres Libres) and informal interviews with experts from the Instituto de Sociología Maurice Lefebvre de la Universidad Mayor de San Andrés and the Consejo Interinstitucional para el Esclarecimiento de Desapariciones Forzadas. We also visited the vigil organized by the PLS, the installations of the Fundación Solón, and the exhibit La Luz de la Memoria at the Museo Nacional del Arte in La Paz. We have stayed in contact with the Asociación de Familiares de Detenidos, Desaparecidos y Mártires por la Liberación Nacional (ASOFAMD) ever since and revisited the vigil in September 2013 and October and November 2014.

2. More generally, the collective perception of the dissolution of traditions and the sense of loss of historical stability in European societies at the end of the nineteenth century and the beginning of the twentieth stimulated social and scientific interest in memory (Antze and Lambeck, 1996).

3. The only written sources we have found regarding the historical memory of the Bolivian dictatorships are reports and testimonies. One of the first reports was from the Bolivian Labor Federation (COB, 1976); the second one was from 2009, titled "Report from Civil Society for the EPU Bolivia" (CBDHDD, 2009); while in 2011 a comparative study was published that examined the government initiatives on memory, truth, and justice carried out in seven Latin American countries, including Bolivia (Garretón, González Le Saux, and Lauzán, 2011). Others include the notes from the Seminario Latinoamericano contra la Impunidad in La Paz in September 2008 (ASOFAMD, 2009); a book on the Harrington Street massacre of January 15, 1981 (ASOFAMD, 2007); *¡Libres! Testimonio de mujeres victimas de las dictaduras* (Movimiento de Mujeres Libertad, 2010); and a book in memory of the student José Carlos Trujillo Orozco (Solón, 2012). This indicated that, unlike the research results from the Southern Cone and even Central America, those from Bolivia have been technical, evaluative, and personal rather than analytical in character.

4. Among the signatories: the Fundación Boliviana contra la Impunidad, the Plataforma de Luchadores Sociales Contra la Impunidad, por la Justicia y la Memoria Histórica del Pueblo Boliviano, the Movimiento Mujeres Libertad, the Taller Luis Espinal, Mujeres por Justicia, the Colectivo de Pensamiento Socialista and the Movimiento Mauricio Lefebvre. All are members of the Coordinadora de Instituciones de Derechos Humanos contra la Impunidad.

5. The demand for trials is not new. In 1968 the socialist politician Marcelo Quiroga Santa Cruz demanded the trial of René Barrientos, and in 1979 he demanded the trial of the dictator Hugo Banzer. Both demands were dismissed by Congress. However, in 1993, Luis García Meza, Luis Arce Gomez, and 43 others were convicted of crimes committed during the dictatorship they had led (*La Razón*, July 15, 2012).

6. The headline read as follows: "Trial Requested against Ex-Military and Mercenaries of the Dictatorship" (*La Razón*, July 24, 2012).

7. Although an important sector of the miners and their families ended up integrated into the coca growers' movement, a new generation of political leaders, such as Evo Morales, without personal experience in the labor movement and the struggle against dictatorships emerged.

8. The expression "indigenous discourse" is used to designate a type of political narrative that invokes precolonial symbols and rituals. It differs both from the term "Indianist," which describes more radically ethnic and separatist positions, and from "indigenist," which refers to the indigenism of the twentieth century, a political-intellectual current of *mestizaje*. For different ideological, political-historical, and cultural meanings of the terms, see Albro (2006), Burman (2011), and Canessa (2006; 2012). Stefanoni (2006) and Postero (2010) have recently spoken of a new "indigenous nationalism."

9. For example, the international meeting of December 21, 2012, at Lake Titicaca. Organized by the Ministry of Foreign Affairs, it resorted to the concept of *pachakuti* to declare new times that could overcome global crises (http://www.cancilleria.bo/node/16; for a critical analysis of this event, see Murillo, Bautista, and Montellano, 2014). To this political-ideological use of cosmological concepts should be added new rituals such as the Aymara New Year and the ancestral wedding, which do not correspond to any particular indigenous culture but represent the attempt to create an "indigenous national culture" (Canessa, 2008; 2012). This is not to imply that these rituals and concepts do not have an existential basis

for many people (Burman, 2011). Our analysis is limited to the use of these concepts and rituals in the institutional political sphere and by the government.

10. This does not mean that Morales understands Tupak Katari in the same way as Indianist activists. Burman (2011) says that for Morales, the Aymara martyr and his dismembered body, symbol of the "national body," and the figure of Simón Bolívar embody the unity of the country, whereas Indianist activists reject this combination.

11. So far, it seems that there is not much effort on the part of the human rights organizations to unite their protests and demands with those of the victims of more recent periods of state repression. Although not formally under a dictatorship, military actions during the "gas war" in El Alto in October 2003 took on unconstitutional, repressive stances, as did the DEA anti-drug war. The military crushing of popular protests, demonstrations, and roadblocks against the exportation of natural gas provoked the death of 72 persons in October 2003 (*La Razón*, September 16, 2012). The Asociación de Víctimas de la Guerra de Gas en Bolivia is demanding the extradition from the United States to Bolivia of former President Gonzalo Sánchez de Lozada and leading members of his government. It complains that economic compensation is lacking for the great majority of affected families (*La Razón*, October 13, 2013). Despite these common demands for justice and compensation, organizations of victims of different regimes have not, as far as we know, significantly collaborated. However, such collaboration may be essential, as the case of Argentina shows (Van Drunen, 2010), to movements' broadening their capacity for interweaving demands based on the crimes committed under the dictatorships with the injustices of neoliberalism and state and military repression of the more recent past. The predominance of the organizations and their demands in the current context may depend on the breadth of their discursive frameworks. This could be a direction for future analysis of historical memory in Bolivia. Another interesting topic would be ethnographic research into the configuration of memory—how long, intermediate, and short-term horizons are combined and juxtaposed in the individual and collective memories of the dictatorships.

6

Colombia's Gallery of Memory

Reexamining Democracy through Human Rights Lenses

Erika Márquez

During a research trip to investigate the effects of state security policies on human rights mobilization in the Colombian Southwest in 2008, I was introduced by activists in the city of Cali to the Gallery of Memory. Part street museum and part popular forum, the Gallery aimed to memorialize victims of human rights violations since the early 1980s. The body of the Gallery included pictures, banners, and newspaper clippings carefully arranged on the ground or hanging from trees. In various sections informally divided among the participant human rights organizations, activists featured a selection of assassinated or disappeared leftist presidential candidates, members of Congress, and militants, along with indigenous or Afro-descendants fallen in paramilitary massacres, students killed by armed forces, and working-class people assassinated by armed forces and falsely presented as guerrillas killed in combat (figure 6.1).

Using a format that resembled the memorialization efforts in postdictatorship Argentina, Chile, and Brazil, the Gallery seemed to belong to the "culture of memory" (Huyssen, 2003) that flourished in Latin America in the 1980s. As in that movement of remembrance and accountability, it aimed at establishing the truth about state-sponsored crimes and, more broadly, being part of a larger mobilization in response to the undemocratic character of the state. As its early promoters point out, the memorialization exercise they proposed was not, or at least was not exclusively, a vehicle for formulating grievances or a space for mourning. The goal was not only to reconstruct the truth about human rights violations but also to connect the past and present structures that allowed these abuses to occur (Cepeda and Girón, n.d.). As the Gallery empowered victims' relatives and fought to make visible the social cost of the crimes, it offered a space in which victims and larger publics converged to reflect on human rights abuses and their structural causes.

Figure 6.1. Disappeared human rights militants memorialized by the Committee in Solidarity with Political Prisoners.
Source: Erika Márquez

In this task of truth reconstruction, the Gallery faced a formidable obstacle: the widespread belief that Colombia, with its almost uninterrupted tradition of popularly elected governments, is a democratic state. Instead, human rights activists suggested that Colombia should be characterized as a formal democracy supported by forms of systematic state terror (MOVICE, 2008). As a result, rather than drawing on the model of Latin America's postdictatorship truth commissions, the almost one dozen organizations that inspired the efforts at memorialization preceding the Gallery under the umbrella Proyecto Colombia Nunca Más said that their goal was to identify the authoritarian structures that allowed human rights violations to continue.

The emergence of a culture of memory through human rights militancy in Latin American postdictatorship countries was, nevertheless, fundamental for the Colombian organizations fighting the undemocratic and repressive practices of the Colombian state. While Colombian institutions remained formally democratic, collectively reconstructing the immediate and remote past was still a crucial exercise in a country where the number of victims of human rights violations was increasing exponentially. In cultivating this tradition, Colombian organizations tapped into memory as a resource for rebuilding community and citizenship ties. Indeed, groups had recognized memory building in terms similar to Jelin's (2003: 2): "Memory has a highly significant role as a cultural mechanism that helps strengthen the sense of belonging to groups or communities. Furthermore, especially for oppressed, silenced, or discriminated groups, the reference to a shared past often facilitates building feelings of self-respect and greater reliance in oneself and in the group." To this extent, remembering atrocities was not only an exercise for adjudicating responsibility in a trial but also a collective process for reconstructing a certain historical reality within and outside contexts of dictatorship.

Examining the work of the Gallery and its contribution to the process of memory making, this work focuses on the first decade of the 2000s as a period of accentuated authoritarian tendencies within Colombia's formally democratic structures. The Gallery exhibits I will review here took place during a period that I have elsewhere (Marquez, 2011) characterized as the "turn to security," a model under which more aspects of everyday life—from the environment to migration—have come to be seen as sources of danger for society or as risks that should be conjured with the instruments of criminal and civil law (Bajc and de Lint, 2011). More clearly than in previous decades, the idea that protest movements constituted a threat to the political order became common sense (Echavarría, 2010; Rojas, 2006).

The turn to security was manifested in the policy known as Democratic Security—a governmental plan, for ensuring economic prosperity through the forced recovery of territories contested by illegal actors, whose chief strategy was discursively separating "good" or compliant citizens from rebellious ones. The Gallery's platform, with its programmatic focus on deconstruction of official truths, became a privileged location for critically engaging this undemocratic policy. By reflecting on the state security policy in the context of larger temporalities and connecting the current form of government with other modes of organizing power, the Gallery became a valuable resource for human rights mobilization. Although local and disconnected from the media, the responses offered by the Colombian human rights movement provided a key asset for understanding the forms that state power assumes as well as the connections between old and new forms of authoritarianism. With its format of itinerant exhibit replicable in different spaces and at different scales, the Gallery emerged as a response of the Movimiento Nacional de Víctimas de Crímenes de Estado (National Victims of State Crimes Movement—MOVICE) to human rights violations that historically had been forgotten and gone unpunished. As part of the human rights repertoire (Tilly, 2006)[1] that fed social mobilization under the turn to security, the Gallery memorialized victims of human rights violations and provided a discourse and a space for building an alternative vision.

A NOTE ON METHODOLOGY

As part of my research on the link between the climate of violence and the security policy that shaped Colombia's government, I had conducted participant observation and interviews with local activists affiliated with the Comité Permanente para la Defensa de los Derechos Humanos (Permanent Committee for the Defense of Human Rights—CPDH), Ruta Pacífica de las Mujeres (Women's Peaceful Route), and the Proceso de Comunidades Negras (Process of Black Communities—PCN). Because of the very risky conditions of their human rights work, I approached these activists through reliable acquaintances who had themselves been involved in political, academic, or human rights defense activity. Through my contacts I was eventually able to conduct participant observation with members of the CPDH and Ruta Pacífica de las Mujeres and interviews with members of the PCN. In addition, I conducted interviews with public officials and with local activists, actors, and educators engaged in the defense of human rights during this period. The Gallery exhibits I attended occurred within the local commemoration of International Human Rights Day on December 10, and they framed recent and old human rights violations as resulting from a security policy that turned critics into enemies. In addition to attending street demonstrations and helping with overall logistics, being part of the exhibits enabled me to observe the activists' and the participants' engagement with each other and with the materials.

Given the sensitivity of the data I intended to collect and the imminent threats that human rights activists faced, I found my interviewees through snowball sampling. Once connected to the organizations, I conducted a number of activities that allowed me to get a better sense of their activities, including, for example, pro bono archival work, regular workshops, and meetings alongside their members. As a native Spanish speaker I was able to conduct all the fieldwork and interviews in Spanish and directly translate these materials into English. In order to maintain confidentiality, I use pseudonyms to refer to activists I interviewed.

While the conditions of human rights militancy in Colombia have historically been adverse for its practitioners, the period in which I conducted the research was particularly problematic for the activists' work because it was being openly attacked by both state and paramilitary actors under the pretense of their affiliation with guerrilla groups. At a time when right-wing paramilitary groups had received amnesties under the state-sponsored demobilization process (2003–2006), activists exercised maximum caution to protect themselves against the persisting threats. Working as a participant observer, I witnessed and to a certain extent experienced the difficult safety conditions that they underwent on a daily basis. For example, during a Gallery exhibit at the Universidad del Valle, a man with features that in activist circles were identified as police- or military-like (almost shaved hair, semiformal clothes, a vigilant attitude, not known by any of the participants) showed up at the exhibit and stared at the activists in a threatening way. The man did not have a visible gun, but his attitude was distinctly intimidating. Eventually one of the activists exchanged glances with the man, almost visually confronting him, and he began slowly leaving the place without abandoning his intimidating demeanor, with the activist following him as if escorting him off the campus. While not objectively confirmed as an act of aggression, this encounter illustrates the challenging conditions under which the activists operated. In the context of the 290 politically motivated killings of human rights defenders that occurred in Colombia between 1996 and 2012 (Comisión Colombiana de Juristas, 2012), it was a reminder of the formidable threats that activists faced in their daily work.

Approaching this reality through the interaction with activists in Cali, I addressed several aspects that, for the purposes of this paper, may be organized as follows: the history of the Gallery, its critique of the turn to security and its human rights–based contribution to democratic forms of citizenship, the significance of the Gallery as a memorialization device, and the ways in which the case of the Gallery of Memory can contribute to the collective-memory field.

FROM MEMORIALIZATION TO MOVEMENT BUILDING

The Gallery of Memory was created in 1995 as an initiative of human rights defenders from the Manuel Cepeda Vargas Foundation, partly to fill a gap in public discussion on what constituted the truth about state crimes in the armed conflict in Colombia. Concurrently with the efforts against impunity of social and human rights organizations, Gallery organizers hoped to contribute to establishing the truth about the conflict's victims, perpetrators, mechanisms, and social costs. In 1995, the foundation, which is dedicated to promoting truth and justice in the cases of the assassinated senator for the Communist Party Manuel Cepeda Vargas (1930–1994) and other victims of human rights violations in Colombia, organized an installation in the Luis Angel Arango Library in Bogotá, where relatives and friends of 40 victims of human rights violations remembered them through their personal effects, writings, and artistic creations (MOVICE, 2008). In each of these exhibits, human rights activists and victims' relatives drew on the personal belongings and intellectual legacies of victims to document their lives, ideas, and political projects; they also created a record with photographs and a card giving the circumstances of the victim's death or disappearance, the alleged perpetrators of the violation, and the current status of the investigation (MOVICE, 2008). Assembling itinerant exhibits of this documentation, they presented the public with a sort of mobile museum that offered a new definition of political violence within the conflict—one that showed that the state, rather than offering protection, victimized and marginalized its political opponents.

In its origins, the Gallery more clearly evoked similar memorialization initiatives such as the Holocaust Museum in Washington, DC, where visitors are presented with aspects of the victim's life (personal effects, ideas, role in the conflict) and confronted as witnesses and as bearers of a duty to prevent the human rights abuses from happening again. Through the accounts of victims it reconstructed the history of the ongoing armed conflict in terms of a narrative that highlighted multiple actors and their motivations and methods and, importantly, a different cartography of the conflict. As a result, a broader account of human rights abuses was offered—one that looked at the consequences of the conflict for public space, social relations, bodies, and other aspects usually ignored in analyses with a more macro-level orientation. As Cepeda and Girón (n.d.) explain, by recovering the victims' belongings, for example, activists attempted to rebuild the educational or political context that had surrounded them and thus illuminated their social networks and, by extension, the contours of their political projects. Through the careful consideration of the victims' experience—on what road or river they were seen for the last time, what authorities or armed actors controlled that area, and why, precisely, the victim was in that particular social or geographic space—activists began to sketch a map of the conflict in terms of that experience.

The initial Gallery of Memory efforts occurred in the context of the early work of human rights and social organizations attempting to make visible the impunity surrounding the egregious state-supported crimes of the previous two decades. Grouped around the platform of the Proyecto Nunca Más, 17 organizations[2] discussed the question of truth for victims of human rights violations in a way that recognized the systematic character of the crimes. The platform also addressed the impossibility of using a transitional justice framework to deal with those crimes, since the situation was one of continued abuses and not of arbitrariness restricted to a specific period. One of the conclusions of this effort was the realization that the continuous and systematic character of human rights violations in Colombia demanded a dual focus on methodology and mobilization. In other words, this effort should not only investigate and shed light on state crimes but also build a large social movement around the human rights violations that have continued to occur in the country. With this precedent, activists and victims' relatives converged in a series of assemblies that discussed, among other things, the need for truth, justice, reparations, and a guarantee of no repetition for victims and their relatives and ultimately came to constitute the MOVICE. Formally created in 2005 with the attendance of more than 800 delegates and parallel regional assemblies, the movement committed itself to leading efforts around collective memory, legal actions, political incidence, mobilization, and visibility through communication.

The MOVICE's programmatic strategy for reconstructing memory and truth were the natural scenario for the establishment of the Gallery of Memory. First in Bogotá and then, toward the early 2000s, in the MOVICE's 19 regional chapters, organizations were increasingly engaged in activities oriented toward memorializing victims of state crimes. They hoped to strengthen their capacity to document and systematize information about these crimes in such a way as to permit the identification of individuals responsible for human rights violations. As a space for compiling and contextualizing data on human rights violations, the Gallery constituted an important element of the movement's activities. In particular, I would suggest, its format provided some flexibility for the movement in allowing diverse organizations to converge on a common arena while maintaining their unique claims and agendas. In contrast to the project of documenting state crimes, which posed significant difficulties in the systematization of information (Centro de Investigación y Educación Popular, 2008), the Gallery offered a relatively open space for making connections among violations without strict reference to a particular scheme for organizing the data.

In the case of the Gallery exhibits I attended, organizations maintained the format of the initial exhibits in that they memorialized individuals through pictures and documents, but instead of memorializing one or several individuals they dedicated space to a number of cases, past and present. They also paid greater attention to cases that touched on the issues they specialized in, such as political prisoners, the regional impact of a specific massacre or violent event, and the killing of public university students. Centrally featuring victims of human rights violations, exhibits were created by organizations whose own members had suffered threats, persecution, and even disappearance because of their activism. In one of the exhibits, the participating organizations included affiliated groups such as the CPDH, the Comité de Solidaridad con los Presos Políticos (Committee in Solidarity with Political Prisoners—CSPP), the NOMADESC Campaña Prohibido Olvidar (NOMADESC Forgetting Is Forbidden Campaign), and the Asociación Nacional de Ayuda Solidaria (National Association of Aid with Solidarity—ANDAS). The other exhibit was mounted by the CPDH, and this one largely memorialized assassinated members of the related political party Patriotic Union.

Despite the risks, activist groups deployed street demonstrations as a way of promoting public participation and consciousness-raising in a variety of city spaces. Both of the Gallery exhibits I participated in took place in emblematic public spaces in Cali, one in the Plaza de Caycedo, in the administrative center of the city, and the other at the Universidad del Valle, the region's first public university and one of the most important in the nation. Loosely following the general format, organizations presented their material in informally divided but complementary sections. Attached to the images, only minimal information was provided—a brief identification of the victim, the circumstances of his or her death or disappearance, and, in a few cases, the possible perpetrators of the violation (figure 6.2).

Figure 6.2.   Gallery of Memory photo display in Cali's Plaza de Caycedo.
Source: Erika Márquez

As in the first Gallery events in Bogotá, the Gallery exhibits in Cali were intended to generate unmediated reflection on the way the project (or projects) of an organized left in Colombia had been and continued to be repressed. With the Gallery, the squares, libraries, and streets where exhibits took place became transitory spaces for formulating a challenge to state violence in that they allowed victims' relatives and activists to represent this violence from their own experience and that of the victims themselves. By relying on the ethical-political appeal of showing up at a given public location—no social media calls, no formal media or poster invitations—Gallery organizers stood up and directly invited others to stand for the memory of the victims.

The context of the Gallery experience was the need to mobilize against state crimes in a framework other than a dictatorship or a full democracy. The violence newly narrated by activists and victims' relatives has been occurring for a long time and continues to the present. Bridging earlier state modalities of violence and more recent ones, Gallery participants formulated a framework that accounted for the mind-sets and practices at the basis of institutionally sanctioned crimes. In particular, activists posed the question of security as a powerful logic underlying the continuing state violence, material and discursive.

CONTESTING THE TURN TO SECURITY

In the shadow of decades of armed conflict, voices defending the need to govern Colombia with a strong hand have become fairly common. Heavily committed to the principle of efficiency, which mandates that the law can be applied even against rights (Aponte, 2006), both the political and the legal system have supported models such as National Security (1970s), Faceless Justice (1990s), and Democratic Security (the first decade of the 2000s). Much as in the first two cases, in the latter the model relies on the argument that there cannot be justice or democracy without a good measure of authority.

When the Democratic Security policy was formulated in 2002 by then-President Alvaro Uribe, the stated goal was to recover the territorial control lost to armed illegal groups including drug traffickers but, most important, the 1960s-formed guerrilla groups—the Marxist-Leninist Fuerzas Armadas Revolucionarias de Colombia (Revolutionary Armed Forces of Colombia—FARC) and the Guevarist Ejército de Liberación Nacional (National Liberation Army—ELN). The right-wing paramilitary force Autodefensas Unidas de Colombia (United Self-Defense of Colombia—AUC) was also targeted in the official discourse of Democratic Security. With the resources and the legitimacy of the so-called Plan Colombia, which the United States and Europe had codesigned and begun to fund during the government of Andrés Pastrana (1998– 2002), the Uribe government launched a comprehensive strategy to, in his terms, consolidate the rule of law that had been compromised by the armed conflict and generalized violence. Democratic Security's stated goal was to ensure the citizen security lost as a result of the conflict and, by way of such security, to guarantee the conditions for economic prosperity through international investment.

Nevertheless, as human rights and social organizations began to document as early as 2003, the security program was executed at a high price. As a key report of Colombian human rights organizations stated (Plataformas, 2008), during the first five years of the Democratic Security policy (2002–2007) serious human rights violations such as extrajudicial executions, disappearances, tortures, and arbitrary detentions committed by state agents almost tripled compared with the previous five years. Not only that, members of social organizations had been disproportionately targeted during this period. At the basis of this human rights crisis seemed to be a pervasive militarization of the relations between state and citizens in which military logics of efficiency displaced existing judicial structures. Indeed, with Democratic Security, the armed forces went through a reorganization that enabled the establishment of the toughened "high-mountain" and mobile battalions, highly professionalized bodies that further weakened ties between the militarized state and local communities.

The other component of the new security program was discursive. Apart from major logistic and institutional improvements, Democratic Security's total war meant a radical change in the way the national situation was conceived and portrayed. Under the new program, the 40-year-long armed conflict was not really an armed confrontation over ideologically divergent models for dealing with Colombia's structural problems of socioeconomic inequality but a criminal upsurge against the Colombian people that had to be militarily repressed. In this view, guerrillas were not combatants, but terrorists, and the conflict was not a confrontation between two armies, but a war of all Colombian society against a terrorist threat.

While Democratic Security received broad support from the United States and the European Union, grassroots movements in Colombia offered a different perspective on its alleged success. Progressive social movements unanimously disagreed with a military solution to the conflict, arguing that this would simply prolong the suffering of militarized communities severely affected by decades of war and divert the discussion from the radical inequality that was the basis of the conflict. As the spokesperson for a national coalition of human rights organizations told me, "Democratic Security promote[d] a militarized security and not a security based on fulfilling people's rights" (interview with Mercedes). Furthermore, social organizations (Proyecto Colombia Nunca Más, 2008) argued that the rhetoric of security that had been used in the framework of the doctrine of national security had been dramatically revamped at the beginning of the 2000s. Whereas security was traditionally understood as a police scheme for isolating an internal enemy, the new security was associated with prosperity. In other words, while national security was the repressive arm of continental dictatorships, democratic security seemed to be the basis of liberal democracy in its advance toward greater economic well-being.

Importantly, social movements observed that, under Democratic Security's total war, they ended up being treated as political enemies. As this same activist told me, "All the accusations . . . by high officials and by the president have generated an increase of threats, persecution, arbitrary detentions, and theft of information from the organizations' offices" to the point that the movements, grassroots organizations, and leaders were considered the ideological branch of the guerrillas. As individuals and as members of historically repressed groups, they saw their political and juridical achievements severely threatened with institutional delegitimation. Furthermore, they understood that the delegitimation of their work presented additional risks and obstacles. One of the activists I interviewed told me that in 2008 the government had accused human rights organizations of being part of the guerrillas' juridical strategy and therefore the organizations had become subject to threats and persecution by paramilitary groups.

In addition, Democratic Security became a threat to the agenda of collective rights and mobilization gained by human rights activists, Afro-Colombians, women, unionists, peasants, indigenous people, and otherwise marginalized populations in Colombia, for they, too, were exposing human rights violations largely justified by running accusations that some of their leaders were guerrilla collaborators. In the view of the organizations, Democratic Security led to what, drawing on the security literature, I call the "securitization of dissent" and laid the foundations for the securitization of society (Bajc and de Lint, 2011). In other words, ostensibly mobilizing a strong rhetorical and military apparatus, Democratic Security commanded a process for legitimating extraordinary means in the name of security.

At this point in the securitization process, the social movements acquired a more central role in mediating the democratic deficit that the implementation of security policies provoked. From widely varied perspectives, movements for the land and for labor rights, women, indigenous people, Afro-descendants, and many others came to reject what was seen as a deep and systematic governmental program to guarantee a certain paradigm of collective security to the detriment of the modicum of liberty gained largely through the constitutional reforms of the early 1990s. Elsewhere in my work on Colombian security policies (Marquez, 2011) I argue that the movement for human rights constituted a social, political, and discursive space for other social movements in Colombia to formulate answers to what some activists called the "humanitarian catastrophe" unleashed by the implementation of extreme forms of securitization, such as arbitrary detention and extrajudicial execution. Here I want to stress that the discursive elements of the human rights tradition, including efforts to memorialize ongoing abuses, facilitated the constitution of a realm of contestation against the security paradigm at a time when security was normalized as official rhetoric and as a government program.

MEMORY AND DEMOCRACY

As the literature on collective memory has shown, the act of memorializing has been both a mnemonic device and, centrally, an intervention in democracy (Gómez-Barris, 2009; Jelin, 1994; 2002; Nora, 1989). Memory not only commemorates the past but also inserts narratives of events into a broader explanatory framework. Through memorialization exercises, memories of the local can become national narratives, and personal remembrance can become tied to the public sphere (Todorov, 2000). Furthermore, by reconstructing an event and their own position within the set of relations that made it possible, those who remember may also grow aware of being entitled to rights, including being the beneficiaries of truth, justice, or reparations as victims of human rights violations (Reátegui, 2009).

At the center of this discussion is the question of citizenship—the relationships between individuals and the state and between them and others in the polis. The Gallery of Memory was constituted as a forum for confronting social views that— whether openly or inadvertently—supported the state's violent legality (Derrida, 1990).[3] For example, in defiance of the broad popular acceptance of Democratic Security, Gallery exhibits under the Uribe administration included a variety of images presenting views critical of the policy (figure 6.3). These images featured security-policy-enabled extrajudicial executions affecting ordinary citizens, as well as the harshly repressed indigenous demonstrations that took place in 2008, when local communities opposed Democratic Security militarization of their territory.

Exposing the crudeness of state-sponsored crimes and the legitimacy of the victims' vital and political project, the organizations and relatives that undertook the process of

Figure 6.3. Images of the 2008 indigenous *minga* (mobilization and march) featured by the Tiberio Fernández Mafla Gallery of Memory. The smaller photos detail clashes between indigenous peoples and armed forces, as well as evidence of an army weapon and a wounded indigenous protester.

Source: Erika Márquez

Figure 6.4. **The Patriotic Union's extermination seen through the party's assassinated leaders.**
Source: Erika Márquez

their collective memorialization openly questioned the state model that endorsed this destruction. Through their references to the connections between human rights violations and the larger political and economic structures that allowed them, participant organizations aimed to make evident the contradictions of a state that incorporated the elements of classic liberal democracy—checks and balances and popular elections—while harshly repressing popular or politically progressive sectors. Evidence of this approach appeared, for instance, in the various photographic references to the popular basis of the Patriotic Union (figure 6.4). Throughout the exhibit, organizers made visual connections between different moments of political repression, including references to ideas of state terrorism, and established links between events through their characterization as massacres, extermination, genocide, or barbarism. Activists referred to various historical moments whose common denominator was state repression and drew on both political and legal judgments to strengthen their case.

Highlighting the violent features that shaped the functioning of the state, activists incorporated into the exhibit references to international human rights decisions against the Colombian state. For example, in the cases of the massacres at La Rochela, Ituango, Pueblo Bello, and Mapiripán, activists pointed to the Inter-American Court of Human Rights' finding that state agents cooperated with and acquiesced in extrajudicial executions and forced disappearances committed by paramilitary groups. Citing more recent cases of extrajudicial executions by members of the armed forces, activists referenced the efforts of national human rights organizations along with the Organization of American States' Inter-American Commission on Human Rights (2007; 2008) and United Nations Office of the High Commissioner for Human Rights (2015) in documenting that members of Colombia's armed forces had repeatedly engaged in the killing of unarmed civilians to make them look like guerrillas killed in combat.

In a case similarly involving coordinated forms of state violence, the Inter-American Court of Human Rights found (Sentence C213 of 2010) that the 1994 assassination of the Patriotic Union Senator Manuel Cepeda Vargas was a state crime that occurred with the joint participation of army and paramilitary members and commanders as part of a pattern of systematic extermination. In that case the surviving members of the party have been petitioning the court to recognize that the Colombian state exterminated or, in their words, committed political genocide against the members of this political party during the 1980s and 1990s. Still ongoing, with 709 opened criminal cases and 265 judicial decisions at the national level (*El Tiempo*, November 11, 2013), this inquiry has brought attention to the plaintiffs' claim that the mass assassination of Patriotic Union members constituted systematic extermination by state agents.

These judicial and human rights inquiries about the persistence of state-sponsored massacres, extrajudicial executions, and systematic extermination of a political party raise the question of the extent to which violence is a constitutive feature of statehood in Colombia. For the human rights organizations, this question echoes what in the tradition of Agamben (1998b) has been characterized as biopolitical—the idea that citizenship rests on the systematic physical or legal elimination of entire segments of the population. Indeed, the Gallery of Memory appears as a radical critique of the Colombian biopolitical regime when it not only stresses the violence on which the state is founded but also raises anew, for its collective reconstruction, the political project that the state has tried to suppress with its violence. Furthermore, this reconstruction is not only an intellectual operation but also a task that is performed in the materiality of public space. If we understand space as encapsulating meanings associated with the events that occur there, we will see that the Gallery not only takes place in a certain public space, but also by virtue of its presence, provides this space with certain meanings and a certain "identity of memory." Following Nora (2009), we could talk about the Gallery as an itinerant "place of memory"—an ordinary space that references signs associated with a certain memory and reproduces this remembrance in a constant way. Examples of such spaces are patriotic or religious monuments but also, as Kaiser (2008) shows, protests or memorialization events taking place in public spaces such as the Mothers of Plaza de Mayo demonstrations in Buenos Aires or the *escraches*—public demonstrations that make former members of the dictatorship and their crimes visible to their neighbors and communities.

As Irazábal (2008) has shown, referring to Latin American cities, it is in deceptively "ordinary" public places that extraordinary political struggles appear. While manifested in everyday public spaces of transit and congregation, such struggles are, ultimately, key domains for negotiating power designs and the larger terms of democracy. Allowing the expression of citizenship forms that Irazábal calls performative, insurgent, and nomadic, public space becomes a privileged arena that enables social struggles to challenge state power. It is in this context that the Gallery, as an intervention in public space, contributes to a bottom-up model of democracy whose boundaries are given not by a single moment of institutional transition from dictatorship to democracy but by a localized, continuous reconstitution of the political. The significance of this intervention appears represented by the fact that the Gallery performs a historical reading of the present, offers an alternative representation of the political, and becomes a vehicle for recreating the public sphere.

THE SIGNIFICANCE OF THE GALLERY OF MEMORY

As an interpretive device, the Gallery of Memory framed Democratic Security measures in a specific historical context and not simply as a manifestation of the current governmental concern to control guerrillas and drug traffickers. In fact, activists spoke about the connection of the current measures with a broader politics of exception reliant on ideas of national security and the internal enemy. In the words of an activist I interviewed (Juan),

> The Democratic Security policy was preceded by something that is very old in Colombia—the Statute of National Security. This statute . . . comes from the 1960s, [and it is] a concept that is heavily influenced by U.S. ideologies about the internal enemy; then, from that point of view, for the government or the ruling classes the enemy is any person who expresses political opposition, who disagrees with government economic policies and uses a legitimate measure, which is the right to protest. [This statute] has a concept of national security not for the defense of national sovereignty and borders but for Colombians themselves, which is to fight social and political expressions, . . . to fight the insurgency, but behind it [the goal] is to fight legal and legitimate organizations. So that's the concept of security that is used. It comes from the concept of national security that has been used since 1965.

While the government repeatedly indicated that, given its focus on economic well-being for all citizens, Colombia's security policy was not a copy of the National Security doctrine, this plea by human rights activists became a common claim across the organizing spectrum. Activists contended that the 2000s Colombian security strategy too closely resembled the earlier version of National Security instituted by the 1978–1982 Julio César Turbay Ayala government through the so-called Statute of Security (Decree 1923 of 1978). Through this regulation, activists recalled, due process was severely limited by a series of draconian administrative measures. The military jurisdiction was granted authorization to judge civilians, the idea of political crimes was suspended through authorization to judge all political prisoners as regular prisoners, liberties of assembly, circulation, expression, and unionization were restricted, new crimes were created, and the penalties for a number of crimes were augmented. Human rights activists drew a parallel between the implementation of this statute, with its more than 8,000 politically motivated detentions, and the Democratic Security operations targeting social movements.

While it had been extended to governments other than Turbay's, this critique intensified during Alvaro Uribe's two presidential terms. In the context of Uribe's Democratic Security policy and the subsequent turn to security, the Gallery of Memory offered an alternative framework for the state's role in sociopolitical violence. By intervening in public space, activists temporarily disrupted available understandings of state crimes and violence as acts typical of the country's "generalized violence" and instead offered a political framework that contextualized human rights violations in a narrative of militancy and state repression. In this narrative, both the state and the assassinated or disappeared militants were provided with agency and incorporated into broader accounts of politically motivated violence. As people passed by the Gallery, some carefully observing the pictures, some skimming through the literature accompanying them, the exhibit organizers answered numerous questions regarding the nature of the exhibit and the identity of the victims. While this was happening, many of the victims suddenly became recognizable to the surprised observers. The activists' talk, representative of their understanding of human rights, addressed not only the victims and the violations but also the connection between these violations, the political motivations behind them, and the state's responsibility in the events.

Activists of the Permanent Committee for the Defense of Human Rights, for instance, stressed that human rights in Colombia were violated as a response to political opposition to governmental practices and policies and not randomly to anyone who exhibited disorderly behavior or isolated oppositional attitudes. From this point of view, human rights violations were conceived as state agents' extreme but routine attempts to silence leaders and militants engaged in effectively criticizing the established order or supporting attempts at popular mobilization. Organized peasants, indigenous people, and unionists were prominent on this list. Throughout the Gallery exhibits, organizations also pointed to the way national human rights crises were connected to geopolitical agendas or transnational corporate interests. In these accounts, the state was depicted as a mediator of transnational corporations that, in order to maintain this foreign investment in the national economy, would practice any form of security even if it led to sacrificing human rights.

Ultimately, the Gallery of Memory exhibits I observed were, foremost, a successful mechanism for initiating an open public dialogue without the intermediation of the mass media. They did not use either the media's predesigned formats or the nongovernmental organization structure to convey their information. While their platform was largely determined by the participating organizations with victims of human rights violations and their relatives, the activists privileged open exposure and dialogue over sloganeering. Locating the Gallery in an open public space facilitated fluid interaction with the exhibit and its content. The organizers did not actively pursue verbal communication with the public but rather made themselves available for conversation when questions or comments came up.

While the point of departure for the organizations hosting the Gallery exhibits was that the state was responsible for action or omission with regard to the denounced violations (and, as suggested above, in many of the cases there were actually verdicts from national and international tribunals), there was also a relative openness for viewers to engage with the exhibited material freely and make their own interpretations. This is interesting because, while activists are often perceived and aggressively portrayed in the media and in conversation as leftist militants, ideological allies of the insurgency, and therefore potential security risks, passersby seemed to approach the exhibit more with expectation than with opposition. Big banners depicting the systematic assassination of Communist Party members were, surprisingly, not met with statements such as "They were asking for it" or "That's what you get when you start messing around with dangerous stuff." Instead, people seemed to observe carefully and sometimes identify familiar figures among the pictures exhibited. Some of them in fact identified the persons depicted, and others wondered what had happened with that case (Was it resolved? Do we know who killed this person? Why was he or she killed?).

This open interpretation was no accident. The human rights organizations involved were more interested in reaching coproduced meanings of human rights than in adopting international human rights standards and instruments without a narrative that made sense of the Colombian sociopolitical context. The meanings they sought were horizontal and communitarian, collective understandings of human rights violations and their context. Using images as opposed to written text was central to this pursuit. Traditional leftist organizations have made extensive use of written media, including pamphlets, flyers, and graffiti. In the Gallery, images were key in motivating the audience to make a connection between human rights violations and the political context of the victim. More than written text, visual language became a space for viewers to fill with their own meanings within the Gallery's overarching narrative. Through this exercise, Gallery organizers created a link between their conceptualization of sociopolitical violence and observers' interpretation of particular instances of violations. By providing plain pictures of victims in a single pose and with identical framing, they created a unified narrative of victims fallen within a similar trajectory of sociopolitical violence. At the same time, by minimizing the fixed meanings supplied by written text, they allowed the audience to participate more closely in the exhibit and its political proposal.

More than a denunciation-based model, this format was oriented to reflect and produce answers to questions about the perpetrators of the violations, the interests that led them to perpetrate these violations, and what should be done about the situation. Organizations did not expect to provide people with a premade model to be applied in their communities for the prevention of new violations. Instead, they were providing an arena for collective reflection that connected the memory of past events with current human rights violations in the framework of undemocratic security policy.

CONCLUSION: DESECURITIZING CITIZENSHIP

I would like to suggest, then, that the Gallery of Memory has provided a modest but powerful forum for understanding and discussing human rights abuses in everyday contexts. Chronicling sociopolitical crimes through a basic display of images, Gallery activists have created a mechanism for engaging passersby in an exercise that, if only momentarily, destabilizes existing narratives of these events. While public space has become highly securitized and designated as an area of street criminality and urban decay, organizers have managed to appropriate street spaces in a way that allows for a continuous flow of pedestrians and relatively limited police presence. In this way, they have opened a participatory channel in the deeply militarized geography of Colombian towns.

Discursively, too, the Gallery became an important forum. Throughout the 2000s, during Alvaro Uribe's government, security became a mantra that, combined with ideas of law-and-order and militarization, made those who voiced it very popular. Even toward the end of Uribe's government, 80 percent of the population in both rural and urban areas supported the policy of strengthening security. The polls did not, however, ask about support for particular measures or how to apply them. For example, they asked "Do you agree with Democratic Security?" but not "Do you agree with extensive wiretapping operations to determine who is a political dissenter?" The Gallery of Memory addressed these gaps. Using accessible references to concrete cases of persecution of persons accused of having ties with insurgent groups, activists contextualized security measures as part of a trend to penalize political dissent. In banners and the captions of images they pointed to the state itself as perpetrating or allowing sociopolitically motivated crimes in the context of severe repression.

Exhibit detail about specific cases involving human rights abuses also served to illuminate the patterns of these actions. For example, in the case of extrajudicial executions or the so-called false positives referenced above, activists borrowed from emerging human rights organizations' reports (Plataformas, 2008) to highlight the connections between the human rights violations committed by military and police agents and the absolute efficacy that Democratic Security policy demanded. Echoing the larger national human rights movement, Gallery organizers articulated the cases memorialized in the exhibit with trends in national defense, criminal justice, and national politics. They made it evident in the exhibit that the context of serious cases of human rights violations was to be found in the framework of the attacks by the ultra-right, state terrorism, and extermination projects centrally portrayed in this particular event.

Through the Gallery of Memory, human rights organizations were able to understand security as a state project with a particular spatiality, historical roots, continuities in time, and trajectory of victimization. Displaying images of cases in which state agents were linked to paramilitary massacres, assassinations, disappearances, and tortures, it was an integral part of the human rights movement's effort to deconstruct the security policy as a discourse that legitimated state violence. Activists showed that the Democratic Security policy drew on a long tradition of political exceptionality in which it was common to appeal to due-process restrictions, administrativization of criminal justice, illegal wiretapping, and the extension of the military jurisdiction to judge civilian offenses. They emphasized that this policy promoted a model of state–civil society partnership to defeat a common enemy and attempted to erase any ideological differences that might undermine that project. As examples of this strategy, women's rights activists pointed to initiatives such as the state-created network of a million civilian informants and the incorporation of 100,000 peasant soldiers into the armed forces. Women, too, were seen as central to the state's security strategy. Martha Giraldo Mendoza (2006) of the Ruta Pacífica de las Mujeres has pointed out that mothers of new peasant soldiers in their graduation ceremony hand their sons their weapons and take an oath offering their sons to the motherland. Through their participation as soldiers' mothers, rural women especially were constituted as bearers of patriotic values, loyal subjects of the state, and producers of the military reserve forces.

In this vein, human rights activists also emphasized that security policies have been key tools of governmentality, creating the self-directed citizens that are instrumental to the consolidation of a deregulated market (Foucault, 1991). Both through coercion and by molding individuals, security policies gave citizenship new meanings. Radically transforming constitutional principles, pushing for toughened legal interpretations, promoting law-and-order approaches in policing and the judiciary, state security endorsed a new model of citizenship in which individuals were state agents in charge of ensuring security.

In defying the state tendency either to criminalize them or to co-opt them, the social organizations in the human rights movement deployed an alternative politics—one that both questioned the exception as a technique of government and pushed for a grassroots-inspired sense of personal and collective security. Incorporating the human rights tradition into their agendas, organizations managed, with an important degree of success, to confront Colombia's "permanent exception" and to continue with their movement agendas while they pursued autonomy and dignity. Drawing on existing repertoires, human rights mobilization in Colombia has articulated a critique of security discourses that has challenged the state conception of rights under security and re-narrativized citizenship in the context of their projects as women, Afro-descendants, and indigenous peoples.

Rather than being a mere survival strategy, the politics of human rights is a mobilization ethos that traverses social movements and counters attempts at securitization through the practice of alternative citizenships. Elements of the human rights tradition including the memorialization of human rights violations have helped to establish a link with existing repertoires and the current political dilemmas posed by securitization. The use of public space, the appeal to memory, the mediation with national and international institutions, and the continued work with grassroots sectors victimized by sociopolitical violence have been critical to transferring this human rights legacy to the arena of Colombian securitized politics.

With the presidential transition from Uribe's Democratic Security to Juan Manuel Santos's government of Democratic Prosperity (2010–2018), it appeared that the emphasis on security as chief public policy would be replaced by concerns with economic growth and development. Instead, Santos's government turned Uribe's largely rural, armed counterterrorist model into an urban scheme based on crime prevention and citizen security. As Guzmán Barney (2013: 37) explains, for Santos's government as for Uribe's, Colombia is at war and therefore needs to maintain an authoritarian police state. Respect for human rights is still compromised by threats against human rights defenders (Programa Somos Defensores, 2015), the killing of social leaders fighting for peasant and environmental rights (Global Witness, 2014), and the use of arbitrary detention and extrajudicial execution (United Nations Office of the High Commissioner for Human Rights, 2015). To this extent, initiatives like the Gallery of Memory remain of the highest significance.

An exercise such as the Gallery also makes an important contribution in the scholarly field of collective memory: it presents the field with the opportunity to observe a pursuit of truth and justice in a situation other than a dictatorship. Confronting the problems of democracy, albeit in its most authoritarian mode, the case of the Gallery makes visible the texture of state violence through the study and the coordinated compilation and presentation of scenarios emerging under both strong authoritarianism and more or less authoritarian forms of democracy. Activists also made connections between different time periods and presidential terms in order to frame events that were part of a highly fragmented political history. Through this exercise, the Gallery offered audiences a clearer picture of events whose violent or authoritarian character was not readily apparent without close analysis. It therefore reminds us of the importance of the nuanced work of collective memory initiatives in accounting for the complex realities of political violence under democracy.

As movements for human rights in Latin America come to operate under democracy, the question arises of the role of the state as it becomes consolidated as a broker in international human rights trials. In Colombia, the 2012 advent of peace negotiations between the national government and the FARC has brought a proliferation of state initiatives promoting the rights of the victims of the armed conflict. These initiatives, which include a law establishing victims' rights, a national truth commission, a center for historical memory, and a national museum for memory in the making, recognize the role of communities as central for achieving truth, justice, and reparations once the peace process is concluded. It remains to be seen what this process of human rights institutionalization will mean for the defense of people's rights. What is clear is that, even if the state assumes a role in organizing this kind of protective service, little transformation will occur if the economic and political structures that allow human rights violations to happen continue unchanged. As other Latin American states move to play a role in the promotion of human rights, both activists and scholars will have to remain vigilant to this turn in the field they have so far been leading.

How human rights activism will maintain its mission in this evolving field also remains to be seen. As I have mentioned, the Gallery's development through organizations affiliated with the MOVICE constitutes an exercise in memorialization that looks beyond the immediate human rights violations to articulate itself with a national movement for justice and truth as it recreates everyday forms of communication and solidarity in the public spaces where it operates. As trials for human rights violations continue, activists will construct a national movement with both national and regional agendas reflective of the plurality of its constituency. In light of the growth of a national human rights movement, the tension with investigative work against impunity will have to be considered in relation to a broader pursuit of truth and justice.

NOTES

The original version of this essay was published in *Latin American Perspectives* 43 (5): 78–98.

1. I use the term "repertoire" in a sense similar to that suggested by Tilly, as the means—vocabularies, tools, and actions—by which protest unfolds.

2. The participant organizations were the Asociación de Familiares de Detenidos Desaparecidos de Colombia (Association of Relatives of Detained Disappeared Persons of Colombia—ASFADDES), the Colectivo de Abogados "José Alvear Restrepo" (José Alvear Restrepo Lawyer's Collective), the Comisión Inter-Congregacional de Justicia y Paz (Inter-Congregational Commission for Peace and Justice), the Fundación Comité de Solidaridad con los Presos Políticos (Foundation Committee in Solidarity with Political Prisoners—CSPP), the Comité Permanente por la Defensa de los Derechos Humanos (Permanent Committee for the Defense of Human Rights—CPDH), the Comisión Interfranciscana de Justicia, Paz y Reverencia con la Creación (Inter-Franciscan Commission for Peace, Justice, and Reverence for Creation), the Corporación Sembrar (Sowing Corporation), the Comité Regional de Derechos Humanos de Santander (Santander Regional Human Rights Committee—CREDHOS), the Fundación Reiniciar (Restarting Foundation), the Colectivo de Derechos Humanos "Semillas de Libertad" (Seeds of Freedom Human Rights Collective—CODEHSEL), the Corporación Jurídica "Libertad" (Freedom Legal Corporation), the Comunidades Eclesiales de Base y Grupos Cristianos de Colombia (Grassroots Church Communities and Christian Groups of Colombia—CEBS), the Humanidad Vigente Corporación Jurídica (Humanity Prevailing Legal Corporation), the Fundación Manuel Cepeda (Manuel Cepeda Foundation), the Asociación Nacional de Usuarios Campesinos Unidad y Reconstrucción (Unity and Reconstruction National Association of Peasant Borrowers—ANUC UR), the Asociación Nacional de Ayuda Solidaria (National Association for Solidary Aid—ANDAS), and the Comunidad de los Misioneros Claretianos de Colombia (Community of Claretian Missionaries of Colombia) (MOVICE, 2008).

3. I use the term "violent legality" in reference to Derrida's interpretation that the law is instituted by virtue of an authority that precedes it and is therefore essentially questionable or even illegitimate. Given Colombia's particularities, I extend this concept to describe the fact that the political order relies on a kind of government that puts itself outside the law and even resorts to violence to enforce it.

Part III

CULTURES OF TRAUMA, HEALING, AND JUSTICE

Roberta Villalón

The chapters in this section of the volume analyze how the wounded cultural background generated by authoritarian regimes and civil wars weighs on processes of pacification, democratization, and societal reconciliation. To begin with, D'Orsi's "Trauma and the Politics of Memory of the Uruguayan Dictatorship" shows how the fractures in the national memory and process of justice are reflected in the personal and familiar lives of Uruguayans who continue to be polarized around old political divides. From a politics of silence and denial to a reopening of the collective lesion, suppressed traumatic memories of a violent past have begun to be brought back into the public realm. The imposed silence was detrimental not only for individuals, whose traumatic experiences could not be resolved at the personal level, but also for the entire society, whose collective trauma could never be addressed. D'Orsi emphasizes the importance of redefining "trauma" (replacing its medical, individualistic meaning with a sociocultural, collective view) in order for scholars to be able to push for political action and processes of memory and justice.

The complexities and nuances of trauma and healing are analyzed in the chapter "Living with Ghosts: Death, Exhumation, and Reburial among the Maya in Guatemala," where Garrard explores how issues of grieving and posttraumatic stress affect both living and dead Mayans. Based on the recent discovery of mass graves and the exhumation and reburial of victims of the 36-year-long civil war, her work examines the role of the supernatural in bereavement, reconciliation, and memory. As in the other countries, struggles to identify the truth about what happened and to whom continue to dominate the political realm in Guatemala, with the difference that here Mayan values, ideas, and cultural practices are involved. With the use of dreams as revelatory and prophetic and the belief that the dead continue to exist in a miasmic sphere in communication with the temporal world, the Maya have experienced violence, murder, and disappearance, and search for the remains of their loved ones as a continuing pursuit of justice between and within life and death. Their discovery of the victims' bodies and performance of the proper rituals of exhumation and reburial has opened the possibility for healing to begin at last.

Regarding the feasibility of reconciliation, Kaiser proposes as a case study Argentina, where after several years of amnesty and impunity, a new phase of trials of the perpetrators of crimes during the dictatorship has begun. Drawing on ethnographic research, she shows that the new court cases have become public spaces that further the development of an increasingly nuanced and complex collective memory about the past. In "Argentina's Trials: New Ways of Writing Memory," Kaiser focuses on the dynamics that emerge between the public attending the hearings, witnesses, allegations, and testimonies in analyzing the courtrooms as sites for the performance and contestation of memory. As the new trials attest to the intricacies of the years of political violence, questions about responsibility, accountability, and the political and moral guilt of both the military and civilians are being raised. The more is learned about how the repressive apparatus worked and the degree of normalization that state terrorism gained, civil society's complicity becomes center stage and the traumatic effects of having directly or indirectly participated in the maintenance of a violent regime are reevaluated.

These three chapters invite readers to pay attention to the cultural sphere with open eyes: sensitive to the silences and contradictions of trauma and healing and to the myriad of social groups that conceptualize and interact with the past and present in diverse ways. For justice and reconciliation to advance, critical thinking, collective responsibility, and social mobilization are key.

Additional readings to complement this section can be found in *Latin American Perspectives* 43 (6) (see Fried Amilivia, 2016; Jara Ibarra, 2016).

7

Trauma and the Politics of Memory of the Uruguayan Dictatorship

Lorenzo D'Orsi

> The dead haunt the living. The past: it "re-bites" [il re-mord] (it is a secret and repeated biting). History is "cannibalistic," and memory becomes the closed arena of conflict between two contradictory operations: forgetting, which is not something passive, a loss, but an action directed against the past; and the mnestic trace, the return of what was forgotten, in other words, an action by a past that is now forced to disguise itself.
>
> —Michel de Certeau, *Heterologies*, 1987

The individual wounds and social fractures produced by state terrorism and the political violence of the cold war period in the Southern Cone have found expression in the language of "trauma." Research on these experiences and the politics of reparations and testimony has made trauma both an object of study and a category of analysis. In this process, the Republic of Uruguay is not an exception: in a country of fewer than 3 million, the repressive powers managed to establish a surveillance system capable of penetrating public places, workplaces, schools, and even families. Its 500,000 exiles, 60,000 imprisoned, and more than 200 disappeared reflect the heavy human cost of the civil-military dictatorship that ruled Uruguay between 1973 and 1985 (Astori et al., 1996; Demasi et al., 2009). One of the features of the dictatorship was the figure of the political prisoner detained and systematically tortured for years. With an average of 31 political prisoners per 10,000 inhabitants, Uruguay was the Latin American country with the most political prisoners in proportion to its population (SERPAJ, 1989). This systematic imprisonment was potentially endless, because once released, people remained subject to almost daily control. The "humble modalities" and "minor procedures" of surveillance and discipline (Foucault, 1978 [1975]: 170) and the systematic practice of torture should be considered not epiphenomena of repression but a pivotal feature of a broader strategy that, by

117

acting on the bodies and minds of individuals, was intended to affect basic social relations, penetrating into families and the rest of society (Scarry, 1985). Thus the "war against subversion" can be understood as a "cultural war" that aimed to shatter the "obviousness" of the social reality that constituted the foundation of collective life (Robben, 2007).

This paper is based on ethnographic fieldwork carried out in Montevideo in 2010.[1] It focuses on the life experiences, both present and past, of former political prisoners and their families and analyzes the changes in the politics of memory that have occurred over time. I adopt a socio-constructive perspective that suggests not considering trauma at the collective and the individual level as the natural and necessary consequence of violence (Prager, 1998). As Jeffrey Alexander (2003) has argued, an event is not traumatic in itself but becomes traumatic when it is recognized (constructed) as such at the social level. Following Alexander, I suggest what he calls "denaturalizing the idea of trauma"[2] in order to understand how the event is framed and decodified—how groups and individuals produce its representations and relate to them. The aim is to show the organizer role played by memory, the collective interference, and the individual effects that are created. The naturalistic approach to social trauma does not allow one to capture the symbolic grammar, the cultural filters, and the political strategies through which the event is locally articulated.

In the first section, therefore, I describe the social procedures by which Uruguay's past became a painful wound that needed to be publicly eviscerated. Although talking about the past still produces sharp polarization, the country has moved from an interpretative frame in which people were asked not to think about the past to one in which the painful experiences have begun to be publicly acknowledged as such. I suggest not viewing this ongoing process of (re)framing the past and (re)membering it as the triumph of truth over falsehood (Villalón, 2013). Rather, this change of narratives, which finds expression in the effort of victims to commemorate the traumatic past, is a slow process of building a new "moral economy"[3] (Fassin, 2011) based on a new sense of collective memory.[4] In the second section, I suggest that the "fractures of memory" (Viñar, 1993) that divide society with regard to the past are not simply divisions between perpetrators of violence and those who suffered from it but also divisions within the community of victims. These fractures divide people over old political dilemmas and the thorny question of talking under torture, address differences between women and men, and penetrate family life, resulting in a lack of communication and divorce. In the third section I show the difficulty of coping with a traumatic past that reappears in the fragmentation of life projects and the loss of perspective. I examine a group of former political prisoners to understand the efforts to readapt to society and the risk of becoming hostage to a past that does not pass. Finally, I discuss the circularity of private telling and public recognition such as the establishment of places of memory and the difficulty of conveying extreme experiences solely through writing and speech.

As I focus on how the past passes through private experiences and historical meanings, I suggest a language sensitive to the moral, social, and cultural features of events and their interpretations. Thus, I believe it is important to de-psychologize the cat-egory of trauma, since the "empire of trauma" (Fassin and Rechtman, 2009 [2007]) evicts victims from history. The psychologization of trauma focuses on the traumatized individual rather than on the situation and overshadows the historical circumstances that produced the suffering and the social specificities that keep it alive (LaCapra, 2001). According to this perspective, trauma can be resolved by removing the painful memory and creating order within the self. Mourning, however, is not an obvious and natural process but intertwined with the dynamics and conditions that make it possible at a social level.[5] My intent is not to deny the relevance of work on the self to restore psychological equilibrium but to better understand the process of framing the violence and the past and to show that these memories are an inextricable tangle of mental, moral, political, and legal enigmas that are often not really resolvable.

THE CONSTRUCTION OF A COLLECTIVE WOUND

While in most of the Latin American countries discussions of violence quickly be-came a central issue, until 2006 Uruguay was the only one in which no trials against the military had taken place. The recognition of what happened has become the site of a struggle in which memory is not the natural consequence of historical experi-ence but a set of opposing cultural and political fields: on the one hand, the military and the traditional political parties claiming that forgetting was an indispensable condition for building the future and, on the other hand, the forces of the Frente Amplio (Broad Front)[6] and the human rights associations postulating the necessity of remembrance and judgment of the perpetrators.

The first postdictatorship governments displayed a strong continuity with the authoritarian regime, establishing a sort of "protected democracy" (Demasi et al., 2009) and favoring a policy of amnesia in which national reconciliation coincided with the elimination of the recent past. The symbol of the policies of impunity that affected the country for almost two decades was the Expiry Law of 1986, through which the state waived prosecution of the military and granted them amnesty sym-metrical to that accorded to political prisoners. The logic behind the law reflected the famous theory of the two demons, according to which society had been the victim of a war between two groups (the military and the Tupamaros) and the coup was merely a response to the guerrilla war (Demasi, 2003).[7] The law had a paralyzing effect, causing denial and silence in both public and private spaces. It can be seen as both a real and a symbolic obstacle to the investigation of abuses perpetrated in the past. Over the years it became the iconic focus of the struggle between two differ-ent collective imaginaries—a struggle not only between different interpretations of episodes of recent history but also between different moral economies, distributions of responsibility, and, ultimately, views of society.

Because of the constant activism of victims and human rights associations, in the latter part of the 1990s traumatic memories began to return to the public agenda.

Among the events that contributed to this was the Marcha del Silencio (Silence March), which took place for the first time on May 20, 1996, and was a commemorative act claiming truth, memory, and justice in contrast to the official ceremonies. A radical change in attitudes toward memory occurred in 2004 with the electoral victory of the Broad Front and the establishment of a research group on the issue of the disappeared. The finding of two bodies was a "memory trigger" that made the existence of systematic violence in Uruguay no longer deniable. Laura, a communist militant tortured for eight months consecutively and imprisoned several times, said (interview, Montevideo, May 18, 2010, my emphasis):

> The clerk of a shop told me, "Once you said that you had been jailed during the dictatorship. When I heard this issue of the two disappeared people I thought about you. Had they ever done anything to you? Did they beat you?" So I started to tell her what happened in the torture, what I experienced, and the woman began to cry and cry; she could not believe it. . . . It was as if, after all these years, a *blindfold had fallen from her eyes*. And it happened like that to many people who knew that there were political prisoners, tortured people and even disappeared ones, but in the depths of their souls they had never really believed it.

After 2005, the approach to the issue of impunity also changed: in 2009 and 2010 there were many landmark verdicts, and the two former dictators, Gregorio Álvarez and Juan María Bordaberry, were sentenced to 30 years in prison.[8] Moreover, the presidential elections in 2009 assumed a symbolic meaning by giving the victory to José Mujica, a former leader of the Tupamaros who had been tortured and imprisoned for more than 10 years. Mujica immediately tried to promote a new policy of mutual coexistence, renewing the image and the role of the armed forces, proposing house arrest for the few detained military, and supporting the necessity to get rid of the "heavy pack" that Uruguayans carried on their backs. This attitude provoked vivid controversy both in the army and among victims because many people interpreted the almost personal dialogue that Mujica established with the military as a repetition of the theory of the two demons. This once again reduced the discourse to only two characters: the military and the Tupamaros. These contrasts show how political divisions affect the interpretations of past events and, in turn, are influenced by the latter. For example, the banner opening the annual Silence March in 2009 read, "There is no reconciliation without truth and justice," in opposition to the approach of the new president.

The Congress has recently passed a law allowing the prosecution for violence perpetrated during the military regime, but the law has been declared partly unconstitutional, leaving the problem of impunity unresolved (Lessa, 2013). In this political and juridical transition the Silence March, dedicated to the disappeared, has assumed an increasingly central role, becoming the event through which people keep attention focused on the past. This commemoration brings together victims and families of different political affiliations, breaking down their isolation. It is a way of building consensus and solidarity around its own truth and its own interpretation of events and is an important part of the mosaic that makes up the national imaginary. Indeed, following Alexander (2003: 142), the collective trauma process can be compared to a linguistic act in which the memory-bearing group manages to spread its own meaning of an event to a wider audience: "Trauma is not the result of a group experiencing pain. It is the result of this acute discomfort entering into the core of the collectivity's sense of its own identity."

The issue of forced disappearance has gradually assumed a dominant position compared with exile, torture, or imprisonment. Disappearance as a metonym[9] for the entire regime must not, however, be seen as a natural reflection of the shape of violence in Uruguay. While this form of violence mainly characterized the Argentine dictatorship, it was much less representative in a country where the disappeared were few compared with the thousands of political prisoners. Traumatic memories do not linearly refer to the past; rather, they are constantly rearranged according to the circumstances of the living present and are mediated by social, political, and cultural filters. In this case, the paradigmatic influence of nearby Argentina is evident in the appropriation of a similar narrative about the disappeared that allowed recognition of the radicalness of the violence suffered, a change in the allocation of responsibility, and the establishment of a bond between the victims and a wider audience. Therefore, the Silence March should not be reduced to a set of public and commemorative acts that reestablish a memory and restore a reality. The symbolic shift encourages us to deconstruct the objectivity of the original traumatic event and adopt the position that collective trauma is a construction based not on the events as such but on their representations. Thus, the blindfold that Laura mentions indicates when and how the event began to be recognized as traumatic in social space—to be lived and felt as traumatic not only by its victims. As Cornelius Castoriadis (1987 [1975]: 390) asserted, a traumatic event "is real as an event and imaginary as a traumatism." The change in narrative experienced in public space should be seen not as the mere triumph of truth but as a conflicted construct that identifies victims, allocates responsibility, establishes new moral economies, and, ultimately, builds a new framework for remembering.[10] Remembering and forgetting are social and contested processes in which personal narratives are embedded. In this respect, the words used by a retired professor who was tortured and imprisoned for four years are eloquent (Mariana, interview, Montevideo, July 8, 2010, my emphasis):

> Telling is not something that depends only on you. There is an interweaving of several causes that create certain circumstances and *certain atmospheres making it possible for your story to have an echo.* Here, for a long time you could not say things, and things had to be not known. Being aware and not telling, knowing as little as possible, are attitudes that remain deeply rooted in the population, because the less you know and say the better! Even for me, starting to tell costs a lot of effort.

In Mariana's words, the time for telling (Ricoeur, 1983) appears neither as an inner, individual time nor as a time proportional to the violence inherent in the event: it is rather a time constructed in accordance with the context through a set of internal and external references. Thus the unresolved case of the disappeared and the Silence March are what has allowed people to keep the memory of denunciation alive and to create a new moral solidarity that can break their isolation and direct their political action.

GENDER AND POLITICAL FRACTURES

Uruguay's memory fractures are not limited to the opposition between the military and the victims. Among the latter, previous ideological and political fractures persist despite the shared experiences of imprisonment and torture, producing a "divided memory" (Contini, 1997) and embedding many interviewees in old dilemmas. Extreme violence and traumatic memories can anchor the communities of victims to the past, hindering the normal flow of events (D'Orsi, 2013). The affiliations and divisions of the various movements that emerged to confront the authoritarian regime (e.g., communists, Tupamaros, Maoists, anarchists, socialists) are still significant today despite the reconfiguration of the political landscape with the birth of the Broad Front. These contrasts emerge in hindsight in the placement of memories, attribution of responsibility, and production of meanings. On the one hand, the ideological and political component played a major role in resisting the hardships of those years by providing a foothold and a support. On the other hand, ideological support was also the cause of deep divisions: first in families in which anticommunist feeling was deeply rooted, where it caused many parents not to visit their children in prison (an extreme case is exemplified by one of my interviewees whose brother was a torturer), and second among former political prisoners, because the ability to withstand torture and not talk under it is still a political issue. Those who provided data are systematically identified in opposing political groups: the Tupamaros accuse the communists and the communists accuse the Tupamaros, producing a vortex of endless controversy. The memory of the coup is still a cause of lacerating divisions: rare episodes of revenge have taken place mainly between former political prisoners and are tied to the thorny question of having talked under torture.

The perpetrators of violence, by contrast, are often seen as mere practical executors and, as a consequence, not considered responsible for their choices and their actions. "The torturer could not do anything in that situation," explained Laura (interview, Montevideo, July 23, 2010), whereas another interviewee pointed out, "You have to understand that the torturer was just an instrument of something bigger than he was: the fault is in the capitalist system" (Sebastián, interview, Montevideo, July 20, 2010). The extreme violence seems to dehumanize the perpetrators in the eyes of the tortured, reducing them to a sort of morally neutral and inevitable phenomenon, while reasons and responsibility are identified within the community of victims (Clemente and Dei, 2005). A memoir by José, an actor jailed for years because of his belonging to the Communist Party, illustrates the intertwining between the inner impulse to exorcise the ghosts of the past and the struggle for memory between communists and Tupamaros (interview, Montevideo, May 4, 2010):

I wrote this book as something personal because writing allowed me to exorcise, to pull things out. Secondly, I wrote to say, "Hi, guys, we too have been there! You are not the only ones! Not just the Tupamaros were there." At that time there was no voice from the party in bookshops. Everything was about the Tupamaros. I was furious and angry with the party. How was it possible that no one had written anything?

The polemic of José's book is thus directed not only at the military world but also at the Tupamaros for allegedly having usurped the dictatorship's memory. This position can be found in the words of several interviewees. The most important testimonial books are those of former guerrillas such as Carlos Rosencof and Mauricio Liscano. While memory has been the focus of the Tupamaros' politics, the Communist Party did not appear to be a container for these experiences: those who died under the dictatorship had simply been fighting for the revolution. Luciana, a former communist militant, explained (interview, Montevideo, July 30, 2010):

> When I came out of prison, I thought there would be someone from the party who would tell me, "Come here, let's talk about your experience and what happened to you." But nobody came. All of us returned to our lives and the life of the party as best we could. I believe that many things remained unsaid and closed in and that this is never healthy. . . . I do not want to be looked on as a heroine, but none of us went through what we went through just for ourselves.

There are also important gender distinctions, because former female political prisoners developed a shared memory. Whereas José wrote his book as an individual act and as a critique of other former prisoners, the collection of women's testimonies *Memoria para armar* (Memory for Building) goes beyond the strictly political dimension to produce a discourse on gender (cf. Ruiz, 2010). Its three volumes (Taller de Género y Memoria, 2001–2003) not only record the experiences of women former prisoners, whose political divisions remain in the background, but also attempt to describe a female universe that until that moment had gone unobserved. Although individual memoirs have been written (e.g., Condenanza, 2002), women's recollections tend to assume a collective character. María Elena, a psychotherapist who was imprisoned as a university student, explained (interview, Montevideo, April 12, 2010):

> For us, prison did not just represent repression. We shared the goods our families gave us, and we taught the new prisoners about life in jail. I believe that this solidarity was really what saved us! Instead, for men, political involvement was what saved them: their resistance passed through ideological exchange and rationalization. . . . After the exile, I met some of my jail-mates, and we became a group. We used to meet and talk, but it wasn't one person telling and the others just listening. One began, another one continued, and another one ended. We made the story all together!

In order to understand this difference in the working of memory, we can first look at the embodiment of cultural codes. Men often followed an ideology of the self linked to the national myth of Uruguay as a country of educated people (Achugar and Caetano, 1992) and to the model of the heroic *macho*, who never suffers moments of weakness (Gutmann, 2003). Fatigue, loss of privacy, and the battle against other prisoners for personal space are the characteristic themes of men's stories. The impossibility of identifying spies also contributed to a feeling of mutual mistrust. Furthermore, while women were confined in barracks, which favored group dynamics, men were jailed in small cells holding two or three. Finally, the violence inflicted on the bodies of the tortured and by the body of the torturer contributed to the shaping of this gender difference. Despite the sharing of political targets, the resistance of men and women assumed different meanings. Matilda (interview, Montevideo, May 12, 2010) well expressed this point: "While men were men who were opposed to men, we were women who were opposed to men. This meant that we opposed as a gender unit, building a feeling of solidarity. While men replied individually, we acted collectively because we felt persecution not just for our political beliefs but also for our being women."

THE BURDEN OF MEMORY IN EVERYDAY LIFE

What Cathy Caruth (1995) calls the "historical power of trauma" pursues its victims long after the events. Silence and withdrawal into oneself in a kind of *insilio* (Perelli and Rial, 1986) are attitudes that can be frequently observed in Uruguay. The trauma of what happened reappears in the reconstruction of the self: in the fragmentation of life projects, loss of perspective, and world-weariness. Torture is different from other traumatic events: it is an attack, through the tortured body, on cultural and social bases (Scarry, 1985). It leaves the individual in a permanent state of uncertainty in which the distinction between memory and imagination is blurred. Those who live through these experiences can no longer freely mark their inner time, as is explained in terms of a recurring dream by José (interview, Montevideo, May 11, 2010):

> I walk down a street and I reach a wall, I climb it and find another wall. When I reach the other wall, I climb up and then climb back down, where I find another wall. I continue to walk and climb up and down, until I sit on top of a wall and start looking in front of me and I see that there are only walls and walls. When I wake up I am tired, as if I had climbed all night.

Many former political prisoners argued that their family members had gone through worse experiences, revealing both a devaluation of themselves and an implicit request for understanding of their eruptions of violence in domestic situations and family intimacy. Of the 17 interviewees who had had stable relationships before being imprisoned, 11 had split soon after their release. In a variety of situations (one or both detained, with or without children), family disintegration testifies to the collapse of the cultural order, the penetration of mistrust and suspicion into interpersonal relationships and their internalization for many years. Diego, a union leader (interview, Montevideo, May 13, 2010) said:

> None of us was prepared to live all that we've been through. I have been married three times, and this also has to do with prison. Couples who have not been destroyed by the military are really rare. The military knew that humiliating the person who remains outside results in creating the belief that the imprisoned person is someone who brings pain and trouble. Some of them told us that we were the guilty ones in all of this.

Many interviewees did not consider themselves victims, or at least no more so than their families. One of the long-term consequences is, indeed, a sense of guilt for having survived and having been unable to cope with events, leaving their partners and children alone. They saw themselves as an unnecessary burden (in the first instance, in economic terms) for their families, who were forced to take care of them while they were in prison or when they could not find jobs once released.

At the end of the 1990s a group of former political prisoners founded an association to help others who were isolated and in economic difficulties. The Centro de Relacionamento y Soluciones Laborales (Social Relations and Employment Solutions Center—CRYS@L) supplied economic aid and tried to create a welcoming space for members. It also advocated for reparations and recognition. It was predominantly male, partly because of the high proportion of male prisoners and partly because women had already been able to establish support groups. Most of its members were people with little social and economic capital and therefore few resources. Through human rights discourse the association provided them with new meanings for their experience. Recognition of the violence they had suffered and their designation as victims allowed them to make sense of their suffering and to cross the threshold of isolation and indifference in which they had been living. Nevertheless, in this process, they also ran the risk of becoming hostage to an image that led to repeating rather than unraveling the past—of being obsessed with their own experience, thus confirming the purpose of the perpetrator of violence: to penetrate and shape the consciousness of the victim. Indeed, most of my interviewees avoided the association because of its strong political activism[11] and its atmosphere of deep melancholy. Andrés, a accountant imprisoned for 5 years and in exile for 10 (interview, Montevideo, July 15, 2010), said:

> Before, I used to go to CRYS@L. Now I go much less because the issue of prison seems the only thing that can exist there. You cannot live with the banner of former political prisoners on your head all the time! Living at CRYS@L means living in nostalgia, and over there I feel stuck in the past. Instead, we must also be able to look to the future and not only live in memories. People can also die from nostalgia.

The issue of loneliness and nostalgia—a nostalgia that can lock a person into an irrevocably lost past, suspended in a "no longer and not yet"—emerged in many of the interviews I conducted. The act of remembering necessarily implies that of forgetting. Memory can be seen as an economy of recollections in which forgetting is part of the process of remembrance (Beneduce, 2007).

Two extremes, therefore, seem to emerge. On the one hand, there are those who deny the importance and influence of this experience, not considering themselves as victims because their families and, in particular, the families of the disappeared had lived through worse situations. On the other hand, there are those who consider their imprisonment the basis of their existence and become living witnesses of history. In different ways, both behaviors are a denial of their own visibility. Not recognizing themselves as victims calls to mind the self-denial and concealment described by Hannah Arendt (1978), but being a "living monument" and a "walking memory" (to use the expressions of some interviewees) also represents a denial of one's biographical flow. Thus, invisibility (due to a lack of meaning or an excess of it) is an expression of practices of extreme violence that destroy the social fabric while fostering the identification of the self and others as "nonpersons."

Simultaneously, between these two opposite positions, there is a continuum of intermediate situations. Mariana, a retired professor who has managed to patch up relations with her anticommunist family and, many years later, has remarried the man she had left after leaving prison, reported (interview, Montevideo, July 9, 2010):

> Some people said it was not worth it, but for me it was. Somehow, I feel I contributed to a better Uruguay like a small grain of sand. . . . I cannot deny that I'm happy to be back to my bourgeois life of university professor: I like to have heating, a car; I like to go to the theater every week; I like a certain kind of food; and I pay attention to pouring coffee in cups of the same set. I like small details. . . . Despite torture I have not been dispossessed of those little joys of life: the two cups, the details, my pleasure in living.

As is shown by the relationship between Mariana and those little "domesticated objects" (De Martino, 1964), which contain biographical fragments and make her feel at home, many interviewees have found new meanings for their experiences by rethinking their relationships with the past, everyday life, and new opportunities.

THE TRANSMISSION OF MEMORY: WORDS AND BEYOND

Telling the traumatic past means being able not only to formulate the experience in words but also to give it a new meaning, to socialize it. Matilda (interview, Montevideo, August 6, 2010, my emphasis) explained, "For those who came back from the torture there is a period in which they *need to tell and retell*. It's like a liberation, as if you could make yourself free through the story and, at the same time, you could also build something." This "need to tell" is well represented by the vast literature about prison, mainly produced after the period of detention (for an overview, see Alzugarat, 2007). All of these books can be seen as what the former political prisoner and literary critic Alfredo Alzugarat calls a *trinchera de papel* (trench of paper), a paper wall erected against oblivion that reveals writing as a social act. The prominent role played by writing partly reflects the profiles of many former political prisoners: among my interviewees there were professors, lawyers, architects, and writers. Furthermore, the great Penal de Libertad, a symbol of the repression that between 1962 and 1985 housed almost 2,800 political prisoners, had a rich library, and during the period of imprisonment reading was the only activity allowed. In this way, as one former prisoner explained, a sort of "man-book fusion" emerged (Alberto, interview, Montevideo, April 17, 2010):

> I read almost 2,000 books in the cell. Reading and studying helped me to survive and to resist. I do not know if you ever read *Fahrenheit 451* by Ray Bradbury. In that story, books were banned but there was a free-zone where people memorized books and ended up becoming themselves books. Well, we were the same, and I had become Lenin's *State and Revolution*.

Telling, as Paul Ricoeur (1983) argued, becomes a duel with time: a way of domesticating history and rewriting the meaning of events. If the act of telling has the power to make history, it is because memory does not just retain the facts but attempts to rebuild meaning. The correct time for remembering (and writing about memories) is always the present, but words are often insufficient to express the loss of meaning that extreme and collective violence produces. The former political prisoner and poet Lucía Fabbri (1989) well expressed this point: "I want to summarize it in a sentence, but to explain it to you I am looking for languages and languages." For Julio, a worker jailed at the age of 16, as for most of my interviewees, telling what happened in prison and during torture was difficult, tiring, and painful, and so they often left the issue unspoken (interview, Montevideo, June 7, 2010):

> What I lived with my children also happened to many of my generation: we did not transmit, we did not say a word, we did not talk about what we lived. . . . maybe to protect them, I really do not know. It is not a topic discussed because, you see, . . . it is a heavy and exhausting thing. And children don't ask.

Finding the "right" time for telling can take a very long time: for Julio, for example, 32 years had not been sufficient to find appropriate words. Most of the writing of the people I interviewed was in fact thought of as a way of conveying their experiences to their children. Leticia, the daughter of an interviewee couple, stressed the necessity to break the silence and the dynamics of secrets that reproduced the logic of violence within the family (interview, Montevideo, April 17, 2010):

> I always thought that the worst defeat for them [the military] was they [referring to her parents' generation] survived, they were free, that this government won the elections, that my generation was born, and that my parents could tell us what they had lived, what they went through, and what happened.

Personal memories have often remained untouched because telling what happened in prison and during torture is tiring and painful. When most interviewees came to terms with the issue of torture, their speech became nebulous, opaque, and apparently self-censored. The memory of extreme violence has more possibilities of expression in a sort of "radioactive transmission," as the psychoanalyst Yolanda Gampel (2000) has suggested, through emotional components, bodily expressions, and silent ways of living the present. One former prisoner said (Sebastian, interview, Montevideo, July 20, 2010),

> I have never told what happened during torture. If you do not live it, it is very difficult to explain and transmit, at least in words. Even with my brother, there was not a specific occasion where I spoke about it with him. But it is the everyday life of years: with signs, gestures, glimpses, silences . . . in some ways we talked about it.

Through gestures and traces it retains, the body may play a pivotal role in communication, becoming a place of testimony. Therefore, the process of embodiment not only speaks about the body itself but also calls into question an existential condition. The silence and the practices of everyday life can tell much more than words. Leonardo, for example, although living in a well-furnished house, has reproduced in his bedroom the poverty of a prison cell, expressing his life experience more effectively than through the words he used in our interviews. Andrés forced me to conduct the interview in midwinter with the window open, and Alejandra came back from the toilet trembling because she had been unable for a moment to open the door. These are different ways of expressing and transmitting what Martin Heidegger called "being-in-the-world," otherwise inexpressible, in which the body becomes a sign of a dismantled memory but also a way of disclosing parts of the story that cannot be told or thought about in other ways (Csordas, 1999). Such is the story of Diego, a union leader imprisoned for nine years who has never been able to find the right words to talk about it to his children. At the end of our meetings he showed me a video of a tango show in a famous Montevideo theater. The last song was dedicated to the loneliness of the political prisoner, and it was sung by his daughter. Thus violence and its memories lurk not just in the transmission of information but in this embodied knowledge where the affective dimension is a precondition for the cognitive one. As Francesca Cappelletto (2003: 256) has put it, "witnesses and non-witnesses seem to be joined by an emotional memory which has a common denominator: the emotive significance of the event." This is the case of a daughter of a couple I interviewed who had adopted her parents' past as her own, becoming the protagonist of their story. During our interviews she suggested which episodes to tell, dictated the timing of the story, corrected the inaccuracies, and burst into tears. The profound violation and the impossibility of putting things in their proper place are thus wrapped in an emotional and bodily habitus (Bourdieu, 1972).

Thinking of the individual and society as ontologically distinct is a fiction of our instruments of knowledge. Even the most intimate memories are entangled in complex historical and social textures. Indeed, the construction of public places and ritual practices for remembering the past can be understood as a process of anchoring the most intimate memories in a collective event (Halbwachs, 1950). The construction of these spaces illustrates the existing power relations and reveals the practices of commemoration to be political acts in a contested space. The policies of amnesia of the 1990s were in fact aimed at making the memories of the victims invisible, marginalizing them and locking them into intimate and private spaces. Even today, the urban spaces of Montevideo reflect this intent. None of the numerous torture centers scattered around the city can be visited. If we exclude the major prisons, we are mostly talking about ordinary buildings that are still the property of the army and are being neglected or have been converted into shops and parking lots. One of the symbols of this great removal is the Punta Carretas Prison,[12] which became famous for the escape of a group of political prisoners including current President José Mujica. Its transformation in 1994 into a shopping mall with a luxury hotel is an embodiment of the policies characterizing that period. It is difficult to get an idea of where the repression took place because there seems to be no trace of those places. From the walls of the Penal de Libertad, carved into with nails, to the torture detention centers hidden in the heart of the city and the *calabozos*[13] with walls written on in blood, none of these places exist or are reported on in any way today. Several former political prisoners are deprived of visual and physical memories because they still do not know where they were tortured.

In contrast, the memorial to the disappeared erected in 2001 by the victims' families and the victory of the Broad Front have encouraged the shaping of urban space through the renaming of streets and the opening of the Museum of Memory (D'Orsi and Rita, 2011; Lessa and Levey, 2012). However, the establishment of places of memory is still difficult because of the powers that are hidden behind bureaucratic obstacles. For instance, the Broad Front government has obstructed the restoration of the Punta de Rieles Prison, a penitentiary for female political prisoners. The project was aimed at preserving one of the symbols of the dictatorship, recovering it as a vehicle of memory, and turning it into a cultural center for the surrounding district. Although a square was inaugurated in 2011, the government decided to reopen the prison, showing that the recognition of violence is still often carried out in opposition to political power. What was sought with the transformation of the prison was the possibility of reinhabiting it, constructing new meanings and being there in a different way. Its reinstatement as a prison represents a repetition of previous dynamics, reanimating the ghosts of the painful past. Inhabiting such places again but in a different way is a way of reintegrating people into history and reopening them to life. Success in building a memory tells us about institutional struggles and public policies but also about intimate stories and private feelings. If there is no room for memory at the collective level, there is no room for the perception of private pain.

CONCLUSION

In these pages I have tried to highlight the relationship between violence, memory, and their historical configurations in Uruguay in an attempt to look at suffering through more than a single lens. The search for meaning that I have tried to depict transcends the boundaries of the definition of "trauma" in individual terms, especially when the events have the profound social, political, moral, and legal implications of the Uruguayan dictatorship. Confronted with such an intricate situation, individual readings of trauma and of memory are not exhaustive. Focusing on the traumatized individual suggests that work on the victim's self is sufficient to overcome the trauma. It reduces the suffering to a universal intrapsychic principle, overlooking the historical and political circumstances that produced it. Since the result of extreme violence and the goal of its perpetrators are to break the victim's bonds with the rest of the world, these aspects cannot be eclipsed either in the interpretation of social scientists or in the discourse of healing. If the experiences of my interviewees are to be understood, the concept of trauma must be rethought as an "in-between" category: "between dimensions of the unconscious and those of history, between individual conflicts and collective tragedies, between private experiences and cultural meanings" (Fassin and Rechtman, 2009 [2007]: 25). The aim is not to replace psychic and individual causality but to include other dimensions of suffering and a plurality of causes of traumatic experience.

For those who lived these experiences, success in sharing stories and in receiving public recognition of what happened has value both therapeutically and morally. The notion of trauma is a universal language that blurs the distinction between criminals and victims in that it can also be used for those who commit violence, obscuring their roles and responsibilities. For example, the former torturer and army captain Jorge Néstor Tróccoli (1996) argued that even torturers such as he suffered from the culture of fear and had traumatic memories. This is not to deny the contradictions of Tróccoli's experiences and the intricacy of their processing in the present but rather to emphasize that the application of the same psychological classification overshadows their history and its contradictions and violates their meaning. It removes the framework in which victims are embedded, distracting attention from categories that haunt them, such as social recognition and justice. The moral eclipse determined by the impunity of the perpetrators thus causes more suffering, preventing the past from remaining in the past. This is the case of José, a taxi driver who lives a few meters away from his psychiatrist torturer, and Alejandra, who often meets one of her jailers at the supermarket. Although justice is inevitably a compromise, it remains a major factor in the recognition of pain and in the restoration of meaning. The lack of justice, symbolic reparations, and places for remembering prevents, in the incisive expression of one of the interviewees, "putting things in their proper place." Forgetting is not necessarily a lack of memory. Nevertheless, in Uruguay, the policies of silence were designed not to process an uncomfortable past but to cut the connection to those events. In this regard, the jurist Richard Terdinam (1993: 108) claimed that "amnesty thus attempts to induce a State-mediated *amnesia*, to upset the process of rememoration, the story told about the past, the very substance of the signification itself." "Making history" and "doing justice" are unavoidable steps for the establishment of a different political and historical regime.

The digestion of trauma is a slow and piecemeal effort requiring de-symbolization and a subsequent re-symbolization in an attempt to "transcend the pain in value"[14] (De Martino, 1958; D'Orsi, 2012). We are talking about a memory that is difficult to pass on (Portelli, 2003b), one in which the trauma process requires a balance between remembering and forgetting and is not an individual matter but a social one. This is not the passive forgetting imposed by institutions in the early years of democracy restoration but, rather, in the words of Paul Ricoeur (2000), "a measured use of remembering" that avoids the excess of amnesia that clears away the past and the excess of memory that haunts people. Although the silence has been broken, discussions about the past still polarize society. The slogan of the last edition of the most recent Silence March—"Where are they? Why this silence?"—is not so different from those from 20 years earlier and shows that the struggle for memory is still going on. The electoral victory of a former Tupamaro, the renaming of the streets and plazas of Montevideo, and the building of monuments and places for discussing the past indicate that Uruguay is a country going through change. We must therefore be able to imagine trauma, both individual and social, within a larger frame capable of expressing its historical, cultural, and political aspects. Taking care of these memories, in fact, means taking care of the significance of history.

NOTES

The original version of this essay was published in *Latin American Perspectives* 42 (3): 162–179.

1. The fieldwork was carried out in Montevideo between March and August of 2010 for the M.A. in anthropology at the Sapienza University of Rome. In order to protect the identity of interviewees, the names reported here are pseudonyms.

2. Although this may seem to deny the radical nature of the violence (Suárez-Orozco, 2000) and may be unacceptable to its victims, who are seeking recognition, it is important to distinguish between the event and its subsequent representation.

3. According to Didier Fassin (2011: 486), moral economies are "the production, circulation, distribution and use of norms and obligations, values, and affects." They characterize a particular historical moment and in some cases a specific group.

4. The concept of collective memory is a meta-memory, a representation (abstraction) that the members of a group produce about a perceived common memory, which is never really shared by all the members of the group (Candau, 1998) but rather constantly imagined in Anderson's (1991) sense.

5. For a deconstruction of this category see Young (1995) and Hacking (1995). On the political consequences of the universalization of trauma see Fassin and Rechtman (2009 [2007]), and for its sociological deconstruction see Alexander (2003).

6. The Broad Front is a coalition of left-wing parties but entertains heterogeneous and often conflicting positions on the issues that emerged with the second referendum against the Expiry Law in 2009 and the subsequent congressional attempt to repeal it.

7. The movement of the Tupamaros had been dismantled before the Congress concluded. By suggesting the equivalence between the guerrillas and the military, the theory is functional

to the traditional political parties because it frees them of any responsibility. Indeed, Juan Maria Bordaberry was the one who put an end to democratic activities, and he came from Sanguinetti's party (Demasi, 2003).

8. The new government bypassed the Expiry Law, considering Bordaberry a civilian who was not protected by the amnesty and excluding from it all the crimes that had been committed before the coup of 1973.

9. A metonym is a figure of speech in which a thing or concept is called by the name of something associated with it in meaning. Metonymy works by the contiguity (association) between two concepts, whereas metaphor is based upon their analogous similarity.

10. A similar approach is taken by Roberta Villalón (2013) in her analysis of memory making in Argentina. Highlighting how the *Nunca Más* report made the experience of some victims more relevant than that of others, she shows that we are not dealing with a binary relation between truth and falsehood in writing the collective story.

11. CRYS@L is a nonparty association but in practice has strong political connotations. The radicalism of many of its militants placed it to the left of the Broad Front, contesting the economic choices of the government, and caused it to lose members who criticized it for acting like a political organization.

12. On this issue, see Guglielmucci and Scaraffuni Ribeiro (2016).

13. *Calabozos* are tiny cells in which the leaders of the Tupamaros were imprisoned for nearly 15 years.

14. "Transcending the pain in value" is a process of objectification that wipes away tears, reintegrates the subject into history, and opens him/her to life again. It is linked to the concept of a "crisis of presence," which De Martino describes as an existential drama with moral, psychological, and cultural dimensions. The "risk of not being here" produces a disturbed sense of self and finds expression in alienation, illness, and emotional disorder (see Saunders, 1995).

8

Living with Ghosts

Death, Exhumation, and Reburial among the Maya in Guatemala

Virginia Garrard

Guatemala is a phantasmagorical land, haunted by its history and the ghosts of its dead. This article explores the meanings of bereavement in Guatemala and the reburials of victims killed during the political violence of that nation's 36-year-long civil war, processes that are simultaneously overtly political and intensely personal. Although more than three decades have passed, bereavement and posttraumatic stress continue to affect many survivors of that dark era, especially since it is only now that a few of the most infamous perpetrators of the violence are being brought to justice. (General Ríos Montt himself was charged and convicted with genocide and crimes against humanity in 2013 but was released after 10 days in prison.) Guatemala has come a long way since the publication in 1998 of the reports of its two truth commissions (the Recuperación de la Memoria Histórica [Recovery of Historical Memory—REHMI], conducted by the Catholic Church, and the United Nations' Comisión de Esclaramiento Histórico [Historical Clarification Commission—CEH]) definitively placed the blame for the vast majority of the killings on the nation's armed forces. But the struggle for a clean historical narrative of what happened during those unhappy years continues, complicated by the conflict among different players for control of what constitutes "truth" and the fact that some of the material evidence of what happened remains underground. Much from this period remains unresolved even as the living move closer to their own more timely demises. It is the object of this work to explore grief and extended bereavement in Guatemala and to examine how a modern scientific quest for justice can intersect with intensely personal and culturally imbedded epistemologies of death and life to mark out pathways to a "usable" historical past.

This work suggests, following Halbwachs (1992), that grief is personal but also a social construction of memory. As Irina Silber (2004: 214) has demonstrated in her work on postwar commemoration in El Salvador, memories of everyday life—

including those of lost loved ones—help construct a history that is embodied (here, literally) in material sites. In El Salvador and Guatemala in particular, there have been many efforts to commemorate those killed during the armed conflicts of the 1970s and 1980s through the work of truth commissions and the creation of murals, statues, and other public artworks to remember and to educate people about the traumatic past. In El Salvador a museum is dedicated to the "image and word" of the war. Commemoration is a public act, and as such it is vitally important in helping to codify a common collective historical memory; it lionizes both victors and victims and singles out history's villains. What is unusual about this task in Central America is that history, in this case, is being written not by the winners but by their victims. This remains true even now, when the narrative of the recent past is being adjudicated and contested by those who won the political war but lost the war of popular collective memory—the generals and those who continue to maintain that the great violence of the 1980s was necessary to "save the country from communism." The national polarization around the May 2013 trial of Ríos Montt, who was convicted of genocide but almost immediately released because of a legal technicality, illustrates that Guatemala's historical memory is still, to some extent, under construction.

The very permanence of commemoration (a materialization of remembrance) in monuments, statues, coins, and other material manifestations serves to affirm the canonization of the historical memory as it is constructed. Yet there is a finality and valedictory quality to it—a suggestion of a completed and perhaps even uncontested historical narrative—that distinguishes it from memorialization (preserving memories of people or events), which speaks more to the memory of individuals and of private loss, a recognition of personhood as much as a brick in the edifice of collective memory. While recognizing that non-Maya in Guatemala face these same challenges, this study focuses on Maya's responses to disappearances and death, including the role that the supernatural plays in bereavement, reconciliation, and historical memory and in the memorialization of loved ones lost to violence.

THE CONTEXT

Although Guatemala's civil struggle was by far the bloodiest of the Central American wars of the 1980s, claiming more lives than the armed struggles in El Salvador and Nicaragua combined, it remains relatively unknown and unremembered by much of the world. Most of the Guatemalan victims died during an intense period of state repression and violence that accelerated sharply between 1981 and 1983—corresponding to the Guatemalan army's scorched-earth campaign against the armed insurgency, a Marxist-inspired guerrilla war involving four distinct movements that unified in 1980 under the umbrella of the Unidad Revolucionario Nacional Guatemalteco (Guatemalan National Revolutionary Unity—URNG). The nadir of this period, now known simply as La Violencia, took place during the de facto presidency of Ríos Montt, under whose leadership the Maya were identified as "internal enemies" of the state. An estimated 150,000 Guatemalans died violently during the armed conflict, nearly half of them, by some accounts, during La Violencia (Bell, Kobrak, and Spirer, 1999).

Of those killed in the early 1980s, the majority (the truth commissions estimate upwards of 80 percent) were Maya, a fact that sharply distinguishes this period from earlier phases of the armed conflict, when its victims tended to be ladino[1] campesinos, trade unionists, students, reformist politicians, and the military's conscripted foot soldiers. The focus of violence on Maya people has given rise to the phrase "the Maya holocaust"—a reference not only to the loss of life but also to the loss of culture as rural Maya exchanged their indigenous identity for that of poor ladinos in order to live in relative anonymity in Guatemala's cities. Taken as a whole, the counterinsurgency campaign of the early 1980s was the worst calamity to befall Mayan life and culture in Guatemala since the sixteenth-century Spanish conquest.

Since the signing of the peace accords in 1996, Guatemala has been engaged in an intense struggle to come to grips with its history. An important aspect of this struggle is the exhumation of massacre victims, their return to their families, and their ritual reburial, in effect repatriating them to their communities. Although the exhumation of massacre victims and other "disappeared" is seen by many as a fundamentally political act, it has deep spiritual significance for the families and communities to which the dead are returned. The recovery of the dead is invested with deep meaning that reaches beyond simple emotional relief. In the words Fredy Peccerelli (2013), the director of Guatemala's forensic institute, the recovery of the dead brings not closure, but empowerment.

While the truth commissions and peace accords have been influential in framing the public debates that have helped establish Guatemala's fragile civil society since the end of the war in 1996, they also paved the way for more local and personal expression of mourning and memory, especially in Maya areas, where state-sponsored violence exacted such a disproportionately heavy toll. In some respects, posttraumatic stress and unresolved grief among the Maya manifests itself as it does in every population, through crippling self-blame, profound anger, interpersonal problems, and continuing and unresolved bereavement. In their work on genocide and collective violence, David Lorey and William Beezley (2002: xv) describe a "cultural history of remembering," by which they mean the "symbols, ritual, language, and use of public spaces in coming to terms with episodes of collective violence and achieving national reconciliation."

The issue of justice remains somewhat outside the discussion here, although it is obviously central to a larger discussion of trauma. Frank Afflitto and Paul Jesilow's (2007) *The Quiet Revolutionaries* speaks precisely to this issue, including the fluid nature of perceptions of justice and the varied ways in which surviving family members (the "quiet revolutionaries" of the title) seek legal redress for wrongs done to their loved ones. In Guatemala the wheels of restorative justice have moved slowly or not at all. This, inevitably, has led to an additional round of disappointment and frustration for powerless people; thus they are more likely to seek remedies at a local level, where community epistemologies and traditional understandings provide more satisfying results. It is at the local level that people have perhaps been most effective in seeking out remedies and continuing to come to grips with the long-term effects of collective violence on their communities. A key aspect of this includes helping to reconcile the dead within the complex Maya worldview, specifically through dreams. This is not to suggest that ladino victims of the war are less afflicted by trauma or haunted by their dreams, but simply to say that this is a rather different story.

DREAMING OF THE DEAD

Dreams may be revelatory and prophetic; they may bring good or bad omens and can guide personal destiny. In Maya culture, spirits and beings of many varieties appear in dreams: earth lords, year-bearers in the solar calendar, dwarf gamekeepers, owners of mountains and volcanoes, giants (sometimes blond and gringo-like in appearance), ancestors and dead relatives, and other supernatural beings (B. Tedlock, 1992: 455). Shamans, bonesetters, and midwives are often called to their vocations in dreams, where they may also learn the specialized epistemologies of their trades: the use of herbs, special prayers, the meanings of sacred stones, and other types of esoteric knowledge (B. Tedlock, 1992: 456). Under normal circumstances, village daykeepers (*ajk'ij* in K'iche') serve as the interpreters of dreams, who can both divine meaning and prescribe remedies for dreams that are obscure or troubling or that demand specific ritual rectification (Colby and Colby, 1981).

So important are dreams that sleeping partners in Maya communities regularly wake one another up to discuss and dissect dreams, while dutiful traditional Maya mothers quiz their children about their dreams every morning (B. Tedlock, 1987: 120). In contrast to dreams in the Western psychoanalytical tradition, Maya dreams are progressive: they foretell the future rather than reiterate the past (Basso, 1987: 87; B. Tedlock, 1992: 458). So salient are dreams in Maya spirituality that dream interpretation has fallen under attack from evangelical pastors (who consider it the work of the devil) and from Catholic Action (which deems it superstition), although some Mayan evangelicals valorize dreams as a direct conduit for God's voice (see Caballeros and Annacondia, 2001; Molesky-Paz, 2006: 155).

According to the ethnolinguist Barbara Tedlock, whose study of the language has helped unlock much of the Maya's rich interior life for outsiders, dreams are understood to fall under three "rules": they may represent the reverse of what may happen in real life, represent reality metaphorically or metonymically, or predict the future (B. Tedlock, 1981: 313). Vicente Stanzione (2003: 50) describes dreams as a liminal space "where the past becomes present and that present knowledge is passed on into the future." Dreams of the dead would fall into a fourth category, being perceived as visitations rather than allegorical representations or wish fulfillment. Tedlock distinguishes between "intertextual" dreams, which embody the myths, symbolism, and expectations that are unique to a given culture, and "contextual" dreams, which are affected by the particular events and circumstances of a given dreamer's life (B. Tedlock, 1992: 468). Dreams and dream interpretation remain a vital element of the Maya worldview today, and nowhere is this more evident than with regard to the dead, who return to terrestrial life through dreams to advise and guide but also cajole and disquiet their loved ones. As Afflitto and Jesilow (2007: 65) note, "Traditional Indians assign profound levels of cosmological and existential significance to dreams; they serve as mechanisms to facilitate the visitation of beings from the spirit world or as a means of telepathic communication via spirit means." While ladinas/os also report the visitation of loved ones in dreams and often use these encounters to determine whether a disappeared person lived or died, Maya dreams give greater credence to the agency of the dead in grieving and reconciliation with the past.

LIVING AMONG THE DEAD

Most Maya today believe that the dead live out their afterlife in a place that is some variation on the Christian heaven. The ancient sacred text known as the *Popol Vuh* describes the afterworld as Xibalba, the dominion of the gods, where the dead dwelt until they could be absorbed into the cosmic life force (D. Tedlock, 1996). The anthropologist Duncan Earle (1986: 143) has observed that in parts of El Quiché some K'iche Maya believe in a bifurcated afterlife that reflects both Christian and Classic Mayan belief systems—half of the soul goes to the underworld (El Mundo) while the other half is reborn after a prescribed period of time in one's immediate descendants. Garrett Cook (2000: 164) describes the floor of the local church and the Stations of the Cross (where the dead are commonly buried) in Santiago Momostenango as serving as a door or gateway to Xibalba, the underworld "inhabited both by the dead and liminal beings," including entities from earlier world orders. The afterlife is a "mirror" of the terrestrial world and preserves its authority and hierarchies. Thus dead elders or relatives retain their status after death (Earle, 1986: 143).

The dead do not cease to exist, then, but live in a realm—heaven—where they maintain an interest in their loved ones in the temporal world. This afterlife communion includes both the long-dead (for example, among the Q'eqchi' of Alta Verapaz, the Classic Maya of antiquity are closely associated with the powerful mountain spirits [Wilson, 1995: 80–121]) and the recently dead, who remain members of the extended family with all the pleasures and tensions that that implies. Communication with the dead takes place regularly in dreams, in which they come to guide, comfort, scold, warn, and reprimand the living (Sparks, 2002). The twentieth day of the Maya calendar cycle (which is still used by many people today) is dedicated to remembering the dead (EPICA, 1996). They are honored and remembered by name, starting with the most recently dead and going back for as many generations as human memory permits (Cook, 1986: 146–147).

RECOVERING THE DEAD

The scorched-earth campaign that left so many tens of thousands of Maya dead or presumed dead posed a special set of metaphysical problems. The nature of the violence that took place during that period and the logistics of counterinsurgency often involved the kidnapping and disappearance of loved ones without the return of a body or any certainty as to its disposition. The Guatemalan military used disappearance as a strategy for avoiding questions about torture or other violations of the rule of law that might have threatened their efforts to subdue the insurgency. The use of forced disappearances and death squads was not a byproduct of counterinsurgency but a specific strategy of it, having as its goal not merely the extermination of politically troublesome individuals but also the subjugation of the general population though fear, intimidation, and psychological pain (Figueroa Ibarra, 1991).

The psychological effects of a loved one's disappearance are unusually pernicious. Survivors may obsess about the lost one's imagined condition of imprisonment or suffering, or they may have unrealistic expectations of reunion even after a very long period of time. Afflitto and Jesilow (2007: 62) write, for example, of a woman who ran outside every afternoon at dusk for more than 15 years to see if her sons were at last returning from the fields. Others have found relief in coming to the realization that their loved ones are dead and free from torture and suffering. Yet even this sense of finality can easily be rattled by uncertainty about when and how loved ones died, whether and how they suffered (far from friends and family), and where and how they were buried.

A further problem was that during La Violencia the army engaged in multiple massacres, killing large numbers of civilians who were thought to be or sometimes actually were sympathetic to the guerrillas. After the massacres, while the survivors fled to the hills, the soldiers typically buried the bodies of the victims in unmarked, mass, clandestine graves. (In 2007 Guatemala had 170 registered "clandestine" cemeteries, a figure that does not include all "ordinary" massacre sites or the large number of common graves located on military installations [Afflitto and Jesilow, 2007: 69].) When the survivors returned, although they knew without a doubt that their loved ones were dead (having often witnessed their murder), they did not know—or, more commonly, were afraid to identify—the locations of their graves and could not, therefore, give them proper burial.

The ritualized disposition of the body of a loved one has important religious and psychological implications in nearly every culture, but in the Maya context proper burial also helps to ensure a happy afterlife and good, ongoing relations with the living. Without proper burial, souls are caught between life and afterlife, in the anthropologist Linda Green's (1999: 77) description "condemned in time between death and the final obsequies." Thus uncertainty about the death or the location of the body of a loved one leaves both the living and the dead in a liminal state that can be worse than death, a source of great anguish on either side of the great divide

(Suazo, 2002). I first became aware of this phenomenon around 2007 while speaking with survivors from Baja Verapaz, who invited me to come and hear death testimonies from their hamlet near Río Negro, where, they reported, there were many dead. Without according the dead their proper status, survivors are unable to establish the postlife relations with them that are essential to the maintenance of family and community coherence and equilibrium.

THE PROCESS OF MOURNING

Elizabeth Jelin and Susana Kaufman (2002: 33), writing about Argentina, note that "a disappearance is a very special kind of wound. What disappears is a human being, a body, but also knowledge and information. Those close to the victim . . . could only say that something happened but could not clearly say what." Women, in particular, seemed to suffer from depression after a death, and they reported imperative dreams about lost fathers and husbands from which they could find no relief until the bodies were located and given proper burial. In the anthropologist Judith Zur's (1998: 224) words, "The armed forces literally expelled people from the world of the living, but as death was not expelled, the spirits cannot be disposed of—they form a new sort of patrol, becoming another terrifying presence, persecuting the living." Therefore exhumation and proper reburial are particularly important. Although communication with the dead does not cease with exhumation, it becomes less painful. We see this clearly demonstrated in a case in which a deceased little girl appeared in a dream to tell her mother just before her clothing was found in a mass grave to say, "Thank you, Mommy, now I am free" (Suazo, 2002: 36). In this context, exhumation and reburial become less an act of closure for the living than a new beginning for the dead.

Between 1992 and 2003 the Fundación de Antropología Forense de Guatemala (Guatemalan Foundation of Forensic Anthropology—FAFG) exhumed 284 massacre grave sites in Guatemala, providing evidence for 669 of the massacres recorded by the CEH (FAFG, 2004). By 2013 the team had recovered the remains of 55,000 people, which it estimates to be only a fraction of the total to be exhumed over the next 10 years. One hundred forty-three of the early exhumation sites were in the Department of El Quiché, a predominantly indigenous region that had borne the brunt of the violence in the early 1980s. The team was originally established by the renowned U.S. forensic anthropologist Clyde Snow and manned by forensic specialists who had been trained to do similar work in Argentina; it is now directed by Fredy Peccerelli, a Guatemalan-American whose family fled Guatemala to avoid the very violence that the FAFG now investigates. By the FAFG's (2012b) definition, a massacre "is an arbitrary mass execution, either selective or indiscriminate, of five or more people at the same time and in the same place. The victims are defenseless—either completely or relatively, in comparison to the victimizer—at the time of the attack."

Although the pace of the massacre excavations has slowed over time, the FAFG continues to work on such projects and remains actively involved in the identification of the remains. Its focus has shifted from the exhumation of massacre sites to the discovery of mass graves in which bodies were dumped by the security forces over a relatively long period of time. It makes a distinction between disappearances in rural and in urban areas, noting that in urban areas the security forces took great pains to obscure their identity, while in rural areas they did not. The discovery of the first of four enormous mass graves of unidentified people in Guatemala City's La Verbena cemetery in late 2009, from which nearly 13,000 bodies have been unearthed, underscores the extent to which political violence transcended geographic boundaries and blurs the lines between individual disappearances and massacres.[2] Other clandestine mass graves have been unearthed in rural areas (especially in and around major military bases) as well as regional cities such as Escuintla, Amatitlán, and Antigua (FAFG, 2012a). In 2010 alone, the FAFG conducted 119 such exhumations (FAFG, 2012c).

THE RITUALS OF REBURIAL

After the forensic material is recorded from a mass grave, the bodies are prepared for reburial. The rituals of reburial are threefold, involving the Christian requiem ritual, traditional Maya rituals for commemorating the dead and purification, and the erection of a public monument of some sort. The following description is a composite drawn from the 1997 documentary *Rub'el Kurus*, produced by the Centro Ak' Kutan, on the reburials that took place in Alta Verapaz and El Quiché:

The process of exhumation is, even in its first steps, a community ritual; villagers work together to clear the brush covering the grave before the team begins its work. When the first bodies are found, a Maya priest offers prayers for the dead and burns incense to help carry the prayers up to heaven. Family members offer prayers at the grave site (FAFG, 2004). After the bodies are identified, either at the grave site or at one of the FAFG's laboratories in Guatemala City, the remains are placed in individual ossuaries and returned to the families in the village. When it is time for the community-wide funeral, the bodies, in small caskets covered with the treasured hand-woven textiles usually placed over the newly dead, are carried through the streets of the village in a public procession, their presence "proclaiming a truth hidden for many years" (FAFG, 2004). A Requiem Mass is celebrated at the local Catholic church, and the full names of the dead are read aloud.[3] (The reading of each name is critical because it helps restore humanity, dignity, and individuality to a massacre victim.) The dead are declared to be martyrs, which places them in an exalted position within the communion of the saints. They are then taken at last to their final rest in the local cemetery. (In some cases, massacre victims are reinterred in their original grave site but properly this time, with respect and full identification.)

Next, led by the priest, the community goes in procession to the site of the massacre, where the survivors, led by a shaman and sometimes members of the religious brotherhood, preside over the Maya aspect of the ritual. They offer prayers, candles, incense, and drumming to honor the dead and to purify the site. Next the community may raise an enormous white cross that some of the men have carried to the site on their shoulders, pouring concrete around its base so that it will serve as a permanent reminder of what happened in this place. On the cross are written the names and dates of birth of all who died, along with the date of the massacre. Finally the group slowly and silently returns to the church.

LETTING THE DEAD "SPEAK FOR THEMSELVES"

Because of the Maya's belief that they can converse with the dead, we have an additional source of documentary material that sheds light on the significance of violent, unresolved death for individuals and their communities. These are the reported words of the dead themselves, who clearly articulate the challenges implicit in the lack of resolution of their deaths and their desire to be restored to their proper place in the cosmos. In the following dreams, most of them recorded by the FAFG as part of the forensic record at specific massacre sites, the dead "speak for themselves":

In Don Juan's dream a woman appears who was brought up out of a clandestine grave. She gets up, grabs her dishes and clothes, and goes over to her family members who are at the edge of the grave. She pulls back her hair from her face and says with happiness in her voice, "*¡Vamos!*—let's go!" (CMC, 2004)

Don Marcelo lost his wife and son in a massacre. . . . He could not bury them in a dignified place because he had to flee to save himself at the time they were killed. Sometimes he dreams of his woman. He sees her from far off, pretty and young. He wants to speak to her, but he cannot. After the exhumation, Don Marcelo dreams again of his wife. She is closer now. He says to her: "Pardon me, my wife, but I have married someone else." "Don't worry," she replies. "I am glad that your wife is there to look out for you; give her my thanks." (CMC, 2004)

Don Domingo's mother has appeared to him various times since her death. Before the exhumation, she came to him to complain: "Son, this old house is no good, I'm very cold." Don Domingo suspected that she was probably right, since she was buried in a clandestine cemetery where the sun never shone. During the days on which the exhumation was taking place, he dreamed again of his mother, and this time she said to him, "Son, please, when they take me out of my old house, don't invite a lot of people over, because I am ashamed." After her body was exhumed but just before her proper reburial, his mother spoke to Don Domingo again: "Son, when you take me over to the new house, invite many people—throw a party!" (CMC, 2004)

A woman lost her husband, son, and three brothers-in-law. The husband came to her in a dream and revealed to her that he was dead and asked that she pay for Catholic masses for the repose of his soul. But the son and brothers-in-law were still alive. (Afflitto and Jesilow, 2007: 65)

After the second unsuccessful effort to exhume Isabel's father-in-law, Don Sebastián, and her son Domingo, Don Sebastián appeared to her in a dream. She saw two figures dressed in white. One of them asked her, "Is my son [Isabel's husband] here?" "No, he went to work," Isabel told the figure. Her father-in-law responded, "Tell him thank you, thank you very much for looking for me, for wanting to give me my place. But tell him not to give up and forget me. It's just that I am here, only I am a little farther up." Upon arising the next morning, Isabel immediately looked for her mother-in-law to tell her about the dream. This made them very content. The bodies were soon exhumed a few meters up from where the forensic team had been working, just as Don Sebastián had told them they would be. (FAFG, 2004)

Doña Pascuala and her daughter Dominga were near us [on the forensic team] when we were working in Río Blanco. They asked us to exhume Don Domingo, their husband and father. We had to tell them that we did not have time to do it because we were working at a different site a little farther away. In the night, Dominga dreamed of her father. She saw a person dressed in white descending into a deep gully. He said, "Daughter, don't be afraid, come down. Don't be afraid. I'm going to help you." Upon arising, she told her mother about the dream. They decided to visit the place that Dominga had dreamed about and leave flowers for the father. They went to the place where they thought he was buried. Doña Pascuala said, "If you dreamed that you have to go down there, then we will go down." They went down into the gully. Underneath some branches they found clothes and skeletal remains. They were convinced that it was their loved one. They told the son to guard the place while they went to find the police. While waiting for them to come back, the boy fell asleep. He dreamed of his father, who said, "Son, you have seen my clothes. You have seen that it's me." (FAFG, 2004)

CONCLUSION: REST IN PEACE

The exhumation and reburial of Maya bodies from the massacres of the 1980s clearly serves a political purpose, which is to provide evidence and moral ballast to the emerging metanarrative of Guatemala's recent political past. The exhumations are a transnational process, often employing foreign scientists and partially funded by a constellation of international agencies. By literally digging up its skeletons, Guatemala is engaging in what the historian Robert Moeller (1996: 1008) has called (in reference to Germany) a "search for a usable past," in which the nation can wrest some kind of meaning out of its national trauma and thus move forward into a better and more just future.

As is the case in many places with a recent traumatic history, the process of constructing a usable past for Guatemala is more about politics than it is about bringing "justice" or satisfaction to the war's many victims. During the Ríos Montt trial, public buses traversed the country with large signs bearing conflicting messages paid for by politicians and interest groups: "No hubo genocidio (There was no genocide)" and "Sí hubo genocidio (Yes, there was genocide)." Even 30 years after the violence, Maya bodies—or the purported absence thereof—demarcate the fault lines of Guatemala's political reality.

Dealing with the dead cannot fail to be a priority, especially in Maya culture, where neither the dead nor the living can move on until some of the problems described above have been resolved. But the discourse that appears in the dream narratives suggests that the exhumations do indeed provide relief and some sense of empowerment to survivors, who can now be sure of exactly what happened to their loved ones. Confidence in the fidelity and reality of communication through dreams with the dead clearly helps to alleviate their grief.

Afflitto and Jesilow (2007: 66) argue that expectations of human behavior regarding bereavement are culturally specific. "Perceived dream communications and relative frequency of ruminations about the missing family members may represent constructive and adaptive coping mechanisms at work, especially for traditional Guatemalans, as opposed to being signs of compromised mental health or symptoms of distress." In some cases, as we have seen, the dead go so far as to instruct their loved ones not only to get on with their lives but also to do so with joy. This is not to say that bereavement disappears but simply that it becomes a thing of the past. Exhumation and reburial open up social and emotional spaces in individual lives and communities where healing of a sort can begin.

It should come as no surprise that dreams play a large part in this process. "One result of the civil war on Maya people . . . [was] an increased emphasis on dreams and visions that enabled them to stay in touch with their own ancestors and the sacred earth on which they live (B. Tedlock, 1992: 471). Tedlock suggests that the revitalization of essential Maya spiritual expression—dreams and their interpretation—seemed to play an essential role in Maya revitalization at large and to promise a return to a "purer" Maya religious expression that predated even the conquest. As an informant explained to the anthropologist Diane Nelson around 1990, "I used to speak against traditional religion. We used to be the worst destroyers of our own culture. But now that I'm more involved, I understand the barbarity I committed and the need to support our traditions" (Nelson, 1991: 14).

It makes sense, then, that in this context the dead would need to be direct and articulate participants in the framing of a new intertextual dream imaginary that emerged around the political project of massacre exhumations. Here, the dead speak not only to bring comfort to themselves and their families but also to bring shame and accountability to those who killed them. Thus the dream narratives of the dead are at once deeply personal and profoundly political: the dreams provide unsolicited testimony to violence, and the dead themselves serve as not-so-mute witnesses to the atrocities that ended their lives.

That this final goal remains elusive is in some ways immaterial: time is on the side of the dead, who have all eternity to wait for justice. Dream testimony has no place in the Guatemala's long march to justice—the idea that the dead can speak on their own behalf falls too far outside the rational norms of legal and scientific proof to serve as any kind of admissible juridical evidence. But in the Maya spiritual world, the voices of the dead, combined with the weight of collective rituals for reburial and mourning, have immense power to help wounded people begin to heal and seek justice. The presence of the dead in the process has been a comfort, the fulfillment of the contextual dreams about which Tedlock writes, and through the dreams the dead themselves actively contribute to the creation of historical memory. As an FAFG report poetically described the recovery of the villages of Chuchucá, Zacapula, and El Quiché: "The cornfield is blooming; the memories are blooming, watered by the rain of grief and sadness, and many questions that, little by little, begin to have an answer. Hope also blooms; the green cornfield announces it" (FAFG, 2004). Both the dead and the living may now begin to rest in peace.

NOTES

The original version of this essay was published in *Latin American Perspectives* 42 (3): 180–192.

1. The word "ladino" is deeply contested, as it can be both a cultural definition (i.e., an indigenous person who abandons an indigenous "lifestyle") and a form of "ethnic" identity, referring to a person who is biologically of mixed indigenous and European descent. I am using the term here simply to mean anyone who does not identify him- or herself as indigenous.

2. Not all the bodies in the La Verbena common mass graves are the victims of political murders; they appear to have been used for many decades and also include paupers and other unidentified corpses.

3. Evangelicals may often take part in these rituals, although they will generally not attend a mass.

9

Argentina's Trials

New Ways of Writing Memory

Susana Kaiser

> You have arrived at a form of absolute, metaphysical torture that is unbounded by time: the original goal of obtaining information has been lost in the disturbed minds of those inflicting the torture. Instead, they have ceded to the impulse to pummel the human substance to the point of breaking it and making it lose its dignity, which the executioner has lost, and which you yourselves have lost.
>
> —Rodolfo Walsh, 1977

During her testimony at one of the hearings examining the case against those accused of the crimes committed at Escuela Superior de Mecánica de la Armada (Navy Mechanics School—ESMA), one of the most notorious clandestine centers for torture and extermination, Lila Ferreyra, the *compañera* of the renowned writer, journalist, and political activist Rodolfo Walsh, quoted him on torture as indicated above. Walsh wrote these words in an open letter to the military junta on the first anniversary of the 1976 military coup, accusing the dictatorship of mass human rights violations.[1] He mailed as many copies of the letter as he could. Ambushed the same day the letter was sent out, he resisted capture, defending himself with the weapon he carried. Apparently, he was already dead when he arrived at ESMA. Thirty-three years later, Ferreyra repeated his words in response to a defense lawyer's asking her why Walsh didn't want to be taken alive. She stated that he knew what torture was and knew about the specific tortures being employed; she recited the fragment of Walsh's letter while looking firmly at the accused, their lawyers, and the public in the courtroom. It was an extremely powerful moment, comparable to a gripping theatrical performance that leaves the audience ecstatic and speechless. The woman sitting next to me grabbed my arm and whispered, "We'll have to read the letter again"—one example of the tone of these trials and the multiple levels on which they connected with the public.

On August 1, 2011, I was attending a hearing on the Plan Sistemático de Apropiación de Menores (Systematic Plan for the Appropriation of Children), the case against those responsible for seizing an estimated 500 children as spoils of war. Some were toddlers kidnapped with their parents; most were born in captivity to prisoners who were later disappeared. As of October 2014, Abuelas de Plaza de Mayo, the organization of activist women searching for their grandchildren, had recovered 115 children. At the request of a defense lawyer, the judge asked the witness, Miguel D'Agostino, to be more precise. He replied: "The only way for you to enter into a concentration camp is through our memories. It's a big effort to narrate this in a way that can be helpful for judging and sentencing. [Memories] are the only way to travel to those times. And they are imprecise." This was another powerful and emotional statement, admitting the limitations and imprecision of survivors' memories while recognizing that, in the absence of confessions from torturers and assassins, the hazy memories of survivors are our only window into what happened in the torture centers three decades ago. The impact of this testimony was obvious in the courtroom.

The last Argentine dictatorship (1976–1983) significantly restructured the economy and imposed a program of state terrorism aimed at eliminating political dissent. It left a legacy of an estimated 30,000 *desaparecidos* (disappeared people). Human rights violations included kidnappings, vicious torture, assassinations, disappearances, "death flights" in which living prisoners were thrown into the ocean, and the stealing of babies. The return to civilian rule set precedents with a truth commission (1983–1984) and trials for the military juntas (1985), which were followed by legalized impunity (1986–1987) and presidential pardons (1989–1990) for many perpetrators.[2] Unyielding campaigns for justice continued; in 2005 the Supreme Court nullified the impunity laws. Three decades after the terror, the wall of impunity is now being torn down. Trials are spreading across Argentina, and hundreds of *represores* and *genocidas* (torturers, assassins, "disappearers" [of people], and their accomplices) are being judged. These historic trials are a leading example of what Sikkink (2011) calls a "justice cascade." Prosecutor Gabriela Sosti (quoted in Dandan, 2012: 16) argues that they are "exceptional because they are trials of history, of the State, not of a common criminal." Noting that the repressors on trial are part of a larger context in which the criminal is the state, she adds that the trials are judging not military officers "but a state policy that became genocidal."

This essay discusses what is unfolding in these trials. I seek to answer a simple question: What memories of the dictatorship are being written at the trials? I argue that these trials are public spaces for collective memory making, political arenas for competing memory battles, and forums in which new information and perspectives about what happened under state terrorism continually emerge. Through the testimonies of survivors and the claims of the defense teams we gain new knowledge about what happened in the time of the terror, the level and scope of the human rights abuses, how the repressive apparatus worked, the everyday "normality" of state terrorism, and society's complicity, including the collaboration of the Catholic hierarchy, corporations, and members of the establishment—the political economy of the repression. In addition to the legal aspects, I am interested in what happens in the courtroom—the performance of the main actors and the public attending the hearings. I look at plaintiffs, the accused, lawyers, witnesses, the perceived impact of the testimonies, and the layers of interaction within publics.

I base my analysis on ethnographic observation of hearings in 2010 and 2011 that were part of two trials that took place in Buenos Aires. The first was the Megacausa ESMA 1 trial, which began in December 2009; the 18 accused were sentenced in October 2011. The second was the Plan Sistemático trial, which began in February 2011; the 8 defendants were sentenced in July 2012. I gathered all the data analyzed here myself, including survivor testimonies, defense allegations, and observations about the performance of different actors and the exchanges within publics. Unless I quote directly, I do not indicate the specific trial or the date of the hearing at which the statements were made, as many were present in several testimonies. First I introduce the concepts that frame my analysis. Next I give some background about the trials and then focus on the hearings, the witnesses, and the testimonies. I conclude with reflections about society's participation in the trials and the potential impact of these legal proceedings on the reconstruction of the nation's collective memories.

CONCEPTUALIZING THE DISCUSSION

These trials took place within a specific historical, mnemonic, cultural, and political environment and at the specific locations where the crimes were committed. These "spatial and temporal coordinates" (Douglas, 2006: 518) shape the writing of history and memory in the courtroom. Location and time characterize emblematic trials for mass political violence. Nuremberg, the first trial for crimes against humanity, took place immediately after World War II, in close proximity to the events being investigated and the locations where the crimes were committed. Fifteen years after the Holocaust, Adolph Eichmann was judged in Israel, far from where the crimes took place but in a place where many Holocaust survivors resided; Milosovic's trial in The Hague was far from both the crimes committed in the Balkans and the victims. The Argentine trials are taking place at the specific locations where the crimes were committed and where many survivors and those who endured the dictatorship live. All Argentines can witness these proceedings firsthand. Criminals are being judged for atrocities that happened three decades ago—at a great temporal remove but in a milieu in which memories of state terrorism have been under construction for many years.

In his seminal study of collective memory, Halbwachs (1980: 157) argued that individuals remember as group members and that each social group's memory has its own spatial and temporal frameworks. Groups battle for the acceptance of their versions of the past, and a society's memories are constantly evolving, subject to manipulation and challenges as well as negotiation and definition in the context of debate (see Fentress and Wickham, 1992; Popular Memory Group, 1982). In Argentina, different memories of the dictatorship compete for hegemony. The hearings become a battlefield for two major memory frameworks: the memories of the victims and those of the perpetrators. Each framework can be explored with Burke's (1989: 107) queries: "Who wants whom to remember what and why? Who wants whom to forget what and why?" If the "whom" is Argentine society, the "what" and "why" are the many versions of this traumatic past and the political motives behind their promotion. As George Orwell (2003: 255) said, "He who controls the past controls the future. He who controls the present controls the past."

As forums for memory writing, the trials make public a combination of known information and new facts. Nothing completely new is discovered about *what* happened, but there is new information about *how* it happened, and many details about the repressive apparatus are revealed. Through these new insights, the hearings provide some answers about *why* it happened. Thus they fulfill a didactic function: memory and history filter into the courtroom, particularly through survivors' voices, turning the hearings into a lesson in history (Douglas, 2006: 515–516). Moreover, survivors' statements about their political affiliations provide essential background information. Previous research had revealed little about the disappeared's political activism, suggesting that, in the transmission of memory, the "ideological, political, or economic causes of the terror had been largely ignored" (Kaiser, 2005: 41). These trials are veritable "memory knots," events that "force charged issues of memory and forgetfulness into a public domain" (Stern, 2006b: 120). In bringing the dictatorship back into the public sphere, the hearings unveil competing versions of the past and grant survivors a space to share their ordeals. The public rendering of victims' private memories, as Thomas (2009: 98) notes, "plays a significant role in the communicative construction of a collective memory," adding another layer to Villalón's (2013) analysis of the truth commission's testimonies and their role in collective memory making. They are a key source for understanding what happened under the reign of terror and the aftereffects of those events.

The brutality of state terrorism is well-known. At the beginning of civilian rule, there was wide sensationalist coverage of the dictatorship's crimes. Horror became a profitable business for the same media corporations that had previously praised the dictatorship (Kaiser, 2005: 149), but still, society learned about unspeakable crimes. The Nuremberg trials, mostly based on documents, had a shocking moment when the prosecution presented a human head with the skull bone removed, shrunken and stuffed; "icons of atrocity" such as this and proofs of barbarism revealed that "civilized" Europeans were shrinking heads like the "primitive" Jivaros in Ecuador (Douglas, 1998: 39, 42–44). Reflecting on 9/11 and our unexamined everyday violence, Scheper-Hughes (2004: 225) observes that "we have faced the terrorist . . . and she is also ourselves." Human beings like us committed those savageries; knowing this magnifies their horror.

At the ESMA 1 and Plan Sistemático trials, icons of atrocity were presented via survivors' accounts and prosecutors' allegations. These fell into two categories, one referring to the brutalities endured by victims (comparable to the above-mentioned shrunken head) and the other, which may appear less blatantly vicious, revealing the coexistence of horror with apparent "normality," such as ESMA's torturers' toasting with their victims to celebrate Christmas. In his analysis of Primo Levi's description of the soccer games between prisoners and SS guards in the Nazi concentration camps, Agamben (2004: 441) says, "This match might strike someone as a brief pause of humanity in the middle of an infinite horror" but "this match, this moment of normality, [was] the true horror of the camp," further arguing that, even if we think "that the massacres are over . . . the match is never over; it continues as if uninterrupted." The trials challenge society to address this facet of the horror. The impact of the atrocities camouflaged by humanity persists in recurrent afterthoughts: Did that really happen? Did torturers really take their victims to a weekend house for a barbecue?

THE TRIALS

I wonder if it is possible to determine exactly who is guilty and responsible for the crimes. Pilar Calveiro (1998) convincingly demonstrates that the camps of torture and extermination cannot be seen as aberrations, isolated from society. Habermas and Michnik (1994: 7) further articulate this idea, claiming that "there is such a thing as collective responsibility for the mental and cultural context in which mass crimes become possible." The trials focus on a few repressors. Is no one else responsible? Are these men the only ones to blame for 30,000 disappeared? Witnesses' testimonies and the allegations of the defense lawyers provide some answers to these questions. We may also wonder which members of society feel guilty and responsible. Krog (2000: 123) identifies categories of guilt formulated by German theologians after World War II that apply to the Argentine context: the criminally guilty, who committed the crimes, including the torturers and those who orchestrated the repression; the politically guilty, including politicians and the political class that supported and benefited from state terrorism; the morally guilty, including those who were passive or paralyzed by fear and allowed the atrocities to happen; and, finally, the metaphysically guilty, who feel guilty for having survived while others did not. If the trials trigger these thoughts in participants, including the accused, the survivors, lawyers, judges, the public in the courtroom, and society in general, how do these reflections shape collective memory making?

THE COURTROOM

The trials are public. Anyone with an ID can get a pass to attend. You only need to answer one question: "Are you here for victims/prosecution or accused/defense?" Your answer determines where you sit. While this separation helps to prevent incidents between two extremely polarized sectors, the requirement to publicly state your affiliation may surprise some people. The hearings for the two trials were held in the main hall of the Comodoro Py courthouse. A glass panel divides the courtroom's ground floor: on one side of the panel are the judges, facing the audience and the legal teams: the victims' team is on the left, where the prosecutor and the plaintiffs' lawyers sit; the right side is for the accused and their lawyers. (With few exceptions, the accused are not present. They can choose to attend, but they are required to be present only for the reading of charges, the verdict, and the sentencing.) The public attending in support of the victims, including survivors and relatives, sits on the other side of the glass. They face the judges, the witness stand, the big screen for teleconference testimonies, the lawyers' backs, and the screens showing what is unfolding in the courtroom. Perpetrators' supporters sit in the balcony with the press. The number of victims' supporters varies from a full house for key testimonies to just a dozen people at other times. I could not assess the public supporting the repressors, but I understand that there is always a loyal group.

Scheffer's (2002: 4–5) description of the English Crown Court points to comparable seating patterns circumscribing conditions of witnessing as a restriction that keeps everybody in place. This arrangement determines the layers of possible links and interactions. Sitting with the victims' supporters, I observed the impact of the testimonies on those close to me. This perspective was not available to the judges, separated from the public by the lawyers, prosecutors, and accused and the glass panel. Nor was it available to the journalists upstairs, who could only observe the reactions of those supporting the accused. At the hearings I attended, journalists did not approach the victims' supporters. Thus contact between publics, judges, victims, the accused, prosecutors, lawyers, and journalists is limited. Although I have concerns about dividing publics, I am aware of the potential disruptions that this separation deters. How would someone feel sitting next to the wife of the person accused of causing the disappearance of her father?

Supporters of victims and accused do not interact in the courtroom. Encounters take place while standing in line to process admission passes, in elevators, in the corridors, and in the cafeteria. Everyone seems to know which side everyone else supports. This is reflected in the way we look at each other and feel observed and scrutinized, the way we silently judge and condemn, for example, when sharing an elevator with intimidating supporters of the repressors. These grandfatherly looking men, most of them retired military officers, appear to me to be capable of committing (and may be responsible for) the same atrocities for which defendants are facing trial. I have been told about repressors' supporters making loud, threatening comments meant to be heard by victims' supporters, including claims that the trials will be forgotten when the current administration leaves office and the accused and/ or condemned will be freed.

Another important level of interaction occurs among the victims' supporters. There are "hearings groupies," quickly integrated by the others, who do not need much time to determine how people attending the trials think, the reasons they are there, and their level of commitment to human rights. Regularly sitting in the victims' section becomes a political act. As the H.I.J.O.S.[3] slogan has it, the accused are "judged by the court, condemned by all of us." This understanding prompts the development of networks, generates trust, and encourages people to open up and share stories and memories, many of which are very personal, illustrating another sphere for collective memory making. There is a palpable feeling of "We're all in this together," "We speak the same language," "I know that you will listen and understand what I need to say." I have heard about disappeared uncles and sisters, accounts of boarding a flight and leaving the country on the point of being abducted, and reports of witnesses' returning to find their homes turned upside down as a warning.

The courtroom turns into a *lieu de mémoire*, a site for the performance of memory. The court hearing, as Scheffer (2002: 5) notes, "is as visible as a play in theatre: one can sit in the higher ranks to gain an overview of the scene or in the first ranks to set eyes on the main characters sweating and stumbling." My experience observing the hearings was like watching a performance with several acts. I observed the whole environment, the performance of the main actors and the public (metaphorically "from the higher ranks"), and focused on witnesses' testimonies (metaphorically "from the first ranks"). Being a researcher aligned with the victims limited what I observed.

THE WITNESSES

Most of the witnesses are survivors; there are also relatives, fellow activists, and people who may have useful information, such as nurses from the hospitals where babies were born and stolen. Survivors have to go back three decades, enter the torture center once again, and face their torturers, in most cases for the first time since the days they were disappeared. It is hard, and there is fear. As Augusto Boal (1998: 162) reminds us, "in crimes of violence, the victim is silenced by death and the witness by fear; . . . even in nonfatal cases, frequently a victim who is also the principal witness stays silent out of fear, becoming doubly a victim." Julio López, who survived his first disappearance during the dictatorship, was disappeared again in 2006 after providing key testimony leading to the sentencing of a major genocide in one of the first trials after the nullification of the impunity laws. It was a clear warning to those daring to testify. Witnesses display amazing courage. They feel the responsibility to testify to seek justice and convict the repressors. Peters (2001: 713) refers to the power of those who survived atrocities and their responsibility to bear witness, arguing that "the militancy in the survivor's voice owes to the battle against oblivion and indifference." Being the voice of the disappeared can be a burden; as Wardi (1992) argues of the children of Holocaust survivors, those who survived the terror have become memorial candles.

Witnesses must remember, and they are afraid of forgetting. Memory is fragile and unreliable. The recollections of survivors who have been testifying since the beginning of civilian rule about events that happened 30 years ago may have changed since they originally spoke to the truth commission or in the trials of the military juntas.

Memory comes and goes, and survivors say "I think" or "I don't remember." Relying on memories to judge historical actions is always problematic, but, in spite of imprecisions, testimonies are always about what people remember having experienced or seen. Moreover, memories may be the only way to achieve access to information.

THE DEFENDANTS

The defense lawyers invoke theories of memory and its unreliability. They refer to survivors' shifting statements, noting that they remember more details with the passage of time, and allude to witnesses' work in reconstructing the events. In doing so, they illustrate the dynamics of the memory construction process and the collective memory of survivors, integrating a mnemonic community. What individuals learn from each other affects the memories they share (Halbwachs, 1980). Defense lawyers often corroborate the atrocities committed. They note that victims were blindfolded to support their claims that survivors' testimonies are unreliable because their situation did not allow them to see anything—a major challenge that survivors face, as portrayed in Ariel Dorfman's play *Death and the Maiden*, in which the protagonist recognizes her torturer and rapist by his voice and smell. To prove their clients' innocence, defense lawyers confirm that decisions about who would disappear in the "death flights" were made on Tuesdays but insist that their clients were not at ESMA during those years. Erasing the phrase "but my client wasn't there" from the record might reveal detailed confessions stated by the perpetrators' own lawyers.

Defense lawyers' aggressive questioning aims to discredit victims' testimonies, often arguing that they are confusing. I have observed witnesses noting the difficulty of understanding what happened without being familiar with the places where the crimes were committed. One survivor responded, "Do you know ESMA? What a pity, my explanation could be much clearer for you" (Plan Sistemático hearing, August 15, 2011).

Many repressors have died or are very old and sick, similar to the Nazi criminals captured and tried decades after their crimes—another instance in which the "efficacy of trying ailing octogenarians" was questioned (Douglas, 2006: 518). But hundreds of them were very young at the time and, now in their sixties, are facing the rest of their lives in jail. Some may be unable to stand trial or claim disability, but there were no instances of the accused's being transferred back and forth from a hospital in the hearings I attended. The repressors present in the courtroom show no remorse or shame. They are indifferent to what is being said, focus their attention on the books they are reading or on their computers, and smile and wave at their supporters, confirming their disregard for the trials. Defense lawyers, most of them court appointed, often match their clients' apathy, reading the newspaper and checking their Facebook pages during hearings. This attitude can be seen as an insult to the victims' supporters sitting behind them and observing their actions but also as a lack of empathy for the clients they must defend.

THE TESTIMONIES

Witnesses' accounts help us to grasp the particulars of society's interaction with state terrorism. Schwarzböck (2007: 66), analyzing films about the dictatorship, notes that we usually judge what happened in the 1970s in terms of what was going on inside the torture centers rather than outside them. This outside is what we must learn more about, and this is one of the historical lessons offered by the trial. The support that certain media gave to the dictatorship is well-known; these organizations often acted as de facto propaganda agencies. Several witnesses commented on this collaboration and named journalists who regularly visited ESMA. Testimonies told of the systematic theft of victims' possessions, ranging from condominiums to refrigerators, including things that belonged to the national patrimony such as Walsh's manuscripts. Some of his unpublished works were read at ESMA by personnel gloating about what they now owned. The dictatorship's disregard for requests from foreign governments was exposed by the French lawyer François Cheron, who was sent to Argentina in 1979 by France's president to inquire about the French nuns Alice Domon and Léonie Duquet, both brutally tortured and disappeared. Cheron testified that two repressors now facing trial welcomed him at the airport and, during dinner, laughed and talked about the "flying nuns"—an obvious reference to the nuns being thrown into the sea on one of the death flights.

Some testimonies are veritable tales of insanity, in the pathological sense of the word. Augusto Boal (1998: 150), describing his experience being tortured by the Brazilian dictatorship, argues that "a scene of torture is a scene of inhuman tragedy" and that "as happens in the great Shakespearian tragedies, the most painful scenes are juxtaposed sometimes with scenes of ridiculous farce." For instance, when he asked why he was being tortured, his torturer replied that it was because he had defamed the nation by denouncing torture in Brazil—a real oxymoron, a torturer telling his victim, "I'm torturing you because you say that we torture." Many of the accounts I heard illustrate this juxtaposition of pain with farce, among them the case of a woman who, while being kidnapped, was forced to sing the popular tango *Caminito*—the torturers and their victim, driving toward ESMA and singing tangos.

ESMA's Casino de Oficiales (Officers' Building), headquarters of the repression, had a glass "office" called La Pecera (the Fish Tank) that allowed officers to monitor what was going on inside. There captives were forced into slave labor, performing a variety of tasks such as falsifying IDs, translating "anti-Argentine" articles published in *Le Monde Diplomatique* or the *New York Times*, and analyzing political documents for the navy officers. According to a survivor, it was "a kind of madness offices in the middle of nowhere" (ESMA 1 hearing, June 17, 2010). ESMA had "branches," one of which was at a house where its leaders hid documents; another was at Admiral Massera's (head of the navy) offices, which he had stolen at gunpoint from prisoners who were later disappeared. Lawyer Cheron testified that Massera offered to have an employee go shopping for his family. Surprised that this young woman wore a necklace with the Star of David in that environment, he asked her why she was working for the navy. Her expression was enough to make him understand the situation. As confirmed later, she had been disappeared at ESMA.

Many torture centers housed maternity wards. Consistent with its strategy of "leaving no trace," Argentina's dictatorship implemented a campaign of systematically seizing babies; it created a "baby factory" in which pregnant prisoners were kept alive until they gave birth. One of the most compelling testimonies I heard was about stolen babies: "Thirty years later, I wonder how we didn't realize that they would keep the babies. They took everything, our goods, our bodies, everything. I couldn't imagine something so atrocious. How can a human being punish another one to the extent of taking away her baby?" (Miriam Lewin, Plan Sistemático hearing, August 2, 2011). These few words summarize the inhumanity of this act as a method for destroying individuals—their "human substance," as Walsh said—and taking everything away from them. ESMA had a sector for pregnant women; physicians collaborating with the navy helped with the deliveries. Cruelty had no limits: the same men who tortured and killed the biological parents of the babies then appropriated some of the babies for themselves. Those given to military families received fancy outfits from Les Bebés, an exclusive store in Buenos Aires. Neighbors of navy personnel have said of the distribution of the babies, "They were given as if they were just little kitties" (Kaiser, 2005: 114).

A state of "normality" can exist under a state of fear. There was a feeling of everyday life as usual, with tourists visiting the country and Argentines traveling around the world. Testimonies attest to the two sides of state terrorism: terror and "life goes on." Examples of this apparent dichotomy constantly emerge. A terrified and paralyzed society chose not to see; everyone knew that something atrocious was happening (Kaiser, 2005). The trials may force many to remove their blinders.

Witnesses remind us that torture centers were located in highly populated areas in the midst of the urban landscape. ESMA is a compound of 35 buildings surrounded by gardens, located in a residential neighborhood facing a wide, high-traffic avenue lined with upscale apartment buildings with terraces overlooking the compound. Survivors mention the "sounds of normal life" surrounding them, like the noises during recesses at the trade school next door. Some people lived right next to a torture chamber where activities were constant and loud. The Casino de Oficiales, where prisoners were housed and tortured, was also the place where officers lived, socialized, and invited their women. The ESMA director had a house there in which his daughter celebrated her fifteenth birthday with a party. This juxtaposition of horror and "normality" also took place outside ESMA. Prisoners were sometimes taken to a weekend house to spend the day and attend a barbecue with the torturers' wives and children. When Argentina won the 1978 World Cup, some prisoners were taken out into the streets, where everyone was celebrating the triumph. What were they supposed to do? Yell out "I'm disappeared at ESMA"? Who would have believed them? Referring to these "field trips," a witness mentioned that there was a lot of going in and out of the torture centers and it was worse being outside than inside: "When you were outside, you knew you were going back" (ESMA 1 hearing, June 14, 2010). Repressors made sure that prisoners were always aware of their vulnerability, telling them what they had done before and would do again. Contact with the outside world included repressors' taking victims to visit their families or going on their own to the captives' homes. One Father's Day, a torturer visited a prisoner's father and took him a tie on behalf of his daughter. Meeting torturers and learning about their relatives' ordeals turned families into hostages, another means of instilling fear.

A survivor testified that, when she arrived at ESMA, she was surprised to see some prisoners wearing makeup, jewelry, and embroidered tunics. She was told that the navy officers liked seeing prisoners well-dressed because it was a sign of their "recovery"—meaning abandoning their political ideas and adopting the repressors' ideology. The navy had a plan to reeducate activists, and many prisoners pretended to go along with it. On occasion the torturers would wake the chained prisoners in the middle of the night and order them to clean up and get dressed, asking them to choose outfits from a storage room filled with goods stolen from the disappeared. Treated as escorts, they were taken to La Costanera, a popular area along the river, for late dinners; they had to pretend to enjoy dinner with their torturers. While listening to this testimony, I couldn't stop thinking about the many Argentines, myself included, having dinner there during those times and the possibility that disappeared women and their torturers might have been sitting at the next table.

The Catholic hierarchy had close ties with the dictatorship and the ESMA torturers. When the Inter-American Commission of Human Rights visited Argentina at the peak of the repression, ESMA's prisoners were hidden on an island owned by the Church appropriately named El Silencio (The Silence). A survivor reported that, while exiled in Europe, her torturer took her on a pilgrimage to the sanctuary of the Virgin of Lourdes. When a prisoner's husband was killed, her 10-year-old daughter was brought to ESMA, where another woman had just delivered a baby. The repressors decided to baptize the girls and took both women and their daughters to an upper-class neighborhood church where the priest, a cousin of one of the torturers, baptized them. The torturers acted as "godfathers" to the girls, making comments like "We hope that these girls won't be as bad as their mothers" (ESMA 1 hearing, June 9, 2010).

The few prisoners who were released were not totally free and lived under constant supervision. If allowed to leave the country, they had to send letters to the repressors letting them know how they were doing—as if they had had a wonderful time together. One survivor testified that after she had settled in Spain she had reported once a month to José Lataliste, the Argentine businessman who owned Mau Mau, the best-known disco in Buenos Aires during the 1970s. Lataliste acted as the navy's overseas parole officer—a link between the business elite and the military, an example of the collaborations that made the horror possible. Similarly, an executive from the Ford Motor Corporation visited ESMA on weekends and participated in torture sessions.

FOOD FOR THOUGHT

In these Argentine trials, a memory-making process is taking place in which different versions of the past compete for hegemony. Survivors' stories allow us to develop a comprehensive account of what went on inside the torture chambers and, most important, its many links with the outside. New knowledge about victims' political activism helps us to understand the reasons for the brutal repression. In spite of silences and denials, confessions are implied in defense lawyers' statements acknowledging the crimes while arguing that their clients "were not there." In the political battles for control of the past, justifying the dictatorship as a holy crusade to defend Christian and Western values is losing ground. What is emerging at the trials confirms that this era was one of the darkest periods in Argentina's history.

The key questions are: Who is watching? How does society participate in this historical process? What are the effects of attending the hearings? How are the media covering the trials? How will the memory work taking place at the trials shape Argentines' collective memories?

The courtroom may be packed or almost empty depending on the day and the relevance of the witnesses. Low attendance may be due to the fact that the trials last many months, the fact that people have to work, lack of interest, fear of facing the truth, or acceptance of an environment of impunity fostered during the years in which laws prevented trials. Human rights organizations encourage society's participation, as do pro-human-rights media and university professors who require students to attend the hearings. With few exceptions, the mainstream media have ignored the trials analyzed here.[4]

We should be concerned about lack of public attendance at the hearings and the limited media coverage. The hearings offer the opportunity to witness the performance of memory in the courtroom, vicariously witnessing, through the testimonies, what went on during the dictatorship. The hearings let the public experience secondhand the suffering of those who were held, tortured, assassinated, or disappeared. And witnessing has effects; becoming aware has political consequences. The responsibility to act is at the core of witnessing (Peters, 2001; Rentschler, 2004).

We can only speculate about the consequences of the hearings for those who attend them or learn about them via the media and what actions this may prompt if witnesses begin to assume responsibility. Judging from what I observed, participating in the hearings seems to be a transformative experience for everyone. I have seen the impact that testimonies have on people—their faces transformed when they leave the courtroom after a long day of hearings. Witnessing these historic trials may prompt support for the process of accountability and an insistence on more information about what happened and why.

The potential long-term effects of the trials and their role in the writing of memories are still open questions. An ongoing process of accountability is taking place across Argentina. As a case study, the analysis of these trials contributes to the development of empirically grounded theory about memory transmission and reconstruction following traumatic political events that happened long ago. Further research should explore what collective memories are being written at the trials, how society gains access to what unfolds there, how society is processing this information, how it affects people's memories of terror, and how these memories shape political action.

The trials are uncovering new information about the links between state terrorism and society. Broadening the discussion to include more than just the genocides on trial might force society to reflect on its role in and responsibility for the terror, and on the political and moral guilt that some may feel. Memory is a dynamic process, and the collective memories of state terrorism will continue to evolve. What is remembered about those years may be changed forever, including how those who lived under terror will answer this simple question from younger generations: What did you do during the dictatorship?

NOTES

The original version of this essay was published in *Latin American Perspectives* 42 (3): 193–206.

1. The ESMA compound now houses a "space for memory," a museum, and several human rights and cultural organizations. The text of Walsh's open letter is inscribed on large glass panels in the compound's park.

2. Law No. 23493, "Full Stop" (December 23, 1986) and Law No. 23521, "Due Obedience" (June 4, 1987); Decrees of Pardon Nos. 1002–05 (October 7, 1989) and 2741–43 (December 30, 1990).

3. Hijos por la Identidad y la Justicia Contra el Olvido y el Silencio (Daughters and Sons for Identity and Justice against Forgetting and Silence) is an organization founded by the adult daughters and sons of the disappeared, murdered political activists, and activists forced into exile. It now includes members without biological ties to direct victims.

4. There was no television broadcast of these trials. A Supreme Court resolution guarantees broadcasts of the beginning and the end of a trial but allows the judge to decide how public the rest of the trial should be. My study of the coverage of these trials in five Buenos Aires newspapers revealed major differences in the number of articles; an analysis of ESMA 1 coverage from the beginning of the trial to the sentencing (November 2009–October 2011) revealed 162 articles in *Página/12*—a pro-human rights publication—and 31 in *Clarín*—the newspaper with the largest circulation in the country (Kaiser, 2014).

Part IV

ARTS, MEDIA, MUSEUMS, AND MEMORY

Roberta Villalón

The chapters in this last section present how artistic and cultural media have emerged in and advanced memory, truth, and justice processes. Cortés's "The Murals of La Victoria: Imaginaries of Chilean Popular Resistance" provides a rich view of a powerful artistic method of advancing counter-hegemonic politics and memory. The case of La Victoria—a paradigmatic neighborhood given that it was the first organized urban occupation of land in Latin America and later on an epicenter of the political left in Chile—shows that popular muralism has helped express, shape, and sustain a collective identity of resistance; record and validate the community's actions against authoritarianism and exclusion; and reassert its sense of self-determination from generation to generation. Inspired by its use by communist groups in other parts of the world and in Chile, activists took up and developed muralism in La Victoria to express the neighborhood's identity as a settlement; promote the ideals of socialism and equality before, during, and after Allende's time; denounce the abuses imposed during Pinochet's military regime; graphically show the various ways in which the neighborhood resisted first the regime and later democratic neo-liberal and reconciliation policies; and reassert the resilience of the community intergenerationally. Cortés's study speaks to the transcendence of art and the collective labor necessary to create and maintain it despite physical and symbolic attempts at silencing and destruction.

Aroni Sulca's "Choreography of a Massacre: Memory and Performance in the Ayacucho Carnival" brings readers a rich ethnography of grassroots mobilizations and cultural performances for memory and justice. Himself a member of the community studied, Aroni Sulca describes the transgenerational transmission of memory at the familial, institutional, and public levels. Once in Lima, survivors of the 1985 massacre in the village of Accomarca, where the state and the Shining Path clashed, insisted on keeping their version of the events alive by sharing them orally with their family members and other survivors in community institutions. More recently, through the traditional art of Carnival performances, survivors and their descendants have represented the massacre publicly and solidified their still unmet claim for justice. The creation and repeated performance of this artistic expression has had deep, embodied emotional effects that have nourished the community's identity, memory, and collective organization.

Schneider and Atencio's "Reckoning with Dictatorship in Brazil: The Double-Edged Role of Artistic-Cultural Production" shows how cultural and artistic forms have worked as catalysts in the emergence of debates about the authoritarian past and promoted a counternarrative to official versions of history. They argue that, despite the late implementation of formal transitional justice measures, Brazil had been developing a culture of memory from the artistic/cultural arena for at least three decades. While they point out that these successful artistic and cultural productions showed how the legacies of the dictatorship and the timid way in which human rights abuses had been dealt with had a negative impact in the present, they suggest that they may have had a less radical effect than once believed. In the context of a culture of reconciliation, watered-down messages of political violence may have fed that ideal rather than creating a counterdiscourse demanding juridical condemnation.

Last, Sierra Becerra's "Historical Memory at El Salvador's Museo de la Palabra y la Imagen" studies the reach and limitations of this initiative on the basis of her own experience as one of its educational programmers and curators. This counter-hegemonic space is devoted to building a more complete civil war history that includes the fate of leftist victims and advances social justice in the present. The Museo de la Palabra y la Imagen (MUPI) archives documents, belongings, and oral histories of activists and promotes memory and identity building through community engagement and popular pedagogy programs inspired by Paulo Freire. Committed to a culture of peace, the MUPI has accomplished a lot with extremely limited resources, but it has had little structural impact given the neoliberal context that has ruled El Salvador and weakened social mobilizations. Through the analysis of this paradigmatic case of a grassroots counter-hegemonic initiative to maintain the memory and identity of Salvadorian guerrillas and other leftist activists in the face of the official silencing of their experiences, the author illustrates the fundamental role that artistic/cultural spaces have in the creation and preservation of collective memory.

These four chapters present a textured understanding of the use of artistic forms and cultural spaces as part of collective memory, truth, and justice processes. Instead of reifying a romanticized view of the arts or prioritizing the cultural domain over the political or legal, this research challenges readers to identify power relations within counter-hegemonic artistic and cultural creations as they inform memorialization and reconciliation.

Additional readings to complement this section can be found in *Latin American Perspectives* 43 (5) (see Feld, 2016; Vilches, 2016; Wilson, 2016; Guglielmucci and Scaraffuni Ribero, 2016) and 43 (6) (see Ulfe and Ríos, 2016; Márquez and Rozas-Krause, 2016).

10

The Murals of La Victoria

Imaginaries of Chilean Popular Resistance

Alexis Cortés
Translated by Margot Olavarria

Muralism is one of the most striking expressions in La Victoria, an emblematic working-class neighborhood in Santiago, Chile (Campos, 2009; Lemouneau, 2015). Murals precisely portray the events that have given La Victoria a central role in the histories of Chilean popular struggles: the land takeover in which it originated in 1957 and the resistance to the military dictatorship of Augusto Pinochet (1973–1989). Both experiences are founded in a story of neighborhood identity that recovers a universe of values associated with the struggle, organization, and solidarity of the popular world, in which the struggle against the dictatorship is understood as an extension of the original epic of the land occupation (Cortés, 2009). The objective of this article is to understand the role of muralism in the construction of the heroic memory that sustains La Victoria's identity.

Since its origin, La Victoria has radiated collective action repertoires for the *pobladores'* (shantytown dwellers') movement (Cortés, 2014). Its muralism is one of the devices that has developed with the most originality because of its contribution to the (re)construction of this working-class neighborhood's collective memory. To understand this role, it is necessary to situate it in the context of the sources and main forms of expression of Chilean muralism, and the first part of this article is dedicated to this task. Following this, I will analyze the relationship of muralism to the dictatorship, showing its consequences for the world of pobladores. Finally, I will assess the importance of muralism in postdictatorship Chile as a mechanism of what could be considered a politics of popular memory.

In preparing this article I have consulted various secondary sources that have helped me to reconstruct the graphic heritage of Chilean and La Victorian muralism. In addition, I have analyzed the murals produced during the commemoration of the fiftieth anniversary of the land occupation in October 2007 and complemented this research with in-depth interviews conducted in the winter of 2008 with 19 pobladores who had lived through the dictatorship in La Victoria.

Muralism appeared in La Victoria as a form of physical support for brief political messages that kept the flame of resistance alive after the coup d'état. Later this expression became increasingly complex, incorporating iconographic references that captured the visual memory of the time of Allende and consolidated its own imaginary associated with political condemnation of the dictatorship. The silence imposed by the military dictatorship was broken in the murals of La Victoria. Pobladores vented their feelings on these surfaces, depicting their daily lives and the abuses they suffered and calling for organization, resistance, and struggle. With the return of democracy, muralism made the neighborhood's historical memory graphic, generating a dialogue between the experience of the land occupation and the resistance to the military dictatorship. A discursive exchange has been generated by the murals that asserts a memory of the *popular* extending the life of the resistance movement in the context of democracy, the transition to which has led to the silencing of certain voices, among them those of the pobladores' movement (Oxhorn, 1994). As occurred during the dictatorship, the murals of La Victoria confront the mechanisms of amnesia set in motion by the official truths imposed by the compromised democratic transition.

CHILEAN MURALISM

Muralism in Chile dates back to the 1930s, when the teachings of Laureano Guevara (1889–1968) opened the way for it at the Escuela de Bellas Artes (Castillo, 2006). Undoubtedly, the Mexican muralism of Rivera, Siqueiros, and Orozco, among others, with its ideas of the socialization of art and the preeminence of collective as opposed to individual work and its large format, also strongly influenced the development of the first generations of Chilean muralists. In fact, the visit of the Mexican muralists Xavier Guerrero and David Alfaro Siqueiros in the 1940s was vitally important for its introduction of new techniques, the production of emblematic murals such as Siqueiros's *Muerte al invasor* (Death to the Invader) in the Escuela México, and the aesthetic-ideological influence of these artists (Bellange, 1995). The 1960s arrival of another Mexican muralist, Jorge González Camarena, left its artistic imprint on the Universidad de Concepción with his mural *Presencia de América Latina* (The Presence of Latin America), in which he "exalts the cultural, racial values of Latin American unity" (Echeverría, 2009: 159).

Although it is possible to count almost a dozen known muralists, it has been argued (see Zamorano and Cortés, 2007) that academic muralism in Chile was limited, despite the definitive movement from easels to walls, in that it never produced groups, generations, or schools that resulted in a pictorial tradition like the one that developed in Mexico. For the same reason, it has been suggested (see Rodríguez-Plaza, 2005) that academic muralism had little influence on the popular muralism that later developed through the joint work of visual artists with the muralist brigades created in the 1960s. However, members of these brigades recognize these artists as their most significant influences, and the brigades' encounters with the academic muralists were some of the most notable artistic conjunctures in recent Chilean history.

According to Marta Traba (2005), from 1960 to 1970 Latin American artists went from being apolitical to being eager to integrate their societies' problems with their aesthetic conceptions. At the same time, the artists suffered in their rebellion with their efforts to solidify their compromise: first, because of the possibility of becoming creators without a public, and second, because of their location on the social ladder: a minority cult group in the context of a multitude that is struggling to survive. In contrast, the intersection of artists with the muralist brigades offered a way of meeting artists' need to contribute to social change at the same time as making possible an encounter with the popular.

The creation of muralist brigades during electoral contests offered Chilean artists an opportunity to go into the streets to express their commitment to the political project that Salvador Allende represented and to paint with the people. Beginning in the mid-1960s, artists such as Luz Donoso, Carmen Johnson, Pedro Millar, Hernán Meschi, Osvaldo Reyes, and Nemesio Antúnez have moved into public space. And, once Allende and the Unidad Popular, with their Chilean path to socialism, were elected, artists set themselves the task of "creating a new culture," an "art for the people," and muralism offered support for that aspiration. "Now art is born from below, like flowers," Roberto Matta declared, arriving in Chile as it was constructing what Allende called a socialism "with the flavor of *empanadas* and red wine" (Grandón, 2011: 10). Matta himself, perhaps the most important painter in Chilean history, painted the mural *El primer gol del pueblo chileno* (The Chilean People's First Goal) with the Ramona Parra Brigade in the working-class district of La Granja. Jose Balmes, Gracia Barros, Guillermo Nuñez, and Francisco Brugnoli also collaborated with brigades to paint murals. Muralist brigades were making their particular contribution to what we could call a "Chilean path to socialist art," and the artistic field recognized its merit not only with collaborations but also by opening the doors to academia—for example, with the exhibit that the brigades presented at the Museo de Arte Contemporáneo, directed by Guillermo Nuñez, in 1971 and the invitation received by the Ramona Parra Brigade to participate in the Paris Biennale of 1973 (which the coup d'état prevented them from doing).

This intersection contributed to the dissemination of an aesthetic proposal that established a strong relationship between art and politics and, therefore, between the artist and society that helped to legitimize an aestheticization of politics and working-class daily life affirming the urban and political identity of the subaltern sectors of Chilean society in the 1970s (Rodríguez-Plaza, 2005). The trend highlighted the hegemony of thematic over aesthetic construction, giving priority to thematic discourse over the aesthetic contemplation of the pictorial experience (Zamorano and Cortés, 2007). Squads that specialized in the use of the mural as a carrier of political messages—brigades such as the Ramona Parra, linked to the Communist Youth, and the Socialist Youth's Elmo Catalán—began to emerge, first with the 1964 presidential campaign of Salvador Allende and later with the 1970 campaign that won him the presidency. At first this work was limited to the tracing of phrases, but it soon led to more elaborate productions signifying the appearance of a specific leftist political imaginary. In the words of one of the founders of the Ramona Parra Brigade, Alejandro "Mono" González (2000),

> A graphic image with pure, flat colors, outlined with thick black lines that modulated the light and shadow of the volume, would emerge in a city averse to color. This concept, in its environment, soon came to dominate the urban architecture when painting a mural took less than a few hours, given its monumental technique and application of color, its attitude, changing as events took place, and its human scale. The walls were simply the artistic support for the contingent.

For Ernesto Saúl (1972), the Chilean muralist brigades were an extremely original experience. Emerging as political publicity, they constructed their political proposal, making the street their own academy. The necessity to paint murals at night, since it was a prohibited activity, allowed the emergence of a fast, direct, and simple art form. For Saúl this was a new form of expression—anonymous and fleeting, for the messages changed with the rhythm of the events that determined their content—that opened the way for an authentic popular art. As the historian Carine Dalmas (2007) confirms, the murals of different brigades contributed to the construction of a socialist imaginary and therefore were historical documents that translated the political and ideological values of the Unidad Popular period and its political tensions.

The visual artist Ebe Bellange (1995: 43), writing about social muralism in the period of Allende's government (1970–1973), emphasized the transformation of mural painting into a form of collective expression in which different social actors (pobladores, students, artists) committed to the process of social change proposed by the Unidad Popular government participated and that assumed a hybrid style with multiple influences:

> Chilean muralism fuses, in simple pictorial expression, the compact and granitic force of Rivera, the dynamism of Siqueiros, the surrealism of Roberto Matta, and the monumentality of pre-Columbian art, all this united through universal symbols such as flowers, hands, faces, leaves, rocks, flags, silhouettes of factories, and stars that represented the worker, family, solidarity, peace, and collective work. The semantics of the visual elements is focused on the totality of the composition and not on the detail.

For her part, Romina Grandón (2011) establishes as direct influences on the muralist brigades the Chilean artists José Venturelli (1924–1988), engraver and muralist; Carlos Hermosilla (1905–1991), illustrator and engraver from Valparaíso; and Pedro Lobos (1919–1968), painter and engraver. One could say that Venturelli had a double influence on brigade muralism. A student of Laureano Guevara at the Universidad de Chile and assistant of David Alfaro Siqueiros in

Chillán, together with Alipio Jaramillo, he left traces of murals all over the world (in Cuba, China, and Europe) and participated in the Experimental Graphics Workshop in Havana (Mansilla, 2003).

Alejandro "Mono" González (2000) recognizes the multiple and heterogeneous origins of brigade muralism:

> They combined the contingent graphics of the silk-screened posters with Pop Art or Op Art designs that the hippies or the Cuban and Polish graphics had made fashionable with Mexican social muralism (with the huge dimensions and realism of Rivera and the features of Siqueiros), often used by Pedro Sepúlveda and his Pedro Lobos Brigade and others; the Cuban advertisements under Batista, which the revolution used on roadside billboards; the Legerism of Fernand Léger, with its workers on bicycles in pure colors outlined in black; the Beatles' *Yellow Submarine*, a lively drawing that some Ramona Parra Brigade murals recreated; and the font from the posters for the film *Spartacus* that the Elmo Catalán Brigade used as its typographic base. One borrows and with that develops a language of one's own, reinvented but used in a new context, another reality with its own concerns.

In addition, with the coup and the systematic erasure of the murals from the Allende period, the production of posters and album covers by designers such as the Larrea brothers (1970–1973) preserved the graphic language of the brigades and visually fueled muralism during the dictatorship in its role as repository of the graphic memory of that time (Castillo, 2006). How did this aesthetic project, emerging from the popular and from a socialist ideology, reinvent itself under the dictatorship? In particular, how was mural painting used in La Victoria to contribute to an epic poem of resistance and as a mechanism for managing the memory and forgetfulness aimed at giving meaning to the present? In other words, how are we to understand muralism as a politics of memory for pobladores?

THE DICTATORSHIP, LA VICTORIA, AND MURALISM

September 11, 1973, opened the way for the military dictatorship of General Augusto Pinochet and with it, a period of systematic violation of human rights in Chile. One of the social groups that suffered the strongest repression of the dictatorship was the pobladores, both selectively, with the death and disappearance of their main leaders, and collectively, with raids, sieges, mass detentions, kidnappings, and the destruction and confiscation of belongings (Comité de Memoria Histórica, 2005).

As Luis Errázuriz (2009: 137) points out, the military coup was not intended solely to exterminate the supporters of the Unidad Popular government but also proposed to dismantle Allende's sociopolitical cultural project, eradicating any type of political or symbolic reminiscence associated with this government. Errázuriz calls this phenomenon an "aesthetic coup": "The intervention of the armed forces was not just interpreted by the citizenry as a political and military event but additionally, in some measure, subjectified and/or perceived aesthetically and socially through the alterations and changes that took place in different areas of visual, aural, and spatial culture." In La Victoria, as in other working-class neighborhoods, physical extermination and the "aesthetic coup" converged. Because of its origin as a land occupation and its strong identification with leftist parties (especially the Communist Party), it was one of the places in which the repressive mechanisms of the regime were concentrated.

Despite the violence inflicted on them, these working-class territories represented the principal foci of resistance to the military dictatorship, mainly through popular protests (Cortés, 2013; Schneider, 1995). As Tomás Moulian (2002 [1998]) points out, it was at dusk that the most intense demonstrations of discontent unfolded in the working-class neighborhoods: *cacerolazos* (pot banging), the honking of car horns, the building of barricades, candlelight vigils, and so on. In this context, La Victoria was transformed into one of the most emblematic bastions of the opposition to Pinochet, and its images traveled the world as an example of the struggle for the recovery of democracy. A distinctive feature of La Victoria was that the dictatorship was framed in such a way as to bring continuity to the memory of the neighborhood's founders, for the experience of the land occupation gave the resistance meaning as an extension of the epic begun in 1957 (Cortés, 2011).

Muralism was one of the mechanisms of diffusion of the identity narrative mobilized to nurture a heroic memory of resistance to the dictatorship. In this period, the mural had various functions, first as the physical carrier of brief political messages aimed at keeping the flame of resistance burning and then as something more graphically complex, combining artistic expression with political condemnation. As a leader of the neighborhood at that time explains (Soledad, interview, La Victoria, 2008),

> The mural allowed us to communicate when a neighbor was killed, when someone was detained and disappeared, when a neighbor was imprisoned, how to make a Molotov cocktail, how to defend oneself—to tell what was happening at the time through a photo, a graphic image posted there, such as when they killed André Jarlán, its significance for us, such a symbolic thing, sacred for the whole La Victoria community.

During the years of dictatorship, the most common images on murals were closed fists, arms being liberated, the military in hostile attitudes, victims of the dictatorship, white doves crying or taking flight—all connected with a brigade imaginary linked to the Chilean left (Gajardo, 1986) and aimed at reclaiming a series of icons that were prohibited by the dictatorship for being linked with the political imaginary of the Allende period. The murals were also an opportunity to vent, a tool for breaking the silence to which the dictatorship had condemned them, a means of communication that allowed the expression of their daily lives, which had been placed under constant threat:

> [The murals] were an opportunity to express rage. One could draw, for example, a soldier firing, one who has you blindfolded, one who is attacking the neighborhood. So for me it was venting on the part of youth. (Sara, interview, La Victoria, 2008)

The murals began as a form of expression, of marking the wall with what you felt, what was bothering you. What you couldn't scream out loud, you started to draw on the walls, and, in fact, it became such a common custom that to this day murals continue to be painted in La Victoria. . . . Besides which, for example, you painted a mural, and the next day it appeared covered with black paint, and you went and painted over that and then painted again because you knew that that mural had touched a nerve for the soldiers. It was a way of making them aware of the things they were doing, that what they were doing was wrong. (Cathya, interview, La Victoria, 2008)

As these testimonials indicate, this artistic expression did not go unnoticed by the dictatorship. The authorities immediately deployed mechanisms aimed at neutralizing the condemnation that pobladores had emblazoned on the walls of La Victoria. An expression that is as intimately linked to the Allende period as this muralism was represented a direct challenge to the regime and therefore could not be permitted, the more so if we consider that a crusade of aesthetic whitewashing of the Unidad Popular's cultural legacy had already begun. What is most noteworthy about this is the pobladores' obstinacy in resisting attempts to erase their historical memory. As Blanca (interview, La Victoria, 2008) explained,

They would paint over the murals. We would get up—later we had whistles, my son here had a band, and he had a *trutruca* [a hornlike Mapuche instrument] and he played it at night, here in the street. Imagine at two in the morning the *trutruca* blasting while we slept with one eye open. . . . "They're coming to raid the neighborhood!" or "They're stealing!" or "They're coming to burn the neighborhood!" . . . And people would come out, and it turned out that they were painting over the murals and others were running away. The trucks would go on ahead and the guys would be left on foot. And it was with stones [that they threw to expel them], and they would leave behind the paint and everything they had brought with them.

La Victoria residents' attitude of not negotiating their sovereignty over the neighborhood is evident in their relationship with the murals and their reaffirmation of certain values considered part of "being from La Victoria": rebellion, struggle, and organization.

During this critical period, muralism can be understood, according to the metaphor used by Allen Feldman (2002: 236), as a "trauma-tropism." Analogous to the reactive curvature of a plant or organism as a result of a wound, muralism is an adaptive collective reaction to a violent situation that gives it new meaning:

Single communities and entire societies can reorganize their identities, histories, and projects around the curvature of chosen prior "historical" wounding, and this would be a socially constructed trauma-tropism. Trauma-tropism is a form of collective memory; more specifically, it is a framework and methodology by which a collectivity recalls the past and places it in a dynamic and formative relationship to the interpretation of the present.

This is because, for Feldman, both the critical memory and the mourning are powerful symbolic counterpoints against the violence of antidemocratic regimes or against other types of human rights violations and in the face of states' and violent organizations' strong capacity to generate amnesia and silence through fear, intimidation, shared trauma, disinformation, and distorted communication.

Muralism was consolidated in this period as a mechanism of memory that not only allowed for resistance to the dictatorship but also created conflict at the level of generating meaning. Murals in the neighborhoods have been recognized as a vehicle of memory that opposes official mechanisms, a powerful symbolic resource for disputing the interpretation of the recent past (Alcatruz, 2004). Muralism allowed for weaving an intergenerational vehicle that related the experience of the founders who took over the land with the residents who defended the neighborhood from the dictatorship. This continuity between these two critical moments in its imaginary is one of the more distinctive elements of La Victoria's narrative of identity. It is well summed up in a testimony from a founding poblador in Morales's *La Victoria de Chile*: "Now young people have followed our path. They are struggling for their rights, For me a mural that was painted in the neighborhood was very touching because it said, 'Our parents gave us the right to housing, let's give them the right to freedom'" (Morales, 1987: 7; figure 10.1).

Figure 10.1. The Ramona Parra Brigade's mural for the fiftieth anniversary of the occupation on the wall of the headquarters of the Communist Youth.
Source: Alexis Cortés

MURALISM IN THE POSTDICTATORSHIP PERIOD

Since the return to democracy, the main goal of muralism has been making graphic the historical memory of the neighborhood, emphasizing the origin myth of the land occupation, especially during the fiftieth anniversary of the event. Images alluding to the occupation are common, among them tents, Chilean flags, unpaved streets, and carts used for transport (figures 10.2 and 10.3), but it is also possible to find murals that commemorate the dictatorship. One mural (figure 10.4) represents an exercise in recursive muralism, for at its center there are two members of the Ramona Parra Brigade painting a mural. Below this image, there is a man with a crate of produce and a woman organizing the community kitchen, an image that recalls the daily life of the neighborhood and one of the most striking repertoires of collective action during the 1980s (Hardy, 1986). In the third part of the mural, there is a painted sign explaining the names of some of the streets.[1] At the right there is an expressionless Che Guevara behind the figure of a poblador with the Chilean flag, symbolizing the connection of the trajectory of La Victoria with the popular struggles of Latin America.

There are also murals combining the origin narrative with the experience of the dictatorship. In the mural of figure 10.5, to the left is a text that states, "What is confirmed is that only struggle and sacrifice grant what capitalist businessmen and their incumbent government deny. Nothing is given to the people," rejecting state

Figure 10.2.   La Garrapata Brigade's mural, showing pobladores with a cart.
Source: Alexis Cortés

Figure 10.3.   Fiftieth-anniversary mural: "50 Years, May They Not Have Been in Vain: History Is in Our Hands."
Source: Alexis Cortés

Figure 10.4.   Muralistas Acción Rebelde's fiftieth-anniversary mural, showing pobladores painting a mural (center) and organizing the community kitchen.
Source: Alexis Cortés

Figure 10.5.   Mural combining the origin narrative and the experience of the dictatorship.
Source: Alexis Cortés

policy and advocating the direct action that characterized the occupation, and a list of residents killed during the dictatorship. In the center of the mural is a sign that represents pobladores' resistance to the dictatorship and a great march in which Salvador Allende participates. To the right is the figure of the priest André Jarlán, killed by a stray police bullet during a protest in the neighborhood, who became a symbol of the struggle against the dictatorship (Verdugo, 1985).

For the sociologist María Emilia Tijoux (2009: 147), "the mural of resistance" in La Victoria appears to focus on artistically transforming history: "Murals of resistance intend to, by their repetition of the inscription, play down the inscription of defeat. Only by *inscribing* defeat in struggle, or death in hope of life, *the repetition is synonymous with new possibility.*" It is worth asking whether the pobladores' persistence on the occupied land could be considered a defeat. Similarly, although the dictatorship represented the defeat of the popular movement that the pobladores identified with and was resisted, often heroically and tragically, and portrayed in murals, this was not an aestheticization of history but a new claim of victory. While, as Tijoux says, the left builds its discourse on the loss of its project, it seems that for this population the project has never been defeated.

As Michel Wieviorka (2006) points out, a social movement that is limited to a representation of itself as a victim tends to go around in circles, unable to project itself beyond the past. Despite everything, a narrative that went beyond victimhood was created in La Victoria, which defined itself not in terms of the loss of anything but in terms of a heroic narrative and a definite set of values that it calls its own and represents in its murals.

Street murals are condemned to a certain transience, often disappearing to give way to others in the same material space. However, is it not precisely this impermanence that gives La Victoria's murals their unique character, their "aura" (Benjamin, 2003)? That aura is associated with their "here and now" character, but it also has a ritual function—connecting the present with the neighborhood's heroic past. Because of this, continuing with Walter Benjamin's metaphors, the murals of La Victoria have not only display value (it is important that they be seen) but also cult value (it is important that they exist). Muralism is at once ephemeral and permanent, for it is constantly being reconstructed and reinterpreted on the walls of the neighborhood. Its permanence comes from its constant reinscription of the present, distinguishing it from the aesthetics of deterioration, which chooses not to establish any set pattern (Traba, 2005). Street muralism has an impact but also carries meaning.

This transience may also give muralism efficacy as an exercise of memory. Murals have, however, survived through photography and postcards, and the local neighborhood council and the neighborhood office of the Department of Community Culture have taken on the task of constructing a registry of the murals painted in the neighborhood over time. At the same time, some murals have survived from the 1980s. There is one very characteristic mural that is renovated annually, with variations. It commemorates André Jarlán (figure 10.6). In its current version, painted by

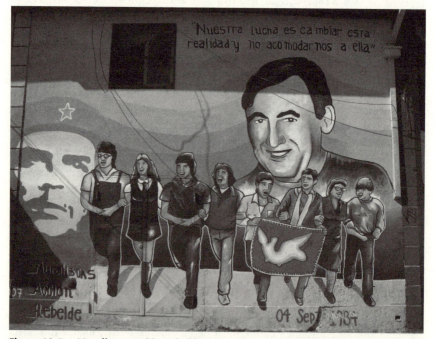

Figure 10.6.   Muralistas Acción Rebelde's mural commemorating André Jarlán and Che Guevara: "Our Struggle Is to Change This Reality, Not Accommodate to It."
Source: Alexis Cortés

the Rebellious Action Muralists, the priest's image is allied with that of Che Guevara, which could be interpreted as a search for continuity of the story of the neighborhood founded with a popular political project at the Latin American level.

A very interesting phenomenon that occurred with the murals that celebrate the 50 years since the occupation is a series of photographs included in the compositions. For Langland (2005: 88) and others, more than an embodiment of memory, these are instruments of the struggle for memory. Whether for its capacity to intervene in the relationship between the written word and truth, for its emotional impact, for its capacity to awaken feelings of personal connection with what is being represented, or for its materiality and reproducibility, "photography has become the quintessential symbol of the loss suffered in the Southern Cone countries and of the persistent struggles for memory that have developed since then." This idea alludes to a well-known photograph by Álvaro Hoppe that is crystallized in one of the murals, taken during the pobladores' march to the Metropolitan Cathedral to mourn Father André (Leiva, 2003: 42).

An element that will be not be explored here but merits mention is the appropriation of muralism by other local groups. The feminist group Mujeres Autónomas (Autonomous Women) employs murals to denounce violence against women, painting the houses of aggressors and converting muralism into an element that blurs the boundary between public and private (Tijoux, 2009). Similarly, soccer fans include muralism in their repertoire of mechanisms for identity affirmation and designation of territories. In the same way, the families of young people who die in tragic circumstances frequently record their deaths with murals. These elements show the capacity of muralism to be appropriated for different discursive purposes and serve as a means of communication for sectors that are deprived of other expressive mechanisms. In this sense, and despite the fact that muralism was originally transient, the repertoire of action of the popular sectors has persisted, constituting itself as one of the main components of the construction of subaltern memory.

For Nelly Richard (2001), the Chilean postdictatorship developed under the sign of reiterated operations of whitewashing the traces of the past, where history is replaced by the flat surface of consensus consecrated to forgetfulness and the suppression of any line of escape from the meaning imposed by the democratic transition. Consensus and the market have been jointly dedicated to a task of "de-narration of memory." Hence her interest in the "residual" as a basis for questioning of the discursive hierarchies of marginal and off-center positions (2001: 15):

> Remembrance needs surfaces for inscription to record on for the relationship to live between mark, texture, and event, releasing new meanings. Where are we to find these surfaces for inscription if transitional Chile has left the broken sequences of history without narrative articulations or story connections? If the ethical rigor of the demand for justice contained in the black-and-white portraits of the detained-disappeared is daily condemned by waves of advertising decidedly hostile to the drama of their meaning?

A response to this question may perhaps be found in muralism, which has served as a consecrator of popular iconographies and imaginaries, a powerful tool for identity construction for the subaltern, and graphic support for political projects intended to represent them. In the case of the Chilean shantytowns, in addition to functioning as a territorial marker, murals make possible a confluence between space and identity and aid in the construction of symbolic boundaries. Brugnoli (2002) also understands this; for him Mapuche muralism has allowed for the visual translation and reinterpretation of this people's identity in the urban context in terms of symbolic and territorial action that defines new forms of "writing" and "reading" both the city and identity itself.

Physical spaces and public spaces have been preferred environments in the struggle for memories and social meanings, particularly in Latin America, with its recent past of political repression and state terrorism (Jelin and Langland, 2003). The marking of places where state violence occurred during the dictatorships has involved the struggle of victims to construct memorials and monuments that recover the lost presence of those who suffered repression. Muralism has been a fundamental tool for subaltern sectors such as Chilean pobladores, victimized by the dictatorship and pushed aside once democracy returned, to convey a memory that rejects any official version of history that silences critical voices in the transition to democracy (Hiner, 2009).

CONCLUSION

The neighborhood identity of La Victoria, to whose reproduction muralism contributes, should not be seen as a mere myth that seeks to essentialize certain cultural traces or as a "vision of the defeated" or a "nostalgia of the anti-dictatorial symbol" (Richard, 2000). It is in constant reconstruction and reinscription in the present, and muralism is an enduring source of hybridization that feeds it (García Canclini, 2009). In its origin, muralism is a product of heterogeneous sedimentations, juxtapositions, and intersections of traditions and ruptures (from Pop Art to Mexican muralism) and continues to reinvent itself in its dialogues with graffiti and with new local meanings and appropriations. As Navarrete and López (2006) point out, graffiti as a form of spontaneous, ephemeral, impersonal, alternative, and clandestine communication has, through its potent urban artifacts, become active or passive resistance to ideological repression. In the case of La Victoria, muralism also functions as a mechanism of collective memory for the maintenance of the neighborhood's collective identity.

Chilean popular muralism, combining political art and the art of memory, has contributed to configuring an urban landscape with a tradition of condemnation of social inequality and violations of human rights, giving a characteristic imprint to Latin American cities (Gorelik, 2007). Although in some cases it has managed to enter the local artistic field, dissolving the boundaries that could have boxed it into being considered mere propaganda or handicraft, and obtained recognition for its aesthetic value—and the murals of Alejandro "Mono" González and the Ramona

Parra Brigade in the Gabriela Mistral Cultural Center or the Santiago Metro subway stations are proof of this—this has not been synonymous with institutionalization. It has no manifesto, for each mural is a manifesto in itself. Although it has distinctive styles, it continues to be fed by new visual proposals, inspirations, and commitments. It continues to propose an aestheticization of politics as the main strategy for inter-pellation and persuasion in everyday urban life.

The murals of La Victoria may be seen as a permanent source of creative renova-tion of muralism in general for their special role in the re-creation of the territorial identity of the neighborhood, proposing a particular signification of the relation-ship between the past, present, and future, acting as one of the main repertoires of pobladores' politics of memory. On the walls of this neighborhood, a new graphic, discursive style problematizes the present and even provides direction for the future. La Victoria muralism has contributed enormously to the iconographic and symbolic nurturance of the imaginary of resistance of the Chilean popular world.

NOTES

The original version of this essay was published in *Latin American Perspectives* 43(5): 62–77.

1. The toponymy of La Victoria is linked to the trajectory of the neighborhood and that of the social movement in Chile and the world. The name of the neighborhood itself refers to the triumph of the land occupation in the face of attempts by the authorities of the time to displace it, and the streets are named after persons prominent in the social struggle or events that are charged with meaning in popular memory.

11

Choreography of a Massacre

Memory and Performance in the Ayacucho Carnival

Renzo Aroni Sulca
Translated by Margot Olavarria

On August 14, 1985, an army patrol under the command of Second Lieutenant Telmo Hurtado massacred 69 indigenous residents, including women, elderly people, and children, of the Accomarca district, in the south-central Andean region of Ayacucho. The massacre was part of the war between the Communist Party of Peru–Shining Path and the state, which began in 1980 and intensified between 1983 and 1985, when towns such as Accomarca, Umaro, and Cayara, supposed bases of support for the Maoist guerrillas in the Pampas River valley, were targeted. The survivors of the massacre were displaced to Lima, where they formed the Asociación de Familiares Afectados de la Violencia Política en el Distrito de Accomarca (Association of Relatives Affected by the Political Violence in the District of Accomarca—AFAPVDA) and became members of the Asociación de Hijos del Distrito de Accomarca (Association of Children of the Accomarca District—AHIDA). Since 2011 they have been remembering the massacre and transmitting their memories to their children in the form of an annual Carnival performance. This article explores the history of the massacre and its choreographed and dramatic representation, seeking to understand why Accomarca migrants annually stage this traumatic experience and how they and their Lima-born children recall and represent that tragedy through art.

My perspective is influenced by my experience as a native Quechua speaker from Ayacucho, a survivor of the war, and an amateur musician, which allowed me to establish rapport with the former Accomarca residents without becoming a subjective constraint on my ethnographic approach. Following Potter and Romano (2012) and as part of this recent history myself, I attempted to show how the massacre was represented in the memories of living subjects. I interviewed the survivors and their children, many of whom are musicians, singers, and dancers in the Accomarca troupe. I observed their rehearsals before the Carnival competition and attended their performances in various contests. Their performance dates to 2011, the year that Accomarca residents demanded the extradition from the United States of retired Major Telmo Hurtado, the person most responsible for the massacre. It was well received from the beginning and continues to draw massive participation of migrants, survivors, and their Lima-born children.

As the Ayacuchan anthropologist Mariano Aronés (2003: 267) has pointed out, this event is remembered "with such clarity—'as if it were yesterday'—because of the number of victims, including children and elderly," and the massive campaign carried out by the press. I would add the pursuit of justice and reparations, by the victims' and survivors' relatives, which has recently led them to organize other forms of remembering. As Cynthia Milton (2014a) points out, atrocities of the past that are hard to express in words are often represented through artistic language, especially in postwar contexts. This article examines the artistic recording of traumatic experiences in the Ayacucho Carnival tradition in Lima, through which the survivors and their children demand justice and reparations from the state for human rights abuses. Carnival and its choreography and music are alternative modes of representation of violence in the experience of the survivors, victims, and their children—a way of publicizing their war experiences and denouncing their consequences.

MEMORY AND PERFORMANCE

From time immemorial, music and dance have been "partners of memory and history" (Taylor, 2011: 23). According to Richard Schechner (2011: 36–37), this involves the acting out of "restored conduct": "Performance means: never for the first time. It means: for the second to the nth time." In other words, performance is an effective device for memory because of its repetition, its constant practice, and its innovation. It brings memory of past events into the present. According to Taylor (2011: 13–14), performance works with two objects: archival memory and repertoire or corporal memory. Archival memory includes materials supposedly resistant to change, such as historical documents, literary texts, archeological remains, bones, videos, and records. The archive "functions through distance, both in temporal and spatial terms," and therefore, "for its capacity to persist through time, the archive is superior to living behavior." In contrast to the archival, which has more "outreach power," corporal memory "circulates through performances, gestures, oral narration, movement, dance, song; in addition, it requires presence. People participate in the production and reproduction of knowledge by 'being there' and being part of its diffusion." Therefore, "Corporal memory, always living, cannot be reproduced in the archive. What the archive possesses is a representation of the living act, through photos, videos, and production notes." Finally, "these two systems of transmission (the archival and the repertoire, among others, such as, for example, virtual or digital systems) transmit knowledge in different ways, sometimes operating simultaneously, sometimes in a conflictive manner."

The survivors of the Accomarca massacre constantly use archival records (research documents, mass graves, remains of burned housing, journalistic reports, visual records, etc.) not only to prove their case in court but also to write the script for the play about the massacre for the Carnival competition. At the same time, young people record this Carnival performance on film to preserve the memory and reconstruct the play in following years. Therefore, archival memory, survivors' oral narrative, and performance reproduce, transmit, and deepen knowledge of the facts in a democratic, popular, and independent way across generations.

THE MASSACRE IN LLOCCLLAPAMPA

According to the testimony of survivors and victims' relatives recorded by the Truth and Reconciliation Commission of 2002–2003, on the morning of the massacre people were carrying out their routine domestic work very early: feeding their livestock, watering the soil for planting, or doing their household chores. A helicopter full of soldiers landed on a plain called Pitecc, adjacent to Accomarca, and under the command of Second Lieutenant Telmo Hurtado the patrol deployed two groups to besiege the town as part of Operation Plan Huancayoc. They gathered the people of the hamlet of Lloccllapampa, forced them into a shack, gunned them down, burned their bodies, and then detonated a grenade so as to leave no remains. The Truth and Reconciliation Commission's final report (CVR, 2003: 159–160) states,

> Besides giving the order to shoot, Telmo Hurtado himself threw a grenade at the places where people were detained and caused the explosion and fire. After the murder, and in order to cover up their responsibility for the crime and give the appearance that it was an attack by the Shining Path, Telmo Hurtado ordered his soldiers to pick up all the elements or substances used.

The massacre occurred at the very beginning of the Alan García Pérez government (1985–1990), which was responsible for systematic human rights violations during the counterinsurgency campaign despite García's promise on taking office on July 28, 1985, "We will not fight barbarism with barbarism." A month after the massacre, military personnel returned to Accomarca to eliminate witnesses before the congressional investigative committee arrived in the town to verify the facts. Hurtado, labeled "the butcher of the Andes" by the press, justified his actions before Congress, stating (CVR, 2003: 162–163):

> You do not experience the acts of war as we who live here do. . . . One cannot trust a woman, an elderly person, or a child. . . . They begin to indoctrinate them at age two or three, by carrying things. . . . Little by little, by dint of deceit, punishment, they win them over to their cause.

Having confessed, he was tried in military court for abuse of authority and sentenced to only six years: then he was released and promoted and remained active until he was arrested in the United States in April 2007 for violating immigration laws while trying to obtain a U.S. visa.

In November 2010, during García's second term (2006–2011), the court tried 29 military personnel for the massacre in Accomarca. The victims' relatives demanded Hurtado's extradition for the trial, and he was finally extradited on July 24, 2011. Although at first Hurtado denied responsibility, in addition to admitting that "systematic extrajudicial executions were committed in the antiterrorist struggle by order of his superiors," he confessed to having assassinated 31 villagers. During the trial, he also reproached another military commander, Lieutenant Juan Rivera Rondón, for killing the other victims: "I am responsible for the death of 31 people; you must have killed the rest, you burned their homes. Both of us participated in the operation" (Mazzei, 2012). Peru's attorney general has requested that the major serve 25 years in prison for his crime.

The victims' organization has engaged in a long battle for truth and justice from the beginning. The massacre has been remembered in different ways over time, both in Accomarca and by the great majority of the displaced survivors and members of the AHIDA. One of these forms of remembrance is the dramatization of the massacre in the Ayacucho Carnival competition organized by the organizations of Ayacucho migrants in Lima. It is the figure of Telmo Hurtado that stands out in this representation, partly because the official memory produced by the state has repeatedly pointed to his individual responsibility. The victims' relatives have continued to condemn him because he was protected by the state with amnesties, mainly during the Alberto Fujimori autocracy, and because he very recently confessed his crimes while accusing others (Burt and Rodríguez, 2015).

THE ACCOMARCA MASSACRE IN THE AYACUCHO CARNIVAL

With the forced migration caused by political violence, artistic and cultural expressions have transcended their local and micro-regional space. Migrants carry them to their places of refuge, including the outskirts of Lima. In 1987, the Ayacucho federation organized the first Carnival competition, called Song for Life. In 1992, a competition involving all 11 provincial federations of Ayacucho called Vencedores de Ayacucho, sponsored by the departmental federation of provincial institutions, was launched in the Plaza de Acho (Huamaní, 2010: 22–23). By participating in the competition, migrants not only constructed spaces for socialization, strengthening ties of solidarity and reciprocity in a context of violence and displacement, but also reconfigured their memories and identities. While the forced migrants were far from home, the symbols, imaginaries, and artistic-cultural repertoires made their hometowns an integral part of the feelings that encouraged them to assemble (Aroni, 2013: 221).

In effect, this process provided symbolic and emotional support in overcoming pain and constructing human dignity. It also involved strategies for survival and alternative political views of the memory of the war that served to (1) counter the image of the Ayacuchan linked to violence and terrorism, (2) construct a communal space within the city as an emotional artistic-cultural refuge from the war and from social exclusion, and (3) subvert hierarchical and authoritarian social relations, for example, by resorting to a playful activity and using it to criticize power.

Chalena Vásquez and Abilio Vergara (1988) describe the Ayacucho Carnival competition as an "integral art" that

> constitutes a favorable socio-artistic medium for the realization of total art: music, dance, poetry, theater. Each area is presented, developing specific languages, interrelated with one another and interdependent. Each artistic area is not self-explanatory: one explains the other and vice versa. Because of this, the concept of "total art" should be understood as "integral art," for the simultaneous presence of artistic areas acquires a more complex and profound aesthetic meaning.

In the Ayacucho Carnival, we see the presentation of music score, choreography, and staging, all part of a complex performance for a massive audience of almost 10,000, mainly Ayacuchans and migrants from other Andean regions. Three or more musicians playing guitar, mandolin, flute, and drums perform the music for the troupe. (Electronic instruments are not allowed.) Two or three women singers accompany the musicians. According to the contest rules, musicians, singers, and dancers must be dressed in the typical dress of Accomarca. The musicians and singers collectively compose and arrange the songs.

Elsa Baldeón, 36, a motorcycle taxi driver and singer in the Accomarca troupe, was one of the massacre's survivors. Seven years old at the time, she witnessed the murder of her grandparents and her uncle, Alejandro Baldeón, from her hiding place: "They killed him in a horrible way: they cut his hand, both arms, his knees, feet, neck. They mutilated him" (interview, March 19, 2014). Speaking of the song "Killing in Accomarca," she said,

> When we sing this song we remember our relatives who lost their lives that year (women, children, and elderly). It is painful for us. We are seeking justice to this day. We are in court, but nothing is happening . . . so we will continue fighting. We compose the songs remembering what we saw in the massacre, asking those who witnessed it what happened.
>
> The song about the killings has a sorrowful musical score. These are the lyrics:

Taytamamallay wañukunkimá
Llaqtamasillay chinkarqunkimá
¿Imataq quchayki qampaqa karqa?
Bala puntampi wañullanaykipaq

Father-mother of mine, you have died
My neighbor you have disappeared
What fault did you have
For you to die from a bullet?

Inocentekunam wañurqunkichik
Mana quchayuqmi chinkarqunkichik
¿Imataq quchayki qampaqa karqa?
Rauraq ninapi rupallanaykipaq

Innocent people died
They disappeared through no fault of their own
What fault did you have
To die in the midst of the fire?

Chunka tawayuq agosto killa, mil novecientos ochenta y cinco
Chunka tawayuq agosto killa, mil novecientos ochenta y cinco
Manaquchayuq taytamamallay qunqayllamanta chinkarillarqa
Manaquchayuq llaqtamasillay qunqayllamanta wañukullarqa

On August 14, 1985
On August 14, 1985
My innocent father and mother suddenly disappeared
My innocent neighbor suddenly died

Chay tragediata yuyarillaspam llapanchurillan purillachkaniku
Chay tragediata yuyarillaspam llapanchurillan purillachkaniku
Justiciatam maskallaniku pirumanaya tarillanikuchu
Justiciatam maskallaniku pirumanaya tarinikuraqchu

Remembering this tragedy, we the children are walking
Remembering this tragedy, we the children are walking
We are seeking justice but have not found it
We are seeking justice but still have not found it

In analyzing the content of another song, "Little Accomarca Soldier," the ethnomusicologist Jonathan Ritter (2013: 1–2) describes songs like this, which narrate "local experiences and attitudes toward the war," as "testimonial songs." These songs commemorate not only the biographical experience of the singer-songwriters but also the collective experience of violence and its aftermath. For some Accomarca migrants, the songs are also a means of protest. "We express our protest through our songs; since we do not find justice, we think that we have to protest through our songs. That is what this song means," says Florian Palacios, 59, son of one of the Accomarca massacre victims (interview, March 15, 2014).

The figures and body movements of the dance in sync with the music make up the choreography of the dance (Mendoza, 2001), which is mainly performed by young people, children of the migrants and survivors of the war. It was rare to see young people dancing in the competition in the 1990s because they were still children. During those years it was mostly their parents and institutional authorities who participated. The young people of today can perform more energetically for the 20 or 30 minutes they are onstage. Accomarca migrants saw the need to transmit to their children not only the experience of the war but also the cultural and musical practices of their village, and for 10 years they have been training the children for the Carnival competition.

According to Florian, the majority of the dancers are young people born in Lima. They participate not only as dancers but also as leaders in organizing rehearsals and in the Carnival competition. For Florian, the feeling that unites these young people is the pain that their parents feel over the loss of their loved ones in the massacre. Florian is the youngest of six children. His mother died young of illness, and his father and his stepmother were killed in the August 14, 1985, massacre. When I interviewed him, he spoke about the "choreography of a massacre" as a form of play and protest in the Carnival: "For us, the 'choreography of the massacre' means . . . that we are outraged that we do not find justice after so many years. That's why we protest; we have fought for more than 29 years. And we do it with our music, singing, and choreography in the Carnival competition. Carnival is play and protest for us" (interview, March 15, 2014). He argues that through the physical and emotional movements of the dance one can rekindle a critical opinion about the human rights abuses committed, be it by the state or by the Shining Path. Memory, protest, and demands for justice stem from this.

On the afternoon of March 16, 2014, the musicians played the Carnival music from a section of the grandstand of the Plaza de Acho, and the young dancers entered. The first 7 minutes of the performance (of a total of 20 minutes) consisted of an imaginary representation of the town of Accomarca and its people, with their feasts and customs: the young people danced, forming geometric figures, and the adults and children re-created planting corn, cooking, collecting cactus fruits, caring for children, and so forth. Suddenly this routine was interrupted by the sound of gunshots coming from the stands. A military patrol entered the stage and gathered the people together, shooting at those who tried to escape. What followed was a drama re-creating the massacre that began with Quechua dialogue between two women, interpreted by singers:

Sofia: Mother Margarita, last night I had a nightmare. Now the army is coming across the Pitecc plain. Let's go hide! They can kill us!

Margarita: Why would they kill us without cause? If you stupidly want to hide, go ahead, but I am staying home.

Lieutenant Telmo Hurtado's order to his troops follows:

Telmo Hurtado: Attention, troops! Soldiers, gather all the people you can find for a meeting. All the people should be led to the tile shack, which is located in the place called Lloccllapampa. That is an order. Understood?

Troops: Yes, Lieutenant Hurtado.

The soldiers beat the villagers and drive them into the shack. Meanwhile, Hurtado and his subordinate encounter a couple of elderly villagers and ask them to accompany them to the meeting. The man answers in his native language, but Hurtado, who does not understand Quechua, interprets his response as an insult:

Telmo Hurtado: Hey, old man, come with me to the meeting in Lloccllapampa!

Elderly man: Wait for me, please. I am going to my house to leave my donkey and his load. Then I will go to the assembly.

Telmo Hurtado: What did you say to me? You have insulted me. Die, old terrorist [*terruco*]! [Bang!]

Elderly woman: Why have you killed my husband, you stupid soldier?

Telmo Hurtado: You die, too, old terrorist woman! [Bang!]

The word *terruco*, used for the sympathizers of Shining Path during the period of political violence, was later applied to other sectors of the population, including human rights defenders, as a stigma, especially during the Alberto Fujimori dictatorship in the 1990s.

In the following scene Hurtado heads to Lloccllapampa, where he orders his troops to kill and burn the bodies of the victims: "Soldiers, aim your weapons! Shoot! [Bang, bang, bang!] . . . Burn the house so that there is no trace" (figures 11.1 and 11.2).

Figure 11.1.   Staging the massacre in the Plaza de Acho, Lima, March 2014.
Source: Luz Enriquez Gerónimo

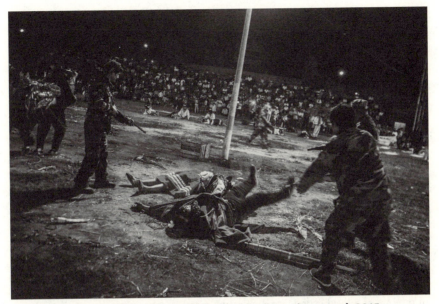

Figure 11.2.   Staging the massacre in Huachipa Stadium, Lima, March 2015.
Source: Diego Vargas Acuña

After the massacre, the lieutenant orders the withdrawal: "Attention, troops! Retreat! March!" The grieving survivors attend to the burial of the dead. The song "Saint Gregory," an old funeral song with prayers for the souls of the deceased that catechist peasants sing to this day, accompanies this scene. Finally, in a whimpering voice Abel Gómez, 30, leader of the Accomarca troupe, calls for justice in memory of the victims of the massacre:

> Our parents have died this way, our innocent countrymen. That is why we Accomarcans are still demanding justice. All of us demand justice in memory of all the dead and disappeared of Accomarca. For all of them, justice for Accomarca! Accomarca lives! Accomarca will not accept defeat!

After the competition I looked for Florian, who portrayed Hurtado in the play. He was dressed in a green uniform, boots, black ski mask, and dark glasses, and his face was painted green and black. How did he feel about playing the part of the military patrol leader who ordered the killing of his father and the other people of his village? He said,

> In the troupe I play the soldier every year, because I know very well how it happened. In addition, I lead the Accomarca victims' association, and I am heading the lawsuit against the military responsible for the massacre. I know enough about how it is going forward, which is what is happening. I, more than anything as an affected person, take on the name of Telmo Hurtado. I play that role to let the public know how the military entered my village, slaughtered the people, sexually abused the women, and burned them alive.

Finally, tearful, he vented his feelings about the impact of playing this role: "I get somewhat annoyed; it's not that I feel liberated. I would feel liberated if justice were done to those responsible for these crimes. When justice punishes all the perpetrators, then I will feel somewhat liberated—but not even then, because our parents no longer exist" (interview, March 15, 2014). While he feels outraged and impotent, at the same time he feels satisfied with himself because he is forcefully protesting and demanding justice for what happened in his village. The performers attempt to represent what occurred in the most realistic way possible to provoke reflection in the audience.

In general, the audience, mainly Ayacuchan migrants, applauded and praised the performance. Some spectators remembered and murmured about their experiences during the war, while others took refuge in silence. Of course, there were also whistles (boos), but rather than discrediting the play they reflected the rivalry between finalist troupes. On this occasion, the troupe from Accomarca won the provincial competition and went on to represent the province in the 2014 Vencedores de Ayacucho contest.

INTERGENERATIONAL MEMORY

In the case of a lived experience such as the massacre, the survivors experience lapses of memory and transmit their experiences to the next generation. Socially and culturally sharing a traumatic experience constructs connections with the generation that has not experienced the process firsthand. This can be called the "communication of memory," and it feeds the imagination and creativity of the "postmemory generation" (Hirsch, 2012). The members of this generation "recognize that the memory received is different from the memory of witnesses and contemporary participants" (Hirsch, 2012: 3). Generational distance establishes a mediated connection with the past wherein a transgenerational narrative is shaped by some traumatic event and communicated through "bodily symptoms," "objects of memory," written text, and oral narratives. This connection is consolidated by the creative and imaginative drive that the past generates in the generations that have not experienced the event firsthand.

Many years of family and community effort in staging the massacre have created an almost generational sensibility and awareness not only of what happened in Accomarca but also of the two decades of Peru's political violence. As the choreography instructor, Juan Avendaño, 50, pointed out, "Since they never experienced this massacre, have not suffered through it, it has been difficult to reach them, but not impossible; today they begin to ask 'Why?' It is necessary that our youth and our children become aware of one of the tragic events that occurred there" (interview, March 16, 2014).

At the same time, there are certain fluid, shared spaces that allow for transgenerational interaction. One is the domestic space, where the most intimate communications flow between parents and children. Another is the communal-institutional space—the AHIDA, where discussion and organization of social and cultural activities for Accomarca migrants takes place. Still another is the public space of the Carnival, with its play and protest. In the communal-institutional space, there is a close relationship between the domestic and the public. The site is much more complex than a collective property, because it weaves a social, affective, and historical relationship. It ensures that private memory becomes public through the multiple sociopolitical, artistic, and cultural activities it organizes. What is said in the domestic space and is difficult to speak about in the public space can be said in the confidence and solidarity of the communal space. Even when these memories are contentious, the communal space allows for negotiation to present a single narrative in the public space. For example, among the victims' and survivors' families, public condemnation of the massacre's legacy is routine. The migrants and the generations of youth that have not lived through the event participate in the play in solidarity but without the same intensity; they are more interested in developing other themes, such as income, education, and sociocultural practices for strengthening the family and the institution. Their agenda is not, however, opposed to that of the victims and survivors, who prioritize issues of human rights, prosecution of the perpetrators, and historical memory. The AHIDA, as the lead organization, incorporates its social bases' demands and represents them in the public space, where the audience is not only the Accomarca community, but also Ayacucho and Lima residents.

In this way, as a social node, the local brings in not only the displaced and survivors from Accomarca in the capital but also the new generations. It is here that the various generations re-create and imagine the urban representation of the social and festive life of their hometown. Similarly, there is a certain continuity in resignifying cultural and musical practices about the lived experiences of their parents in Accomarca. The young people and the children know and participate in the production of patron saints' feasts and Carnival competitions, and there they socialize—forming social ties and even finding marriage partners, becoming self-aware about assuming, practicing, and maintaining the cultural legacy of their parents, and organizing intergenerational cultural and sporting events for those born in Accomarca and Lima.

One of these young people is Abel Gómez, leader of the Accomarca troupe for the past five years. Although he was born in Accomarca, he migrated to Lima just after graduating from high school to work as a blacksmith. When he organized the young people to participate in the Carnival competition in 2011, he said, "Many young people didn't even know about Accomarca, but as children of Accomarca migrants they began to participate, and many of them even met each other there, in the rehearsals and competitions. The youth are more united now. That's also an incentive, a human resource. They are now not only youth or children; they come together" (interview, March 19, 2014).

However, beyond the family and the institutional space, the Carnival space explicitly offers young people and children the possibility of receiving cultural and historical knowledge from their parents. This intergenerational interaction takes place not only through bilingual spoken language (Quechua-Spanish) but also through bodily expression such as dance and music, as a device of memory and identity that renews the collective experience of violence and its consequences in the Accomarca community. In this sense, the Carnival space is also an effective site for the transmission of trauma. In the Carnival, the traumatic experience is transported to other public spaces such as the Ayacucho Carnival in the Plaza de Acho. Other publics exist there—Andeans from various regions and people from Lima. In one way or another, the representation of the massacre in the Carnival reactivates the spectators' memories, for many of them were also victims or survivors of armed conflict. They comment on what they are seeing in relation to what they have lived through in their villages. In this way they also share their experiences and respond to their children's anxieties about the remembered and experienced scenes of armed conflict.

CONCLUSION

In post-conflict Peru, the function of the memory of violence goes far beyond oral testimony, construction of memorials, and commemorations of the recent past. Violence and its scars are expressed through a diversity of cultural productions contextualized in historical and political processes often in the pursuit of truth and justice. Peasants' memory of the massacre and its traces is reflected in grassroots social organizations and activities that include victims and migrants in everyday life and in spaces of cultural production such as the troupe competitions. By focusing on the social and cultural frameworks of the memory of victims and survivors, we can go beyond the global humanitarian "never again" discourse and its memorials and museums. Musical and theatrical performance is an important resource for analyzing how social and historical remembrances of armed conflict find collective creative expression in different generations and societies in post-conflict contexts such as that of Peru.

The remembrance of the recent past flows through music and dance, which involve the body itself as the raw material of corporal and social memory. While the song lyrics condense the narrative of the lived and remembered event, what brings consistency and density to that narrative is the dance and the drama, in which a tragic history is renewed and re-created. The music allows interaction that evokes memory; the dance involves a more sensitive disposition of the body, inviting intergenerational participation-solidarity-confidence to dignify the lives of the dead and the living, to remember and protest.

Finally, with the performance of this massacre in the Ayacucho Carnival competition Accomarcans evoke their memories of the past as a guide for the construction of a better future. They call into question our recent past through the atrocious experience they have lived through, exposed in a Carnival performance by survivors, victims' relatives, and, most of all, their children. They seek to transmit those experiences through intergenerational interaction in the time and space of the Carnival. Denied recognition as witnesses, survivors, and victims of the massacre while impunity prevails for its perpetrators, they seek justice in this shared initiative.

The original version of this essay was published in *Latin American Perspectives* 43 (6): 41–53.

12

Reckoning with Dictatorship in Brazil

The Double-Edged Role of Artistic-Cultural Production

Nina Schneider and Rebecca J. Atencio

In 1986, a little over a year after their military stepped aside for a civilian president, Brazilians were riveted by a telenovela that dramatized the contemporary political moment. Titled *Roda de Fogo* (Wheel of Fire), the drama featured a cast of villains from the military as well as the economic and political elite. One of the subplots revolved around a young woman named Maura, a former political prisoner struggling with whether to confront the man who had tortured her years earlier. *Roda de Fogo* made history by discussing political torture before a mass audience, many of whose members first became aware of the issue by watching the hit telenovela. It also invited spectators to extrapolate Maura's dilemma to that of their country: should Brazil, like Maura, confront police and military torturers? *Roda de Fogo* aired in the context of Brazil's political transition, a time when the state took virtually no steps to reckon with the dictatorial past, thus exemplifying how artistic-cultural production can help fill the void by raising questions that were not being discussed in the political and legal domains. The case of *Roda de Fogo* illustrates the central concern of this article: what role has artistic-cultural production played in Brazil's history of reckoning with the military past?

Latin Americanist scholars in the field of memory studies have increasingly focused on the role of artistic-cultural production—works of literary fiction and testimony, film, plays, television shows, art installations, and memory sites—in the remembrance of authoritarian or conflictual pasts.[1] For the sociologist Elizabeth Jelin (2003: 25), cultural goods are an important manifestation of or vehicle for memory work (what she calls the "labors of memory"), for through them "social agents . . . try to 'materialize' the meanings of the past." Steve Stern (2010: xxii) emphasizes that memory studies allow us to research the "underexplored 'hearts and minds'"— people's emotions. He suggests conceiving of memory as an interactive, dynamic struggle allowing us to transcend the abstract dichotomy between a top-down, elite perspective and a "bottom-up perspective that sees its obverse" (xxiii). In a similar vein, other scholars have called attention to the fact that artistic-cultural works may constitute a necessary alternative or complement to official truth-telling projects such as truth commissions, particularly in Argentina, Chile, and Peru (Atencio, 2014; Bilbija and Payne, 2005; Kaiser, 2002; Milton, 2007; 2014a; Rosenberg, 2010; Stern, 2010; 2012).

While a full elaboration is beyond the scope of this article, we argue that the relationship between "transitional justice" and "collective memory" remains under-theorized, in particular with regard to artistic-cultural productions. "Transitional justice" refers to a larger set of official accountability measures including prosecutions, truth commissions, reparations, forms of memorialization, and education.[2] While the complex concept of "collective memory" has the benefit of focusing on culture as the social and cultural everyday practices of society as a whole—the state and civil society—it tends to be rather vague. The cultural historian Peter Burke (2004: 58), for one, observes that it remains unclear when it is justifiable to generalize from personal memory to a collective or national memory. Most scholars concur that multiple memories coexist. There is less consensus, however, as to how to evaluate the relative influence of a given interpretation of the past or the relationship between competing memories. Steve Stern (2010: xxix) suggests historicizing memory struggles and their dynamic nature. He contends that memory studies often fail to take into account the "wider political, economic, and cultural contexts" (xxii). Whereas most works analyzing artistic-cultural productions after mass violence tend to relate exclusively to the collective memory approach, assuming it as an abstract given regardless of the historical evidence and political context, reckoning histories or so-called transitional justice accounts tend to ignore the role of culture and focus narrowly on legal and political initiatives. In sum, publications that connect the role of art, "collective memory," and the reckoning history (or transitional justice) process are lacking. Myopic scholarly analyses—focusing narrowly on either the political reckoning history or artistic-cultural artifacts—are insufficient to grasp the complex dynamics experienced in postauthoritarian countries. While Stern and other scholars have called for moving beyond top-down binaries, this article combines disciplinary approaches in order to transcend the boundaries between artistic-cultural work, history, and politics.

A look at the way memory of dictatorship has been constructed through artistic-cultural production is particularly illuminating in the Brazilian case. Whereas a focus on official reckoning mechanisms alone might lead one to conclude that Brazil lacked a culture of memory until recently, broadening the perspective to include artistic-cultural production reveals a long record of grappling with the dictatorship and its legacies. For three decades, artistic-cultural productions—along with the central protagonists of the memory struggle, the families of the dead and disappeared as well as human rights groups—has helped keep the memory question alive in Brazil while the state failed to address it.

Postauthoritarian Brazil's reckoning history has received considerably less attention than that of other Latin American countries. The scholarship available focuses on the roles of the Brazilian state and its official responses (particularly in the form of reparations and, more recently, the National Truth Commission) and of international law (the Inter-American Court of Human Rights). In this article, we focus on the critical role that artistic-cultural production plays in reckoning with Brazil's authoritarian past. The first section explains that Brazil's protracted and complex political transition was fundamentally shaped by the 1979 Amnesty Law, which was the product of widespread popular mobilization, on the one hand, and tight control from those parts of the military regime negotiating a highly constrained process of political opening, on the other. The second section summarizes Brazil's comparatively late and less radical posttransition accountability measures, including an extensive, if frequently criticized, reparations program and various state-sponsored artistic-cultural memory projects from 2006 on. The third section then contrasts these official responses with other, cultural ones, providing an overview of the construction of memory in best-selling testimonies as well as in telenovelas and fiction film.

Drawing on the analysis of these three means of cultural production, the fourth section presents what we call the "double-edged role of artistic-cultural production." This discussion leads us to conclude that while it may not be possible to draw causal connections between artistic-cultural production and official truth-seeking, compensation, and legal reckonings with dictatorship, culture deserves greater attention in reckoning histories or so-called "transitional justice studies" (see, e.g., Rush and Simic, 2014). Conversely, cultural memory studies profit from more attention to the historical context and the sociopolitical interests that shape the struggle over memory.

The empirical facts in Brazil are—and this is what is striking and what is the core point of the article—that the cultural production on reckoning was early and pervasive at a time when political measures initiated by the state were absent. In the Brazilian process these measures were not complementary at first; the Truth Commission was established only in 2012, and none of the Brazilian perpetrators has ever been punished. A conservative approach that takes into account only official reckonings might lead one to believe that Brazil has lacked a culture of memory, at least until recently. Widening the scope to include cultural production, however, provides a different view, one of a long tradition of reckoning with the dictatorship.

FROM DICTATORSHIP TO DEMOCRACY

While cross-country comparisons are complex, the history of political transition in Brazil differed from that of other Latin American countries in terms of both time span and nature. Brazil's transition was long and gradual, initiated in 1974 by the military president Ernesto Geisel's policy of *distensão* (literally "depressurization" [Montero, 2005: 20]). Scholars diverge about the end date of the dictatorial period, whether it was 1985, when the first civilian but not directly elected president and former regime collaborator José Sarney took office; or 1988, with the Brazilian Constitution; or 1989, with the first direct presidential election. Some even regard the transition as incomplete (Teles and Safatle, 2010). The generals engineered a very controlled democratization process (Gaspari, 2004), which, however, was partly a victory of massive popular mobilization (the socially and ideologically broad amnesty movement) as the regime's popularity declined in the 1970s (Alves, 1985; Lamounier, 1980: 7).

In Brazil, the transition to democracy and subsequent memory politics were hugely influenced by the amnesty question. In 1979, six years before the formal return to democracy, the Brazilian regime promulgated an amnesty law that covered not only the members of its own security forces but also parts of the opposition. Political prisoners who had been involved in the armed struggle, participated in attacks on other persons' lives ("blood crimes"), or been charged with establishing illegal parties were excluded, however. This was done grudgingly after months of nationwide mobilizations by large sectors of civil society demanding amnesty for all political exiles and prisoners. At the time Brazil was still under military rule and memories of state violence were still fresh. For this reason, the Brazilian amnesty could be—and was—promoted as a victory for civil society (even as human rights groups saw it as a defeat) and a gesture of national conciliation. Even though at its height the national amnesty campaign and some influential political exiles had demanded punishment—not amnesty—for state torturers, much of civil society desired reconciliation and ultimately chose to celebrate the blanket amnesty rather than to mobilize against it.[3] Even some of those who spoke out most passionately about the need for punishment in the months preceding the law's passage (e.g., Fernando Gabeira [Atencio, 2015]) fell silent on the subject almost immediately thereafter.

After the passage of the Amnesty Law, the demands for truth and justice that had formerly animated parts of the amnesty movement (Fico, 2009: 1; Reis Filho, 2004: 46) were overshadowed by more future-oriented concerns. The formerly massive popular mobilization was redirected into other political projects and forms of organization. New parties were being formed (including the Partido dos Trabalhadores [Workers' Party—PT]), Brazilians took to the streets in 1984 to demand—unsuccessfully—direct presidential elections, and throughout the 1980s a variety of civil society movements emerged, including the women's, gay, and black movements, along with environmentalist groups. Civil society and the left reorganized, but reckoning with the past was no longer a key demand for either. One might have expected the left—reconstituted in the PT, the Partido da Social Democracia Brasileira (Brazilian Social Democracy Party—PSBD), and other parties—to push for truth and justice, but instead it "joined the game of 'let's forget' dictated by the old right" (Seligmann-Silva, 2010: 60). According to Seligmann-Silva, 1985 represents less the end of the dictatorial period than the collapse of the left: "I wouldn't say that in 1985 there occurred a pact between the right and left. What happened was more serious: it was a kind of drawing together and almost fusion of the two."

OFFICIAL RECKONINGS WITH DICTATORSHIP IN BRAZIL

Overall, the Brazilian state took accountability measures in a slow and gradual process lacking a clear point of rupture with the authoritarian past (for an overview on the reckoning history in Brazil consult Barahona de Brito, Gonzalez-Enriquez, and Aguila, 2001: 119–161; Mezarobba, 2007; Payne, Abrão, and Torelly, 2011; Pereira, 2005). Until 2006, most state initiatives deliberately targeted individual victims rather than Brazilian society as a whole, and, as Pereira (2005: 163) has noted, governments (the Lula government being no exception) seemed afraid to publicize memory-making initiatives. The lack of "transparency" has also been a key point raised by critics of the National Truth Commission (*O Estado de São Paulo*, June 14, 2013). Brazil has so far resisted (especially international) pressure to hold torturers criminally accountable.[4] In lieu of criminal trials, Brazil initially sought to redress dictatorship-era human rights crimes through a two-step reparations program (1995/2002) and official truth-seeking and memory initiatives including the recent National Truth Commission. However, these initiatives did not come easily but resulted from the families' of victims and their supporters' decade-long struggle (Coimbra, 2001: 11–19; Mezarobba, 2007; Santos, Teles, and Teles, 2009: 472–495; SEDH, 2007: 32–33).

In 1995 the state passed the Law of the Disappeared, which established reparations for the families of the killed and disappeared; the burden of proof, however, still fell upon the families. In 2002, a second program known as the Amnesty Commission (Law No. 10.559/02) extended reparations from those affected by death and disappearance to survivors of torture and dismissal not covered by the 1995 law, a much larger group of victims (Abrão and Torelly, 2011a: 443–485; 2011b: 217; Ministério da Justiça, 2008: 39–51; 2009: 110–149). In contrast to its predecessor reparations commission, the Amnesty Commission itself investigates complaints.[5] While the president of the Amnesty Commission, Paulo Abrão, and his colleague, Marcelo Torelly (2011b: 444), regard the reparations program as the "linchpin of transitional justice" in Brazil and a starting point for further accountability measures, Glenda Mezarobba (2007: 307–308, 322, 359) has criticized it for its unfair payment procedure and the individualization of the victims, disconnecting them from society as if compensation were a private rather than a public gesture. The very name—"Amnesty," instead of "Reparations," Commission—associates reparations payments with the conciliatory framework set by the 1979 amnesty. Since 2007, however, the Amnesty Commission has tried to change the meaning of "amnesty" from "impunity and forgetting" to "freedom and reparations" and "reparations and memory" (Abrão, 2012; Abrão and Torelly, 2012). Under Abrão's leadership it has, furthermore, developed into the primary official institution to mobilize for prosecutions (Abrão, 2012: 30; Schneider, 2014).

Truth-seeking measures prior to the National Truth Commission included a vital commission with limited personal and financial support to investigate the past human rights crimes—the Comissão Especial sobre Mortos e Desaparecidos Políticos (Special Commission on the Dead and Disappeared Political Activists), also established by the 1995 Law of the Disappeared. While the military regime first denied deaths and disappearances altogether and only later acknowledged some cases as "excesses" rather than a systematic state practice (Green, 2010: 209, 219–222), the 1995 law officially acknowledged murder victims, and President Fernando Henrique Cardoso issued an official apology, albeit a timid one (Schneider, 2014).

The Brazilian state abandoned its "politics of silence" only in 2006, when the federal government started honoring the left-wing opposition groups that bore the brunt of human rights crimes. During the second Lula administration, Paulo Vannuchi, then human rights minister, launched two major culture-oriented initiatives: The Right to Memory and Truth (2006) and Memories Revealed (2009), projects that encompassed educational programs, monuments, museum exhibits, and official reports. The most important of these official reports from the mid-2000s is that of the Special Commission of the Dead and Disappeared, titled *O direito à memória e à verdade* (for analysis see Atencio, 2014). The state's new politics of memory—another important shift in Brazil's reckoning process, which for the first time addressed society as a whole, making torture a public rather than a private concern (Schneider, 2011a)—clearly operated on the cultural level: instead of pressuring for prosecutions, it championed the remembrance of victims.[6] Since 2008, the previously mentioned Amnesty Commission has also fostered public memory work, partly in response to the criticism leveled at the reparations procedures and their effect of privatizing rather than publicizing the question of torture. Abrão began bringing the amnesty sessions to different Brazilian cities and making them public by means of what are called "amnesty caravans," often accompanied by artistic-cultural events related to the dictatorship (Abrão and Torelly, 2011b: 465; Ministério da Justiça, 2009: 110–149). The Amnesty Commission has furthermore published numerous reports and books, kick-started renewed discussions about impunity, and been a driving force behind the so-called Amnesty Memorial currently under construction in Belo Horizonte (Peixoto, 2013).

Many important accountability measures, however, remain to be developed, among them institutional reforms within the military, the police, and the judiciary, and criminal charges against the perpetrators. Whenever individual statesmen have attempted to move beyond reparations, truth-seeking, and memory initiatives and to challenge impunity, they have ultimately faced defeat. Vannuchi, for example, encountered major resistance when he demanded that the 1979 Amnesty Law be reconsidered and when creating the National Truth Commission (Schneider, 2011c: 164–170). The fate of Vannuchi's more ambitious attempts at radical steps demonstrates that bold legal-political steps have so far been opposed by powerful sectors within the state, including the armed forces, the Supreme Court, and the Defense and Foreign Ministries.

Not all the blame rests with the state, however. The lack of public mobilization for the clarification and punishment of past torture has also been a decisive factor, since Brazil lacks a movement with broad appeal similar to the Madres de Plaza de Mayo in Argentina (Abrão and Torelly, 2011a: 227, 237–239, 244; Pereira, 2000: 224). Empirical evidence from Latin America has shown that transitional justice processes cannot be reduced to one-directional, top-down policies and that civil society plays a key role in addressing the authoritarian past (Jelin, 2007; Stern, 2006; 2010). But what if neither the state nor the larger public takes an interest in addressing the military past through legal-political mechanisms, as until 2012, when the National Truth Commission started its work, has been the case of Brazil? Before 2006 the state failed to launch official memory campaigns (Schneider, 2011a), and memory work in Brazil has been largely reduced to the private realm, that of marginalized victims and their families supported by the Catholic Church, lawyers, and local and global human rights activists (Coimbra, 2001: 12; Green, 2010; Pinheiro, 1997; Santos, Teles, and Teles, 2009). Besides the governments' silencing of torture prior to 2006 and a widespread public approval of police aggression,[7] some scholars note the public perception that the repression was less intense relative to that of its South American neighbors and that in the eyes of ordinary Brazilians the violence of the present is more pressing than that of the past; in 1997 police killings in São Paulo amounted to triple the victims under the whole dictatorship (Brito, 2001: 119–160; Pereira, 2000: 233–234, 228).

Still, it would be misleading simply to interpret public lack of interest in torture and punishment as a benevolent attitude toward the military regime. The larger public's lack of enthusiasm for and mobilization around the clarification of violence and punishment contains many shades of grey, as a look at the cultural arena reveals.[8] The proliferation and popularity of artistic-cultural works, such as published testimonies as well as telenovelas and films that engage the dictatorial period point, to a larger phenomenon in Brazil: a tendency to address past human rights crimes outside the institutional sphere.[9]

CULTURAL RECKONINGS WITH DICTATORSHIP IN BRAZIL

A conventional approach that takes into account only official reckonings such as the one outlined above might lead one to believe that Brazil has lacked a culture of memory, at least until recently. Widening the scope to include cultural production, however, provides a different view: one of a long tradition of reckoning with the dictatorship. Immediately after the passage of the Amnesty Law, former guerrillas began publishing their testimonies of armed struggle. The first and most influential were Fernando Gabeira's *O que é isso, companheiro?* (What's Going On Here, Comrade?, 1979) and Alfredo Sirkis's *Os carbonários* (The Carbonari, 1980). These survivors of dictatorship, who had experienced armed struggle and often imprisonment, torture, and exile, told the side of the story that had been suppressed during many years of censorship of the newspapers, television, and radio. Gabeira, a member of MR-8 (October 8 Revolutionary Movement), provided the first inside look at the kidnapping of U.S. Ambassador Charles Elbrick, arguably the most successful guerrilla operation and the only one to gain popular sympathy; he also recounted the several months he spent in political prisons, including the torture he endured and witnessed. Sirkis, whose book came out six months later, recounted his own trajectory from high school student activist to member of the Vanguarda Popular Revolucionária (Revolutionary Popular Vanguard—VPR). He had participated in not one but two successful revolutionary kidnapping operations involving foreign dignitaries (the Swiss and German ambassadors). His account became a cult classic on how to become a revolutionary.

Both books were huge hits, attaining every measure of commercial and critical success. At a time when the book-publishing industry was suffering a downturn, they flew off the shelves, requiring multiple reprintings. Each occupied the best-seller list for months and eventually won the prestigious Jabuti literary prize in the "best autobiography/memoir" category. Gabeira's, the more popular of the two, sold 200,000 copies in the first five years after it was launched. By comparison, the Archdiocese of São Paulo's unauthorized report on torture, *Brasil Nunca Mais* (one of the best-selling books of all time), sold 200,000 in two years. *Companheiro* did not achieve the same readership, but its success was considerable nevertheless. Together with dozens of similar accounts, they laid the foundation of the left's memory of the armed struggle and the dictatorship's repression (Atencio, 2014; Martins Filho, 2009).[10] The success of the two works and the flood of testimonies that followed belie the notion that memory work was entirely absent in the wake of the Amnesty Law.

Even more far-reaching than published testimonies are telenovelas and film. After 1985, full-length novelas and shorter miniseries gradually began to revisit the period. The 1986 novela *Roda de Fogo*, described earlier, was the first to address torture. Yet, significantly, the novela did not dramatize the period itself. That "first" fell to *Anos Rebeldes* (Rebel Years) in 1992. That miniseries, inspired partly by Sirkis's testimony, presents a typical story of star-crossed lovers: the idealist João is caught between his calling in radical politics and his passion for Maria Lúcia, an individualist who dreams of a traditional middle-class life. The plot follows the lives of the two romantic leads and their group of high school friends from 1964 to 1979, reimagining key historic moments such as the coup, the student protests of 1968 and the subsequent hardening of the regime in December of that year, and the return of political exiles to Brazil with the 1979 Amnesty Law. *Anos Rebeldes* pioneered the dramatization of political violence and censorship on Brazilian television, although it simultaneously played down the brutality of the security forces.[11] The result was a hit: the program drew 30 million viewers during its initial broadcast and inspired spin-off products including an LP of its soundtrack and a paperback book. The miniseries, which features scenes of protest marches from the 1960s, has been rerun several times on Globo's regular and paid channels—most recently in May and June of 2013, not coincidentally while protests swelled around the issues of rising public transportation costs, endemic corruption, and other injustices.[12]

Anos Rebeldes broke the taboo and opened the floodgates for discussing the dictatorship on prime-time television (Atencio, 2011). Globo followed up with several other novelas and miniseries, as well as other kinds of programming. One of the most popular was the novela *Senhora do Destino* (Lady of Destiny), which tells the story of a woman's search for a daughter who went missing during a protest march in 1968. The first four episodes are set in the dictatorship period (most of the novela takes place in the present) and feature stronger scenes of violence than *Anos Rebeldes*, including a scene of sexual violence. Other networks have followed Globo's lead in revisiting the dictatorship: rival network SBT broadcast the relatively less successful 2011 *Amor e Revolução* (Love and Revolution), a love story set against the backdrop of the harshest years of the dictatorship, which ran at the time the Brazilian Congress was debating the law to create the National Truth Commission, and TV Cultura featured the 2009 *Trago Comigo* (I Carry It with Me), a four-episode miniseries in which a former guerrilla decides to revisit his past by staging a play about it.

Cinema has provided another space for the public to engage the memories of dictatorship. The corpus of works is vast and heterogeneous, with great variations in sophistication and quality as well as commercial and critical success. Nevertheless, two important characteristics are evident: the attempt to create memories of the dictatorship and an increasing emphasis on the legacies of the authoritarian period in the present. While genres run the gamut, the political thriller and documentary (including fiction-documentary hybrids) are particularly well represented (Seligmann-Silva, 2010).

Many if not most of these films seek to restore dignity to the victims. Often they do so through the focus on real-life people and their suffering. Director Sérgio Rezende dramatized the lives of Carlos Lamarca, a former military officer who joined the resistance and was ultimately killed, and Zuleika Angel Jones, an internationally renowned fashion designer whose dogged pursuit of the truth about what happened to her son ended in a suspicious car accident, in the 1994 *Lamarca* and the 2006 *Zuzu Angel*, respectively. Helvécio Ratton's 2006 film *Batismo de Sangue* (Blood Baptism) retells the story of Frei Tito de Alencar Lima, who survived the torture chamber only to commit suicide in Paris (in Brazil, suicides are included in the official count of deaths caused by the dictatorship). Not all films feature real-life victims; others tell the stories of fictional characters. One of the first and most successful was Roberto Farias's 1983 film *Pra Frente Brasil* (Onward Brazil) about two apolitical brothers who inadvertently get sucked into the vortex of the political repression. More recently, Caio Hamburger's critically acclaimed 2006 film *O ano que meus pais saíram de férias* (The Year My Parents Went on Vacation) presents the brutality and terror of the dictatorship period as seen through the eyes of a young boy.

In surveying cinematic production since transition, one notes a growing emphasis on the legacies of dictatorship in the present.[13] Rather than a simple dramatization of the authoritarian period, these films explore the effects of impunity in the present and the timidity of Brazil's official reckoning process, as well as the factors contributing to them, such as the left's reluctance to push the issues of memory and justice. An excellent example is Beto Brandt's 1998 *Ação entre amigos* (Friendly Fire), in which a torture survivor, dissatisfied with the impunity resulting from the amnesty, persuades three of his former comrades to impose their own form of justice on the man who tormented them during the dictatorship. More recently, in Tata Amaral's 2012 film *Hoje* (Today), a woman receives a reparations check for the political disappearance of her husband, and his unexpected reappearance symbolizes how the dictatorial past continues to haunt Brazil's present. The film's message was all the more poignant because of the timing of its release, which came at the time when the Brazilian Congress was debating the National Truth Commission (Atencio, 2014). Lúcia Murat's 2013 *A memória que me contam* (The Memory They Tell Me) explores the role of the 1960s generation in contemporary Brazil and particularly the inability of the left to remedy the inequalities it denounced decades ago despite its rise to political power. Other Murat films, including the 1986 *Que bom te ver viva* (How Nice to See You Alive), featuring interviews with female torture survivors, and the 2005 *Quase dois irmãos* (Almost Brothers), depicting contemporary violence and social injustice as legacies of dictatorship, also fit into this category and illustrate how filmmakers have produced cultural reckonings with the dictatorial period.

THE DOUBLE-EDGED ROLE OF ARTISTIC-CULTURAL PRODUCTION IN RECKONING WITH DICTATORSHIP

Brazil has a robust tradition of artistic-cultural production that engages with the dictatorial period, one that dates back at least to the 1979 Amnesty Law. In a society in which official responses have been timid and where there was little effort by the state before 2006 to generate discussion about the past, cultural producers have stepped in and offered testimonies, telenovelas, films, and other works in an effort to "'materialize' the meanings of the past" (to reprise Jelin's words). Yet what is the role of this vast and varied cultural production and the "labors of memory" it performs in the reckoning with the military dictatorship and its legacies?

In an important sense, artistic-cultural production that revisits the authoritarian past or explores the legacies of dictatorship in the present has the potential to promote further memory work within society. For the most part, the creative works described in the preceding section have served to draw or renew attention to the authoritarian past. Cultural works have the potential to disseminate and validate counter memories of the authoritarian past, thereby helping to contest the official narrative put forth by the dictatorship. While artistic-cultural production cannot rectify impunity, many individual works invite Brazilians to critically rethink the systematic human rights violations of the dictatorship. In this sense, cultural works constitute a privileged arena in which alternative memories can circulate and trigger discussion (Atencio, 2011; 2014). They denounce dictatorship-era political torture, murder, and disappearance and, through storytelling, humanize and arguably restore dignity to the victims of the repression, mitigating the stigma of "terrorists." Novelas and films bring the past to a new audience, one of massive proportions thanks to the packaging of memory as "entertainment" (Bilbija and Payne, 2005: 6). *Anos Rebeldes*, for example, attracted an audience 50 times the size of the readership of Brazil's first truth report. While the numbers for cinema are not as high, they are still substantial. Moreover, their entertainment value has allowed them to reach people who might otherwise avoid the dictatorial past as "too political."

Of course, cultural production is not a monolith, and there is a vast spectrum of ideologies represented. By its very nature as creative expression it allows for multiple meanings and interpretations, not all of which are necessarily consistent with promoting memory work and the human rights message of "never again." As the critic Márcio Seligmann-Silva (2010: 66) explains, Brazilian televisual and cinematographic engagements with the dictatorship period all too often encourage "catharsis in its negative sense, producing an effect of forgetting." He contends that while cultural production can serve as a vehicle for constructing memories of past trauma, the memories constructed have "little political density."

Anos Rebeldes is a case in point. On the one hand, the miniseries promotes the human rights message of "never again" through protagonists, including João and Maria Lúcia, who forcefully denounce torture and other human rights crimes. On the other hand, it tends to play down the harsh realities of life under dictatorship in numerous ways, including by presenting military characters as benevolent father figures, by avoiding showing scenes of torture or other forms of violence, and by portraying the one violent death of a main character as the result of a tragic accident rather than the product of systematized violence. The result is a watered-down depiction of the political violence, a kind of "repression lite" (Atencio, 2011: 52). Moreover, because the conflict between dictatorship and opposition is presented as the backdrop for a romance between the guerrilla João and his apolitical girlfriend Maria Lúcia, romance invariably overshadows—and mutes—political issues. João's political activism matters in the plot primarily because it creates tension in his relationship with Maria Lúcia. Similarly, when another main character in the series, Heloísa, is tortured, the focus is placed on the tension that her predicament causes with her father (a dictatorship financier). The state's abuse of power over the individual is reduced to a familial conflict, thereby draining it of its political significance.[14] While the "repression lite" message in *Anos Rebeldes* must certainly be recognized and contested, it does not necessarily negate, but rather coexists uneasily with, the "never again" message in the miniseries.

Yet it is not just in this sense of transmitting competing meanings or messages that cultural works can cut both ways. Culture is one force among many that influences how societies remember a painful past, and its influence is double-edged. Looking at the larger picture and comparing it with official truth-seeking, reparations, or legal reckoning mechanisms, cultural memory work's power is limited to raising awareness and providing "moral condemnation." This moral condemnation can mobilize accountability demands by acting as a stepping stone to juridical condemnation, but it can also demobilize them if treated as a mechanism for *bypassing* juridical condemnation. In Brazil, the latter possibility seems to predominate in that popular enthusiasm for "hit" books, films, and novelas denouncing the dictatorship does not seem to translate into popular enthusiasm for human rights trials. In this sense, consumption of cultural works about the dictatorship does not challenge, but arguably supports, the paradigm of reconciliation imposed by the 1979 Amnesty Law. Bearing in mind Brazil's history of political transition, public lack of interest in the question of torture and the widespread reception of guerrilla memoirs, telenovelas, and movies do not represent a paradox but rather make perfect sense.

This double-edged role of culture (as one form of reckoning among others) and its contribution to the reconciliatory amnesty framework is especially evident in the case of the guerrilla testimonies discussed earlier. These works played a critical role in contesting the official version of the repression (as a dirty war against terrorism) at a time when the regime was still in power. Yet a careful look at Gabeira's and Sirkis's books reveals that, for all their denunciation of torture, they are curiously silent about the Amnesty Law and the extension of its benefits to torturers; in fact, both former guerrillas would eventually come to *defend* impunity (Atencio, 2014). Their denunciations of political torture, murder, and disappearance notwithstanding, these two iconic books have done much to reinforce the framework of reconciliation imposed by the Amnesty Law (Atencio, 2014; Avelar, 1999; Reis Filho, 1997).

While, especially in the context of the Chilean and South African truth and reconciliation commissions, the term "reconciliation" was often invoked in a positive way associated with a "new social contract" following a period of violence (Hazan, 2010: 34–39), the empirical history of Brazil's reckoning process paints a different picture. As in many other Latin American countries, "reconciliation" became a euphemism for impunity, leading scholars to use alternatives like "social reconstruction" instead (Roht-Arriaza and Mariezcurrena, 2006: 12).

CONCLUSION

Assuming that cultural strategies shape reckoning processes, form peoples' memories and thoughts about past human rights crimes, and deserve to be studied, what are the possible advantages and disadvantages of cultural memory work in dealing with the authoritarian past? Critics could argue that cultural tactics are insufficient, most importantly, when the state evades its own responsibility for systematic crimes and fails to punish perpetrators. Similar accusations have been made against nonretributive measures, which critics see as "cheap" substitutes for prosecutions (Subotić, 2012: 120).

While the role of artistic-cultural productions in contexts of democratic transition should not be overemphasized, it certainly forms part of any serious, comprehensive study about long-term processes of reckoning with the military past and has larger implications for both scholars and practitioners. Official responses do not take place in a vacuum but rather are conditioned by their social, political, and cultural milieu. In certain cases, artistic-cultural works may even interact more concretely with official steps, such as when a film engages with the reparations program for the disappeared (as in the case of *Hoje*) or when state actors sponsor cultural memory policies (Atencio, 2014). Artistic-cultural production can furthermore serve as an alternative and less official form of truth telling (Atencio, 2014; Bilbija and Payne, 2005; Milton, 2007; 2014a).

Yet does the act of agenda setting—of making the military past a frequently discussed and publicly visible issue—advance the quest of memory, truth, and justice, especially if the way the history of the dictatorship is told is perpetually subject to romanticism or manipulation? Does it perhaps rather fill a void left by arguably half-hearted or belated accountability measures and, most important, impunity? In the specific Brazilian context, it appears to strengthen the amnesty framework ("reconciliation") rather than to undermine or overcome it (mobilizing for punishment). This article's central argument is that the function of cultural and memory work is double-edged, requiring a close reading of both the portrayal of violence in each cultural work and the larger historical and political context of each country's case.

In theoretical terms, we conclude that just as official responses do not take place in a vacuum but are conditioned by their social, political, and cultural milieu, so cultural production occurs in a specific historical context in which different agents struggle over how to read the past. Only by combining these two approaches can we research both the dynamic interrelations in a memory struggle and the meaning of cultural productions in a specific reckoning process, because, contrary to the framework of scholarly disciplines, "real life" is not compartmented but an integrated whole. We agree with Stern (2010: xxii) that memory studies, on the one hand, and reckoning histories, on the other hand, benefit from taking into account the "wider political, economic, and cultural contexts" of memory struggles over a violent past, and we suggest testing this holistic methodological approach in other cases.

Most postauthoritarian societies have also used cultural forms of engaging with the dictatorial past. Taking a holistic approach that combines cultural work and the larger historical context, what role has cultural memory work played in other postauthoritarian societies at different junctures in their reckoning processes? In Argentina and Chile, the millions of citizens who struggled for memory, truth, and justice initiatives faced different kinds of challenges. While the Full Stop Law and the Law of Due Obedience hindered prosecutions in Argentina for nearly a decade, Chile never officially revoked its amnesty law. Even though the Brazilian experience with amnesty was unique (it was both demanded from below and highly controlled by the military), the general question can be raised: Have not other postauthoritarian countries struggled against discourses of "reconciliation" in comparable ways, preventing a clear condemnation of the authoritarian past? Future scholarship can build upon the already substantial research on individual creative works and countries to investigate and theorize more fully what role cultural production has played in transition processes throughout Latin America—not as an isolated question but taking an integrated view of artistic-cultural production alongside truth seeking, reparations, and trials.

NOTES

The original version of this essay was published in *Latin American Perspectives* 43 (5): 12–28.

1. We use the term "memory" in a broad sense, referring to the remembering of historical events in the form of material objects and social practices in both the public and the private sphere.

2. Following Ruti Teitel (2003: 69), we define transitional justice as "the conception of justice associated with periods of political change, characterized by legal [and, we add, political and cultural] responses to confront the wrongdoings of repressive predecessor regimes."

3. The historian Daniel Aarão Reis Filho (2001), himself a former guerrilla, warns that the amnesty became associated with a series of myths, one of which pertains to the amnesty as being "reciprocal" (to the mutual benefit of repressive agents and former guerrillas), given that only perpetrators enjoyed de facto amnesty.

4. Since the condemnation of the Brazilian state by the Inter-American Court of Human Rights in late 2010, the São Paulo federal court has been filing criminal charges against a few convicted torturers, including the notorious Colonel Carlos Alberto Brilhante Ustra.

5. Marcelo Torelly made this point in a talk he delivered at Tulane University on December 4, 2013, titled "Amnesty and Transitional Justice in Brazil after Twenty Years of Democratic Rule of Law: Why Now?"

6. A prime example of these policies is the Resistance Memorial, inaugurated in 2009 in downtown São Paulo. The memorial has been extremely popular, likely because its slick aesthetic and tech-heavy concept is designed to appeal to the masses. For a critique of the memorial, see Atencio (2013).

7. According to a 2010 study by the Núcleo de Estudos da Violência at the University of São Paulo, 47.6 percent of the interviewees "completely agreed" that evidence extracted under torture should be used in criminal trials, while only 11.2 percent "completely disagreed" (Saito, 2013).

8. A more detailed analysis of the Brazilian amnesty debate reveals that those who favor impunity do not necessarily defend the military regime or wish to deny the military past (Schneider, 2011b: 47–49).

9. The institutional sphere refers to accountability mechanisms including truth seeking (truth commissions, inquiry commissions); official apologies; reparation payments; symbolic reparations such as political apologies, punishment, and institutional reforms; and purges within the judiciary, the military police, and the armed forces.

10. These include, to cite but a few of the best-known, Álvaro Caldas's *Tirando o capuz* (Taking Off the Hood, 1981), Herbert Daniel's *Passagem para o próximo sonho* (Ticket to the Next Dream, 1982), and Alex Polari's *Em busca do tesouro* (In Search of the Treasure, 1982). Such books found a wide readership in the late 1970s and early 1980s, especially among a new generation of Brazilians coming of age during the years of political opening.

11. The most powerful scenes involve Heloísa, a friend of the romantic leads who becomes involved in the armed struggle. In one, she reveals the marks of torture on her body to her stunned father, a regime apologist; in another, she is gunned down by security forces in a dramatic death scene. In addition to such fictional renderings, the show includes never-before-seen period footage of security forces violently suppressing protesters in the streets (for a complete analysis, see Atencio, 2011).

12. The original broadcast also coincided with real-life protests demanding the impeachment of then-President Fernando Collor (see Atencio, 2011: 60–63).

13. For an extensive albeit partial list of films that deal with the Brazilian military dictatorship, see Seligmann-Silva (2010: 66–67 n. 1).

14. The scholarship on how artistic-cultural production intervenes in transitional processes in multiple Latin American countries is vast. See, for example, Jelin and Longoni (2005), Bilbija and Payne (2005; 2011), Avelar (1999), Lazzara and Unruh (2009), Masiello (2001), Ros (2012), and Hite (2013).

13

Historical Memory at El Salvador's Museo de la Palabra y la Imagen

Diana Carolina Sierra Becerra

The cemetery was covered with a blanket of mangos. Cleotilde López, an 86-year-old union organizer, firmly gripped her cane as she led me through a hilly labyrinth of disorganized and discolored crosses. She stopped at the tomb of Mélida Anaya Montes, former president of the Asociación Nacional de Educadores Salvadoreños (National Association of Salvadoran Educators). With vivid detail, she recounted how she and her fellow teachers, the majority women, had organized massive strikes in 1967, 1968, and 1971 (Almeida, 2008: 91–93), but then the excitement in her voice dwindled. She cried as she recounted the murder of her nephew—massacred by government soldiers in a university protest in 1975. He died denouncing the military occupation of his campus.

López had witnessed an era in El Salvador in which unions, student groups, human rights and refugee organizations, and Christian base communities mobilized to build a society free of exploitation.[1] In 1980, after decades of military dictatorship and repression against nonviolent civilian movements, organizers formed a guerrilla coalition, the Frente Farabundo Martí para la Liberación Nacional (Farabundo Martí National Liberation Front—FMLN). The brutal civil war that followed (1980–1992) resulted in the death of approximately 75,000 people, the vast majority killed by state and paramilitary forces.

Survivors of state repression struggle on unequal terms to preserve the memory of their loved ones and achieve a measure of justice (Guzmán Orellana and Mendia Azkue, 2013). Legal impunity protects war criminals. A week after the United Nations Truth Commission published its 1993 report on human rights violations committed during the war, the right-wing legislature passed amnesty laws to prohibit the investigation and prosecution of the crimes documented. In 2013 the Instituto de Derechos Humanos de la Universidad Centroamericana (Human Rights Institute of the Central American University) challenged the constitutionality of the amnesty laws, and disputes are ongoing (Thale, 2013). Although a 1996 educational reform permitted school curricula to address recent history, public schools often lack the educational tools and training to critically teach the history of state violence. Textbooks, moreover, often reproduce highly misleading narratives of the war. For example, a history text for high school students frames the war as an "ideological confrontation" between the Soviet Union and the United States, a framing that has been discredited as an ideological product of the cold war (Grandin, 2004; MINED, 2009: 221).

Fortunately, the testimonies and personal files of activists like Cleotilde López find refuge at the Museo de la Palabra y la Imagen (Museum of the Word and Image—MUPI) in San Salvador. Labeled the "museum of rebellions" (Lindo, 2015), the MUPI documents the history and collective memories of peasants, indigenous peoples, workers, and women in social movements, among others. It denounces systemic inequality and human rights abuses and illuminates the history of collective struggle to promote social change.[2] This intervention departs from the historic role of museums in upholding ruling-class hegemony (Hein, 2000; Hooper-Greenhill, 1992).[3]

Memory plays an important role in shaping social justice movements (Langland, 2013; Straubhaar, 2015). Activists analyze the oppressive systems and collective struggles of the past in order to shape the strategies, identities, and analysis of current movements. In El Salvador, leftist organizations have drawn on collective memories to situate their movements within a larger history of struggle.[4] Postwar movements, however, struggle to transmit the collective memories of older activists to younger generations. A quarter century of neoliberalism has undermined the foundations for collective action (Alarcón Medina and Binford, 2014: 529).

The MUPI has assumed the task of transmitting collective memories across generations. Some scholars have identified this intergenerational transmission as "postmemory" (Hirsch, 2008).[5] In its educational programs, the museum centers collective memory in the production of history and provides people with the tools to build a democratic El Salvador—linking memory to conscientious action. This progressive museum model encourages critical historical analysis and empowerment—the latter defined as the representation, participation, and skill building of the oppressed (Chávez, 2007; Winn, 2012: 69). However, popular pedagogy is limited in a political context characterized by relatively low levels of social movement mobilization.

As a curator and educational programmer at the MUPI since 2013, I have observed firsthand its successes and challenges in promoting historical memory. This experience may be instructive for practitioners of memory who are looking for appropriate models and pedagogical methods. Furthermore, it may encourage scholars of collective memory to place their skill sets at the service of public institutions seeking to keep memories of collective action alive.

A BRIEF HISTORY OF THE MUPI

During the war, the MUPI's founder, Carlos Henríquez Consalvi, under the pseudonym "Santiago," served as the announcer of Radio Venceremos (Radio We Shall

Triumph), "the official voice of the FMLN." The radio station denounced human rights violations, broadcasted educational programs, reported FMLN military operations, and summarized local and international news (Henríquez Consalvi, 1992; López Vigil, 1992). After the signing of the Chapultepec peace accords, he began collecting testimonies about military-led massacres. These materials, along with audiovisuals of Radio Venceremos, came to form the original MUPI archive. "Every day we go and seek out the public; we haven't lost what we learned in the mountains," he said (OJO! Media Collective, 2012). The MUPI organizes exhibitions, talks, debates, workshops, festivals, and film forums at its headquarters in San Salvador and nationwide. It publishes books, comic books, magazines, and coloring books; produces cartoon animations, documentaries, and board games; broadcasts the radio show *Tejiendo la memoria* (Weaving Memory); and shares these materials with schoolteachers and community educators to help address the limitations of national curricula. This approach contrasts with museum curators' more common tendency to privilege academic forms of communication (Gurian, 2006: 150).

The first MUPI publication was *Luciérnagas en El Mozote* (Fireflies in El Mozote), which documented an infamous 1981 rural massacre (Amaya, Danner, and Henríquez Consalvi, 1996). Days after the massacre, Henríquez Consalvi had interviewed the survivor Rufina Amaya, who testified that the government's Atlacatl Battalion under the command of Colonel Domingo Monterrosa had murdered approximately 800 peasants. Soldiers raped, impaled, burned, and decapitated their victims. Throughout the 1980s the Reagan administration and the right-wing party, Alianza Republicana Nacionalista (National Republican Alliance—ARENA), whose founder had organized death squads, repeatedly denied the massacre (Danner, 1993; Grandin, 2015; Preston, 2013: 65). Exhumations later removed all doubt; one mass grave alone held the remains of 143 children under the age of 12 (Danner, 1993).

To build its archive, the MUPI initiated a public campaign in 1996 titled "Contra el caos de la desmemoria" (Against the Chaos of Un-memory). Via community radio, it invited civilians to donate materials related to the war. When respondents insisted that the museum also focus on broader national themes, the MUPI extended its conservation and programmatic efforts to include Salvadoran literature and art and prewar social movements. The archive currently contains the documents of important historical figures such as the activists and writers Prudencia Ayala and Roque Dalton. An extensive photography and film archive houses 50,000 images and thousands of hours of audiovisual footage. Researchers are invited to consult these materials in order to produce new interpretations of Salvadoran history. The importance of this public campaign cannot be overstated. El Salvador had no history museums in the early postwar period. For example, the only anthropology museum closed down after an earthquake in 1986 and did not reopen until 2001. Furthermore, according to Henríquez Consalvi, both rightist and leftist parties were uninterested in memory efforts. For many politicians, although for different reasons, the armed conflict represented a moral defeat: for the right its memory threatened to highlight its systematic human rights abuses, while for the left it represented the defeat of social movements (Hernández Rivas, 2015: 5–6).

The efforts of the original campaign continue. One of the treasures archived includes the personal photographic negatives of Archbishop Oscar Romero, which he had handed to his friend Santos Delmi Campos de Cabrera only months prior to his assassination. In 2010, on the thirtieth anniversary of Romero's death, Campos de Cabrera donated the collection to the MUPI. Through the photographs, viewers literally see through the lens of the young priest, who photographed the local religious celebrations of the poor, visited prisoners, and admired his country's volcanic landscapes. From this collection, the MUPI curated the exhibit *Romero, voz y mirada* (MUPI, 2011b). Romero was a proponent of liberation theology, which advocated collective mobilization to eliminate the "structural sin" of poverty (Gutiérrez, 1999 [1973]; Lernoux, 1980; Smith, 1991). He had denounced the military's repression of peasants and the urban poor in the late 1970s. A death squad bullet pierced his heart on March 24, 1980, as he was saying mass; the previous day he had demanded that the army stop killing civilians. The number of visitors to the exhibit increased around the time of his beatification in May 2015, a time when activists were insisting on raising the question of who killed him and why (*Contrapunto*, May 20, 2015).[6] In this way, even seemingly nonpolitical photographs provided an opportunity to discuss how the prewar history of state repression is remembered and why it matters in the present.

Romero's murder and its remembrance remain central to present-day Salvadoran political struggles. Although the FMLN party has won the past two presidential elections (2009 and 2014), right-wing sectors retain significant power to shape public discourse about national history. In late 2014, former San Salvador Mayor Norman Quijano of the ARENA party renamed an important street after Major Roberto D'Aubuisson, the founder of ARENA and the death squads and the intellectual architect of Romero's murder according to the United Nations Truth Commission (1993: 119). Quijano dismissed the evidence of human rights violations: "Look, I do not call it the truth commission, I call it the commission of lies. . . . All too frequently we Salvadorans have the tendency to invoke the past when it's convenient for us" (*Canal Genteve*, November 24, 2014). Up and down the street, graffiti artists stenciled skulls and wrote: "Ni calle, ni camino, con nombre de asesino" ("No street, no road with the name of a murderer."[7] In contrast, wealthy neighborhoods in San Salvador paid tribute to D'Aubuisson through public commemorations reflective of ARENA efforts to "recognize the virtues of the major" and to "rescue his political history within national life." In 2009 ARENA sought to have its "maximum leader" D'Aubuisson posthumously receive one of the highest honors in the country, "most worthy son," though the motion failed after protesters occupied the National Assembly building (*TCS Noticias*, February 5, 2009).

POSTWAR POPULAR EDUCATORS

During the mid-to-late twentieth century, popular education became an important tool for building social justice in Latin America. Paulo Freire, the best-known theorist and practitioner of popular pedagogy, developed methodologies for eradicating illiteracy and equipping the poor with the skills to challenge the hierarchies that sustain their oppression. He criticized the "banking method" of education for treating students as empty vessels in which to deposit information and encouraging student passivity. Instead, he argued, popular educators should treat the experiences of students as a source of knowledge and pose questions that can be resolved through collective reflection and action (Freire, 1973a: 36, 47; McLaren and Giroux, 1997; Zinn and Macedo, 2005: 64–65). Popular education examined the way power shaped the production of knowledge and human relationships more broadly (Freire, 1970; Trouillot, 1995).

In El Salvador, popular education was central to sustaining mass organizing before and during the war. In the Chalatenango department, organizers pioneered popular education as civilians resettled areas under FMLN control. The *poderes populares locales* (popular local powers) or community councils democratically coordinated education efforts (Cruz, 2011). Popular educators linked the eradication of illiteracy to individual empowerment and collective political participation (Hammond, 1998; Pearce, 1986). Historically, rural people endured higher levels of poverty and illiteracy (especially among women) than city dwellers. Literacy campaigns taught participants about their capabilities and rights. Education often led peasant women to challenge domestic violence and reflect on their situation (Rivera et al., 1995; interviews, Azucena Quinteros, Rosa Rivera, Domitila Ayala, Esperanza Ortega, San Salvador and Arcatao, May 2015). The wartime educator and academic María del Carmen Cruz (2004) argued that popular pedagogy promoted a horizontal relationship between teacher and student, the exchange of experiences, the discovery of community values and problems, criticism of social realities, and efforts to transform collective livelihoods.

In the postwar period, popular education lives on in the museum. MUPI educators transmit historical memory and organize participatory activities in order to *concientizar* (raise consciousness) about the role of oppression and violence, both overt and structural, in shaping El Salvador's past and present.[8] Participants are encouraged to reflect upon the way this history has touched their own lives. In teaching the history of how ordinary people have worked together to change their life circumstances and the country itself, the MUPI hopes to inspire participants about their own capabilities. In order to translate consciousness into action, the MUPI holds training sessions to equip people with the skills to address the concerns of their communities. It has drawn key elements from popular education—politicized education, consciousness raising, participatory learning, and community engagement—to address postwar realities. Collective memory is a central component of its educational programs.

All education is inherently political, differing only in the interests it serves. However, popular education need not be *partisan*, and many theorists have insisted that it must not promote allegiance to parties and leaders (Zinn, 1990 [1970]: 52, 295). For example, the MUPI has never endorsed any political party, including the

FMLN. It has exercised complete autonomy over its educational content, and its staff members are not FMLN party militants. Prior to the FMLN's 2009 electoral victory, however, the MUPI did pressure the right-wing government for funding, and currently it has a working relationship with the Secretariat of Culture, which is directly linked to the FMLN presidency.[9] The latter institution partially funds transportation costs to bring children from the countryside to the MUPI, and the party has supported other non-MUPI memory initiatives.[10]

TEACHING THE HISTORY OF STATE REPRESSION

The MUPI has engaged the public with two events that have arguably been the most definitive for twentieth-century El Salvador: the 1932 revolt and massacre and the 12-year-long civil war. On January 22, 1932, thousands of indigenous and nonindigenous peasants declared themselves the rightful owners of the land and, alongside leaders such as Julia Mojica and Feliciano Ama, occupied villages and military barracks in western El Salvador. The insurrection was the largest in Latin America during the Great Depression. In response, President General Maximiliano Hernández Martínez and the National Guard massacred 10,000–30,000 people in a country with a total population of 1.5 million; the exact figure is debated because of the scarcity of sources, the absence of a body count, and a long-standing leftist discourse that cites 30,000 victims (Anderson, 1971). From an analysis of available documents, including leftist organizational and government correspondence, Gould and Lauria-Santiago (2008) argue that the number is probably closer to 10,000.

In the early 1990s, Henríquez Consalvi and Gould traveled to rural villages in western El Salvador to collect the testimonies of elders, and those oral histories provided the basis for the documentary *1932: Cicatriz de la memoria* (1932: Scar of Memory) and the book *To Rise in Darkness: Revolution, Repression, and Memory in El Salvador, 1920–1932* (Gould and Lauria-Santiago, 2008).[11] With this research, the MUPI has produced two exhibits and a guide for educators and organized countless history education workshops and film forums. Recently, public school teachers recommended to the Ministry of Education that the documentary be part of the national high school curriculum.[12] In the film forums, museum personnel have facilitated discussions about key themes of the documentary and its current relevance. The MUPI has measured the impact of film forums via participant observation and outreach.[13] Hernández and Doño (2008: 40) observed that indigenous elders have been encouraged to share their stories and garnered community respect from it. Indigenous organizations have used the documentary to launch political platforms such as protests against the omission of indigenous people from the 2007 national census and demands for land and education.

Both the documentary and the book examined the collective memories of landowners and peasants. They approached history on three levels: what happened, how people from that specific historical moment understood and acted upon their situation, and how people, experientially connected to the event or not, remembered it. This last element, commonly termed "collective memory," has implications for identity, power, and justice in the present (French, 1995). The MUPI's approach to historical memory draws from both the study of history and collective memory (for the strengths of historical approaches in the study of memory see Serbin, 2006: 188–189).

The relationship between what happened and the collective memory of it is complex. Memories may be more or less accurate but are always shaped at least in part by present-day power and interests (Olick and Robbins, 1998: 110–111). For example, for decades the official history of 1932 reflected oligarchic and military interests. Elite narratives that equated being Indian with being communist and backward have cast a long shadow. During the civil war, death squads named after General Martínez continued to hunt down "communist" peasants. As is its custom, the ARENA party initiated its 2014 presidential campaign in the historically indigenous department of Sonsonate. Meters from a humble monument that marks an indigenous mass grave, members sang their official anthem, "Yes to the homeland, no to communism" (*La Prensa Gráfica*, October 3, 2013).[14]

Gould and Lauria-Santiago (2008) have also pointed to the way elite narratives about 1932 have shaped the collective memories of indigenous peasants themselves. Indigenous peasants interviewed often presented a dichotomy between themselves and *ladino* (nonindigenous) communist "instigators." Here the collective memory of later generations and even some survivors is in conflict with the worldviews of many of the participants in the 1932 revolt. Indigenous peasants such as Francisco Sanchéz led labor organizations that articulated their own local visions of Marxism (Gould and Lauria-Santiago, 2008: 161, 178–180). Understandably, in the light of the trauma, many indigenous communities have distanced themselves from communism in order to delegitimize a state that justified its actions in terms of eliminating a communist threat. Nonetheless, recognizing indigenous peasants as radicals in their own right complicates standard narratives about who led the revolt and why it happened. It challenges both ladino leftists who treated urban Communist Party militants as the real architects of the revolt (for a parallel case in Guatemala see Grandin, 2004) and elites who characterized peasants as incapable of intervening politically on their own behalf. A distinct yet complementary elite narrative reduces the insurrection to "looting" and thus strips peasants of their political agency (for a critical discussion, see Gould and Lauria-Santiago, 2008: 180, 193–194).

In the case of the 1932 revolt, differences in historical interpretation have not blocked important alliances between the MUPI and indigenous communities. Each year the MUPI provides educational materials for annual commemorations and coordinates with indigenous leaders to implement educational programs in their local schools and museums. In other words, the larger picture—the rights of victims and their families, the trauma and violence inflicted on indigenous communities, their exclusion from national histories, and their continued invisibility—has not been lost even though differences of historical interpretation may exist. The commitment to justice is the basis of the alliance.

In February 2015, the MUPI inaugurated the exhibit *1932*, which explored the socioeconomic inequalities of early twentieth-century El Salvador, including the working conditions that women workers faced on the coffee plantations, and introduced a new gendered focus: the impact of terror on indigenous women (Sierra Becerra, 2015; MUPI, 2015). The exhibit challenged elite narratives about 1932 via the testimonies of indigenous peasants who participated in the insurrection and survived the massacre.[15] Aware of the problems of dominant narratives, the curators highlighted the conditions and events preceding the massacre, the reasons participants revolted, how the state responded, and the long-term impact on indigenous communities.[16] In addition, the exhibit provided an opportunity for discussions about national identity and justice for victims of state repression. At least 3,500 public school students visited the exhibit in 2015, and it continues to travel through the country's 14 departments and to be part of commemorations of the massacre (figure 13.1).

Exhibits are more effective when they are accompanied by participatory activities that cater to diverse learning styles and empower youth to share their newly acquired knowledge. This latter point is especially important because it gives participants the skills to publicly share and engage with collective memory, and helps counter hierarchies of knowledge production and access between the museum and the given population. For example, in May 2015 Anna Theissen and I facilitated a five-hour workshop at the Náhuat Pipil Community Museum in Izalco, where we trained 20

Figure 13.1.   Indigenous elders from Nahuizalco visiting the *1932* exhibit.
Source: Diana Carolina Sierra Becerra

students aged 14 to 23 to become exhibit guides in their local museum. The museum is based in the historically indigenous department of Sonsonate, where the massacres of 1932 were heavily concentrated. Participants represented the rural villages of Na-huizalco, Pushtán, and Carrizal.

The MUPI's didactic guide informed the methodologies of the workshop (Sierra Becerra et al., 2015). In Part 1 the topic was introduced through a film forum on the *1932* documentary. In Part 2, students practiced guiding their peers through a specific exhibit panel, receiving constructive criticism about public speaking. Part 3 used role-playing to promote understanding of the choices that the historical ac-tors of 1932 faced. Participants playing the role of coffee workers drew information from the exhibit to discuss their working conditions and what equality and respect meant to them. From this discussion, participants presented a list of labor demands to the landowner. Afterward, Theissen and I summarized the parallels between their role-playing and the historical realities of labor organizing. In the final activity, each group made a collective drawing to represent what 1932 meant to them and why it was important to remember the event. This portion was especially moving because many participants had direct familial ties to the events of 1932.

The workshop also addressed insecurities and feelings of inferiority among young people. At the beginning of the workshop, one young woman stated, "I'm sorry, I'm not used to talking too much or expressing myself in groups." In her many years as a MUPI educator, Theissen has observed that rural participants, particularly women, are more doubtful about their capabilities than urban participants. This behavior is rooted in what Freire called the "banking method" of education and in historical class, gender, ethnic, and urban-rural inequalities. MUPI facilitators have therefore developed techniques sensitive to the needs of semiliterate groups and encouraged the participation of women. By the conclusion of this workshop we noted that the young woman quoted above was much more vocal.

THE POWER OF TESTIMONY

Testimonies have been a key tool for denouncing state violence and teaching the history of the civil war and have proved a captivating entry point for young people accustomed to thinking of history as the memorization of rote facts. Through testi-monies, the MUPI aims to present history not as an abstract concept or collection of dates but as a lived experience. Historically, testimonies have provided oppressed Latin Americans with a medium for articulating their identities and political visions (Dulfano, 2004; Maier, 2004). While testimonies should be critiqued like any other historical source, the MUPI treats testimonies as a source of knowledge that deserves serious consideration, a point that popular educators have advocated for quite some time (High, 2015). As many have commented, testimonies and oral histories are not just about what happened but about the meanings that ordinary people assign to their extraordinary experiences (Portelli, 1998).

The MUPI has drawn from the collective memory of activists, combatants, and civilians to tell the history of the civil war. In particular, it addresses why and how people were radicalized; why the state, paramilitaries, and landowners violently repressed civilian movements; and what the social movement participants, including FMLN combatants, hoped to accomplish. Public school teachers have reported that their students struggled to "understand the causes that gave rise to the civil war in El Salvador," to "differentiate between structural causes and immediate causes," and to understand key turning points before and during the war. This confusion was perhaps due to textbooks that obscure the structural inequalities and human actions that culminated in the outbreak of the war (MINED, 2009: 221–223).

While right-wing narratives absolve state and paramilitary forces of human rights abuses, a mainstream human rights discourse has created a moral equivalency between state/paramilitary and insurgent violence. "Hegemonic discourses of human rights" have framed the popular armed struggle as a *locura* (madness) rather than the "outcome of decades of socioeconomic injustice, militarization, and oligarchic repression" (Alarcón Medina and Binford, 2014: 529). Within this logic, the insurgency is put on "a par with the army and the repressive security forces" (526). For example, some present-day residents of El Mozote have attributed the military-led massacre there to the FMLN (525). However, the Truth Commission reported that government forces and right-wing death squads committed 85 percent of acts of violence and the guerrillas 5 percent (United Nations Truth Commission, 1993). This basic disparity refutes the common argument that the scale of the violence was the same on all sides, but textbooks tend to imply a moral equivalency between state and guerrilla violence and between the destruction of economic infrastructure and violence against people (MINED, 2009: 225, 228, 231). This discourse is also evident in other countries that have experienced state violence and remains fairly common in scholarly accounts of the cold war (e.g., Brands, 2010). In the case of postapartheid South Africa, history education based on "both sides of the story" similarly ignores the historical roots of current inequalities and constructs a moral equivalence between enforcers and resisters of apartheid in order to promote "national unity." Such narratives have upheld "color-blind" racism (Teeger, 2015). Even when Salvadoran textbooks do not explicitly equate right-wing and left-wing violence, a lack of clarity about the civil war inhibits understanding and prevents people from challenging the oppressive conditions that have shaped El Salvador.

The exhibit *La historia de Chiyo* (The Story of Chiyo) illustrates how the MUPI has challenged the aforementioned narratives. It traced the wartime childhood of Lucio (Chiyo) Vásquez via passages from his testimony *Siete gorriones* (MUPI, 2011a; Vásquez, 2012). The exhibit narrated key moments before, during, and after the civil war, including the rise of Christian base communities and the influence of liberation theology, the repression of peasant movements, the role of the FMLN and Radio Venceremos, the signing of the 1992 peace accords, and life in the postwar period. When Chiyo was seven, government soldiers murdered his brothers Hilario and Chepe at a 1979 protest. Hilario and Chepe had joined the peasant movement that fought for land rights and education. A year later the National Guard murdered their mother, Feliciana, and their pregnant sister, Teodora, outside their home. Three more siblings, Hubert, Romero, and Juan, later died fighting for the FMLN. In total, Chiyo lost six of his nine siblings. At the age of nine Chiyo joined the FMLN and worked with Radio Venceremos (*Contrapunto*, November 10, 2014). In the guerrilla camps, popular educators taught him to read and write.

Chiyo now works at the MUPI as a cultural promoter, traveling throughout the country mounting exhibits and sharing his testimony. In an interview, Chiyo illuminated how state violence pushed peasants toward armed struggle. His remarks below are representative of the experiences that he usually shares with young people: "The armed forces and the oligarchy obeyed the orders of the North Americans to exterminate *their own people*, in a rush to supposedly detain communism, when in reality they practiced *pure* terrorism. . . . My adult brothers were aware that a clear confrontation with the dictatorial government was coming and that only armed struggle remained ahead" (*Contrapunto*, November 10, 2014). "They made war on us" is a common explanation among peasants. In fact, most date the start of the war not to 1980 (the year in which the FMLN was formed) but to the 1970s, when the repression escalated against peasant organizations. In other words, the war began when the state declared activists military targets. Peasant memories are supported by historical evidence: counterinsurgency programs and paramilitary agencies in El Salvador were established a decade before the formation of the first guerrilla group in 1970, and many activists seriously debated the advisability of armed struggle late into the 1970s (Almeida, 2008: 127, 140, 167–168; Grandin, 2006: 95; McClintock, 1985: 41, 59, 204).

In his book, Chiyo (Vásquez, 2012: 190–192) foregrounded the daily wartime experiences of the rank and file from their collective pain and solidarity to their critiques of the top leadership. He recalled the death of his brother Hubert, a fellow combatant: "You don't have your family close by and you only look for solitude. And in that solitude I overcame my pain. And then you have no other choice but to resign yourself and receive the consoling message of your other comrades. . . . Because there, one dead comrade [represented] a death for everyone, a fallen child was everyone's child. Having that consciousness hurts" (117–118). In addition, he discussed how the practice of solidarity enabled the peasant insurgency to survive against all odds: "We faced an absolutely unequal war, and with the power of our joy we knew how to defeat the most powerful technology: the arms of the United States in the hands of the Salvadoran army. . . . Only a smile and solidarity saved us at the hour of death" (*Contrapunto*, November 10, 2014). When Chiyo shares his convictions he defies urban stereotypes of apolitical and stupid peasants. Furthermore, it is difficult for audiences to forget the way he speaks about his loved ones and their sacrifices to build a more just society.

With a guitar in hand, Chiyo has captured the attention of teenagers who minutes prior had expressed boredom. Sitting in a circle, they intently listen and ask critical questions about the meaning of justice: "Why don't you kill the man who did that to your family?" Although Chiyo knows the officers—commander Eliseo Canales (who is still alive) and soldier Adán Guevara—who murdered his mother and sister, he does not want to "stain his hands" (Vásquez, 2012: 40). I "picked up a gun, but to protect life," he argued. In other words, his vision of justice extends beyond personal revenge. Instead, he encourages young people to pick up a pencil or a guitar to express themselves (advice that is in part shaped by the current reality of youth recruitment to violent gangs that extort and kill poor people).

The MUPI guestbook reveals how historical memory related to the civil war has impacted young visitors (Sandra Guevara, guest book entry, San Salvador, July 20, 2013):

> I never thought that I could be so inspired and impressed, but the lives of peasants during the armed conflict are truly unforgettable; there is so much to see with the photos of Monsignor Romero and of Radio Venceremos; the memories of the armed conflict have taken me into a time machine; through their gazes I witness the suffering of each person who lived during that period.

Given that the war ended less than 25 years ago, it is not uncommon for visitors to share a direct connection to the exhibited history. One adult visitor expressed her relationship to "Amada Libertad" (Beloved Liberty), a woman FMLN combatant and poet who died in combat, as follows: "This afternoon I arrived at the MUPI and saw your things in an exhibition. I have remembered you so much with that little shirt; thank you to the museum for making known what women warriors were and are like" (Angélica, guest book entry, San Salvador, July 16, 2013). Situating individual loss within a historical context of state violence can serve as a form of healing and as a means for older activists to tell their stories to younger people.[17] The MUPI makes a special contribution in affirming the histories of its visitors.

CULTIVATING "CULTURES OF PEACE"

How can memory be translated into practice? Transmitting historical memory is only one component of making it relevant. The second component is providing participants with the skills required for political participation. In present-day El Salvador, young people are disproportionately impacted by poverty, undocumented migration, and gang violence; young women and LGBTQ youth are especially vulnerable to sexual and gender-based violence (United Nations Children's Fund, 2014: 35, 46, 140; United Nations High Commissioner for Human Rights, 2011: 10). In response, the MUPI organizes leadership training on human rights via public debates, film, and the creative arts. "Youth learn to analyze their daily problems as they relate to human rights. You notice a change," says Theissen. These programs enable participants to reflect on their own realities and learn from their peers (cf. Freire, 1973b: 49). In short, young people are motivated to work collectively to envision nonviolent solutions to their personal and collective problems, a key component of popular pedagogy that attempts to link knowledge to action.

In June 2015 the MUPI launched its "Schools of Peace" project, which consists of workshops directed at public school students and teachers. The three-year program is being implemented in 10 municipalities in the city of San Salvador and involves 1,250 students and 135 teachers. At "creative fairs" students are encouraged to join youth-led collectives that practice photography, theater, juggling, drumming, Andean music, and artisanal jewelry. The youth educators in the collectives have previously worked with the MUPI. Each group embarks on a long-term collective project using its chosen medium to explore alternatives to violence in its community. While learning specific skill sets, participants are working to build peace, which is defined not as the maintenance of order in the face of poverty and inequality, but rather as a life free from exploitation, oppression, and violence.

The project also trains teachers via nine workshops, composed of eight five-hour sessions each. The MUPI program coordinator Claudia Anay García describes its goals: "We hope that the teachers will recognize their own violent attitudes, the ones they exercise at work or in their family life, and understand the changes that can be generated once those attitudes are changed" (e-mail correspondence, June 2015). Educators learn theoretical and practical components of "cultures of peace" that they can implement in their schools. People need to analyze "their daily behavior" to live "a dignified life," argues Theissen (e-mail correspondence, August 2015). This approach takes its cues from Freire and others who have long challenged the authoritarian dynamics that formal educators may reproduce (Freire, 1970: 59; Gramsci, 1971).

CHALLENGES

The MUPI accomplishes a lot with few resources, but Theissen raises the question of individual versus structural change: "You perhaps change something for the young man, but you really don't change anything in the structure, nor do you change where he lives. . . . Many [participants] said that the [MUPI programs] were their areas of rest, [a chance] to breathe, but when they returned again to their neighborhoods, there they faced violence" (interview, San Salvador, May 2015). She added, "I am totally convinced that structural changes are necessary." Therefore, we must ask where and how participants will channel their newly acquired skills and knowledge about historical memory.

After decades of neoliberal policies, the mobilizing power and influence of social movements has greatly diminished. Such an observation is not meant to dismiss how a new generation of organizers, often alongside revolutionaries from the civil war era, continues to struggle. But the level of progressive mobilization is much lower than it was a quarter century ago. Popular education is an essential tool, but it alone cannot build or substitute for social movements that will confront the elites and institutions responsible for violence and oppression. It would be unfair to expect the MUPI to carry out its popular education programs *and* build the social movements that can transform Salvadoran policies and institutions. This problem is not unique to the

MUPI: theorists and practitioners of popular pedagogy have long sought to address it. As popular education theorists argue, practice is as important as the reflection that it inspires (Barreiro, 1974: 30; Freire, 1970; 1973a; 1973b). In July 2015 I raised the question of the relationship between theory and practice with members of the International Coalition of Sites of Conscience, a network of organizations dedicated to history and human rights education to address current injustices. The coalition has a Latin America network in which the MUPI participates. In an online forum open to all members, participants discussed where such institutions fit into the larger picture of social justice. How can museums work with social movements and grassroots organizations whose goal is to transform the institutions that produce the violence we denounce? How can educational organizations promote the self-organization of their target audiences?

The nonprofit structure also impacts the work of museums. Funders, both public and private, often dictate the agenda and approach of museum programs (INCITE!, 2007). These agendas and approaches often reproduce class and racial hierarchies between museum staff and their participants (see the unexamined assumptions in Winn, 2012). The MUPI is financially constrained because funding is often specified for programs that have a finite time frame rather than for sustaining the museum as a whole or paying its staff, which results in a cyclical scramble to secure funding sources that are predominantly based in the United States and Europe. Many funders only accept applications in English, thus excluding staff that lack the appropriate language skills or time to only write grants.

Museums can, however, make unique contributions. They can assist grassroots organizations in the education of their own membership and the larger public and provide a space to develop a community forum and political platform (Cameron, 1971). For example, the District Six Museum in South Africa links its educational work about apartheid and forced displacements to current anti-gentrification campaigns (Layne, 2008). Museums can also issue statements in support of specific reforms. For instance, curators at the National Museum of Colombia have advocated reparations to black people even though national policies oppose such measures (Lleras, 2012). Museums are especially relevant because neoliberal policies continue to slash funding for public programs and history education in public schools. But when the museum closes at the end of the workday, who will be left to translate consciousness into action? Social movements can be the vehicles for people to articulate popular demands and build the organizational power of oppressed sectors. An alliance between museums and social movements seems more important than ever.

CONCLUSION

Salvadoran organizers planted the seed of popular pedagogy during the country's civil war, and those roots have extended into the postwar period. In contrast to the historic role of hegemonic museums, the MUPI documents the collective memories of social movement participants in order to denounce systemic inequality and human rights abuses. Ultimately, older activists share their collective memories in order to guide new struggles. Popular pedagogy is used to disseminate and critically engage younger generations with historical memory. Historical memory can valorize subaltern knowledge and critically interrogate the meanings we assign to the past. When linked to a popular pedagogical approach, historical memory can bridge generational divides and empower participants to address the needs of their own communities. In the words of Chiyo Vásquez, the museum should present alternatives "and a vision of El Salvador where we all belong" (interview, San Salvador, June 2013). The MUPI model, including its pedagogy and community partnerships, may be particularly useful for those interested in the practice of memory work.

This case study highlights several major challenges, however. In addition to noting the obvious financial constraints under which the MUPI operates, I have called attention to a perennial dilemma of popular education praxis as it relates to historical memory. At its best, popular education links collective reflection to action. Yet the strength of popular education is diluted in a political context in which social movements are weak and fragmented. While the museum may successfully transmit historical memory, participants may struggle to find avenues, such as organizations and social movements, in which to apply their knowledge. In contrast, when historical memory is transmitted in a social movement context, the revolutionary bud may blossom.

NOTES

The original version of this essay was published in *Latin American Perspectives* 43 (6): 8–26.

1. In Christian base communities, ordinary people applied the teachings of the bible to their own lives and used collective action to improve their living conditions.

2. Since the 1970s, some scholars have pressed museums to interpret themes of public importance, fulfill "ethical responsibilities outside the museum" such as supporting social justice, and improve the "quality of people's lives" (Cameron, 1971; Marstine, 2011: 12–14; Weil, 2002: 9). This approach complements the initiatives of institutions such as the MUPI.

3. For example, the European "universal museum" reproduced the racism of the imperial state and echoed "ceremonial practices of accumulation display" (Duncan and Wallach, 1980: 449).

4. The FMLN portrayed its armed struggle as a reenactment of the 1932 peasant revolt and named itself after Farabundo Martí, a Communist Party leader who supported the revolt (Lindo-Fuentes, Ching, and Lara-Martínez, 2007: 255). In the 1970s and 1980s, nationalist ideologies of *mestizaje* (race-mixture) contributed to the omission by most leftists of indigenous participation in that revolt (Gould, 2001).

5. Hirsch writes of "postmemory" as a "structure of inter- and trans-generational transmission of traumatic knowledge and experience" through stories, images, and behaviors (2008: 106). For example, Salvadoran youth use social media to connect to their parents' revolutionary past (Alarcón, 2014: 492).

6. Marissa D'Aubuisson is a longtime activist and a founder of the Romero Foundation. She has played a key role in demanding that her brother be held accountable for the murder of Archbishop Romero.

7. In recent years the right has appropriated mural painting in an attempt to promote tourism and divorce the medium from its historic role in expressing collective memory (Heidenry, 2014: 133).

8. Johan Galtung (1969) coined the term "structural violence" to describe the way a social structure or institution prevents people from fulfilling their basic needs, such as obtaining food and shelter.

9. In 2005 Henríquez Consalvi publicly questioned the lack of support from the Consejo Nacional de Cultural (National Council of Culture—CONCULTURA), a branch of the Ministry of Education and Inclusion. That public pressure pushed CONCULTURA to support the traveling MUPI exhibitions that are housed at the Red de Casas de Cultura (Network of Cultural Houses) (Hernández Rivas, 2015: 31). The network is composed of more than 130 "cultural houses" (DeLugan, 2008: 181).

10. Recently the FMLN has supported civilian training in "the rescue of historical memory" (FMLN, 2016).

11. To watch the film and other MUPI documentaries, visit https://www.youtube.com/watch?v=mLZTTxddCZg.

12. A total of 2,443 teachers participated in workshops to discuss national curricula (MINED, 2013).

13. From 2003 to 2007 more than 16,000 people had participated, including 2,200 elementary school students 5,700 high school students, 370 teachers and community educators, and 5,200 members of the general public, including indigenous communities (Hernández and Doño, 2008: 42).

14. For the lyrics in their entirety, visit http://arena.org.sv/partido/marcha/.

15. The exhibit was made possible by funding from the Rackham Program in Public Scholarship (formerly known as Arts of Citizenship) at the University of Michigan.

16. Collective memories highlight that the massacre forced indigenous women to survive in silence, generated fear of political organizing, accelerated the decline of the Nahuat-Pipil language, and heightened ethnic discrimination, particularly toward women who wore native dress (Gould and Lauria-Santiago, 2008: 253, 257; Sierra Becerra, 2015).

17. In a parallel case, Canadian aboriginal inmates have used history in group therapy sessions in order to "understand their circumstances, how they came to be damaged," and how "the legacy of historical processes of oppression remain as threats to personal and collective wellbeing" (Waldram, 2014: 377). In contrast, unresolved trauma among Salvadoran war survivors has hurt familial relationships and helped produce a negative group culture (Dickson-Gómez, 2002: 416).

Conclusion

Complexities, Controversies, and the Value of Collective Memory and Social Justice

Roberta Villalón

A second wave of memory, truth, and justice mobilizations has been spreading in Latin America since the turn of the century. The push to address unresolved human rights violations perpetrated in the region's recent history has resulted in the (re) opening of trials of perpetrators and a more complex understanding of past and present violence and inequalities. The resilient collective efforts that have fed these processes have also gained depth. Richer collective memories and the achievement of (at least partially) successful outcomes have provided movements a clear sense that not all their efforts have been in vain. Justice, reconciliation, and social equality may not be at all possible, but they are ideals worth pursuing.

This volume comprises a theoretical contribution to the field of memory studies by focusing on the politics of framing collective memory, truth, and justice processes in Latin America from a critical epistemology from below. The research is intended to challenge systems and practices of inequality and contribute to community efforts to generate social change for justice. The contributors dismantle inequalities of knowledge and power by critically pointing to controversies, inconsistencies, and complexities of memory, truth, and justice processes. Their studies allow for a more nuanced comprehension of past violence, breaking up simplistic interpretations that pair victims and victimizers, left and right, pre- and post-conflict, truth, and injustice to instead explore the grey areas in between and reveal the misleading effects of dichotomous rationalizations.

The research presented here motivates reflection for action. In part I, "Framing Collective Memory: Counter-Hegemonic and Master Narratives," Crenzel's work on Argentina's famous *Nunca Más* report dares readers to deconstruct current dominant accounts despite the fact that they were originally the symbol of resistance, and he calls for deliberation about how societies can ultimately reach an understanding of a divisive past that is all-inclusive without being dismissive or oppressive. Similarly,

221

Salvi asks about the possibility of reconciliation of parties that are politically polarized (the Argentinean military and human rights organizations' members) yet morally bound together under a newly reconstructed ideal of universal victimhood and
national unity. Is this an unintended consequence that puts into question the actual
willingness of the parties to reach a point of reconciliation? Is it a historical irony
that brings up a stalemate impossible to overcome? Relatedly, Hiner and Azócar
raise questions about the unexpected outcomes of all-encompassing human rights
regimes, which, in the case of Chile, imposed a reconciliatory culture where it was
not appropriate (in the realm of family violence). Are forgiveness and unity always
desirable? Can justice mean something else? All of these studies challenge readers to
develop more nuanced, critical research that looks into the controversies of memory,
truth, and justice processes.

In part II, "Defining Historical Periods, Blame, and Reparation," researchers
suggest readers to question typical narratives about Latin America's conflictive past.
Poblete's analysis of Chile's transition, García Jerez and Müller's work on the distinction between long-term and short-term memory in Bolivia, and Márquez's study of
Colombia's Gallery of Memory disrupt the conventional pairing of violence with
military regimes. The violence that is to be resisted and repaired is linked in Chile to
neoliberal capitalism and its implementation during both military and democratic
governments, and in Bolivia to the colonial oppression of indigenous communities.
In Colombia the responsibility for human rights violations is questioned because
of the fact that conflict has continued despite declarations of a postwar time and
because of the ambivalent role of the state in perpetrating, promoting, and denying
violence. The analyses presented by these authors emphasize the need to rethink political strategies with regard to justice and equality, and academic tactics with regard
to the historical and political focus of research projects. Can there be a collective
memory in an individualistic, consumerist culture? Can there be justice without the
recognition and reparation of colonial inequalities and their legacies? Can processes
of memory, justice, and reconciliation advance in contexts of ongoing violence in
ambiguous democracies? Can the state or any other party involved in the perpetration of violence be exempted of responsibility and justice be accomplished?

In part III, "Cultures of Trauma, Healing, and Justice," readers are also called
to broaden their inquiries and dismiss prevailing explanations. The research by
D'Orsi and Garrard defies mainstream ideas about how to move forward after
highly traumatic violent events. In his analysis of Uruguay's long-awaited process of
memory and justice, D'Orsi moves away from an individualistic understanding and
psychological treatment of trauma to a collective and sociopolitical one, and makes
readers wonder how a balance between forgetting and an obsession with the past can
be achieved in a context with old, decaying, suppressed wounds. Garrard's research
highlights the general lack of a cultural relativist approach in both the politics and
the scholarship of memory and justice. In exploring the experiences of the Maya, she
ponders parallel dynamics of healing and justice: while they are finding the physical
remains of their dead and enacting their rituals to allow them to rest in peace and,

thus, for the living to close a chapter of lingering horror, Guatemala's most notorious killers and repressors remain not charged and free. Questions about the imperfect memory, truth, and justice processes within wounded cultural backgrounds are also raised by Kaiser. Analyzing the new trials in Argentina, she dares readers to assume their responsibility as part of a whole that is arguably accountable for the horrors of the past: with limited media coverage, low attendance at court hearings, and minimal following, will the effects of this new advancement of judicial proceedings be far too limited to be significant at all?

In part IV, "Arts, Media, Museums, and Memory," readers are invited to focus on the power relations underlying artistic creations and cultural spaces related to processes of memory, truth, and justice. Cortés tests the equalization of political art and propaganda by explaining how muralism creatively connects past, present, and future. Art is traversed with power, and vice versa, but such a connection can denounce and transcend social inequalities and violence, while reproducing collective identity and political citizenship. Similarly, Aroni Sulca points to the perseverance of survival, of the resignification of individual and collective being in a context that may have been labeled as post-conflict but in reality continues to amass pain, injustice, and resistance. The currency of cultural productivity in Peru, like that of muralism in Chile, is testament of the central role that memory art has had in justice and reconciliation processes.

Schneider and Atencio, however, challenge readers not to overvalue the power of artistic or cultural creations. While it is true that they can help advance memory, truth, and justice processes, their real effect may be tamed. In Brazil, the popular success of artistic/cultural productions goes hand in hand with the absence of legal processes for addressing human rights violations. Artistic and cultural media are relevant, but not enough to achieve justice. Sierra Becerra also ask readers to be cautious. Counter-hegemonic grassroots museums and cultural spaces have been excellent means to feed memory, truth, and justice processes, and they have represented strong links between past, present, and future struggles. But again, they are not all that is necessary to reach a fair resolution to the legacies of conflict and current violence. El Salvador's wider, neoliberal context with weak and fragmented social movements limits the potential of initiatives like MUPI's. Thus, artistic creations, be they murals, carnivals, telenovelas, films, popular museums, or memory spaces, can become formidable tools to advance memorialization and reconciliation through wounded cultures, but can only be fully effective if they are accompanied by other legal/political measures and unrelenting civil mobilization that work to bring justice to all.

All together, this volume leaves readers with a realistic panorama of where the complex and contradictory memory, truth, and justice processes in Latin America are, with their glow and their murkiness, together with an acute sense of historicity and collective agency. Contemporary inequalities and injustices are not to be simply interpreted as empty of history or passively accepted as unavoidable. Social mobilization not only allows for change, however minimal, but also builds collective identity and a sense of being. Power relations affect us all. Taking action changes the meaning of our personal and communal lives and, more important, leads to the purposeful construction of our realities. Memories cannot be suppressed, and the pursuit of justice continues to run strong despite all efforts to settle without a fair resolution.

This compilation stands out for recognizing the complexities and controversies of collective memory, truth, and justice processes, while at the same time emphasizing their extraordinary value for dismantling oppressive practices and violent structures of inequality. Together with the 16 authors of this volume, I hope that this critical scholarship contributes to furthering collective efforts to achieve social justice in the region and beyond.

References

Abrão, Paulo. 2012. "The struggle over the meaning of amnesty in Brazil," pp. 23–33 in Marcelo D. Torelly (ed.), *Justiça de transição e Estado Constitucional de direito: Perspectiva teórico-comparativa e análise do caso brasileiro*. Belo Horizonte: Fórum.

Abrão, Paulo and Marcelo D. Torelly. 2011a. "As dimensões da justiça de transição no Brasil, a eficácia da Lei de Anistia e as alternativas para a verdade e a justiça," pp. 212–248 in Payne, Abrão, and Torelly (eds.), *A anistia na era da responsibilização*.

———. 2011b. "The reparations program as the linchpin of transitional justice in Brazil," pp. 443–485 in Félix Reátegui (ed.), *Transitional Justice: Handbook for Latin America*. Brasília and New York: Brazilian Amnesty Commission, Ministry of Justice / International Center for Transitional Justice.

———. 2012. "Resistance to change: Brazil's persistent amnesty and its alternatives for truth and justice," pp. 152–181 in Lessa and Payne (eds.), *Amnesty in the Age of Human Rights Accountability*.

Achugar, Hugo and Gerardo Caetano (eds.). 1992. *Identidad uruguaya: ¿Mito, crisis, o afirmación?* Montevideo: Ediciones Trilce.

Acuña, Carlos, Inés González Bombal, Elizabeth Jelin, Oscar Landi, Luis Quevedo, Catalina Smulovitz, and Adriana Vacchieri. 1995. *Juicio, castigos y memorias: Derechos humanos y justicia en la política argentina*. Buenos Aires: Nueva Visión.

Acuña, Carlos and Catalina Smulovitz. 1995. "Militares en la transición argentina: del gobierno a la subordinación constitucional," pp. 153–202 in Carlos Acuña (ed.), *La nueva matriz política argentina*. Buenos Aires: Nueva Visión.

Adorno, Theodor W. 1973 (1966). *Negative Dialectics*. Translated by E. B. Ashton. New York: Continuum Press.

———. 1978 (1951). *Minima Moralia: Reflections from a Damaged Life*. Translated by E. F. N. Jephcott. London: Verso.

Afflitto, Frank and Paul Jesilow. 2007. *The Quiet Revolutionaries: Seeking Justice in Guatemala*. Austin: University of Texas Press.

Agamben, Giorgio. 1998a. *Quel che resta di Auschwitz: L'archivio e il testimone (Homo Sacer III)*. Turin: Bollati Boringhieri.

———. 1998b. *Homo Sacer: Sovereign Power and Bare Life*. Stanford, CA: Stanford University Press.

———. 2004. "The witness," pp. 437–442 in Nancy Scheper-Hughes and Philippe Bourgois (eds.), *Violence in War and Peace*. Oxford: Blackwell.

———. 2009. *Lo que queda de Auschwitz*. Valencia: Pre-Textos.

Agger, Inger and Soren Jensen. 1997. *Trauma y cura en situaciones de terrorismo de estado*. Santiago: ILAS/CESOC.

Alanes, Olga. 2012. "Contextualización histórica de las dictaduras militares en Bolivia," pp. 61–82 in Vincenty and Zapata (eds.), *Contextualización de la antropología física forense en Bolivia*.

Alarcón Medina, Rafael. 2014. "'Dreaming the dream of a dead man': memory, media, and youth in postwar El Salvador." *Dialectical Anthropology* 38: 481–497.

Alarcón Medina, Rafael and Leigh Binford. 2014. "Revisiting the El Mozote massacre: memory and politics in postwar El Salvador." *Journal of Genocide Research* 16: 513–533.

Albó, Xavier. 2009. "Larga memoria de lo étnico en Bolivia, con temporales oscilaciones," pp. 19–40 in John Crabtree, George Gray Molina, and Laurence Whitehead (eds.), *Tensiones irresueltas: Bolivia, pasado y presente*. La Paz: Plural Editores.

Albro, Robert. 2005. "'The water is ours, Carajo!': deep citizenship in Bolivia's water war," pp. 249–271 in June Nash (ed.), *Social Movements: An Anthropological Reader*. London: Basil Blackwell.

———. 2006. "Bolivia's 'Evo Morales phenomenon': from identity to what?" *Journal of Latin American Anthropology* 11: 408–428.

———. 2009. "Democracy's labor: disjunctive memory in a Bolivian workers' union." *Latin American Perspectives* 36 (5): 39–57.

Alcatruz, Paula. 2004. "Aquí se pinta nuestra historia: el muralismo callejero como acercamiento metodológico al sujeto histórico poblador." *Anuario de Pregrado en Historia Universidad de Chile 2004*, 1–17.

Alexander, Jeffrey. 2003. *The Meanings of Social Life: A Cultural Sociology*. Oxford: Oxford University Press.

———. 2004. "Toward a cultural theory of trauma," pp. 1–30 in Jeffrey Alexander, Ron Eyerman, Bernhard Giesen, Neil J. Smelser, and Piotr Sztompka (eds.), *Cultural Trauma and Cultural Identity*. Berkeley: University of California Press.

Alexander, Jeffrey, Ron Eyerman, Bernhard Giesen, Neil J. Smelser, and Piotr Sztompka (eds.). 2004. *Cultural Trauma and Cultural Identity*. Berkeley: University of California Press.

Almarez, Alejandro et al. 2012. *Bolivia MAScarada del poder: Por la recuperación del proceso del cambio por los pueblos indígenas y los trabajadores*. Buenos Aires: Herramienta.

Almeida, Paul D. 2008. *Waves of Protest: Popular Struggle in El Salvador, 1925–2005*. Minneapolis: University of Minnesota Press.

Alonso, Ana María. 1994. "The politics of space, time, and substance: state formation, nationalism, and ethnicity." *Annual Review of Anthropology* 23: 379–405.

Altamirano, Carlos. 2007. "Pasado presente," pp. 17–33 in Lida, Gutiérrez Crespo, and (eds.), *Argentina, 1976*.

Alves, Maria H. Moreira. 1985. *State and Opposition in Military Brazil*. Austin: University of Texas Press.

Alzugarat, Alfredo. 2007. *Trincheras de papel: Dictadura y literatura carcelaria en Uruguay*. Montevideo: Ediciones Trilce.

Amaya, Rufina, Mark Danner, and Carlos Henríquez Consalvi. 1996. *Luciérnagas en El Mozote*. San Salvador: Museo de la Palabra y la Imagen.

Amnesty International. 2010. "Bolivia: documentos militares deben ser entregados para que se haga justicia en casos de desapariciones forzadas del pasado." Índice AI: AMR 18/003/2010.

———. 2012. "Bolivia: autoridades deben otorgar reparaciones integrales a víctimas de violaciones de derechos humanos durante regímes militares y autoritarios." Press release, August 21.

Anderson, Benedict. 1991. *Imagined Communities*. London: Verso.

Anderson, Thomas P. 1971. *Matanza: El Salvador's Communist Revolt of 1932*. Lincoln: University of Nebraska Press.

Andreozzi, Gabriele (ed.). 2011. *Juicios por crímenes de lesa humanidad en Argentina*. Buenos Aires: Atuel.

Antze, P. and M. Lambeck (eds.). 1996. *Tense Past: Essays in Trauma and Memory*. London: Routledge.

Aponte, Alejandro. 2006. *Guerra y derecho penal de enemigo: Reflexión crítica sobre el eficientismo penal de enemigo*. Bogotá: Ediciones Jurídicas Gustavo Ibáñez.

Arce, Luz. 2004. *Inferno: A Story of Terror and Survival in Chile*. Madison: University of Wisconsin Press.

Arendt, Hannah. 1978. *The Life of the Mind*. New York: Harcourt Brace.

———. 1994. "Organized guilt and universal responsibility," pp. 121–131 in *Essays in Understanding 1930–1954*. New York: Harcourt Brace.

———. 2007. "Responsabilidad colectiva," pp. 151–159 in *Responsabilidad y juicio*. Barcelona: Paidós.

Arias, Arturo and Alicia del Campo. 2009. "Introduction: memory and popular culture." *Latin American Perspectives* 36 (5): 3–20.

Arnson, Cynthia (ed.). 1999. *Comparative Peace Processes in Latin America*. Stanford, CA: Stanford University Press.

———. 2012. *In the Wake of War: Democratization and Internal Armed Conflict in Latin America*. Washington, DC: Woodrow Wilson International Center for Scholars.

Arnson, Cynthia, Ariel C. Armony, Catalina Smulovitz, Gaston Chillier, Enrique Peruzzotti, and Giselle Cohen. 2009. *La "nueva izquierda" en América Latina: Derechos humanos, participación política, y sociedad civil*. Washington, DC: Woodrow Wilson International Center for Scholars.

Aronés, Mariano. 2003. "El proceso de desmilitarización en Ayacucho," pp. 266–288 in Ludwig Huber (ed.), *Centralismo y descentralización en Ayacucho*. Lima: IEP.

Aroni, Renzo. 2013. "Sentimiento de *pumpin*: música, migración y memoria en Lima, Perú." Master's thesis, Universidad Nacional Autónoma de Mexico.

Arquidiócesis de São Paulo. 1985. *Brasil: Nunca mais*. Petrópolis: Vozes.

Arthur, Paige. 2009. "How transitions reshaped human rights: a conceptual history of transitional justice." *Human Rights Quarterly* 31: 321–367.

ASOFAMD (Asociación de Familiares de Detenidos, Desaparecidos y Mártires por la Liberación Nacional). 2007. *La masacre de la calle Harrington: Para que no se olvide, 15 de enero de 1981*. La Paz: Creart Impresores.

———. 2008. *Informe sobre las desapariciones forzadas en Bolivia*. La Paz: Capítulo Boliviano de Derechos Humanos, Democracia y Desarrollo.

———. 2009. *Voces latinoamericanos contra la impunidad: Seminario internacional contra la impunidad*. La Paz: Garza Azul.

Assmann, Jan. 2008. "Communicative and cultural memory," pp. 109–118 in Astrid Erll and Ansgar Nünning (eds.), *Cultural Memory Studies: An International and Interdisciplinary Handbook*. Berlin: de Gruyter.

Astori, Daniel et al. 1996. *El Uruguay de la dictadura (1973–1985)*. Montevideo: Ediciones de la Banda Oriental.

Atencio, Rebecca J. 2011. "A prime time to remember: memory merchandising in Globo's *Anos Rebeldes*," pp. 41–68 in Bilbija and Payne (eds.), *Accounting for Violence*.

———. 2013. "Acts of witnessing: site-specific performance and transitional justice in post-dictatorship Brazil." *Latin American Theatre Review* 46 (2): 7–24.

———. 2014. *Memory's Turn: Culture and Transitional Justice in Brazil*. Madison: University of Wisconsin Press.

———. 2015. "Reconciliation or resistance? Fernando Gabeira's *O que é isso, companheiro?* and the Amnesty Law." *Luso-Brazilian Review* 52 (2): 99–115.

Avelar, Idelber. 1999. *The Untimely Present: Postdictatorial Latin American Fiction and the Task of Mourning*. Durham, NC: Duke University Press.

Aylwin, Patricio. 1992. *La transición chilena: Discursos escogidos marzo 1990–1992*. Santiago: Editorial Andrés Bello.

Badaró, Máximo. 2009. *Militares o ciudadanos: La formación de los oficiales del Ejército Argentino*. Buenos Aires: Prometeo.

Bajc, Vida and Willem de Lint. 2011. *Security and Everyday Life*. New York: Routledge.

Baldez, Lisa. 2002. *Why Women Protest: Women's Movements in Chile*. Cambridge: Cambridge University Press.

Barahona de Brito, Alexandra. 1997. *Human Rights and Democratization in Latin America: Uruguay and Chile*. Oxford: Oxford University Press.

———. 2001. "Truth, justice, memory, and democratization in the Southern Cone," pp. 119–160 in Barahona de Brito, González-Enríquez, and Aguilar (eds.), *The Politics of Memory*.

Barahona de Brito, Alexandra, Carmen Gonzalez-Enriquez, and Paloma Aguila (eds.). 2001. *The Politics of Memory: Transitional Justice in Democratizing Societies*. Oxford: Oxford University Press.

Barreiro, Julio. 1974. *Educación popular y proceso de concientización*. Buenos Aires: Siglo XXI.

Barrios, Raúl. 1992. "Militares y democracia en Bolivia: entre la reforma o la desestabilización." *FASOC* 8 (3): 1–10.

Basile, Teresa. 1989. "Aproximaciones al 'testimonio sobre la desaparición de personas' durante la dictadura militar y la democracia argentinas." *Cuadernos Angers* 2 (2): 45–63.

Basso, Ellen. 1987. "The implications of a progressive theory of dreaming," pp. 86–104 in Barbara Tedlock (ed.), *Dreaming: Anthropological and Psychological Interpretations*. Cambridge: Cambridge University Press.

Bell, Christine and Catherine O'Rourke. 2007. "Does feminism need a theory of transitional justice? An introductory essay." *International Journal of Transitional Justice* 1: 23–44.

Bell, Patrick, Paul Kobrak, and Herbert F. Spirer. 1999. *State Violence in Guatemala, 1960–1996: A Quantitative Reflection*. Washington, DC: AAAS Science and Human Rights Program.

Bellange, Ebe. 1995. *El mural como reflejo de la sociedad chilena*. Santiago: LOM/CESOC.

Beneduce, Roberto. 2007. *Etnopsichiatria: Sofferenza mentale e alterità fra storia, dominio e cultura*. Rome: Carocci.

Benjamin, Walter. 2003. *La obra de arte en la época de su reproductibilidad técnica*. Mexico City: Itaca.

Bickford, Louis. 2000. "Humans rights archives and research on historical memory: Argentina, Chile, and Uruguay." *Latin American Research Review* 35 (2): 160–182.

Bietti, Lucas. 2009. "Entre la cognición política y la cognición social: el discurso de la memoria colectiva en Argentina." *Discurso y Sociedad* 3 (1): 44–89.

Bilbija, Ksenija and Leigh A. Payne (eds.). 2005. *The Art of Truth-Telling about Authoritarian Rule.* Madison: University of Wisconsin Press.

———. (eds.). 2011. *Accounting for Violence: Marketing Memory in Latin America.* Durham, NC: Duke University Press.

Blofield, Merike and Liesl Haas. 2005. "Defining democracy: reforming the laws on women's rights in Chile, 1990–2002." *Latin American Politics and Society* 47 (3): 35–68.

Bloxham, Donald. 2001. *Genocide on Trial: War Crimes Trials and the Formation of Holocaust History and Memory.* Oxford: Oxford University Press.

Boal, Augusto. 1998. *Legislative Theater.* New York: Routledge.

Boesten, Jelke. 2012. "The state and violence against women in Peru: intersecting inequalities and patriarchal rule." *Social Politics: International Studies in Gender, State, and Society* 19: 361–382.

Bortoluci, Jose and Robert Jansen. 2013. "Toward a postcolonial sociology: the view from Latin America," pp. 199–229 in Julian Go (ed.), *Postcolonial Sociology* (Political Power and Social Theory, vol. 24). Bingley, UK: Emerald Group Publishing.

Bourdieu, Pierre. 1972. *Esquisse d'une théorie de la pratique.* Geneva: Droz.

———. 1977. *Outline of a Theory of Practice.* New York: Cambridge University Press.

———. 1984. *Distinction: A Social Critique of the Judgment of Taste.* Cambridge. MA: Harvard University Press.

Brands, Hal. 2010. *Latin America's Cold War.* Cambridge, MA: Harvard University Press.

Brienza, Lucía. 2009. "Relatos en pugna sobre el pasado reciente en Argentina: las visions militares sobre los años setenta desde Alfonsín hasta el primer gobierno de Menem." *Revista Temáticas* 17 (33/34): 73–104.

Brugnoli, Valeria. 2002. "Trazos urbanos de una identidad." *Revista Chilena de Antropología Visual,* no. 2, 85–96.

Bunster, Ximena. 1985. "Surviving beyond fear: women and torture in Latin America," pp. 297–327 in June Nash and Helen Safa (eds.), *Women and Change in Latin America.* South Hadley, MA: Bergin and Garvey.

Burgos, Elizabeth. 1998 (1983). *Me llamo Rigoberta Menchú y así me nació la conciencia.* Mexico City: Siglo XXI.

Burke, Peter. 1989. "History as social memory," pp. 97–113 in Thomas Butler (ed.), *Memory: History, Culture, and the Mind.* Malden, MA: Blackwell.

———. 2004. *Varieties of Cultural History.* Cambridge, UK: Polity Press.

Burman, Anders. 2011. *Descolonización aymara: Ritualidad y política (2006–2010).* La Paz: Plural Editores.

Burt, Jo-Marie. 2013. "The new accountability agenda in Latin America: the promise and perils of human rights prosecutions," pp. 101–141 in Hite and Mark (eds.), *Sustaining Human Rights in the Twenty-first Century.*

Burt, Jo-Marie and María Rodríguez. 2015. "Justicia, verdad y memoria: el proceso penal para el caso de la masacre de Accomarca," pp. 135–168 in Ludwig Huber and Ponciano del Pino (eds.), *Políticas en justicia transicional: Miradas comparativas sobre el legado de la CVR.* Lima: IEP.

Caballeros, Harold and Carlos Annacondia. 2001. *Victorious Warfare: Discovering Your Rightful Place in God's Kingdom*. Nashville, TN: Thomas Nelson.

Calveiro, Pilar. 1998. *Poder y desaparición: Los campos de concentración en Argentina*. Buenos Aires: Ediciones Colihue.

Cámara de Diputados. 1993. "Sesión 42, 19 enero." Santiago: Cámara de Diputados de la República de Chile.

Cameron, Duncan. 1971. "The museum, a temple or the forum." *Curator* 14 (March): 11–24.

Campos, Luis. 2009. "Los murales de La Victoria: efectos de sentido y lugar." *Actuel Marx*, no. 8, 129–142.

Candau, Joël. 1998. *Mémoire et identité*. Paris: Presses Universitaires de France.

Canessa, Andrew. 2006. "Todos somos indígenas: towards a new language of national political identity." *Bulletin of Latin American Research* 25: 241–263.

———. 2008. "Celebrando lo indígena en Bolivia: unas reflexiones sobre el año nuevo Aymara," pp. 39–48 in Carmen Martínez (ed.), *Repensando las identidades y políticas indígenas en América Latina*. Quito: FLACSO.

———. 2012. *Conflict, Claim, and Contradiction in the New Indigenous State of Bolivia*. Working Paper 22. DesiguALdades.net. Berlin: Freie Universität.

Cappelletto, Francesca. 2003. "Long-term memory of extreme events: from autobiography to history." *Journal of the Royal Anthropological Institute* 9 (2): 241–260.

Caruth, Cathy. 1995. "Trauma and experience: introduction," pp. 3–12 in C. Caruth (ed.), *Trauma: Explorations in Memory*. Baltimore: Johns Hopkins University Press.

Castillo, Eduardo. 2006. *Puño y letra: Movimiento social y comunicación gráfica en Chile*. Santiago: Ocho Libro Editores.

Castillo, Juan Carlos. 2012. "Is inequality becoming just? Changes in public opinion about economic distribution in Chile." *Bulletin of Latin American Research* 31 (1): 1–19.

Castoriadis, Cornelius. 1987 (1975). *The Imaginary Institution of Society*. Cambridge, UK: Polity Press.

CBDHDD (Capítulo Boliviano de Derechos Humanos, Desarrollo y Democracia y Comunidad de Derechos Humanos). 2009. *Informe de la sociedad civil para el EPU Bolivia: Un informe sobre los derechos humanos en Bolivia*. La Paz: CBDHDD/CDH.

Centro de Estudios Legales y Sociales. 2011. *Hacer justicia: Nuevos debates sobre el juzgamiento de crímenes de lesa humanidad en Argentina*. Buenos Aires: Siglo Veintiuno Editores.

Centro de Investigación y Educación Popular. 2008. *Noche y niebla: Marco conceptual banco de datos de derechos humanos y violencia política*. 2d edition. Bogotá: CINEP.

Cepeda Castro, Ivan and Claudia Girón Ortiz. n.d. "La Galería de la Memoria." *Desaparecidos*. http://www.desaparecidos.org/colombia/galeria/comple.html (accessed December 10, 2015).

Chávez, Lisa. 2007. "Vietnamese women's museums: a form of resistance." *Asian Women* 23 (December): 107–127.

Chizuko, Ueno and Jordan Sand. 1999. "The politics of memory: nation, individual, and self." *History and Memory* 11 (2): 129–152.

CIPAE (Comité de Iglesia para Ayudas de Emergencia). 1990. *Paraguay Nunca Más*. Asunción: CIPAE.

Clavero, Carolina. 2009. *El despertar de una nueva conciencia: Memoria de lucha contra la violencia doméstica en Uruguay (1984–2002)*. Montevideo: OBSUR.

Clemente, Pietro and Fabio Dei (eds.). 2005. *Poetiche e politiche del ricordo*. Rome: Carocci.

CMC (Solidaridad y Comisariato de las Misiones de Holandesa). 2004. *Se levantan: El camino hacia una sepultura digna*. Amsterdam: Solidaridad CMC de Holandesa.

CNVD (Comisión Nacional de Verdad y Reconciliación). 1991. *Informe de la Comisión Nacional de Verdad y Reconciliación.* Santiago de Chile: Ediciones del Ornitorrinco.

COB (Central Obrera Boliviana). 1976. *Informe: Violación de los derechos humanos en Bolivia.* La Paz: COB/ASOFAMD.

Cohen, Stanley. 2001. *States of Denial: Knowing about Atrocities and Suffering.* Cambridge, UK: Polity Press.

Coimbra, Cecília Maria Bouças. 2001. "Tortura ontém e hoje: resgatando uma certa história." *Psicologia em Estudo* 6 (April): 11–19.

Colby, Benjamin N. and Lore M. Colby. 1981. *The Daykeeper: The Life and Discourse of an Ixil Diviner.* Cambridge, MA: Harvard University Press.

Collins, Cath. 2010. *Post-Transitional Justice: Human Rights Trials in Chile and El Salvador.* University Park: Pennsylvania State University Press.

Collins, Patricia Hill. 2000. *Black Feminist Thought: Knowledge, Consciousness, and the Politics of Empowerment.* New York: Routledge.

Comisión Colombiana de Juristas. 2012. "Listado de víctimas de violencia sociopolítica en Colombia, julio de 1996 a mayo de 2012." http://www.coljuristas.org/documentos/cifras/cif_2012-06-26.pdf (accessed December 1, 2015).

Comité de Memoria Histórica. 2005. *Tortura en poblaciones del Gran Santiago (1973–1990).* Santiago: Corporación José Domingo Cañas.

CONADEP (Comisión Nacional sobre la Desaparición de Personas). 1983–1984. "Actas." MS, Buenos Aires.

———. 1984. *Nunca Más: Informe de la Comisión Nacional sobre la Desaparición de Personas.* Buenos Aires: EUDEBA.

———. 2006. *Nunca Más: Informe de la Comisión Nacional sobre la Desaparición de Personas.* 2d edition. Buenos Aires: EUDEBA.

Condenanza, Maria. 2002. *La espera.* Montevideo: Editorial Senda.

Conferencia Episcopal de Chile. 1984. *El renacer de Chile.* Santiago: Conferencia Episcopal de Chile.

Connell, Raewyn. 2007. *Southern Theory: The Global Dynamics of Knowledge in Social Sciences.* Cambridge, UK: Polity Press.

Contini, Giovanni. 1997. *La memoria divisa.* Milano: Rizzoli.

Convicción. 1983. "Documento final de la Junta Militar sobre la guerra contra la subversión y el terrorismo." April 29, special supplement, 1–4.

Cook, Garrett W. 1986. "Quichean folk theology and Southern Maya supernaturalism," pp. 139–154 in Gary Gossen (ed.), *Symbol and Meaning beyond the Closed Community: Essays in Mesoamerican Ideas.* Albany: State University of New York Press.

———. 2000. *Renewing the Maya World: Expressive Culture in a Highland Town.* Austin: University of Texas Press.

Cook, Rebecca J. (ed.). 1997. *Derechos humanos de la mujer: Perspectivas nacionales e internacionales.* Bogotá: Profamilia.

Correa Sutil, Jorge. 1999. "La Cenicienta se queda en la fiesta: el poder judicial chileno en la década de los 90," pp. 281–315 in Drake and Jaksic (eds.), *El modelo chileno.*

Cortés, Alexis. 2009. "'Nada por caridad': toma de terrenos y dictadura, la identidad territorial de La Población La Victoria." Master's thesis, IUPERJ/UCAM.

———. 2011. "Da memória traumática ao relato heróico: o papel da violência na identidade de bairro da Población La Victoria em Santiago do Chile." *Sociedade e Cultura* 14: 257–367.

————. 2013. "A struggle larger than a house: *pobladores* and *favelados* in Latin American social theory." *Latin American Perspectives* 40 (2): 168–184.

————. 2014. "El movimiento de pobladores chilenos y la población La Victoria: ejemplaridad, movimientos sociales y el derecho a la ciudad." *EURE (Santiago)* 40 (119): 239–260.

Crenshaw, Kimberle. 1991. "Mapping the margins: intersectionality, identity politics, and violence against women of color." *Stanford Law Review* 43: 1241–1299.

Crenzel, Emilio. 2008. *La historia política del Nunca Más: La memoria de las desapariciones en Argentina*. Buenos Aires: Siglo XXI.

Cruz, María Angélica. 2004. *Iglesia, represión y memoria: El caso chileno*. Madrid: Siglo XXI.

Cruz, María del Carmen. 2004. "Orígenes de la educación popular en Chalatenango: una innovación popular." *Estudios Centroamericanos* 671: 897–925.

————. 2011. "A discussion with María del Carmen Cruz Senovilla, Professor in the Education Department, Universidad Centroamericana, José Simeón Canas, El Salvador." Berkeley Center for Religion, Peace, and World Affairs, July 10. https://berkleycenter .georgetown.edu/interviews/a-discussion-with-maria-del-carmen-cruz-senovilla-profes sor-in-the-educationdepartment-universidad-centroamericana-jose-simeon-canas-el-sal vador (accessed September 1, 2015).

Csordas, Thomas. 1999. "Embodiment and cultural phenomenology," pp. 143–162 in G. Weiss and F. H. Haber (eds.), *Perspectives on Embodiment: The Intersection of Nature and Culture*. London: Routledge.

Curtis, Bruce. 2002. "Surveying the social: techniques, practices, power." *Histoire Social/Social History* 25 (69): 83–108.

Curtis-Fawley, Sarah and Kathleen Daly. 2005. "Gendered violence and restorative justice: the views of victim advocates." *Violence against Women* 11: 603–638.

CVR (Comisión de la Verdad y Reconciliación). 2003. "Informe final, Tomo 7, Caso Accomarca." http://www.derechos.org/nizkor/peru/libros/cv/vii/215.pdf (accessed December 16, 2014).

Da Silva Catela, Ludmila. 2001. *No habrá flores en la tumba del pasado: La experiencia de reconstrucción del mundo de los familiares de desaparecidos*. La Plata: Al Margen.

————. 2010. "Pasados en conflicto: de memorias dominantes, subterráneas y denegadas," pp. 99–123 in Ernesto Bohslansky, Marina Franco, Mariana Iglesias, and Daniel Lvovich (eds.), *Problemas de historia reciente del Cono Sur*, vol. 1. Buenos Aires: Universidad Nacional de General Sarmiento/Prometeo.

Dalmas, Carine. 2007. "As brigadas muralistas da experiência chilena: propaganda política e imaginário revolucionário." *História* 26 (2): 226–256.

Daly, Kathleen and Julie Stubbs. 2006. "Feminist engagement with restorative justice." *Theoretical Criminology* 10 (1): 9–28.

Dandan, Alejandra. 2012. "Lo que se viene." *Página/12*, July 22, 16.

Danner, Mark. 1993. *The Massacre at El Mozote*. New York: Vintage.

Davis, Diane. 2008. "Challenges of violence and insecurity: beyond the democracy-development mantra." *ReVista: Harvard Review of Latin America*, Winter. http://www.revista.drclas.harvard .edu (accessed January 25, 2015).

Degregori, Carlos Iván. 1999. "Movimientos étnicos, democracia y nación en Perú y Bolivia," pp. 159–225 in Claudia Dray (ed.), *La construcción de la nación y la revolución ciudadana en México, Guatemala, Perú, Ecuador y Bolivia*. Guatemala City: FLACSO.

del Pino, Pociano. 2014. "Ayacuchano cinema and the filming of violence: interview with Palito Ortega Matute," pp. 153–175 in Milton (ed.), *Art from a Fractured Past*.

DeLugan, Robin María. 2008. "Census, map, museum (revisited): El Salvador's postwar transnational magination." *Identities* 15: 171–193.

De Martino, Ernesto. 1958. *Morte e pianto rituale nel mondo antico: Dal lamento pagano al pianto di Maria.* Turin: Einaudi.

———. 1964. "Apocalissi culturali e apocalissi psicopatologiche." *Nuovi Argomenti,* nos. 69–71, 105–141.

Demasi, Carlos. 2003. "¿Cuáles dos demonios?" *Memorias* 1. http://www.paginadigital.com.ar/articulos/2003/2003quint/noticias18/1204711-7.asp.

Demasi, Carlos et al. 2009. *La dictadura cívico-militar.* Montevideo: Ediciones de la Banda Oriental.

Derrida, Jacques. 1990. "The force of law: 'The Mystical Foundation of Authority.'" *Cardozo Law Review* 11C: 919–1045.

Desmond Arias, Enrique and Daniel M. Goldstein. 2010. *Violent Democracies in Latin America.* Durham, NC: Duke University Press.

Dezalay, Yves and Bryant Garth. 2002. *The Internationalization of Palace Wars: Lawyers, Economists, and the Contest to Transform Latin American States.* Chicago: University of Chicago Press.

Diario de las Madres de Plaza de Mayo. 1984. "CONADEP: los desaparecidos no se archivan." 1 (1): 6–7.

———. 1985. "Las trampas del Nunca Más." 1 (2): 7.

Díaz Bessone, Ramón. 1998. *In memoriam.* Buenos Aires: Ediciones del Círculo Militar.

Dickson-Gómez, Julia. 2002. "The sound of barking dogs: violence and terror among Salvadoran families in the postwar." *Medical Anthropology Quarterly* 16: 415–438.

Do Alto, Hervé. 2005. "What will the victory of Morales mean?" *International Viewpoint* 4 (December): 16–19.

Donzelot, Jacques. 1991. "The mobilization of society," pp. 169–179 in Graham Burchell, Colin Gordon, and Peter Miller (eds.), *The Foucault Effect: Studies in Governmentality.* Chicago: Hemel Hempstead.

Dooner, Patricio. 1989. *Iglesia, reconciliación y democracia.* Santiago: Editorial Andante.

D'Orsi, Lorenzo. 2012. "Apocalissi culturali e economie della memoria," pp. 153–156 in A. M. Sobrero (ed.), *Il cannocchiale sulle retrovie.* Rome: CISU.

———. 2013. "In Uruguay non poteva piovere: tempi e racconti della dittatura uruguaiana tra il 1973 e il 1985," pp. 67–92 in F. Dei and C. Di Pasquale (eds.), *Esplorazioni etnografiche tra guerra e pace.* Pisa: Pacini.

D'Orsi, Lorenzo and Carla Rita. 2011. "Luoghi per ricordare: la memoria della tragedia a Montevideo." *Anuario de Antropología Social y Cultural en Uruguay* 2010–2011: 67–79.

Dosh, Paul. 2002. "Peace after terror: reconciling justice and the rule of law in Argentina, El Salvador, and Guatemala." *Latin American Perspectives* 29 (4): 98–104.

Douglas, Lawrence. 1998. "The shrunken head of Buchenwald: icons of atrocity at Nuremberg." *Representations* 63 (Summer): 39–64.

———. 2006. "The didactic trial: filtering history and memory into the courtroom." *European Review* 14: 513–522.

Drake, Paul and Ivan Jaksic (eds.). 1999. *El modelo chileno: Democracia y desarrollo en los noventa.* Santiago: LOM.

Dubet, François. 2012. *¿Para qué sirve realmente un sociólogo?* Buenos Aires: Siglo Veintiuno Editores.

Duhalde, Eduardo. 1999. *El Estado terrorista argentino: Quince años después, una mirada crítica.* Buenos Aires: EUDEBA.

Dulfano, Isabel. 2004. "*Testimonio*: present predicaments and future forays," pp. 81–96 in Linda S. Maier and Isabel Dulfano (eds.), *Woman as Witness: Essays on Testimonial Literature by Latin American Women*. New York: Peter Lang Publications.

Duncan, Carol and Alan Wallach. 1980. "The universal survey museum." *Art History* 3: 448–469.

Dunkerley, James. 1984. *Rebellion in the Veins: Political Struggle in Bolivia, 1952–1982*. London: Verso.

Dussel, Inés, Silvia Finocchio, and Silvia Gojman. 1997. *Haciendo memoria en el país de Nunca Más*. Buenos Aires: EUDEBA.

Earle, Duncan. 1986. "The metaphor of the day in Quiché: notes on the nature of everyday life," pp. 155–172 in Gary Gossen (ed.), *Symbol and Meaning beyond the Closed Community: Essays in Mesoamerican Ideas*. Albany: State University of New York Press.

Echavarría, Josefina. 2010. *In/Security in Colombia: Writing Political Identities in the Democratic Security Policy*. Manchester: Manchester University Press.

Echeverría, Albino. 2009. "Mural 'Presencia de América Latina' del pintor mexicano Jorge González Camarena." *Atenea (Concepción)*, no. 500, 157–166.

Eckstein, Susan and Manuel M. A. Garretón. 1989. *Power and Popular Protest: Latin American Social Movements*. Berkeley: University of California Press.

ECLAC (Economic Commission for Latin America and the Caribbean). 2013. *Economic Survey of Latin America and the Caribbean: Three Decades of Uneven and Unstable Growth*. Santiago: United Nations Publications.

———. 2014. *Compacts for Equality: Towards a Sustainable Future*. Santiago: United Nations Publications.

Edwards, Alice. 2011. *Violence against Women under International Human Rights Law*. Cambridge: Cambridge University Press.

Ellner, Steve. 2012. "The distinguishing features of Latin America's new left in power: the Chávez, Morales, and Correa governments." *Latin American Perspectives* 39 (1): 96–114.

———. (ed.). 2014. *Latin America's Radical Left: Challenges and Complexities of Political Power in the Twenty-first Century*. Lanham, MD: Rowman and Littlefield.

Ensalaco, Mark. 1994. "Truth commissions for Chile and El Salvador: a report and assessment." *Human Rights Quarterly* 16: 656–675.

EPICA (Ecumenical Program on Central America and the Caribbean, Center for Human Rights Legal Action). 1996. *Unearthing the Truth: Exhuming a Decade of Terror in Guatemala*. Washington, DC: EPICA and CHRLA.

Errázuriz, Luis Hernán. 2009. "Dictadura militar en Chile: antecedentes del golpe estético-cultural." *Latin American Research Review* 44 (2): 136–157.

Evans, Rebecca. 2007. "Treating poorly healed wounds: partisan choices and human rights policies in Latin America." *Human Rights Review*, April–June, 249–278.

Eyerman, Ron. 2004. "The past in the present: culture and the transmission of memory." *Acta Sociológica* 47 (2): 159–169.

Fabbri, Lucía. 1989. *Qué diré de la cárcel*. Montevideo: Centro de Integración Cultural.

FAFG (Fundación de Antropología Forense de Guatemala). 2004. *Reconocimiento: La memoria de las víctimas del conflicto armado*. Guatemala City: FAFG.

———. 2012a, "Forced disappearances." http://www.fafg.org/Ingles/paginas/ForcedDisappearances. html.

———. 2012b. "Masacres." http://www.fafg.org/paginas/masacres.htm.

———. 2012c. "Informe Programa PAJUST." http://www.fafg.org/pagTemas/2011/Marzo/Informe_ Programa_PAJUST.html.

Fassin, Didier. 2011. "A contribution to the critique of moral reason." *Anthropological Theory* 11: 481–491.

Fassin, Didier and Richard Rechtman. 2009 (2007). *The Empire of Trauma*. Princeton, NJ: Princeton University Press.

Faulk, Karen. 2013. *In the Wake of Neoliberalism: Citizenship and Human Rights in Argentina*. Stanford, CA: Stanford University Press.

Feld, Claudia. 1998. "Cómo la televisión argentina relata hoy el período de la dictadura militar (1976–1983)." Ph.D. diss., Université de París-VIII.

———. 2001. "La construcción del 'arrepentimiento': los ex represores en la television." *Entrepasados*, nos. 20–21, 35–54.

———. 2016. "Constructing memory through television in Argentina." *Latin American Perspectives* 43(5): 29–44.

Feldman, Allen. 2002. "Strange fruit: the South-African Truth Commission and the demonic economies of violence," pp. 234–265 in Bruce Kapferer (ed.), *Beyond Rationalism: Rethinking Magic, Witchcraft, and Sorcery*. New York: Berghahn Books.

Fentress, James and Chris Wickham. 1992. *Social Memory*. Oxford: Blackwell.

Ferree, Myra Marx. 1990. "Beyond separate spheres: feminism and family research." *Journal of Marriage and Family* 52: 866–884.

———. 2010. "Filling the glass: gender perspectives on families." *Journal of Marriage and Family* 72: 420–439.

Fico, Carlos. 2009. "A negociação parlamentar da anistias de 1979 e o chamado 'perdão aos torturadores.'" https://www.passeidireto.com/arquivo/3076396/13-a-negociacao-parlamentar-da-anistiade-1979-e-o-chamado-perdao-dos-torturador (accessed June 14, 2010).

Figueroa Ibarra, Carlos. 1991. *El recurso del miedo: Ensayo sobre el estado y el terror en Guatemala*. San José, Costa Rica: Programa Centroamericano de Investigaciones, Secretaría General del CSUCA / Editorial Universitaria Centroamericana.

FMLN (Frente Farabundo Martí de Liberación Nacional). 2016. "Memoria histórica prepara colectivo de rescate de la histórica," *Prensa FMLN*, May 15. http://www.fmln.org.sv/sv/oficialv3c/index.php/noticias/noticias-fmln/492-memoriahistorica-prepara-colectivo-de-rescate-de-la-historica (accessed May 20, 2016).

Fontán, Dionisia. 1985. "*Nunca Más*: un libro que el periodismo ha silenciado." *El Periodista de Buenos Aires* 1 (30): 38.

Fontana, Lorenza Belinda. 2013. "On the perils and potentialities of revolution: conflict and collective action in contemporary Bolivia." *Latin American Perspectives* 40 (3): 26–42.

Foro de Buenos Aires por la Vigencia de los Derechos Humanos. 1973. *Proceso a la explotación y a la represión en Argentina*. Buenos Aires: Foro de Buenos Aires por la Vigencia de los Derechos Humanos.

Foucault, Michel. 1978 (1975). *Discipline and Punish: The Birth of the Prison*. New York: Pantheon Books.

———. 1991. "Governmentality," pp. 87–104 in Graham Burchell, Colin Gordon, and Peter Miller (eds.), *The Foucault Effect: Studies in Governmentality*. Chicago: University of Chicago Press.

———. 2011 (1975). "Film in popular memory: an interview with Michel Foucault," pp. 252–253 in Jeffrey Olick, Vered Vinitzky-Seroussi, and Daniel Levy (eds.), *The Collective Memory Reader*. New York: Oxford University Press.

Franceschet, Susan. 2003. "'State feminism' and women's movements: the impact of Chile's Servicio Nacional de la Mujer on women's activism." *Latin American Research Review* 38 (1): 9–40.

Franco, Jean. 1992. "Gender, death, and resistance: facing the ethics vacuum," pp. 104–118 in Juan E. Corradi, Jessica Weiss Fagen, and Manuel Antonio Garretón (eds.), *Fear at the Edge: State Terror and Resistance in Latin America*. Berkeley: University of California Press.

Frazier, Lessie Jo. 2007. *Salt in the Sand: Memory, Violence, and the Nation-State in Chile, 1890 to the Present*. Durham, NC: Duke University Press.

Freire, Paulo. 1970. *Pedagogy of the Oppressed*. Translated by Myra Bergman Ramos. New York: Continuum.

———. 1973a. "Education as the practice of freedom," pp. 1–61 in Myra Bergman Ramos (ed.), *Education for Critical Consciousness*. New York: Continuum.

———. 1973b. *Extensión o comunicación: La concientización en el campo*. Mexico City: Siglo XXI.

French, Scot A. 1995. "What is social memory?" *Southern Cultures* 2 (1): 9–18.

Freud, Sigmund. 1919. *Totem and Taboo: Resemblances between the Psychic Lives of Savages and Neurotics*. New York: Collier.

Fried Amilivia, Gabriela. 2009. "Remembering trauma in society: forced disappearance and familial transmissions after Uruguay's era of state terror (1973–2001)" in Noel Packard (ed.), *Sociology of Memory: Papers from the Spectrum*. Cambridge: Cambridge Scholars Press.

———. 2016. "Sealing and unsealing Uruguay's transitional politics of oblivion: waves of memory and the road to justice, 1985–2015." *Latin American Perspectives* 43(6): 103–123.

Fuentes, Claudio. 1999. "Partidos y coaliciones en el Chile de los '90: entre pactos y proyectos," pp. 191–222 in Drake and Jaksic (eds.), *El modelo chileno*.

Funes, Patricia. 2001. "*Nunca Más:* memorias de las dictaduras en América Latina," pp. 43–61 in B. Groppo and P. Flier (eds.), *La imposibilidad del olvido: Recorridos de la memoria en Argentina, Chile y Uruguay*. La Plata: Al Margen.

Gajardo, Patricio. 1986. "Los murales de La Victoria." *Araucaria*, no. 35, 8–9.

Galtung, Johan. 1969. "Violence, peace, and peace research." *Journal of Peace Research* 6: 167–191.

Gampel, Yolanda. 2000. "Reflections on the prevalence of the uncanny in social violence," pp. 48–69 in A. Robben and M. Suárez-Orozco (eds.), *Cultures under Siege: Collective Violence and Trauma*. Cambridge: Cambridge University Press.

García Álvarez, Jacobo. 2009. "Lugares, paisajes y políticas de memoria: una lectura geográfica." *Boletín de la A.G.E.* no. 51, 175–202.

García Canclini, Néstor. 2009. *Culturas híbridas*. Mexico City: Debolsillo.

García Jerez, Francisco A. 2012. "The skin of the city: remembering Bolivian dictatorships in the streets of La Paz." Master's thesis, University of Aberdeen.

García Linera, Álvaro. 2006. "El capitalismo andino-amazónico." Le Monde Diplomatique, edition Chile. http://www.lemondediplomatique.cl/El-capitalismo-andino-amazonico.html (accessed February 2, 2014).

Garretón Kreft, Francisca, Marianne González Le Saux, and Silvana Lauzán. 2011. *Políticas públicas de verdad y memoria en 7 países de América Latina (Argentina, Bolivia, Brasil, Chile, Paraguay, Perú y Uruguay)*. Santiago de Chile: Programa Derechos Humanos y Democracia/Centro de Derechos Humanos/Facultad de Derecho.

Garretón, Roberto. 1988. "La evolución política del régimen militar chileno," pp. 147–185 in Guillermo O'Donnell, Philippe Schmitter, and Laurence Whitehead (eds.), *Transiciones desde un gobierno autoritario*, vol. 2, *América*. Buenos Aires: Paidós.

Gaspari, Elio. 2004. *A ditadura encurralada*. São Paulo: Companhia das Letras.

Giesen, Bernhard. 2004. *Triumph and Trauma*. Boulder: Paradigm.

Giraldo Mendoza, Martha Elena. 2006. "La Ruta Pacífica de Mujeres de Colombia y las mediaciones femeninas," pp. 19–33 in *Octavo Foro de los Derechos Humanos: Derechos humanos y objetivos del milenio*. Barcelona: Cooperacció.

Gitlin, Todd. 1980. *The Whole World Is Watching: Mass Media in the Making and Unmaking of the New Left*. Berkeley: University of California Press.

Gledhill, John. 2000. *Power and Its Disguises: Anthropological Perspectives on Politics*. Sterling, UK: Pluto Press.

Global Witness. 2014. "Deadly environment." https://www.globalwitness.org/en/campaigns/environmental-activists/deadly-environment/ (accessed December 1, 2015).

Go, Julian. 2013. "Introduction: Entangling postcoloniality and sociological thought," pp. 3–31 in Julian Go (ed.), *Postcolonial Sociology* (Political Power and Social Theory, vol. 24). Bingley, UK: Emerald Group Publishing.

Goffman, Erving. 1974. *Frame Analysis: An Essay on the Organization of Experience*. New York: Harper and Row.

Gómez-Barris, Macarena. 2009. *Where Memory Dwells: Culture and State Violence in Chile*. Berkeley: University of California Press.

González, Alejandro. 2000. "El arte brigadista." *abacq*. http://www.abacq.net/imagineria/arte4.htm (accessed May 9, 2014).

González Bombal, Inés. 1995. *"Nunca Más:* el juicio más allá de los estrados," pp. 193–216 in Acuña, Bombal, Jelin, Landi, Quevedo, Smulovitz, and Vacchieri (eds.), *Juicio, castigos y memorias*.

González Bombal, Inés and Oscar Landi. 1995. "Los derechos en la cultura política," pp. 147–192 in Acuña, Bombal, Jelin, Landi, Quevedo, Smulovitz, and Vacchieri (eds.), *Juicio, castigos y memorias*.

Gorelik, Adrián. 2007. "Las metrópolis latinoamericanas, el arte y la vida: arte y ciudad en tiempos de globalización." *Aisthesis*, no. 41, 36–56.

Gould, Jeffrey L. 2001. "Revolutionary nationalism and local memories in El Salvador," pp. 138–171 in Gilbert M. Joseph (ed.), *Reclaiming the Political in Latin American History: Essays from the North*. Durham, NC: Duke University Press.

Gould, Jeffrey L. and Aldo Lauria-Santiago. 2008. *To Rise in Darkness: Revolution, Repression, and Memory in El Salvador, 1920–1932*. Durham, NC: Duke University Press.

Graham, B., G. J. Ashworth, and J. E. Tumbridge. 2000. *A Geography of Heritage: Power, Culture, and Economy*. Oxford: Oxford University Press.

Gramsci, Antonio. 1971. *Selections from the Prison Notebooks of Antonio Gramsci*. Translated by Quintin Hoare and Geoffrey Nowell Smith. New York: International Publishers.

Grandin, Greg. 2004. *The Last Colonial Massacre: Latin America in the Cold War*. Chicago: University of Chicago Press.

———. 2005. "The instruction of great catastrophe: truth commissions, national history, and state formation in Argentina, Chile, and Guatemala." *American Historical Review* 110 (1): 46–67.

———. 2006. *Empire's Workshop: Latin America, the United States, and the Rise of the New Imperialism*. New York: Metropolitan.

———. 2015. "Did Bill O'Reilly cover up a war crime in El Salvador?" *The Nation*, February 9. http://www.thenation.com/article/did-bill-oreilly-cover-war-crime-el-salvador/ (accessed September 1, 2015).

Grandin, Greg and Thomas Miller Klubock. 2007. "Editors' introduction." *Radical History Review* 97: 1–10.

Grandón, Romina. 2011. "Brigada Ramona Parra: muralismo político y debate cultural en la Unidad Popular." Licenciado thesis, Universidad Alberto Hurtado.

Grecco, Jorge and Gustavo González. 1990. *Argentina: El ejército que tenemos.* Buenos Aires: Sudamericana.

Green, James N. 2010. *We Cannot Remain Silent: Opposition to the Brazilian Military Dictatorship in the United States.* Durham, NC: Duke University Press.

Green, Linda. 1999. *Fear as a Way of Life: Mayan Widows in Rural Guatemala.* New York: Columbia University Press.

Guglielmucci, Ana and Luciana Scaraffuni Ribeiro. 2016. "Site of memory and site of forgetting: the repurposing of the Punta Carretas Prison." *Latin American Perspectives* 43(5): 131–144.

Gurian, Elaine H. 2006. "Noodling around with exhibition opportunities: the potential meaning of exhibition modalities," pp. 150–161 in *Civilizing the Museum: The Collected Writings of Elaine Heumann Gurian.* New York: Routledge.

Gutiérrez, Gustavo. 1999 (1973). *A Theology of Liberation: History, Politics, and Salvation.* Translated by Sister Caridad Inda and John Eagleson. Maryknoll, NY: Orbis Books.

Gutmann, Matthew (ed.). 2003. *Changing Men and Masculinities in Latin America.* Durham, NC: Duke University Press.

Guzmán, Álvaro. 2012. "Desaparición forzada de personas 1964–1982," pp. 93–98 in Vincenty and Zapata (eds.), *Contextualización de la antropología física forense en Bolivia.*

Guzmán, Patricio. 2010. *Nostalgia de la luz.* Atacama Productions.

Guzmán, Virginia, Amalia Mauro, and Kathya Araujo. 2000. "La violencia doméstica como problema público y objeto de políticas." Proyecto FONDECYT No. 96033. Santiago: Centro de Estudios de la Mujer.

Guzmán Barney, Alvaro. 2013. "Seguridad ciudadana y seguridad del estado," pp. 19–41 in Alexandra Abello Colak and Pablo Emilio Angarita Cañas (eds.), *Nuevo pensamiento sobre seguridad en América Latina: Hacia la seguridad como un valor democrático.* Medellín: CLACSO/Universidad de Antioquia.

Guzmán Orellana, Gloria and Irantzu Mendia Azkue. 2013. *Mujeres con memoria, activistas del movimiento derechos humanos en El Salvador.* Bilboa: HIGOA.

Haas, Leisl. 2010. *Feminist Policymaking in Chile.* University Park: Pennsylvania State University Press.

Habermas, Jürgen and Adam Michnik. 1994. "Overcoming the past." *New Left Review* 203 (January/February): 3–16.

Hacking, Ian. 1995. *Rewriting the Soul: Multiple Personality and the Sciences of Memory.* Princeton, NJ: Princeton University Press.

Halbwachs, Maurice. 1950. *La mémoire collective.* Paris: Presses Universitaires de France.

———. 1980. *The Collective Memory.* New York: Harper and Row.

———. 1992. *On Collective Memory.* Chicago: University of Chicago Press.

———. 2004. *Los marcos sociales de la memoria.* Barcelona: Anthropos.

Hale, Charles. 2008. *Engaging Contradictions: Theory, Politics, and Methods of Activist Scholarship.* Los Angeles: University of California Press.

Hammond, John L. 1998. *Fighting to Learn: Popular Education and Guerrilla War in El Salvador.* New Brunswick, NJ: Rutgers University Press.

Harding, Sandra. 1998. *Is Science Multicultural? Postcolonialisms, Feminisms, and Epistemologies.* Bloomington: Indiana University Press.

Hardy, Clarisa. 1986. *Hambre + diginidad = Ollas comunes*. Santiago: PET.

Harvey, David. 2005. *A Brief History of Neoliberalism*. Oxford: Oxford University Press.

Hayner, Priscilla. 1994. "Fifteen truth commissions, 1974 to 1994: a comparative study." *Human Rights Quarterly* 16: 597–655.

———. 2001. *Unspeakable Truth: Confronting State Terror and Atrocity*. New York: Routledge.

Hazan, Pierre. 2010. *Judging War, Judging History: Behind Truth and Reconciliation*. Stanford, CA: Stanford University Press.

Heidenry, Rachel. 2014. "The murals of El Salvador: reconstruction, historical memory, and whitewashing." *Public Art Dialogue* 4 (1): 122–145.

Hein, Hilde S. 2000. "Museum typology," pp. 17–26 in *Museum in Transition: A Philosophical Perspective*. Washington, DC: Smithsonian Institution Press.

Henríquez Consalvi, Carlos. 1992. *La terquedad del izote: La historia de Radio Venceremos*. Mexico City: Editorial Diana.

Herman, Judith. 2005. "Justice from the victim's perspective." *Violence against Women* 11: 571–602.

Hernández Rivas, Georgina. 2015. "Cartografía de la memoria." Ph.D. diss., Universidad Complutense de Madrid.

Hernández Rivas, Georgina and Milton Doño. 2008. "Memoria en movimiento: experiencias sobre memoria histórica a través de audiovisuales dirigidos al sistema educativo y las comunidades indígenas." *Trasmallo: Identidad, Memoria, Cultura* 3: 36–42.

Herzog, Kirstin. 1993. *Finding Their Voice: Peruvian Women's Testimonies of War*. Philadelphia: Trinity Press International.

High, Steven (ed.). 2015. *Beyond Testimony and Trauma: Oral History in the Aftermath of Mass Violence*. Vancouver: University of British Columbia Press.

Hiner, Hillary. 2009. "Voces soterradas, violencias ignoradas: discurso, violencia política y género en los Informes Rettig y Valech." *Latin American Research Review* 44 (3): 50–74.

———. 2012. "Historizar la violencia puertas adentro: el caso de la Casa Yela y la violencia de género en Talca, 1964–2008." Ph.D. diss., Universidad de Chile.

———. 2013. "Mujeres entre 'la espada y la pared': violencia de género y Estado en Chile, 1990–2010," pp. 249–276 in Consuelo Figueroa (ed.), *Chile y América Latina: Democracias, ciudadanías y narrativas históricas*. Santiago: RIL.

Hirsch, Marianne. 2008. "The generation of postmemory." *Poetics Today* 29 (1): 103–128.

———. 2012. *The Generation of Postmemory: Writing and Visual Culture after the Holocaust*. New York: Columbia University Press.

Hirsch, Marianne and Valerie Smith. 2002. "Feminism and cultural memory: an introduction." *Signs* 28 (1): 1–19.

Hite, Katherine. 2013. *Politics and the Art of Commemoration: Memorials to Struggle in Latin America and Spain*. New York: Routledge.

Hite, Katherine and Mark Ungar (eds.). 2013. *Sustaining Human Rights in the Twenty-first Century: Strategies from Latin America*. Washington, DC: Woodrow Wilson International Center for Scholars / Johns Hopkins University Press.

Hooper-Greenhill, Eilean. 1992. "What is a museum?," pp. 1–23 in *Museums and the Shaping of Knowledge*. London: Routledge.

Howard, Rosaleen. 2010. "Language, signs, and the performance of power: the discourse struggle over decolonization in the Bolivia of Evo Morales." *Latin American Perspectives* 37 (3): 176–194.

Htun, Mala. 2003. *Sex and the State*. New York: Cambridge University Press.

Huamaní, Edilberto. 2010. "El concurso del carnaval Vencedores de Ayacucho." *Pariwana* 2 (1): 22–23.

Hudson, Barbara.2002. "Restorative justice and gendered violence." *British Journal of Criminology* 42: 616–634.

Human Rights Watch. 2014. "World Report 2014, Bolivia." http://www.hrw.org/world -report/2014/countrychapters/bolivia (accessed December 7, 2014).

Hurtado, Javier. 1986. *El Katarismo*. La Paz: Hisbol.

Huyssen, Andreas. 2000. "Present pasts: media, politics, amnesia." *Public Culture* 12 (1): 21–38.

———. 2003. *Present Pasts. Urban Palimpsests and the Politics of Memory*. Stanford, CA: Stanford University Press.

Hylton, Forrest and Sinclair Thomson. 2007. *Revolutionary Horizons: Past and Present in Bolivian Politics*. London: Verso.

INCITE! Women of Color Against Violence and Nadia Elia (eds.). 2007. *The Revolution Will Not Be Funded: Beyond the Non-Profit Industrial Complex*. Brooklyn, NY: South End Press.

Inter-American Commission on Human Rights. 2007. *Informe preliminar de la misión internacional de observación sobre ejecuciones extrajudiciales e impunidad en Colombia*. http:// www.dhcolombia.info/IMG/Informe_misionobservacion_ejecuciones.pdf (accessed December 1, 2015).

———. 2008. "Informe anual." http://www.cidh.oas.org/annualrep/2008sp/cap4.Colombia. sp.htm (accessed December 1, 2015).

Irazábal, Clara (ed.). 2008. *Ordinary Places/Extraordinary Events: Citizenship, Democracy and Public Space in Latin America*. New York: Taylor and Francis.

Izaguirre, Inés. 1992. *Los desaparecidos: Recuperación de una identidad expropiada*. Cuaderno 9. Buenos Aires: Instituto de Investigaciones Gino Germani, Facultad de Ciencias Sociales, Universidad de Buenos Aires.

Jaggar, Alison. 2008. *Just Methods: An Interdisciplinary Feminist Reader*. Boulder: Paradigm.

Jara Ibarra, Camila. 2016. "The Demobilization of Civil Society: Posttraumatic Memory in the Reconstruction of Chilean Democracy." *Latin American Perspectives* 43(6): 88–102.

Jaspers, Karl. 1998. *El problema de la culpa: Sobre la responsabilidad política alemana*. Barcelona: Paidós.

Jelin, Elizabeth. 1994. "The politics of memory: the human rights movements and the construction of democracy in Argentina." *Latin American Perspectives* 21 (2): 38–58.

———. 1995. "La política de la memoria: el movimiento de derechos humanos y la construcción de la democracia en Argentina," pp. 101–146 in C. Acuña Bombal, Jelin, Landi, Quevedo, Smulovitz, and Vacchieri (eds.), *Juicio, castigos y memorias*.

———. 2001. *Los trabajos de la memoria*. Buenos Aires: Siglo XXI.

———. 2002. *Los trabajos de la memoria*. Madrid: Siglo XXI.

———. 2003. *State Repression and the Labors of Memory*. Minneapolis: University of Minnesota Press.

———. 2007. "Public memorialization in perspective: truth, justice, and memory of past repression in the Southern Cone of South America." *International Journal of Transitional Justice* 1 (1): 138–156.

Jelin, Elizabeth and Ana Longoni (eds.). 2005. *Escritura, imágenes y escenarios ante la represión*. Madrid: Siglo XXI.

Jelin, Elizabeth and Susana Kaufman. 2002. "Twenty years after in Argentina," pp. 31–41 in David E. Lorey and William Beezley (eds.), *Genocide, Collective Violence, and Popular*

Memory: The Politics of Remembrance in the Twentieth Century. Wilmington, DE: Scholarly Resources.

Jelin, Elizabeth and Victoria Langland. 2003. "Las marcas territoriales como nexo entre pasado y presente." pp. 1–18 in Elizabeth Jelin and Victoria Langland (eds.), *Monumentos, memoriales y marcas territoriales.* Madrid: Siglo XXI.

Jensen, Silvina. 2004. "Suspendidos de la historia/exiliados de la memoria: el caso de los argentinos desterrados en Cataluña (1976–. . .)." Ph.D. diss., Universidad Autónoma de Barcelona.

Johnson, Michael. 2007. "Domestic violence: the intersection of gender and control," pp. 257–268 in Laura O'Toole, Jessica Schiffman, and Margie Kiter Edwards (eds.), *Gender Violence: Interdisciplinary Perspectives.* 2d edition. New York: New York University Press.

Kaiser, Susana. 2002. "*Escraches*: demonstrations, communication, and political memory in post-dictatorial Argentina." *Media, Culture and Society* 24: 499–516.

———. 2005. *Postmemories of Terror: A New Generation Copes with the Legacy of the "Dirty War."* New York: Palgrave Macmillan.

———. 2008. "The struggle for urban territories: human rights activists in Buenos Aires," pp. 70–196 in Irazábal (ed.), *Ordinary Places/Extraordinary Events.*

———. 2014. "Argentinean torturers on trial: how are journalists covering the hearings' memory work?," pp. 242–257 in Barbie Zelizer and Keren Tenenboim-Weinblatt (eds.), *Journalism and Memory.* New York: Palgrave Macmillan.

Keck, Margaret and Kathryn Sikkink. 1998. *Activists beyond Borders: Advocacy Networks in International Politics.* Ithaca, NY: Cornell University Press.

Kirkwood, Julieta. 1990 (1986). *Ser política en Chile: Los nudos de la sabiduría feminista.* Santiago: Editorial Cuarto Propio.

Klein, Herbert S. 2011. *A Concise History of Bolivia.* New York: Cambridge University Press.

Klein, Naomi. 2007. *The Shock Doctrine: The Rise of Disaster Capitalism.* New York: Metropolitan Books.

Kohl, Benjamín. 2010. "Bolivia under Morales: a work in progress." *Latin American Perspectives* 37 (3): 107–122.

Koonings, Kees and Dirk Kruijt (eds.). 1999. *Societies of Fear: The Legacy of Civil War, Violence, and Terror in Latin America.* London: Zed Books.

———. 2004. *Armed Actors: Organised Violence and State Failure in Latin America.* London: Zed Books.

Krog, Antjie. 2000. *Country of My Skull: Guilt, Sorrow, and the Limits of Forgiveness in the New South Africa.* New York: Three River Press.

LaCapra, Dominick. 2001. *Writing History, Writing Trauma.* Baltimore: Johns Hopkins University Press.

Lamounier, Bolivar. 1980. *Voto de desconfiança: Eleições e mudança na política no Brasil, 1970–1979.* Petrópolis: Vozes.

Langland, Victoria. 2005. "Fotografía y memoria," in Elizabeth Jelin and Ana Longoni (eds.), *Escrituras, imágenes y escenarios ante la represión.* Madrid and Buenos Aires: Siglo XXI.

———. 2013. *Speaking of Flowers: Student Movements and the Making and Remembering of 1968 in Military Brazil.* Durham, NC: Duke University Press.

Larraín, Pablo. 2008. *Tony Manero.* Fábula Productions.

Layne, Valmont. 2008. "The District Six Museum: an ordinary people's place." *The Public Historian* 30 (1): 53–62.

Lazzara, Michael J. and Vicky Unruh (eds.). 2009. *Telling Ruins in Latin America.* New York: Palgrave Macmillan.

Lazzarato, Maurizio. 2009. "Neoliberalism in action: inequality, insecurity, and the reconstitution of the social." *Theory, Culture, and Society* 26 (6): 109–133.

Leal-Guerrero, Sigifredo. 2015. "'The Holocaust' or 'the Salvation of Democracy': Memory and Political Struggle in the Aftermath of Colombia's Palace of Justice Massacre." *Latin American Perspectives*, 42(3): 140–161.

Lechner, Norbert and Pedro Güell. 1999. "Construcción social de las memorias en la transición chilena," pp. 185–210 in Amparo Mendez Carrión and Alfredo Joignant (eds.), *La caja de Pandora: El retorno de la transición chilena*. Santiago: Planeta.

———. 2006. "Construcción social de las memorias en la transición chilena," pp. 17–46 in Elizabeth Jelin and Susana Kaufman (eds.), *Subjetividades y figuras de la memoria*. Buenos Aires: Siglo XXI.

Leiner, Martin and Susan Flämig (eds.). 2012. *Latin America between Conflict and Reconciliation*. Göttingen: Vandenhoeck and Ruprecht.

Leiva, Gonzalo. 2003. *Álvaro Hoppe: El ojo en la historia*. Santiago: Colección Imaginario.

Lemouneau, Carine. 2015. "A propósito de las pinturas murales en Chile entre 1970 y 1990: archivar, referenciar, construir." *Bifurcaciones*, no. 20, 1–17.

Lernoux, Penny. 1980. *Cry of the People: The Struggle for Human Rights in Latin America—The Catholic Church in Conflict with U.S. Policy*. London: Penguin.

Lessa, Francesca. 2013. *Memory Politics and Transitional Justice in Argentina and Uruguay: Against Impunity*. New York: Palgrave Macmillan.

Lessa, Francesca and Cara Levey. 2012. "Memories of violence and changing landscapes of impunity in Uruguay, 1985–2011." *Encounters* 5: 137–168.

Lessa, Francesca and Leigh A. Payne. 2012. *Amnesty in the Age of Human Rights Accountability: Comparative and International Perspectives*. Cambridge: Cambridge University Press.

Levitsky, Steven and Kenneth M. Roberts. 2011. *The Resurgence of the American Left*. Baltimore: Johns Hopkins University Press.

Lida, Clara Eugenia, Horacio Gutiérrez Crespo, and Pablo Yankelevich. 2007. *Argentina, 1976: Estudios en torno al golpe de Estado*. Mexico City: Colegio de México.

Lindo, Roger. 2015. "El museo de las rebeldías." *Confidencial*, March 6. http://www.confidencial.com.ni/articulo/21919/el-museo-de-las-rebeldias (accessed September 1, 2015).

Lindo-Fuentes, Héctor, Erik Ching, and Rafael Lara-Martínez. 2007. *Remembering a Massacre in El Salvador: The Insurrection of 1932, Roque Dalton, and the Politics of Historical Memory*. Albuquerque: University of New Mexico Press.

Lira, Elizabeth (ed.). 1994. *Psicología y violencia política en América Latina*. Santiago: ILAS/CESOC.

Lira, Elizabeth and María Isabel Castillo. 1993. "Trauma político y memoria social." *Psicología Política*, 6: 95–116.

Lira, Elizabeth and Brian Loveman. 1998. "La política de reconciliación: discursos, sacramentos y pragmatismo." Paper presented at the conference Legacies of Authoritarianism: Cultural Production, Collective Trauma, and Global Justice, Madison, WI.

Lira, Elizabeth and Isabel Piper (eds.). 1996. *Reparación, derechos humanos y salud mental*. Santiago: ILAS/CESOC.

Lleras, Christina. 2012. "Doors being open: rights of Afro-descendants in the National Museum of Colombia." *Curator* 55: 327–342.

López Vigil, José Ignacio (ed.).1992. *Las mil y una historias de Radio Venceremos*. San Salvador: UCA Editores.

Loraux, Nicole. 1989. "De la amnistía y su contrario," pp. 27–52 in Y. Yerushalmi et al. (eds.), *Usos del olvido*. Buenos Aires: Nueva Visión.

Lorenzo, G. Ángel. 2011. "Marcha indígena por el TIPNIS en Bolivia: ¿más que un simple problema?" *Revista Andina de Estudios Políticos* 9: 1–17.

Lorey, David E. and William Beezley. 2002. "Introduction," pp. xi–xxxiii in David E. Lorey and William Beezley (eds.), *Genocide, Collective Violence, and Popular Memory: The Politics of Remembrance in the Twentieth Century*. Wilmington, DE: Scholarly Resources.

Loveman, Brian and Elizabeth Lira. 2000. *Las ardientes cenizas del olvido: Vía chilena de la reconciliación política, 1932–1994*. Santiago: LOM.

———. 2002. *El espejismo de la reconciliación política: Chile 1990–2002*. Santiago: LOM/ DIBAM / Universidad Alberto Hurtado.

———. 2005. *Políticas de reparación: Chile 1990–2004*. Santiago: DIBAM / Barros Arana.

Lynch, Horacio and Enrique Del Carril. 1985. *Definitivamente nunca más: La otra cara del informe de la CONADEP*. Buenos Aires: FORES.

Macauley, Fiona. 2006. "Judicialising and (de)criminalising domestic violence in Latin America." *Social Policy and Society* 5 (1): 103–114.

Maier, Linda S. 2004. "The case for and case history of women's testimonial literature in Latin America," pp. 1–17 in Linda S. Maier and Isabel Dulfano (eds.), *Woman as Witness: Essays on Testimonial Literature by Latin American Women*. New York: Peter Lang Publications.

Malloy, James and Eduardo Gamarra. 1988. *Revolution and Reaction: Bolivia, 1964–1985*. New Brunswick, NJ: Transaction Books.

Mannheim, Karl. 1952. "The sociological problems of generations," pp. 286–320 in *Essays on the Sociology of Knowledge*. London: Routledge.

Mansilla, Luis Alberto. 2003. *Hoy es todavía: José Venturelli, una biografía*. Santiago: LOM Ediciones.

Mantilla, Julissa. 2007. "'Sin la verdad de las mujeres la historia no estará completa': perspectiva de género en la Comisión de la Verdad y Reconciliación del Perú," pp. 1–55 in Anne Pérotin Dumon (ed.), *Historizar el pasado vivo en América Latina*. http://www.historizarel pasadovivo.cl/downloads/mantilla.pdf (accessed July 25, 2011).

Marchesi, Aldo. 2001. *Las lecciones del pasado, memoria y ciudadanía en los informes Nunca Más del Cono Sur*. Montevideo: Facultad de Humanidades y Ciencias de la Educación.

———. 2005. "Vencedores vencidos: las respuestas militares frente a los informes 'Nunca Más' en el Cono Sur," pp. 175–207 in Eric Herschberg and Felipe Agüero (eds.), *Memorias militares sobre la represión del Cono Sur: Visiones en disputa en dictadura y democracia*. Madrid: Siglo XXI.

Markarián, Vania. 2006. *Idos y recién llegados: La izquierda uruguaya en el exilio y las redes transnacionales de derechos humanos 1967–1984*. Mexico City: Uribe y Ferrari Editores.

Márquez, Erika. 2011. "Citizenship in times of exception: the turn to security and the politics of human rights in Valle del Cauca, Colombia." Ph.D. diss., University of Massachusetts– Amherst.

Márquez, Francisca and Valentina Rozas-Krause. 2016. "Occupying and reclaiming a national historical monument: the Casa Central of the Universidad de Chile." *Latin American Perspectives* 43(6): 54–74.

Márquez, Nicolás. 2004. *La otra parte de la verdad*. Buenos Aires: Argentinos por la Memoria Completa.

Marstine, Janet. 2011. "The contingent nature of museum ethics," pp. 3–24 in Janet Marstine (ed.), *Routledge Companion to Museum Ethics: Redefining Ethics for the Twenty-First-Century Museum*. New York: Routledge.

Martins Filho, João Roberto. 2009. "The war of memory: the Brazilian military dictatorship according to militants and military men." *Latin American Perspectives* 36 (5): 89–107.

Marx, Karl. 1845. *Thesis on Feuerbach*. Marx/Engels Internet Archive. https://www.marxists
.org/archive/marx/works/1845/theses/theses.htm (accessed December 1, 2014).

Masiello, Francine. 2001. *The Art of Transition: Latin American Culture and Neoliberal Crisis*. Durham, NC: Duke University Press.

Mayorga, René Antonio. 1978. "National-popular state, state capitalism, and military dictatorship in Bolivia: 1952–1975." *Latin American Perspectives* 5 (2): 89–119.

Mazzei, Gabriel. 2012. "'¡Tú también mataste!', dijo Hurtado a Rivera Rondón." *La República*, September 21. http://larepublica.pe/21-09-2012/tu-tambien-mataste-dijo-hurtado-rivera-rondon (accessed December 14, 2014).

McClintock, Michael. 1985. *The American Connection*. Vol. 1. *State Terror and Popular Resistance in El Salvador*. London: Zed Books.

McIlwaine, Cathy and Caroline Moser. 2001. "Violence and social capital in urban poor communities: perspectives from Colombia and Guatemala." *Journal of International Development* 13: 965–984.

McLaren, Peter and Henry A. Giroux. 1997. "Writing from the margins: geographies of identity, pedagogy, and power," pp. 16–41 in Peter McLaren (ed.), *Revolutionary Multiculturalism: Pedagogies of Dissent for the New Millennium*. Boulder: Westview Press.

Medina, Fernando and Marco Galván. 2014. *Sensibilidad de los índices de pobreza a los cambios en el ingreso y la desigualdad: Lecciones para el diseño de políticas en América Latina, 1997–2008*. Estudios Estadísticos 87.

Mejías, Sonia Alda. 2007. "La participación de las fuerzas armadas en la revolución democrática del MAS: el proyecto de Evo Morales," pp. 445–472 in Isidro Sepúlveda (ed.), *Seguridad humana y nuevas políticas de defensa en Iberoamérica*. Madrid: Instituto Universitario "General Gutiérrez Mellado"/UNED.

Mendoza, Jorge. 2016. "Reconstructing the collective memory of Mexico's dirty war: ideologization, clandestine detention, and torture." *Latin American Perspectives* 43(6): 124–140.

Mendoza, Zoila. 2001. *Al son de la danza: Identidad y comparsas en el Cuzco*. Lima: Fondo Editorial de la Pontificia Universidad Católica del Perú.

Menjívar, Cecilia. 2011. *Enduring Violence: Ladina Women's Lives in Guatemala*. Berkeley: University of California Press.

Merry, Sally Engle. 2008. *Gender Violence: A Cultural Perspective*. Hoboken, NJ: Wiley Blackwell.

Mezarobba, Glenda. 2007. "O preço do esquecimento: as reparações pagas às vítimas do regime militar (uma comparação entre Brasil, Argentina e Chile)." Ph.D. diss., University of São Paulo.

Mignolo, Walter. 2012. *Local Histories/Global Designs: Coloniality, Subaltern Knowledges, and Border Thinking*. Princeton, NJ: Princeton University Press.

Mignone, Emilio. 1984. "No hubo errores, no hubo excesos." *Nueva Presencia* 7 (388): 7.

———. 1991. *Derechos humanos y sociedad: El caso argentino*. Buenos Aires: CELS.

Mills, Charles W. 1959. *The Sociological Imagination*. New York: Oxford University Press.

Milton, Cynthia. 2007. "At the edge of the Peruvian truth commission: alternative paths to recounting the past." *Radical History Review* 98: 3–33.

———. (ed.). 2014a. *Art from a Fractured Past: Memory and Truth-Telling in Post–Shining Path Peru*. Durham, NC: Duke University Press.

———. 2014b. "Art from Peru's fractured past," pp. 1–34 in Milton (ed.), *Art from a Fractured Past*.

MINED (Ministerio de Educación). 2009. "La guerra civil," pp. 221–232 in Chester Rodolfo Urbina Gaitán and Waldemar Urquiza (eds.), *Historia 2: El Salvador*. San Salvador: MINED.

———. 2013. "Propuestas metodológicas planteadas por los docentes para desarrollar o fortalecer los conocimientos y habilidades que resultaron difíciles para los estudiantes en la PAES [Prueba de Aprendizaje y Aptitudes para Egresados de Educación Media], 2013." Ministry of Education. http://www.mined.gob/sv/ (accessed February 23, 2016).

Ministério da Justiça. 2008. *Relátorio annual da Comissão de Anistia*. Brasília: Ministério da Justiça.

———. 2009. "Especial: as caravanas da Anistia." *Revista Anistia: Política e Justiça de Transição* 2: 110–149.

Moeller, Robert G. 1996. "War stories: the search for a usable past in the Federal Republic of Germany." *American Historical Review* 101: 1008–1048.

Molesky-Paz, Jean. 2006. *Contemporary Maya Spirituality: The Ancient Ways Are Not Lost*. Austin: University of Texas Press.

Montero, Alfredo P. 2005. *Brazilian Politics*. Cambridge, UK: Polity Press.

Morales, Carlos. 1987. *La Victoria de Chile*. Santiago: La Llama.

Moreiras, Alberto. 1993. "Postdictadura y reforma del pensamiento." *Revista de Crítica Cultural*, no. 7 (May).

Morris, Stephen A. and Charles Blake (eds.). 2010. *Corruption and Politics in Latin America: National and Regional Dynamics*. Boulder: Lynne Rienner.

Moulian, Tomás. 1998. *Chile actual: Anatomía de un mito*. Santiago: LOM.

MOVICE (Movimiento Nacional de Víctimas de Crímenes de Estado). 2008. "Historia de la Galería de la Memoria." http://www.movimientodevictimas.org/versionantigua/index .php?option=com_k2&view=item&id=2672:historia-de-lagaler%C3%ADa-de-la-memo ria&Itemid=381 (accessed November 15, 2015).

———. 2015. "Historia: antecedentes Proyecto Colombia Nunca Más." http://www.mov imientodevictimas.org/?q=content/historia (accessed December 1, 2015).

Movimiento de Mujeres Libertad. 2010. *¡Libres! Testimonio de mujeres víctimas de las dictaduras*. La Paz: Plural Editores.

MUPI (Museo de la Palabra y la Imagen) 2011a. "La historia de Chiyo." http://issuu.com/ mupi/docs/expo_chiyo_web (accessed September 1, 2015).

———. 2011b. "Romero, voz y mirada." http://issuu.com/mupi/docs/romero (accessed September 1, 2015).

———. 2015. "1932." https://issuu.com/mupi/docs/1932_a6719d6b9904a5 (accessed August 10, 2016).

Murillo, Mario. 2012. *La bala no mata sino su destino: Una crónica de la insurrección popular de 1952 en Bolivia*. La Paz: Plural.

Murillo, Mario, Ruth Bautista, and Violeta Montellano. 2014. *Paisaje, memoria y nación encarnada: Interacciones ch'ixis en la Isla del Sol*. La Paz: PIEB.

Naples, Nancy. 2003. *Feminism and Method: Ethnography, Discourse Analysis, and Activist Research*. New York: Routledge.

Nash, June. 1993. *We Eat the Mines and the Mines Eat Us*. New York: Columbia University Press.

Navarrete, Rodrijo and Ana Maria López. 2006. "Rayando tras los muros: graffiti e imaginario político-simbólico en el Cuartel San Carlos (Caracas, Venezuela)," pp. 39–61 in Pedro Pablo Funari and Andrés Zarankin (eds.), *Arqueología de la represión y la resistencia en América Latina 1960–1980*. Córdova: Encuentro Grupo Editor / Universidad Nacional de Catamarca.

Nelson, Diane. 1991. "The reconstruction of Mayan identity." *Report on Guatemala* 12 (2): 6–7, 14.

Ni Aoláin, Fionnuala. 2009. "Women, security, and the patriarchy of internationalized transitional justice." *Human Rights Quarterly* 31: 1005–1085.

Ni Aoláin, Fionnuala, Dina Haynes, and Naomi Cahn. 2011. *On the Frontlines: Gender, War, and the Post-Conflict Process*. London: Oxford University Press.

Nietzsche, Friedrich. 2010 (1874). *On the Use and Abuse of History for Life*. Arlington, VA: Richer Resources Publications.

Nino, Carlos. 1997. *Juicio al mal absoluto: Los fundamentos y la historia del juicio a las juntas del proceso*. Buenos Aires: Emecé.

Nora, Pierre. 1989. "Between memory and history: Les lieux de mémoire." *Representations* 26: 7–24.

———. 2002. "Reasons for the current upsurge in memory." *Transit* 22 (1): 4–8.

———. 2008. *Les lieux de mémoire*. Montevideo: Ediciones Trilce.

———. 2009. *Rethinking France: Les lieux de mémoire*. Vol. 3, *Legacies*. Chicago: University of Chicago Press.

O'Donnell, Guillermo. 2004. "Why the rule of law matters." *Journal of Democracy* 15 (4): 32–46.

OJO! Media Collective. 2012. "An interview with Carlos Henríquez 'Santiago' Consalvi." May 1. https://www.youtube.com/watch?v=sYmxLAZKxQ4 (accessed September 1, 2015).

Olick, Jeffrey. 2007. *The Politics of Regret: On Collective Memory and Historical Responsibility*. New York: Routledge.

Olick, Jeffrey and Joyce Robbins. 1998. "Social memory studies: from 'collective memory' to the historical sociology of mnemonic practices." *Annual Review of Sociology* 24: 105–140.

Olsen, Tricia, Leigh Payne, and Andrew Reiter. 2010. "The justice balance: when transitional justice improves human rights and democracy." *Human Rights Quarterly* 32: 980–1007.

Orellana Aillón, Lorgio. 2006. "Nacionalismo, populismo y régimen de acumulación en Bolivia: hacia una caracterización del gobierno de Evo Morales." *Socialismo o Barbarie*, December, 83–105.

Orwell, George. 2003. *1984*. Centennial edition. New York: Plume, Hartcourt Brace.

Oxhorn, Philip. 1994. "Where did all the protesters go? Popular mobilization and the transition to democracy in Chile." *Latin American Perspectives* 21 (3): 49–68.

Palacios, Daniel. 2011. "La reforma procesal penal en Chile: nuevos agentes, sus trayectorias y la reestructuración de un campo." *Política* 49 (1): 43–70.

Partnoy, Alicia. 1998. *The Little School: Tales of Disappearance and Survival*. Berkeley, CA: Cleis Press.

Payne, Leigh A., Paulo Abrão, and Marcelo D. Torelly (eds.). 2011. *A anistia na era da responsibilização: O Brasil em perspectiva internacional e comparada*. Brasília and Oxford: Ministry of Justice / Oxford University.

Pearce, Jenny. 1986. *Promised Land: Peasant Rebellion in Chalatenango, El Salvador*. London: Latin American Bureau.

Peccerelli, Fredy. 2013. "Documenting the Guatemalan armed conflict and its victims." Paper presented to the conference Impunity, Justice, and the Human Rights Agenda, Austin, TX, February 7.

Peixoto, Paulo. 2013. "Memorial da anistia em BH deverá ser inaugurado pelo governo em 2014." *Folha de São Paulo Online.* http://www1.folha.uol.com.br/poder/1194215 -memorial-da-anistia-em-bh-devera-ser-inaugurado-pelo-governo-em-2014.shtml (accessed June 10, 2013).

Pereira, Anthony W. 2000. "An ugly democracy? State and rule of law in postauthoritarian Brazil," pp. 217–235 in Peter R. Kingstone and Timothy J. Power (eds.), *Democratic Brazil: Actors, Institutions, and Processes.* Pittsburgh: University of Pittsburgh Press.

———. 2005. *Political (In)justice: Authoritarianism and the Rule of Law in Brazil, Chile, and Argentina.* Pittsburgh: University of Pittsburgh Press.

Perelli, Carina and Juan Rial. 1986. *Demitos y memorias políticas.* Montevideo: Ediciones de la Banda Oriental.

Peters, John Durham. 2001. "Witnessing." *Media, Culture and Society* 23: 707–723.

Philips, Kendall (ed.). 2004. *Framing Public Memory.* Tuscaloosa: University of Alabama Press.

Phillips-Amos, Georgia. 2016. "A dystopian climate for transitional justice: naming recent violence in Medellín." *Latin American Perspectives* 43(5): 99–111.

Pinheiro, Paulo S. 1997. "Popular responses to state-sponsored violence in Brazil," pp. 261–280 in Douglas A. Chalmers, Carlos M. Vilas, Katherine Hite, Scott B. Martin, Kerianne Piester, and Monique Segarra (eds.), *The New Politics of Inequality in Latin America: Rethinking Participation and Representation.* Oxford: Oxford University Press.

Pion-Berlin, David and Craig Arceneaux. 1998. "Tipping the civil-military balance: institutions and human rights policy in democratic Argentina and Chile." *Comparative Political Studies* 31: 633–661.

Plataformas de la Sociedad Civil Colombiana de Derechos Humanos y Paz. 2008. *Informe para el examen periódico universal.* Bogotá: Plataformas de la Sociedad Civil Colombiana de Derechos Humanos y Paz.

PLS (Plataforma Luchadores Sociales Bolivia). 2012. "A treinta años de la masacre sangrienta de Todos Santos." http://plataformaluchadoressocialesbolivia.blogspot.com/2012/10/a-treinta-anos-de-la-masacre-sangrienta.html (accessed December 8, 2014).

Poblete, Juan. 2012. "La productividad del afecto en un contexto postsocial," pp. 55–72 in Mabel Moraña and Ignacio Sánchez Prado (eds.), *El lenguaje de las emociones: Afecto y cultura en América Latina.* Madrid and Frankfurt: Iberoamericana / Vervuert.

———. 2015a. "A sense of humor and society in three Chilean comedies." in Juan Poblete and Juana Suárez (eds.), *Humor and Cinema in Latin America.* New York: Palgrave (forthcoming).

———. 2015b. "Subordinated memory and liberatory spectatorship in Latin American cinema: on Fernando Eimbcke's *Temporada de patos.*" *Global South*, Fall, n.p.a.

Popular Memory Group. 1982. "Popular memory: theory, politics, method," pp. 205–252 in Richard Johnson et al. (eds.), *Making Histories: Studies in History-writing and Politics.* London: Hutchinson.

———. 2011 (1998). "Popular memory: theory, politics, method," pp. 254–260 in Jeffrey Olick, Vered Vinitzky-Seroussi, and Daniel Levy (eds.), *The Collective Memory Reader.* New York: Oxford University Press.

Portelli, Alessandro. 1998. "What makes oral history different?," pp. 32–42 in Robert Perks and Alistair Thomson (eds.), *The Oral History Reader.* New York: Routledge.

———. 2003a. "Memoria e identidad: una reflexión acerca de la Italia postfascista," pp. 165–190 in Elizabeth Jelin and Victoria Langland (eds.), *Monumentos, memoriales y marcas territoriales.* Madrid: Siglo XXI.

———. 2003b. "Non era una storia da tralasciare," pp. 393–406 in Toni Morison (ed.), *Amatissima*. Milano: Frassinelli.

Postero, Nancy. 2007. "Andean utopias in Evo Morales's Bolivia." *Latin American and Caribbean Ethnic Studies* 2: 1–28.

———. 2010. "Morales's MAS government: building indigenous popular hegemony in Bolivia." *Latin American Perspectives* 37 (3): 18–34.

Potter, Claire and Renee Romano. 2012. *Doing Recent History: On Privacy, Copyright, Video Games, Institutional Review Boards, Activist Scholarship, and History That Talks Back*. Athens: University of Georgia Press.

Prager, Jeffrey. 1998. *Presenting the Past: Psychoanalysis and the Sociology of Misremembering*. Cambridge, MA: Harvard University Press.

Preston, Keith. 2013. *El Salvador: A War by Proxy*. London: Black House Publishing.

Programa Somos Defensores. 2015. *Los nadies: Informe enero-junio, Sistema de Información sobre Agresiones contra Defensores y Defensoras de DD.HH. en Colombia*. Bogotá: Programa No Gubernamental de Protección a Defensores de Derechos Humanos.

Proyecto Colombia Nunca Más. 2008. "En palabras de Uribe: de la seguridad nacional a la 'Seguridad Democrática,'" September 29. http://prensarural.org/spip/spip.php?article1538 (accessed December 1, 2015).

Proyecto Interdiocesano de Recuperación de la Memoria Histórica. 1996. *Guatemala: "Nunca Más."* Guatemala City: Proyecto Interdiocesano de Recuperación de la Memoria Histórica.

Puente, Rafael. 2011. *Recuperando la memoria: Una historia crítica de Bolivia*. La Paz: Plural Editores.

Quinalha, Renan. 2013. *Justiça de transição: Contornos do conceito*. São Paulo: Outras Expressões.

Quintana, Juan R. 1998. "Las relaciones civiles-militares en Bolivia: una agenda pendiente." *FASOC* 13 (1): 22–46.

Reátegui Castillo, Félix. 2009. "Las víctimas recuerdan: notas sobre la práctica social de la memoria," pp. 17–39 in Centro Internacional para la Justicia Transicional (ed.), *Recordar en conflicto: Iniciativas no oficiales de memoria en Colombia*. Bogotá: Centro Internacional para la Justicia Transicional.

Reis Filho, Daniel Aarão (ed.). 1997. *Versões e ficções: Seqüestro da história*. São Paulo: Ed. Fundação Perseu Abramo.

———. 2001. "A anistia recíproca no Brasil ou a arte de reconstruir a história," pp. 131–137 in Janaína Teles (ed.), *Mortos e desaparecidos: Reparação ou impunidade?* São Paulo: Humanitas and FFLCH/USP.

———. 2004. "Ditadura militar e sociedade: as reconstruções da memória," pp. 29–52 in Daniel A. Reis, Marcelo Ridenti, and Rodrigo P. Sá Motta (eds.), *O golpe e a ditadura militar: 40 anos depois (1964–2004)*. Bauru: EDUSC.

Rentschler, Carrie A. 2004. "Witnessing: US citizenship and the vicarious experience of suffering." *Media, Culture and Society* 26: 296–304.

Richard, Nelly. 1993. *Masculino/femenino*. Santiago: Francisco Zegers Ediciones.

———. 1998. *Residuos y metáforas: Ensayos de crítica cultural sobre el Chile de la transición*. Santiago: Editorial Cuarto Propio.

———. 2000. *La insubordinación de los signos: Cambio político, transformaciones culturales y poéticas de la crisis*. Santiago: Editorial Cuarto Propio.

———. 2001. *Residuos y metáforas: Ensayos de crítica cultural sobre el Chile de la transición*. Santiago: Editorial Cuarto Propio.

———. 2004 (1998). "Cites/sites of violence: convulsions of sense and official routines," pp. 15–30 in *Cultural Residues: Chile in Transition*. Translated by Alan West-Durán and Theodore Quester. Minneapolis: University of Minnesota Press.

———. 2006. "Presentación," pp. 9–14 in Nelly Richard (ed.), *Políticas y estéticas de la memoria*. Santiago: Editorial Cuarto Propio.

———. 2007. *Fracturas de la memoria: Arte y pensamiento crítico*. Buenos Aires: Siglo XXI Editores Argentina.

———. 2008. *Feminismo, género y diferencia(s)*. Santiago: Palinodia.

Ricoeur, Paul. 1983. *Temps et récit 1*. Paris: Seuil.

———. 1999. *La lectura del tiempo pasado: Memoria y olvido*. Madrid: Universidad Autónoma de Madrid.

———. 2000. *La mémoire, l'histoire, l'oubli*. Paris: Seuil.

———. 2003. *La memoria, la historia, el olvido*. Madrid: Trotta.

———. 2006. "Memory—forgetting—history," pp. 9–19 in Jorn Rusen (ed.), *Meaning and Representation in History*. Oxford: Berghahn Books.

Rigney, Ann. 2012. "Reconciliation and remembering: (how) does it work?" *Memory Studies* 5: 251–258.

Ríos, Marcela, Lorena Godoy, and Elizabeth Guerrero. 2003. *¿Un nuevo silencio feminista?* Santiago: CEM / Cuarto Propio.

Ritter, Jonathan. 2013. "Carnival of memory: songs of protest and remembrance in the Andes." *Smithsonian Folkways*. http://www.folkways.si.edu/magazine/2013_spring_summer/from_the_field. aspx (accessed December 15, 2014).

———. 2014. "The 'voice of the victims': testimonial songs in rural Ayacucho," pp. 217–253 in Milton (ed.), *Art from a Fractured Past*.

Rivera, Ana Kelly, Edy Arelí Ortiz Cañas, Liza Domínguez Magaña, and María Candelaria Navas (eds.). 1995. *¡¿Valió la pena?! Testimonios de salvadoreñas que sobrevivieron la guerra*. San Salvador: Editorial Sombrero Azul.

Rivera Cusicanqui, Silvia. 2003 (1984). *Oprimidos pero no vencidos: Luchas del campesinado aymara y qhechwa 1900–1980*. La Paz: Aruwiyiry.

Robben, Antonius C. G. M. 2007. *Political Violence and Trauma in Argentina*. Philadelphia: University of Pennsylvania Press.

Rodríguez-Plaza, Patricio. 2005. "Estética, política y vida cotidiana: el caso de la pintura callejera chilena." *Bifurcaciones*, no. 3. http://www.bifurcaciones.cl/003/Rodriguez-Plaza.htm (accessed May 9, 2014).

Roht-Arriaza, Naomi and Javier Mariezcurrena (eds.). 2006. *Transitional Justice in the Twenty-First Century: Beyond Truth versus Justice*. Cambridge: Cambridge University Press.

Rojas, Cristina. 2006. "The securitization of citizenship under Colombia's Democratic Security policy." *Center for Research on Latin America and the Caribbean Bulletin* 5 (5): 1–4. http://www.yorku.ca/cerlac/bulletins/bulletin_colombia_citizenship_2006.pdf (accessed December 1, 2015).

Rojas, María Teresa. 2000. "Reflexiones y creaciones: la memoria en el arte," pp. 297–301 in Mario Garcés, Pedro Milos, Myriam Olguín, Julio Pinto, María Teresa Rojas, and Miguel Larentis Urrutia (eds.), *Memoria para un nuevo siglo: Chile, miradas a la segunda mitad del siglo XX*. Santiago: LOM Ediciones.

Rojkind, Luis. 2004. "La revista controversia: reflexión y polémica entre los argentinos exiliados en México," pp. 239–243 in P. Yankelevich (ed.), *Represión y destierro: Itinerarios del exilio argentino*. La Plata: Al Margen.

Roniger, Luis and Mario Sznajder. 1999. *The Legacy of Human Rights in the Southern Cone: Argentina, Chile, and Uruguay*. New York: Oxford University Press.

Ros, Ana. 2012. *The Postdictatorship Generation in Argentina, Chile, and Uruguay: Collective Memory and Cultural Production*. New York: Palgrave Macmillan.

Rosenberg, Fernando. 2010. "Derechos humanos, comisiones de la verdad y nuevas ficciones globales." *Revista de Crítica Latinoamericana* 35 (69): 91–114.

Ross, Fiona C. 2003. *Bearing Witness: Women and the Truth Commission in South Africa*. London: Pluto.

Ruiz, Carlos. 2000. "Democracia, consenso y memoria: una reflexión sobre la experiencia chilena," pp. 15–21 in Nelly Richard (ed.), *Políticas y estéticas de la memoria*. Santiago: Editorial Cuarto Propio.

Ruiz, Marisa. 2010. *Ciudadanas en tiempos de incertidumbre*. Montevideo: Doble-Clic.

Rush, Peter and Oliver Simic (eds.). 2014. *The Arts of Transitional Justice: Culture, Memory, and Activism after Atrocities*. Berlin: Springer.

Sader, Emir. 2008. "The weakest link? Neoliberalism in Latin America." *New Left Review* 52: 5–31.

Sagot, Montserrat. 2010. "Peace begins at home: women's struggles against violence and state actions in Costa Rica," pp. 221–235 in Elizabeth Maier and Nathalie Lebon (eds.), *Women's Activism in Latin America and the Caribbean: Engendering Social Justice, Democratizing Citizenship*. New Brunswick, NJ: Rutgers University Press.

Saito, Bruno Y. 2013. "Marcas da violência." *Valor Econômico*, June 5. http://www.valor.com.br/cultura/3187050/marcas-da-violencia (accessed July 3, 2013).

Salvi, Valentina 2011a. "The slogan 'Complete Memory': a reactive (re)-signification of memory of the disappeared in Argentina," pp. 43–61 in Francesca Lessa and Vincent Druliolle (eds.), *The Memory of State Terrorism in the Southern Cone*. New York: Palgrave.

———. 2011b. "La memoria institucional de Ejército Argentino sobre el pasado reciente (1999–2008)." *Revista Militares e Política*, no. 8, 39–54.

———. 2013. *De vencedores a víctimas: Memorias militares sobre el pasado reciente en la Argentina*. Buenos Aires: Biblos.

Sánchez, Magaly R. 2006. "Insecurity and violence as a new power relation in Latin America." *Annals of the American Academy of Political Science* 606: 178–195.

Santos, Cecilia MacDowell. 2005. *Women's Police Stations: Gender, Violence, and Justice in São Paulo, Brazil*. New York: Palgrave.

Santos, Cecilia MacDowell, Edson Teles, and Jamaina de Almeida Teles (eds.). 2009. *Desarchivando a ditadura: Memoria e justiça no Brasil*. 2 vols. São Paulo: Editora Hucitec.

Sarlo, Beatriz. 2005. *Tiempo pasado: Cultura de la memoria y giro subjectivo, una discusión*. Buenos Aires: Siglo XXI.

Saúl, Ernesto. 1972. *Pintura social en Chile*. Santiago: Ediciones Quimantú.

Saunders, George R. 1995. "The crisis of presence in Italian Pentecostal conversion." *American Ethnologist* 22: 324–340.

Scarry, Elaine. 1985. *The Body in Pain: The Making and Unmaking of the World*. New York: Oxford University Press.

Schechner, Richard. 2011. "Restauración de la conducta," pp. 31–50 in Diana Taylor and Marcela Fuentes (eds.), *Estudios avanzados del performance*. Mexico City: Fondo de Cultura Económica.

Scheffer, Thomas. 2002. "Exploring court hearings: towards a research design for a comparative ethnography on 'witnessing in court.'" Department of Sociology On-line Publications,

Lancaster University. http://www.lancaster.ac.uk/fass/sociology/research/publications/papers_alpha.htm#st (accessed February 13, 2015)

Scheper-Hughes, Nancy. 2004. "Violence foretold: reflections on 9/11," pp. 224–226 in Nancy Scheper-Hughes and Philippe Bourgois (eds.), *Violence in War and Peace*. Oxford: Blackwell.

Schild, Verónica. 2007. "Empowering 'consumer-citizens' or governing poor female subjects? The institutionalization of 'self-development' in the Chilean social policy field." *Journal of Consumer Culture* 7: 179–203.

Schneider, Cathy. 1995. *Shantytown Protest in Pinochet's Chile*. Philadelphia: Temple University Press.

Schneider, Nina. 2011a. "Breaking the 'silence' of the military regime: new politics of memory in Brazil?" *Bulletin of Latin American Research* 30: 198–212.

———. 2011b. "The Supreme Court's recent verdict on the Amnesty Law: impunity in post-authoritarian Brazil." *European Review of Latin American and Caribbean Studies* 90: 39–54.

———. 2011c. "Truth no more? The struggle over the National Truth Commission in Brazil." *Iberoamericana* 42: 164–170.

———. 2014. "Waiting for a meaningful apology: has the Brazilian state apologised for authoritarian repression?" *Journal of Human Rights* 13 (1): 1–16.

Schudson, Michael. 1989. "The past in the present versus the present in the past." *Communication* 2: 105–113.

Schwarzböck, Silvia. 2007. *Estudio crítico sobre* Crónica de una fuga. Buenos Aires: Picnic Editorial.

Scott, Joan W. 1992. "Experience," pp. 22–40 in Judith Butler and Joan W. Scott (eds.), *Feminists Theorize the Political*. New York: Routledge.

Secretaría General de Gobierno. 1996. *Informe de la Comisión Nacional de Verdad y Reconciliación sobre Violación a los Derechos Humanos en Chile 1973–1990*. Vol. 1. Santiago: Secretaría General de Gobierno. http://www.gob.cl/informe-rettig/.

SEDH (Secretaria Especial dos Direitos Humanos). 2007. *Direito à memória e à verdade: Comissão especial sobre mortos e desaparecidos políticos*. Brasília: SEDH.

Seligmann-Silva, Márcio. 2010. "Narrativas contra o silêncio: cinema e ditadura no Brasil." *Letterature d'America* 130: 59–89.

Senado. 1993. "Sesión 14, 16 noviembre." Santiago: Senado de la República de Chile.

———. 1994. "Informe de la Comisión de Constitución, Justicia y Reglamento, Sesión 3, 15 diciembre." Santiago: Senado de la República de Chile. Retrieved at: http://www.leychile.cl/Navegar?idLey=19325.

Sennet, Richard. 1998. "Disturbing memories," pp. 11–25 in Patricia Fara and Karalyn Patterson (eds.), *Memory*. Cambridge: Cambridge University Press.

Serbin, Ken. 2006. "Memory and method in the emerging historiography of Latin America's authoritarian era." *Latin American Politics and Society* 48 (3): 185–198.

SERNAM (Servicio Nacional de la Mujer). 1995. *Violencia intrafamiliar y derechos humanos*. Santiago: SERNAM.

———. 2009. *Detección y análisis de la violencia intrafamiliar en la Región Metropolitana y La Araucanía*. Documento de Trabajo 121. Santiago: SERNAM.

SERPAJ (Servicio Paz y Justicia). 1989. *Uruguay:* Nunca Más, *informe sobre las violación de los derechos humanos (1972–1985)*. Montevideo: Altamira.

Sharrat, Sara. 2011. *Gender, Shame, and Sexual Violence*. Farnham, Surrey: Ashgate Publishing.

Shayne, Julie (ed.). 2014. *Taking Risks: Feminists, Activism, and Activist Research in the Americas*. Albany: SUNY Press.

Sierra Becerra, Diana Carolina. 2015. "Resistant women: indigenous women remember El Salvador's 1932 insurrection." *History Workshop Online*, March 9. http://www.history workshop.org.uk/resistant-women-indigenous-women-remember-el-salvadors-1932-insur rection/ (accessed September 1, 2015).

Sierra Becerra, Diana C., Pedro Durán, Rafael Lara-Martínez, and Georgina Hernández. 2015. "Guía didáctica sobre el levantamiento y la masacre de 1932." Museo de la Palabra y la Imagen. http://issuu.com/dcsierra/docs/guia_didactica_sobre_1932__el_salva (accessed September 1, 2015).

Sikkink, Kathryn. 2011. *Justice Cascade*. New York: W. W. Norton.

Sikkink, Kathryn and Carrie Booth Walling. 2006. "Argentina's contribution to global trends in transitional justice," pp. 301–324 in Roht-Arriaza and Mariezcurrena (eds.), *Transitional Justice in the Twenty-First Century*.

———. 2007. "The impact of human rights trials in Latin America." *Journal of Peace Research* 44: 427–445.

Silber, Irina. 2004. "Commemorating the past in postwar El Salvador," pp. 211–229 in Daniel J. Walkowitz and Lisa Maya Knaur (eds.), *Memory and the Impact of Political Transformation in Public Space*. Durham, NC: Duke University Press.

———. 2011. *Everyday Revolutionaries: Gender, Violence, and Disillusionment in Postwar El Salvador*. New Brunswick, NJ: Rutgers University Press.

Silva, Eduardo. 2009. *Challenging Neoliberalism in Latin America*. Cambridge: Cambridge University Press.

Silva, Patricio. 2002. "Memoria colectiva, miedo y consenso: psicología política," pp. 185–209 in Kees Koonings and Dirk Kruijt (eds.), *Las sociedades del miedo: El legado de la guerra civil, la violencia y el terror en América Latina*. Salamanca: Universidad de Salamanca.

Sivak, Martín. 2001. *El dictador elegido: Biografía no autorizada de Hugo Bánzer Suárez*. La Paz: Plural Editores.

Sjoberg, Gideon, Elizabeth A. Gill, and Leonard D. Cain. 2003. "Countersystem analysis and the construction of alternative futures." *Sociological Theory* 21: 210–235.

Smith, Christian. 1991. *The Emergence of Liberation Theology: Radical Religion and Social Movement Theory*. Chicago: University of Chicago Press.

Sokoloff, Natalie and Ida Dupont. 2005. "Domestic violence at the intersections of race, class, and gender: challenges and contributions to understanding violence against marginalized women in diverse communities." *Violence against Women* 11: 38–64.

Solón, Pablo. 2012. *El "Jó" en la piedra: Los restos que no desaparecen*. La Paz: Fundación Solón.

Somos. 1984. "Sábato enfrentó a Alfonsín: el shock de *Nunca Más*." 8 (408): 6–11.

Sparks, Garry. 2002. "A proposed framework for inter-religious interaction by Christians toward Native American spiritualities." M.S., University of Chicago School of Theology.

Stahler-Sholk, Richard, Harry E. Vanden, and Mark Becker (eds.). 2014. *Rethinking Latin American Social Movements: Radical Action from Below*. Lanham, MD: Rowman and Littlefield.

Stahler-Sholk, Richard, Harry E. Vanden, and Glen D. Kuecker (eds.). 2008. *Latin American Social Movements in the Twenty-first Century: Resistance, Power, and Democracy*. Lanham, MD: Rowman and Littlefield.

Stanzione, Vincent. 2003. *Rituals of Sacrifice: Walking the Face of the Earth on the Sacred Path of the Sun*. Albuquerque: University of New Mexico Press.

Stefanoni, Pablo. 2006. "El nacionalismo indígena en el poder." *Observatorio Social de América Latina* 19: 37–44.

Stephen, Lynn. 1994. *Hear My Testimony: Maria Teresa Tula, Human Rights Activist of El Salvador*. Boston: South End Press.

Stephenson, Marcia. 2002. "Forging an indigenous counterpublic sphere: the Taller de Historia Oral Andina in Bolivia." *Latin American Research Review* 37 (2): 99–118.

Stern, Steve. 2004. *Remembering Pinochet's Chile*. Durham, NC: Duke University Press.

———. 2006a. *Battling for Hearts and Minds: Memory Struggles in Pinochet's Chile, 1973–1988*. Durham, NC: Duke University Press.

———. 2006b. *Remembering Pinochet's Chile: On the Eve of London 1998*. Durham, NC: Duke University Press.

———. 2010. *Reckoning with Pinochet: The Memory Question in Democratic Chile, 1989–2006*. Durham, NC: Duke University Press.

———. 2012. "The damned and the authentic: the ambivalence of human rights in film and society." Keynote speech at the Historical Justice and Memory Conference, Melbourne, Australia, February 13–17.

———. 2014. "The artist's truth: the post-Auschwitz predicament after Latin America's age of dirty wars," pp. 255–276 in Milton (ed.), *Art from a Fractured Past*.

Stiegler, Bernard. 2010. *For a New Critique of Political Economy*. Cambridge, UK: Polity.

Straubhaar, Rolf. 2015. "Public representations of the collective memory of Brazil's Movimento dos Trabalhadores Rurais Sem Terra." *Latin American Perspectives* 42 (3): 107–119.

Stubbs, Julie. 2007. "Beyond apology?: domestic violence and critical questions for restorative justice." *Criminology and Criminal Justice* 7 (2): 169–187.

Sturken, Marita. 1997. *Tangled Memories: The Vietnam War, the AIDS Epidemic, and the Politics of Remembering*. Berkeley: University of California Press.

Suárez-Orozco, Marcelo. 2000. "Interdisciplinary perspectives on violence and trauma," pp. 1–41 in A. Robben and M. Suárez-Orozco (eds.), *Cultures under Siege: Collective Violence and Trauma*. Cambridge: Cambridge University Press.

Suazo, Fernando. 2002. *La cultura maya ante la muerte: Daño y duelo en la comunidad achí de Rabinal*. Guatemala City: Equipo de Estudios Comunitarios y Acción Psicosocial.

Subotić, Jelena. 2012. "The transformation of international transitional justice advocacy." *International Journal of Transitional Justice* 6: 106–125.

Sutton, Barbara. 2015. "Collective memory and the language of human rights: attitudes toward torture in contemporary argentina." *Latin American Perspectives* 42(3): 73–91.

Sutton, Barbara and Kari Marie Norgaard. 2013. "Cultures of denial: avoiding knowledge of state violations of human rights in Argentina and the United States." *Sociological Forum* 28: 495–524.

Taller de Género y Memoria ex-Presas Políticas. 2001–2003. *Memoria para armar*. 3 vols. Montevideo: Senda.

Taylor, Diana. 2011. "Introducción: performance, teoría y práctica," pp. 7–30 in Diana Taylor and Marcela Fuentes (eds.), *Estudios avanzados del performance*. Mexico City: Fondo de Cultura Económica.

Tedlock, Barbara. 1981. "Quiché Maya dream interpretation." *Ethos* 9: 313–330.

———. 1987. "Zuni and Quiche dream sharing and interpretation," pp. 105–131 in Barbara Tedlock (ed.), *Dreaming: Anthropological and Psychological Interpretations*. Cambridge: Cambridge University Press.

———. 1992. "The role of dreams and visionary narratives in Mayan cultural survival." *Ethos* 20: 453–476.

Tedlock, Dennis. 1996. *Popol Vuh: The Mayan Book of the Dawn of Life*. New York: Simon and Schuster.

Teeger, Chana. 2015. "'Both sides of the story': history education in post-apartheid South Africa." *American Sociological Review* 80: 1175–1200.

Teitel, Ruti. 2003. "Transitional justice genealogy." *Harvard Human Rights Journal* 16: 69–94.

Teles, Edson and Vladimir Safatle (eds.). 2008. "Editorial note: transitional justice globalized." *International Journal of Transitional Justice* 2 (1): 1–4.

———. 2010. *O que resta da ditadura: A exceção brasileira.* São Paulo: Boitempo.

Terdinam, Richard. 1993. *Present Past: Modernity and the Memory Crisis.* Ithaca, NY: Cornell University Press.

Thale, Geoff. 2013. "Amnesty under Fire in El Salvador: Legal Challenges and Political Implications." *Washington Office on Latin America*, October 21. https://www.wola.org/ analysis/amnesty-under-fire-in-el-salvador-legal-challenges-and-political-implications/ (accessed September 1, 2015).

Thomas, Günter. 2009. "Witness as a cultural form of communication: historical roots, structural dynamics, and current appearances," pp. 89–111 in Paul Frosh and Amit Pinchevski (eds.), *Media Witnessing.* London: Palgrave Macmillan.

Thomson, Sinclair. 2003. "Revolutionary memory in Bolivia: anticolonial and national projects from 1781 to 1952," pp. 117–134 in Merilee Grindle and Pilar Domingo (eds.), *Proclaiming Revolution: Bolivia in Comparative Perspective.* Cambridge, MA: Harvard University Press.

Ticona Alejo, Esteban. 1996. *CSTUB: Trayectorias y desafíos.* La Paz: CEDOIN.

Ticona Alejo, Estéban, Xavier Albó, and Roberto Choque Canqui. 1996. *Jesús de Machaqa: La marka rebelde.* La Paz: CIPCA/CEDOIN.

Tijoux, María Emilia. 2009. "La inscripción de lo cotidiano: los murales de la población La Victoria." *Actuel Marx*, no. 8, 143–153.

Tilly, Charles. 2006. *Regimes and Repertoires.* Chicago: University of Chicago Press.

Tinsman, Heidi. 1995. "Los patrones del hogar: esposas golpeadas y control sexual en Chile rural, 1958– 1988," in Lorena Godoy et al. (eds.), *Disciplina y desacato: Construcción de identidad en Chile, Siglos XIX y XX.* Santiago: Ediciones SUR/CEDEM.

———. 2002. *Partners in Conflict: The Politics of Gender, Sexuality, and Labor in the Chilean Agrarian Reform, 1950–1973.* Durham, NC: Duke University Press.

Todorov, Tzvetan. 2000. *Los abusos de la memoria.* Barcelona: Paidós.

Traba, Marta. 2005. *Dos décadas vulnerables en las artes plásticas latinoamericanas, 1950–1970.* Buenos Aires: Siglo XXI.

Tróccoli, Jorge Néstor. 1996. *La ira de Leviatán: Del método de la furia a la búsqueda de la paz.* Montevideo: CAELUM.

Trouillot, Michel-Rolph. 1995. *Silencing the Past: Power and the Production of History.* Boston: Beacon Press.

Trubek, David M. and Alvaro Santos (eds.). 2006. *The New Law and Economic Development: A Critical Appraisal.* Cambridge: Cambridge University Press.

Ulfe, María Eugenia and Vera Lucía Ríos. 2016. "Toxic memories? The DINCOTE Museum in Lima, Peru." *Latin American Perspectives* 43(6): 27–40.

Unión Cívica Radical Representatives. 1983. "Actas." MS, Buenos Aires.

United Nations Children's Fund. 2014. *Hidden in Plain Sight: A Statistical Analysis of Violence against Children.* New York: UNICEF.

United Nations High Commissioner for Human Rights. 2011. *Discriminatory Laws and Practices and Acts of Violence against Individuals Based on Their Sexual Orientation and Gender Identity.* New York: UN General Assembly.

United Nations Office of the High Commissioner for Human Rights. 2015. "Report A/HRC/28/3/Add.3." http://www.ohchr.org/EN/HRBodies/HRC/RegularSessions/Ses sion28/Documents/A_HRC_28_3_Add_3_ENG.doc (accessed December 1, 2015).

United Nations Truth Commission. 1993. *From Madness to Hope: The 12-Year War in El Salvador.* New York: UN Security Council.

Valdés, Teresa. 1988. *Venid, benditas de mi padre: Las pobladoras, sus rutinas y sus sueños.* Santiago: FLACSO.

Valdés, Teresa and Marisa Weinstein. 1993. *Mujeres que sueñan: Las organizaciones de pobladoras en Chile, 1973–1989.* Santiago: FLACSO.

Van Cott, Donna Lee. 2005. "'A reflection of our motley reality': Bolivian Indians' slow path to political representation," pp. 49–98 in Donna Lee Van Cott (ed.), *From Movements to Parties: The Evolution of Ethnic Politics.* New York: Cambridge University Press.

Van Drunen, Saskia. 2010. *Struggling with the Past: The Human Rights Movement and the Politics of Memory in Post-Dictatorship Argentina (1983–2006).* Amsterdam: Rozenberg Publishers.

Vásquez, Chalena and Abilio Vergara. 1988. *Chayraq!: El carnaval ayacuchano.* Ayacucho: CEDAP/TAREA.

Vásquez Díaz, Lucio Atilio. 2012. *Siete gorriones.* San Salvador: Museo de la Palabra y la Imagen.

Verbitsky, Horacio. 1987. *Veinte años de proclamas militares.* Buenos Aires: Editora 12.

———. 1995. *El vuelo.* Buenos Aires: Planeta.

Verdugo, Patricia. 1985. *André de La Victoria.* Santiago: Aconcagua.

Vezzetti, Hugo. 2002. *Pasado y presente: Guerra, dictadura y sociedad en la Argentina.* Buenos Aires: Siglo XXI.

Vich, Victor. 2014. "Violence, guilt, and repetition: Alonso Cueto's novel *La hora azul*," pp. 127–138 in Milton (ed.), *Art from a Fractured Past.*

Vidaurrázaga, Tamara. 2007. *Mujeres en rojo y negro, reconstrucción de la memoria de tres mujeres miristas.* Concepción: Ediciones Escaparate.

Vilches, Patricia. 2016. "Andres Wood's *Machuca* and *Violeta Went to Heaven*: The geographical spaces of conflict in Chile." *Latin American Perspectives* 43(5): 45–61.

Villalón, Roberta. 2013. "Framing extreme violence: collective memory-making of Argentina's Dirty War," pp. 298–315 in Celine-Marie Pascale (ed.), *Social Inequality and the Politics of Representation: A Global Landscape.* Newbury Park, CA: Pine Forge/Sage.

———. 2014. "Latina battered immigrants, citizenship, and inequalities: reflections on activist research," pp. 245–277 in Shayne (ed.), *Taking Risks.*

———. 2015. "The resurgence of collective memory, truth, and justice mobilizations in Latin America," *Latin American Perspectives* 42(3): 3–19.

———. 2016a. "The complexities of memory, truth and justice processes: artistic and cultural resistance," *Latin American Perspectives* 43(5): 3–11.

———. 2016b. "The resilience of memory, truth and justice processes: justice, politics and social mobilizations," *Latin American Perspectives* 43(6): 3–7.

Viñar, Marcelo. 1993. *Fracturas de memoria.* Montevideo: Ediciones Trilce.

Vincenty, Claudia and Luis Castedo Zapata (eds.), *Contextualización de la antropología física forense en Bolivia: Estudio de casos—desapariciones forzadas.* La Paz: IIAA.

Vivanco Roca Rey, Lucero de and Genevieve Fabry. 2013. "Introducción: las memorias y la tinta," pp. 13–29 in Lucero de Vivanco Roca Rey (ed.), *Memorias en tinta: Ensayos sobre la representación de la violencia política en Argentina, Chile y Perú.* Santiago: Ediciones Universidad Alberto Hurtado.

Waldram, James B. 2014. "Healing history? Aboriginal healing, historical trauma, and personal responsibility." *Transcultural Psychiatry* 51: 370–386.

Wardi, Dina. 1992. *Memorial Candles: Children of the Holocaust.* New York: Routledge.

Webber, Jeffery R. 2010. "Bolivia in the era of Evo Morales." *Latin American Research Review* 45: 248–260.

———. 2011. *From Rebellion to Reform in Bolivia: Class Struggle, Indigenous Liberation, and the Politics of Evo Morales*. Chicago: Haymarket Books.

Weil, Stephen E. 2002. "Museums: can and do they make a difference?," pp. 55–74 in *Making Museums Matter*. Washington, DC: Smithsonian Institution Press.

Weine, Stevan. 2006. *Testimony after Catastrophe: Narrating the Traumas of Political Violence*. Evanston, IL: Northwestern University Press.

Wielandt, Gonzalo and Carmen Artigas. 2007. *La corrupción y la impunidad en el marco del desarrollo en América Latina y el Caribe: Un enfoque centrado en derechos desde la perspectiva de las Naciones Unidas*. Políticas Sociales 139.

Wieviorka, Michael. 2006. *La violence*. Paris: Hachette Littérature.

Wilde, Alexander. 1999. "Irruptions of memory: expressive politics in Chile's transition to democracy." *Journal of Latin American Studies* 31: 473–500.

Wilson, Kristi M. 2016. "Building memory: museums, trauma, and the aesthetics of confrontation in Argentina." *Latin American Perspectives* 43(5): 112–130.

Wilson, Richard. 1995. *Maya Resurgence in Guatemala: Q'eq chi' Experiences*. Norman: University of Oklahoma Press.

Winn, Alisha R. 2012. "The Remembering St. Petersburg Oral History Project: youth empowerment and heritage preservation through a community museum." *Transforming Anthropology* 20 (1): 67–78.

Young, Allan. 1995. *The Harmony of Illusions: Inventing Post-Traumatic Stress Disorder*. Princeton, NJ: Princeton University Press.

Zalaquett, José. 1988. "Confronting human rights violations committed by former governments: principles applicable and political constraints," pp. 23–69 in Aspen Institute (ed.), *State Crimes: Punishment or Pardon*. Queenstown, MD: Aspen Institute.

———. 1992. "Balancing ethical imperatives and political constraints: the dilemma of new democracies confronting past human rights violations." *Hastings Law Journal* 43: 1425–1438.

———. 1999. "Procesos de transición a la democracia y políticas de derechos humanos en América Latina," pp. 105–134 in Lorena González (ed.), *Presente y futuro de los derechos humanos*. San José: Instituto Interamericano de Derechos Humanos.

Zamorano, Carlos. 1984. "*Nunca Más*, testimonio vivo de la represión: el libro de la CONADEP." MS, Buenos Aires.

Zamorano, Pedro and Claudio Cortés. 2007. "Muralismo en Chile: texto y contexto de su discurso estético." *Universum (Talca)* 2 (22): 254–274.

Zerubavel, Eviatar. 1996. "Social memories: steps toward a sociology of the past." *Qualitative Sociology* 19: 283–299.

Zinn, Howard. 1990 (1970). *The Politics of History*. Champaign: University of Illinois Press.

Zinn, Howard and Donaldo Macedo. 2005. *Howard Zinn on Democratic Education*. Boulder: Paradigm Publishers.

Zur, Judith N. 1998. *Violent Memories: Mayan War Widows in Guatemala*. Boulder: Westview Press.

Index

Page references for illustrations are italicized.

Barbie, Klaus, 82
Barrientos, René, 81, 92n5
Barrios, Raúl, 84
Barros, Gracia, 163
Batismo de Sangue (film), 197
Bellange, Ebe, 164
Benítez, Mario Aguado, 33
bereavement: character of, 133; Maya
  beliefs and practices, 136–44; muralism
  as mechanism of resistance and, 168;
  psychological effects of disappearances
  and, 138; unresolved grief, 133, 135–36,
  138
Bilbao, Josefina, 50, 53
Bloque Independiente, 86
Boal, Augusto, 151, 153
Bolívar, Simón, 88, 93n10
Bolivia: historical memory research, 80–81,
  92n3; national initiatives, 77, 82–83;
  political practice contradictions, 77,
  79; political violence in, 77, 81–82, 90,
  93n11; politics of memory, influences
  on, 83–91; social organizations' justice
  demands, 77, 78, 83, 84, 93n11;
  violence and drug trafficking, 10n7
"Bolivia: Thirty-Three Years since the Todos
  Santos Massacre" (manifesto), 84
Bolivia Labor Federation (Central Obrera
  Boliviana, COB), 82, 86, 87, 92n3
books, as artistic-cultural productions,
  195–96
Bordaberry, Juan María, 120, 131–32nn7–8
Brandt, Beto, 198
Brasil Nunca Mais (Archdiocese of São
  Paulo), 196
Brazil: artistic-cultural productions on
  reckoning in, 189, 195–202; democratic
  transition and justice, 190, 191–95;
  disappearances, 14, 194, 196; public
  perception of repression in, 195; trial
  testimonies and torture descriptions,
  153; violence associations, 10n7
Brilhante Ustra, Carols Alberto, 202n4
Broad Front, 119, 120, 122, 129
Brugnoli, Francisco, 163
Bunster, Ximena, 45
burial/reburial rituals, 138–41

Cabrera, Guillermina, 35
Caldas, Álvaro, 202n10
Camarena, Jorge González, 162
Caminito (song), 153
Campos de Cabrera, Santos Delmi, 208
Canales, Eliseo, 216
Cantuarias, Eugenio, 53
capitalism, 68, 70–71, 74, 88. *See also*
  neoliberalism
Cappelletto, Francesca, 128
Carapintada rebellion, 34
carbonários, Os (Sirkis), 195–96, 200
Cardoso, Fernando Henrique, 194
Caridi, José, 34
Carloto, Estela, 18
Carnival performances. *See* Ayacucho
  Carnival
Catholic Church: Chilean democratic
  transitions and reification of, 46, 47–48;
  Chilean family policy issues, 46, 51, 53;
  Guatemalan truth commission reports
  of, 133; Maya dream traditions and
  opposition of, 136; Maya reburial ritual
  roles of, 140–41; political violence and
  complicity of, 20, 146, 155
Central Obrera Boliviana (COB), 82, 86,
  87, 92n3
Centro de Relacionamento Soluciones
  Laborales (CRYS@L), 125
Cepeda Vargas, Manuel, 99, 107
Che Guevara, Ernesto, 81, 82, 169, *170,
  172,* 173
Cheron, François, 153
children: abductions and disappearances
  of, 4, 23, 30n21, 146, 154; deaths of,
  35, 177, 207; intergenerational memory
  transmission to, 126–28, 186–88, 206;
  massacre justification as distrust of, 179;
  massacre survivor experiences, 151, 181–
  82, 183, 214–16; matrimonial family
  definitions and rights of, 53
Chile: artistic-cultural productions and
  national memory construction, 70–73;
  authoritarian judicial system, 49;
  democratic transition, 46, 47–48;
  family policies and family violence

ESMA (Escuela Superior de Mecánica de la
Armada), 145, 147, 149–55
Espinal, Luis, 82
Espinoza, Pedro, 57n7
Esquivel, Adolfo Pérez, 17
exhumations, 135, 139–44
Expiry Law, 119

Fabbri, Lucía, 127
Fábrica Militar de Pólvoras y Explosivos of
Villa María attack, 42n17
Familiares de Desaparecidos y Detenidos
por Razones Políticas, 15
Familiares y Amigos de Muertos por la
Subversión (FAMUS), 32–33
families: Chilean public policy debates
on, 52–53; divorce laws, 56; and
domestic violence, 45–46, 50–56,
209; intergenerational transmission
of memory, 186–88, 206; judicial
processes and courts for, 53, 55, 56;
political fractures of, 122; prisoner
normality and relationships with, 155;
reparations to, 193; as social oppression
support, 58n10; state repression of,
117, 118, 155; survivors' guilt and,
125, 126
family (domestic) violence, 45–46, 50–56,
209
Farias, Roberto, 197
Favaloro, René, 17
Federación de Mineros, 86
Federaciones del Trópico, 87
Federación Sindical de Trabajadores
(FSTMB), 86
Federal War, 89
Feldman, Allen, 167–68
Fernández Meijide, Graciela, 17, 29n15
Ferrari, León, 24–25, 26
Ferreyra, Lila, 145
"50 Years, May They Not Have Been in
Vain: History Is in Our Hands" (mural),
170, *170*
films, 25, 70–73, 179, 197–200, 207, 210
"Final Document of the Military Junta
on the War against Subversion and
Terrorism" ("Documento final de la

Junta Militar sobre la guerra contra la
subversión y el terrorismo"), 16, 32, 33
Flores Pedregal, Carlos, 82
FMLN (Frente Farabundo Martí para la
Liberación Nacional), 205, 206–7, 208,
210, 214–15, 219n4
Fontanarrosa, Roberto, 30n27
forgetting and forgetfulness: consumption
as replacement for, 66, 68, 70–73;
memory impasse conditions, 63, 64;
state-mediated amnesia, 119, 129, 130,
162, 168, 192; as trauma process, 117,
126, 131
forgiveness, 38, 39, 48, 58n11
Foro de Estudios sobre la Admnistración de
Justicia (FORES), 22
Foucault, Michel, 7
Franco, Jean, 45
Frei, Eduardo, 47, 49, 54
Freire, Paulo, 208–9, 213, 217
Frente Amplio (Broad Front), 119, 120,
122, 129
Frente Farabundo Martí para la Liberación
Nacional (FMLN), 205, 206–7, 208,
210, 214–15, 219n4
Frente Patriótico Manuel Rodrìguez
(FPMR), 48
Fuerzas Armadas Revolucionarias de
Colombia (FARC), 102, 113
Fujimori, Alberto, 9n4, 180, 184
Full Stop Act, 23, 201
Fundación contra la Impunidad, 84
Fundación de Antropología Forense de
Guatemala (FAFG), 139–40
Fundación Paz Ciudadana, 58n8

Gabeira, Fernando, 192, 195–96, 200
Galeano, Eduardo, 30n27
galleries, 6, 83, 129, 134, 218. *See also*
Gallery of Memory
Gallery of Memory: democracy
contributions, 104–8, 113; description
overview and purpose, 95–96, 102;
exhibition history, 95, *96*, 99–101, *101*,
111–12; founding of, 99; human rights
activism risks, 98–99; security policy
critiques, 102–4, *105*, 108–9, 111;

Index 265

Levi, Primo, 149
Light of Memory, The (exhibition), 83
Liscano, Mauricio, 123
"Little Accomarca Soldier" (song), 182
Lloccllapampa massacre, 179–80, 184
Lobos, Pedro, 164
Long, Hilario F., 17
López, Cleotilde, 205, 206
López, Julio, 151
López, Santiago, 29n10
Lübbert, Orlando, 70
Luciérnagas en El Mozote (Amaya, Danner, and Henríquez Consalvi), 207
Lucioni, Ana, 32, 36, 38
Lucioni, Oscar, 41n3
Luder, Ítalo, 28n3

Madres de Plaza de Mayo, 15, 17, 18, 22, 41–42n8, 107
Malajunta (Aliverti), 25, 26
Marcha del Silencio, 120–21
Marchant, Patricio, 64
Mariani, Isabel, 18
Martí, Farabundo, 219n4
Martínez de Perón, María Estela, 14, 19
Martínez de Perón, María Isabel, 22
martyrdom, 22, 36, 37, 82, 88–90, 140
Marxism, 34, 48, 86–88, 90, 102, 211
MAS (Movement for Socialism, Bolivian government): national initiatives, 82–83; political practice contradictions, 77, 79; politics of memory policies, 83–91
massacres: Bolivian, 81–82, 90, 95; as Christian value system consequence, 24–25; Columbian gallery exhibitions featuring, 106, 107, 111; definitions, 129; denials of, 143; Guatemalan victim exhumations and reburials, 135, 139–43; Peruvian, 177–80, 181, 184, 185, 186; Peruvian performance reenactments, 180–88, *184, 185;* Salvadorian, 207, 210, 214–16, 220n16. *See also* genocides
Massera, Emilio Eduardo, 42n12, 153
maternity wards, 154
Matta, Roberto, 163, 164
Maya (Guatemalan indigenous people): afterlife beliefs, 137, 138; burial rituals,

138–39; counterinsurgency policies and victimization of, 134–35, 138; dead remembrance events, 137; dreams and visitations from dead, 136–37, 141–42, 143–44; exhumation of massacre victims, 135, 139–43; posttraumatic stress/unresolved grief, effects of, 135, 138; reburial rituals, 140–41; restorative justice, unresolved, 135–36
media, 29n18, 82, 145, 150, 153, 156
Memoria Completa, 31, 35–39
memorialization spaces: Carnival performances and sites as, 186–87; definition and descriptions, 134; museums and galleries as, 6, 83, 129, 134, 218; purpose of, 5, 94–96, 107, 112, 174; for victims of subversive terrorism, 31–32, 36–37, 39. *See also* commemoration; Gallery of Memory
memorials and monuments: Argentine pro-military, 31; Bolivian, 82, 83; Brazilian, 194, 202n6; museums and galleries as, 83, 129, 134; prisons as, 129, 157n1; reburial rituals with, 141
Memoria para armar (Taller de Género y Memoria), 123
memória que me contam, A (film), 198
memorias de la represión, Las (Jelin), 63–64
Memories Revealed, 194
memory, overview: archival, 178; artistic creations and cultural spaces contributing to, 6; authoritarian control of, 168; commission reports as vehicle for, 24–27; for community rebuilding, 96–97; corporal/repertoire, 178; cultural goods as vehicles/labors of, 6, 189, 198; emblematic, 44, 46, 63; externalization of, 69; fractures of, 118, 122; gender violence and, 44–47; guilt and construction of, 149; influences on, 211; intergenerational transmission of, 126–28, 186–88, 206; intersectionality of, 44; irruptions of, 73–74; leftist organizations using historical, 206; memory impasse oscillation process, 63, 64; mobilization of truth, justice and, 1–6, 221; muralism for construction

About the Contributors

Renzo Aroni Sulca is a Ph.D. student in the history department at University of California, Davis.

Rebecca J. Atencio is an associate professor in the Department of Spanish and Portuguese of Tulane University.

María José Azócar is a Ph.D. student in sociology at the University of Wisconsin–Madison and an investigative affiliate at the Universidad Diego Portales, Chile.

Alexis Cortés teaches sociology at the Universidad Alberto Hurtado, Chile.

Emilio Crenzel is a professor of sociology at the Universidad de Buenos Aires and a researcher at the Consejo Nacional de Investigaciones Científicas y Técnicas in Argentina.

Lorenzo D'Orsi holds a Ph.D. in cultural anthropology from the University of Milan-Bicocca.

Francisco Adolfo García Jerez is a professor in the Department of Social Sciences at the Universidad del Valle, Colombia.

Virginia Garrard is a professor of history and religious studies, and the Director of LLILAS Benson Latin American Studies and Collections at the University of Texas, Austin.

Hillary Hiner is an assistant professor of history at the Universidad Diego Portales, Chile.

Susana Kaiser is a professor of media studies and Latin American studies at the University of San Francisco.

Erika Márquez is a lawyer and political sociologist. She is a professor at the Universidad Icesi, Facultad de Derecho y Ciencias Sociales, Departamento de Estudios Sociales, Calle 18 No. 122–135, Cali, Colombia.

Juliane Müller is a lecturer in the Department of Cultural and Social Anthropology at the University of Munich, Germany.

Juan Poblete is a professor of literature and Latin/o American cultural studies at the University of California, Santa Cruz.

Valentina Salvi is a researcher at the Consejo Nacional de Investigaciones Científicas y Técnicas, and the Director of Núcleo de Estudios sobre Memoria CIS-CONICET/IDES in Argentina.

Nina Schneider is a senior research fellow at the Global South Study Center of the University of Cologne, Germany.

Diana Carolina Sierra Becerra is a doctoral candidate in history and women's studies at the University of Michigan.

Roberta Villalón is a Fulbright Scholar, an associate professor of Sociology and the Chairperson of the Sociology and Anthropology Department at St. John's University, New York City.